Female
of
the
Species

Female of the Species

M. KAY MARTIN

BARBARA VOORHIES

1975

COLUMBIA UNIVERSITY PRESS—NEW YORK & LONDON

Library of Congress Cataloging in Publication Data

Martin, M   Kay, 1942–
  Female of the species.

  Bibliography: p.
  Includes index.
  1. Women. 2. Sex role. I. Voorhies, Barbara,
1939–   joint author. II. Title.
GN294.M37   301.41′2   74-23965
ISBN 0-231-03875-5
ISBN 0-231-03876-3 pbk.

TO
MARGARET MEAD

A continuing pioneer
in the anthropological study
of sex and gender.

Preface

This book is the outcome of a course we first offered at the University of California, Santa Barbara, in the fall of 1971. Both the course and the present work grew out of an attempt to utilize the approach of traditional anthropology in the examination of the position of women at the species level. This is an enormous task, and one that is being seriously undertaken for the first time by a number of scholars in many places. We hope our own contribution will aid in furthering interest in the topic, and that it will stimulate long neglected research on women.

Although we have consistently tried to examine the issues in this book as objectively as possible, we must note that the work contains a fundamental underlying bias: We recognize that differences between men and women, in terms of sexual activity and social behavior, are important in the daily lives of human beings in every society. These differences are in part the result of fundamental biological variation between the sexes. We are committed to the proposition, however, that culture rather than biology plays the more critical role in determining those features of behavior which ultimately dichotomize the sexes.

We recognize that the underscoring of sexual differences is crucial to the economic success and social continuity of many human societies, but we also hold that the cultural promotion of such differences in industrial ones is an increasingly maladaptive and hence vanishing phenomenon. In our society we must begin to minimize the importance of sex where sexual activity is not relevant. This deemphasis on a person's sexual and other phenotypic characteristics will allow for the successful cultivation of individual potentials that are otherwise culturally suppressed. We are on the threshold of a new cultural era in which, perhaps more than ever before, the creative and intellectual efforts of the entire species will be simultaneously and intensively utilized.

The disposition of work was as follows: Martin contributed chapters 1 and 6–11, and Voorhies chapters 2–5.

A number of people have contributed significantly to the genesis of this work. We are especially grateful to Beth Dillingham for stimulating our interest in this subject and to Thomas G. Harding for encouraging us to pursue this interest as an academic course. We also thank our students for their enthusiasm for this material, which we first shared with them. Several people offered insightful comments on various portions of the manuscript. We are indebted to Donald E. Brown, Eleanor Leacock, Denise O'Brien, George Spindler, Louise Spindler, Charlotte Symons, and innumerable anonymous reviewers for their comments. Jé Goolsby skillfully drew the illustrations. Arlene Bogardus and Pat Griffith ungrumblingly typed and retyped various drafts. Finally we thank our editors, John Moore and Leslie Bialler, and designer Jennifer Roberts, for their considerable help.

One of us (M.K.M.) received a Summer Faculty Research Fellowship from the Academic Senate, U.C.S.B., in partial support of this project. We are grateful for this assistance.

Finally we thank our parents, Russell and May Martin, and Alfred and Dorothy Voorhies, whose socialization efforts allowed us the necessary latitude to perceive alternative goals within the more traditional bounds of womanhood.

January 1975   M.K.M.
                                                           B. V.

Acknowledgments

Figures 2-5 and 2-6 are redrawn with permission from John Money, "Psychosexual Differentiation." In *Sex Research: New Developments,* edited by John Money, pp. 3–23, 1965. Copyright © Holt, Rinehart and Winston.

Figure 2-8 is redrawn with permission from W. A. Schonfeld, "Primary and Secondary Sexual Characteristics." *American Journal of Diseases of Children* 65.

Figure 3-1 is reproduced with permission from John Garcia, "I.Q., The Conspiracy." *Psychology Today,* June 1972. Copyright © Ziff-Davis Publishing Company.

We express our thanks for the photographs that were generously supplied, with permission to reproduce them:

To Elizabeth and Robert Fernea for Plate 6
To Andrew and Marilyn Strathern for Plates 3, 4, and 5
To the University of Washington Press for Plates 1 and 2, reproduced from Jane Goodale, *Tiwi Wives,* 1971. Copyright © University of Washington Press.

Material from the following sources has been reprinted by kind permission of the publishers or authors:

Women's Role in Economic Development, by Ester Boserup. By permission of George Allen and Unwin and St. Martin's Press.

"The Position of Women in a Pastoral Society," by Marguerite Dupire. In *The Position of Women in a Pastoral Society.* Originally published by the University of California Press; reprinted by permission of The Regents of the University of California.

Guests of the Sheik, by Elizabeth Fernea. Reprinted by permission of Doubleday and Co., Inc., Inc., A Watkins Inc., and the author.

Sex and Temperament in Three Primitive Societies, by Margaret Mead. Copyright © 1963 by William Morrow & Co., Inc.

Marilyn Strathern, *Women in Between,* by permission of Academic Press, Inc. Copyright © 1972 by Academic Press.

Contents

A map of the societies mentioned in
this book appears on pages 90–91

Female
of
the
Species

The Quintessence of Sex

CHAPTER ONE

This book investigates over one-half of humanity, not only from the perspective of today's diverse societies, but from the dim beginnings of the species itself. The goal of this ambitious adventure is neither a political statement nor an Amazonian call to arms, but to gain a clear understanding of the myriad definitions and functions of female and male behavior, and of the way societies manipulate sex to achieve efficient adaptations to their physical and social environments.

One of the reasons why females are of interest is that they have been so seldom chosen as the object of rigorous, comprehensive study in the social sciences. Anthropology is no exception in this respect. This discipline has typically treated females and their activities as peripheral to the mainstream of cultural systems and cultural evolution. This consistent bias in scientific reporting is perhaps best viewed as a function of the culture in which these bodies of theory developed, rather than of any sexist conspiracy. It is becoming apparent to an increasing number of scholars, however, that cultural bias in a science purporting to be free of it has resulted in serious distortions in our understanding of human behavior. The recent sense of urgency to examine female roles anew is attributable not only to the swelling ranks of women anthropologists, but also to the growing sophistication of anthropology as a science.

Another reason for studying the female of the species is that roles assumed by males and the cultural functions of sex itself are cast in fresh perspective. Vital questions, such as the nature of ancient society or the determinants of primitive kinship systems, remain in anthropological theory. Many of these may be answerable with a thorough understanding of the way basic sex criteria are utilized to bring human interactions and social groups in tune with specific environments.

But we must begin at the beginning. It is first necessary for us to define what we mean by sex, female, and male, and to note the role culture plays in our conceptions of sex-specific behaviors.

SEX: BIOLOGY OR SOCIAL LEARNING?

For most of us, the differences between men and women seem fairly obvious and simple. One of the first things we learn as children is that there are physical differences in their size and strength, in the appearance of their genitals, and subsequently in their reproductive roles. Such overt differences are thought to be absolute and immutable. Euroamericans conceptualize a humanity divided in half on the basis of biological criteria.

But other more covert sexual attributes attach themselves to these dichotomous categories as well. Males and females, we are often told, have fundamentally different temperaments, desires, emotional qualities, personalities, learning abilities, and aptitudes. Some argue that observed differences in these areas are also the result of biological inheritance—that males and females have evolved to fulfill complementary rather than equal roles in society, and that these differences in potential are genetically imprinted. Others would protest strongly that such measurable differences as exist are both the cause and effect of differential child-rearing practices in our culture. They would argue that male and female infants are born with similar potentials, but that parents and other socializing agencies impose different standards of sexual behavior on their offspring in accordance with cultural guidelines.

The argument over the determinants of sex-specific behavior has sometimes been referred to summarily as the nature-nurture dichotomy. More and more scholars are coming to the conclusion, however, that sex identity is not all that simple—that feminine and masculine behavior cannot be explained away as being solely the result of biology or solely the result of social conditioning. When we look at men and women in societies throughout the world, for example, some features of their respective behaviors seem to be fairly constant, but others show such diversity that they appear at times to be mutually contradictory. When we observe sexual differences in specific behaviors even within the limited context of our own society, it is impossible to determine where biology ends and social learning begins.

All available evidence, then, seems to indicate that sexual differences are better represented as variable points on a broad continuum than as polar opposites. Sex has multiple determinants, which include basic genetic potentials contained in the body cells, cultural information contained in the brain cells, and a critical union of these two sources of information which guides the development and renewal of the adult organism.

In this book we shall recognize both biological and cultural aspects of sex, reserving for a time the question of their relative weights in the generation of dichotomous behaviors. We demarcate features known to have a genetic basis as a person's *physical sex* or *phenotypic sex*. This allows us to isolate anatomical females from anatomical males for the purpose of study. In contrast, those features that appear to have their foundation in cultural instruction, and that reflect preferred role behaviors, are referred to as a person's *social sex* or *gender*. An important thing to remember about these two variables of sex is that they are themselves continuous rather than absolute phenomena. People, for example, are not uniform, but diverge in the extent to which they conform to the ideal phenotype (or, rarely, even the typical genetic pattern) of their sex. As we shall see, cultures vary even in the number of physical sexes recognized. Further, the physical and social sex a person assumes are not always parallel. Again, the degree of symmetry is variable. An anatomical male may, for example, assume a largely female gender role, and vice versa.

In summary, sex refers to a division of humanity into two or more categories on the basis of both biological and cultural criteria. Sex distinctions may be most profitably viewed as points on a continuum with acceptable ranges of deviation, rather than as absolute phenomena. The recognition of males and females is universal, but the typical behaviors assigned to them vary greatly from one society to the next.

SEX AS A CULTURAL PROCESS

Although inheritance and learning appear to be jointly operative in the production of male and female behaviors, one basic feature distinguishes them as causal factors. Genetic determinants of sex-specific behavior are consistent for the species as a whole, whereas learned determinants are differentially molded and expressed by each culture. For example, females in America, Uruguay, China, and Nigeria begin with a largely identical inventory of structural and chemical traits that prepares them for their unique reproductive and nurturant functions. Such consistencies, when found in a great number of human societies, would seem to indicate features that confer some adaptive advantage on the species itself. Other features of overt behavior, however, show considerably less uniformity. Women may be powerful or powerless, dependent or independent, scholars or domestics, as their cultures require. These features of sex-specific behavior show infinite variety, and appear always to confer an adaptive advantage to a specific population in a specific ecological niche. That is, in order to guarantee a degree of conformity sufficient for the survival of people in a given economic and social environment, every culture imposes upon its members definite prejudices about the nature of human nature and the nature of women and men. So logical do these patterns for behavior appear, and so reinforced are they by society, that people tend to see them as inevitable, unalterable, and universal human qualities.

Common features of womanhood the world over may have their basis in genetic determinants, or they may be so crucial to human culture as a whole that they are consistently taught to young females in every society. Here the line between genetic and cultural inheritance, as noted above, is often impossible to draw. We can say with greater confidence, however, that features of womanhood which diverge from one society to the next are *wholly* dependent on learning. The ability of culture to mold our conception of what is "natural" or "normal" behavior for females is immense. In the chapters that follow, we shall consider this variation along several parameters.

Reproductive and Social Groups. Because of their intensive relationship with offspring both before and after birth, females are often more closely identified with reproduction and child-care than are males. Women everywhere marry, have babies, and together with their children form the core of family and kinship groups. In American society the *nuclear* family—a married or conjugal pair and their offspring—predominates as the approved sexual and reproductive unit and as the primary socializing agency. Descent through one's father and mother is reckoned equally or *bilaterally* (literally, two sides). In other words, an individual believes that both parents make equal contributions to his/her biological and social inheritance. Couples typically strike out on their own after marriage, segregating themselves physically as a new unit by setting up a household separate from either set of parents. Anthropologists call this type of residence *neolocal*.

The creation of small, monogamous, and independent family units—a pattern prevalent in industrial societies—strongly colors our conceptions of appropriate sex behaviors. The relative isolation of young men and women from their respective kinsmen after marriage, for example, casts them into a rather intense relationship of mutual dependency. Males and females in our society have traditionally been taught that the sexes are fundamentally different in both temperament and aptitudes, and that their respective roles should therefore be complementary rather than equal. Since ideally there are only two adults in the nuclear household to perform all of the tasks necessary for its survival, and since women are more temporally committed to and spatially limited by reproduction, males have assumed the role of provider. The economic, social, and political horizons of women have been proportionately limited to the household. Despite the increasing assumption of these responsibilities by nonkinship agencies (i.e., nursery schools, housekeeping services), American men and women still tend to agree that the home, rather than "the world outside," is the natural and proper arena for female energies and female aspirations.

There is an old saying that one cannot change the ingredients without altering the flavor. It is in this spirit that we shall consider the position of women in non-Western and especially non-industrialized, agrarian, herding, and foraging societies. With the latter types of adaptations, the small nuclear family as we know it is generally not an efficient economic or social unit. Rather, the conjugal units of *several* related individuals are often joined together to form a larger food-producing and food-sharing group. Such extended kinship groups are widespread in the non-Western world. Although they serve similar functions as our simple dyadic families, they recruit many more people, and with different criteria.

The social organization of non-Western societies is often a source of confusion to beginning anthropology students, not only because their kinship groups are large and complex, but also because such groups are typically based upon the recognition of links between only *one* parent and his/her offspring at the expense of the other parent. Thus, the criterion of sex becomes particularly exaggerated in importance.

In some societies, individuals of both sexes trace their biological and social inheritance through their mother *only*. Although the father is usually recognized as playing some role in conception, he is not a member of his child's (maternal) kinship group, and hence not of particular social importance. Descent groups that recruit their membership through maternal links are called *matrilineal* (literally, mother's line). Members of each matrilineal group or *matrilineage* share descent from a common ancestress (i.e., mother, mother's mother, mother's mother's mother, etc.). Since links through females are accorded primary importance, many matrilineal societies require that a man leave the locality of his birth at marriage and go to live with the relatives of his wife. This type of residence, called *matrilocal*, keeps a core of related females (grandmothers, mothers, sisters, daughters, granddaughters) together in one locality, along with their imported husbands. As we shall see in later chapters, societies in which women form the locus of social groups permit them much greater latitude in extradomestic activities and power than do many others.

In other societies the opposite situation prevails: individuals trace their biological and social inheritance through paternal links only. This type of kinship system is called *patrilineal* (literally, father's line). All members of a *patrilineage* share descent from a common male ancestor (father, father's father, etc.). Patrilineal systems differ from our own in that they socially disregard the mother and her kinsmen. All children of a married couple belong to the father's social group. As in the case of matrilineal societies, patrilineal ones typically benefit by keeping the members of their kinship groups in one locality. The immediate implication of these rules for women is that they must leave their own kinsmen at marriage and spend the major part of their lives in the company of comparative strangers—their husband's relatives. As we shall see, patrilineal societies are often highly male-dominant, and in some cases may even require the strict segregation of women from public life.

Bilateral, matrilineal, and patrilineal systems are ideal structures with many possible variations in human cultures. Although all family and kinship groups assume a responsibility for biological and cultural reproduction, they achieve these similar functions in ways that require alternate definitions of appropriate male and female behaviors. The number of lovers a woman has before and after marriage, the number of husbands she may serially or simultaneously acquire, the importance she attaches to child-bearing, the extent of her emotional or physical dependency on males, and whether she will learn to compete or cooperate with other women are all a function of adaptive social groups and the ideologies they promote to ensure their own survival.

Economic and political ramifications that flow from these distinct social systems must also be considered.

Production, Power, and Authority. Why societies differ with respect to family, kinship, and social groups relates directly to the way they make their living. In addition to providing for the biological and social continuity of a culture, such groups compose the basic units of production as well. We feel that the exact nature of economic production has an important determining influence upon the nature of political and social relations, including the variable status positions of women and men.

In American society, for example, the nuclear family has evolved as a sort of minimal corporation in an industrial economy that depends upon a large and mobile work force. Large *unilineal* (literally one line, either matrilineal or patrilineal) kinship groups, once adaptive in our agrarian past, have been eroded by the conditions of urban life. The isolated male-female dyad with offspring arose as the most efficient unit of both production and consumption. What this traditionally meant for women is their assumption of dependent, subordinate roles in relation to males, whose monopolization of economic tasks outside the home complements the domestic autonomy of women. Industrialized America, in addition to the basic division of labor by sex, of course also relies upon complex nonkinship groups, such as large, highly structured corporations, to maintain the existing economy. Women in our society have been steadily invading these formerly male domains. Interestingly, changes are concomitantly taking place in our ideas about the fundamental aptitudes and temperaments of men and women.

The importance of economic factors in the way we view the sexes becomes even more apparent when we consider the very different ways that women are regarded in other societies. The division of labor by sex is defined anew by each of the world's cultures. Every society has fairly explicit ideas about what is "men's work" and what is "women's work," and there is a tendency for such labor allocations to be rationalized on the basis of alleged natural aptitudes. There are, of course, biological constants. Males tend, on the average, to be more robust than females in both size and strength. Further, the act of reproduction for males involves no necessary extended commitment to the pre- or immediately post-natal development of the infant, and no temporary loss of productive efficiency.

It has been pointed out in cross-cultural studies (see D'Andrade 1966) that male subsistence activities are typically those which are physically most strenuous, and which involve the greatest mobility from the vicinity of the household. Murdock (1937) tabulated the types of productive tasks assigned to men and women for a large sample of nonindustrial societies of varying complexity. He found that the subsistence activities most commonly associated with males are hunting, fishing, trapping, herding, and the clearing of agricultural lands. Women, in contrast, are typically responsible for the gathering of wild food plants and the tending and harvesting of crops. Secondary activities also reflect the sexual dichotomy between the provision of protein and vegetable foods in the diet. Males occupy themselves with the production of tools for food-getting, such as weapon-making, net-making, boat building, stone-working, and so forth. Female activities, however, center around food preparation, the making of storage containers, and the maintenance of clothing. The delegation to women of tasks associated with the household is certainly related to their availability as childbearers and child-rearers.

Despite obvious similarities in the types of economic activities assumed by the sexes worldwide, there are surprising differences in their relative productive importance. Our own cultural philosophy holds that males are the natural providers. As we shall see, however, this is not a universal notion. Women in societies with certain types of production provide the bulk of food not only for themselves, but for their children and husbands as well. Although men and women seem anatomically favored, either structurally or as a matter of convenience, for specific kinds of jobs, the environment and the technology available for its exploitation determines which sex is economically featured in any given society. These same factors play the primary role in selecting the social groups that are most efficient for organizing productive activities. Later, we shall offer a theory for predicting the occurrence of matrilineal and patrilineal varieties of kinship groups in certain ecological niches.

Economic factors are critical to our consideration of female lifestyles, then, because questions of whether basic groups in society are founded on the principle of maternal, paternal, or bilateral links relate so intimately to male-female relationships. In America, for example, the isolation of women from significant participation in institutions outside the home has sharply limited their access to authority and power in the larger society.

But many are quick to point out that men are the world's warriors and politicians. Does this mean that males are everywhere dominant, or that the monopolization of such roles has a basis in our primate past? This is certainly a question that we want to consider in some detail. Throughout our discussion of this issue, however, it will be essential to keep the distinction between *power* and *authority* in mind. Power refers to the ability to coerce others toward desired ends, whereas authority refers to legitimate or legal power. A survey of human societies shows that positions of authority are almost always occupied by males. Technically speaking, there is no evidence for matriarchy, or rule by women, Amazonian or otherwise. Of even greater significance, however, is that the assignment of power and authority may vary independently. Leadership positions are generally occupied by males, but power may attach itself to either sex. This is especially well illustrated by matrilineal societies, in which senior women assign public offices to males, but may reserve the actual decision-making for themselves.

In our investigation we shall therefore often have to look beneath the surface hierarchies of group officials to find the real locus of power. In most cases, we shall find that power attaches itself to those who control the distribution of food or wealth, irrespective of sex.

OUR APPROACH

We have so far stressed that what are often conceived of as absolute categories of reality, namely male and female, are in fact dynamic rather than static phenomena. But it is not enough to note diversity; our task is to understand it. We must therefore examine the female range of the sexual spectrum from the contrasting perspectives of biology, primate social life, behavioral differences in our own society, and the infinitely diverse profiles of womanhood in other cultures.

There are two major themes unifying this discussion. The first chapters deal with the interaction of biological and social factors in the determination of behavioral differences between the sexes. We begin with a brief discussion of sex as a biological process. First, we examine the attributes of the mammalian form of sexual reproduction and compare it with other forms of reproduction. Second, we investigate the developmental process by which a person assumes a sexual identity. This process involves the interaction of several physiological and social factors, and is not simply cast in one stroke as is popularly believed.

We shall then go on to analyze several personality characteristics which are differentially expressed by each sex in our own society. For each trait we shall examine some non-Western societies to discover whether the Western pattern is universally typical of humans or if it is restricted to certain societies. We shall also be concerned with the development of these sex-linked behaviors during the growth and maturation of the individual. The delineation of unlike patterns of trait development for each sex often sheds light on the complex origins of sex-linked traits.

In the final chapter concerned with the biosocial theme, we investigate a few societies that recognize *more* than two sexes in their populations, or that permit a person to choose between gender roles that are congruent or not congruent with his/her physical sex. These situations underscore our conclusion that behavioral traits correlated with sex are predominantly determined by society and secondarily by biology.

The dominant theme in the latter part of the book, beginning with chapter 5, is that the nature of human sex roles has an adaptive advantage for society, and that these adaptations correlate with group ecology. During human evolution several major ecological adjustments have occurred, and each of these favors significantly different sex roles. We discuss past and present theories of sex roles and human evolution, after which we analyze the major shifts in human ecology.

We begin the discussion of the origin and development of sex differences with an examination of the behavior of animals closely related to ourselves. Monkeys and apes are ideal for a general study of sex behavior because their reproductive systems are very much like those of humans. In fact, because of many close biological similarities between these animals and humans, several popular authors have argued that behavior observed in one particular species of nonhuman primate accounts for human behavior. We reject this approach; but we do feel it is instructive to witness the lability of sex-linked behavior of animals as it correlates with environment. Surely if the sex roles of apes vary in correlation with their environments, we can expect an even greater variation in humans, who rely so significantly on social learning.

In chapter 6 we correlate the changing conception of male and female in the development of anthropological theory with a discussion of theories on the origin of human society. During the nineteenth century, women were often identified as the architects of ancient marrige, kinship, and political relations. This position was reversed sharply in the present century, with its emphasis on male dominance, territoriality, and aggression as cornerstones of human society. Whereas the establishment of family, moral, and religious orders were once attributed to the restraining influences of women, males are currently given credit for both the establishment and evolutionary progression of culture. We explore the notion that modern theories have developed to some extent in reaction to those of the previous century, and we offer a new synthesis.

Five ecological adaptations, representing various levels of organizational complexity in world cultures, are then considered in depth. These are foraging, horticulture, agriculture, pastoralism, and industrialism. For each preindustrial category, we analyze a cross-cultural sample of societies to identify prevailing patterns of ideal sex behavior. We then correlate these with productive, demographic, political, and social variables. In addition, we present a case study for each adaptation considered. These profiles of women in individual societies are intended not as prototypes of female lifestyles, but as qualitative illustrations of the quantitative cross-cultural data that precede them.

The first ecological adjustment we examine is that of foraging. This term refers to an economy based on the collection of foods by hunting, fishing, and gathering, in the absence of cultivation or the keeping of domesticated animals. These societies are often said to be male-dominant in both economic and social spheres. In the chapter on foraging, we examine the general applicability of this model in cross-cultural perspective. Gathering by women is found generally to contribute a more substantial portion of food to the diet in societies at this level than does hunting by men. Likewise, links through females may sometimes provide the central organizing principle in kinship relations and in the allocation of authority. We conclude that there is no necessary one-to-one correlation between productive and social dominance. Relations among the sexes in foraging societies are highly egalitarian.

Societies depending primarily upon cultivation for their subsistence display tremendous variation in the assignment of economic and social roles to women and men. In the chapter on horticulture, we investigate sex role differentiation in societies employing hand tools for farming activities. The status of women appears to be directly related to the level of economic productivity and to the nature of kinship and social organization. Women are found to be dominant in cultivative activities, but to enlist the labor of males in relation to the increasing importance of farming products in the subsistence base. Although women enjoy a considerable degree of economic independence in all horticultural societies, their social status is often diminished in situations where descent is reckoned through males.

Agriculture is a category we reserve for intensive farming—that is, for cultivation involving irrigation or the use of domestic animals for organic fertilizer and for attachment to the plow. These techniques are often associated with high yield, population density, urbanization, and the development of complex political units. The analysis reveals agricultural communities to be overwhelmingly male-oriented in both production and social organization. In contrast, the labor of women tends to be spatially and conceptually identified with the household. We conclude that the males' usurpation of cultivative tasks, which accompanied intensive farming, occurred in response to the demands for continual heavy field labor and the concomitant demand for continual processing and preparation of cereal foods in the household by women. The combination of these factors favored a distinction between domestic and extradomestic labor, and the isolation of women from the productive sphere of activity.

Pastoral societies depend heavily on products of domesticated animals for their subsistence. These societies are almost universally characterized by patrilineal descent, and reserve for males the dominant positions in both economic and social status. We find, however, that sex roles are not static variables, but fluctuate predictably with the relative importance of herding and cultivation.

Our review of women's roles in many different societies demonstrates that the relative positions of women and men are not crystallized into typical sex patterns, but in fact vary widely in response to many interacting social and biological factors. We use these insights as we investigate gender roles as they have developed, and as they are developing, in industrialized societies.

Industrialism presents a very different social environment. Gender roles, like many other social features, are undergoing change in response to these new conditions. In the final chapter, we examine the effect of industrialism on the gender roles of the United States and the Soviet Union. The effects of industrialism have taken different forms in each of these two nations. Consequently, the histories of alteration in gender roles have followed different courses in each area. Yet our comparison of these historical developments permits us to identify the social processes that are apparently operative in both social systems. After we identify the social processes that are underway, we make predictions about the future development of gender roles in these and other industrialized nations.

Sex as a Biological Process

CHAPTER TWO

The fundamentally different functions that males and females perform in the reproductive cycle stem from the anatomical differences, familiar to everyone, that are at the core of the differentiation of humans into two sexes. Less well understood, however, is the significance of sexual reproduction for humanity as a whole, or how an individual acquires a sexual identity.

The evolution of the process of sexual reproduction has had widespread effects on the organic world. Humans are among many organisms that reproduce in this way. Nevertheless, there are other forms of reproduction that have been successful over a long evolutionary period, and we shall be particularly interested in comparing the advantages of the various forms. Such a discussion launches a line of inquiry that we shall pursue throughout the book: to investigate the adaptive advantage of various sociocultural forms of human sex differences in different environments. We shall begin this task by examining the advantages of sexual reproduction as a system; later on we shall investigate the advantages of human elaborations on the male-female theme. Most of this book, of course, is concerned with the sex differences in behavior rather than those in physiological reproduction. Yet, they are inextricably interrelated. In this chapter we shall first examine the evolutionary origin of sex— what is sex? when did it arise during the course of evolution? what advantages does it bestow on evolving organisms?—in order to put human sex differences in the context of all other living organisms.

In the second section we shall deal with human sexual identification—how is the sex of an individual determined? how is human sex identity developed during a person's growth to maturity? This topic, too, demands an understanding of both physiological-developmental and social processes. Our initial concern, however, will be with the more strictly biological side of the issue. We shall deal in later chapters with the process and results of sex-typing. That is, the way in which people learn their sex identities.

SEX AND EVOLUTION

Biologists believe the first organisms that lived on earth, over a billion years ago, reproduced asexually. These organisms each consisted of one autonomous cell. Many unicellular organisms today reproduce by cell division, and this may have been the method of the earliest organisms. In this process the parent cell rearranges its constituent material so that when it fissions each daughter cell is complete. As a result, the two daughter cells are identical to each other and are carbon copies of the parent. The parent is self-sacrificing in this process.

When multicellular organisms evolved, at least 500 million years ago, radical variations in the organization of basic life processes occurred. One important new development was that cell division became the main mechanism for the development and growth of organisms, each of which began as a single cell. Some multicellular organisms developed new means of *asexual* reproduction, whereas others developed *sexual* reproduction.

There are two common forms of asexual reproduction in multicellular organisms. One of these is *vegetative*. In this form a new organism is generated from a part of the parent organism's body. This occurs in both plants and animals, although it is most common in plants. Plant cuttings or runners (Fig. 2-1A), which develop into new plants, are examples. The budding phenomenon of the *Hydra*, a tiny aquatic organism, is an example of vegetative reproduction in an animal (Fig. 2-1B). During budding, a parent *Hydra* forms a new offspring by growing a projection, which eventually separates from the parent.

The second type of asexual reproduction is the formation of single reproductive cells, called *spores*, each of which develops without fertilization into a separate organism. Such plants as molds and mushrooms reproduce by means of spores.

Sexual reproduction evolved when some multicellular organisms began producing specialized, incomplete cells (*gametes*) that united to form a new individual. These cells are incomplete because each has only half of the message-bearing units (*genes*) necessary for the life of an organism. The full component of genetic material can be restored only by the union of two gametes. Today sexual reproduction is found in almost all animals and is the only form of reproduction among the vertebrates. Its essential feature is that each new organism inherits half of its genetic material from each of two different sex cells. This means that the genes of a population are reshuffled with every new generation.

The ramifications of this are often astounding. For example, a single human couple is theoretically capable of producing 64 trillion genetically different children (Carr 1970:11). Each child a couple produces will therefore automatically be genetically unique, except under the relatively unusual circumstances in which two or more individuals develop from the same fertilized egg.

A comparison of asexual and sexual forms of reproduction reveals that each is particularly suited to perpetuating life in a specific type of environment. Asexual reproduction is uniparental and offspring are ordinarily genetically identical to the parent. Thus both individuals have the same *genotypes*. Since offspring are carbon copies of their parents the genetic line is perpetuated in a highly conservative fashion. This is an advantage to organisms that live in relatively unchanging environments. (It becomes a disadvantage, however, in environments that change rapidly.) Today many asexually reproducing organisms are found in relatively stable environments such as the sea or deep soils.

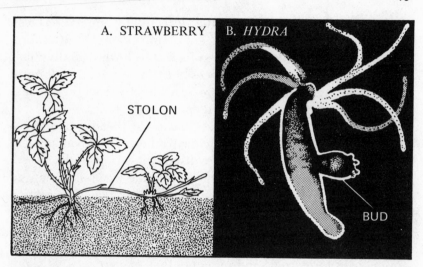

Figure 2–1. Vegetative reproduction.
A. In the strawberry the shoot system affects vegetative reproduction. Shoots known as stolons, growing along the surface of the ground, may develop new root systems and establish a new plant.
B. A parent *Hydra* with developing bud. Eventually the bud will sever itself completely from the parent and become a new individual (after Simpson *et al.* 1957:358, 359).

Sexually reproducing organisms never produce offspring that are genetically identical to their parents, since parental genes are always reshuffled in the formation of a new individual. Several disadvantages result. For one, it is less efficient, in terms of resource utilization, if there are two organisms involved in the completion of each reproductive cycle. Some types of sexually reproducing organisms avoid this situation. In these, a single individual is capable of producing both male and female gametes. Many flowering plants are like this.

A second disadvantage is that some experiments in genetic recombination must be sacrificed in the continuing evolution of a group of organisms. Charles Darwin was the first to recognize this situation. His principle of natural selection is based on the observation that reproduction is differential, not random. Some organisms reproduce successfully and pass on their genes to their descendants. Others are less successful and their genes are eventually removed from the descendent population. The continuous production of new genetic mixes in sexually reproducing organisms frequently results in the birth of individuals that are not reproductively successful. This is another form of wastage of living matter which results directly from the endless variety of genetic recombinations produced.

Despite these disadvantages sex is a widespread and successful means of reproduction. Obviously there are advantages to this process that outweigh the disadvantages just discussed. The primary advantage is that survival of the group is enhanced in certain environments by the high degree of genetic variation produced in each generation. This is particularly adaptive for organisms living in environments that undergo rapid changes. For this reason sexually reproducing organisms are especially common in terrestrial environments that remain relatively unstable over long periods of time.

An analogy may help clarify the comparison between asexual and sexual reproduction. Let us imagine that a population of organisms can be represented by a pile of beans and natural selection by a sieve. If the beans represent the result of asexual reproduction they will all be the same size and shape. Most beans pass freely through the sieve; that is, they are not removed from the population by the process of natural selection. These beans are well fitted to the environment. If a sieve with smaller holes is substituted for the first one, it is probable that few, if any, beans will fall through. Changing the sieve is analogous to a rapid change in the environment; it is a change to which the bean population cannot readily respond. The continuance of the bean population is in serious jeopardy.

If the original pile of beans represents the result of sexual reproduction, the pile will contain beans of a variety of shapes and sizes. Some of these will pass through the first sieve, whereas others will not. Substitution of sieves will allow passage of some other beans and the retention of some. In both cases, however, many beans will fall through and thus be able to perpetuate the bean population.

In most sexually reproducing organisms a single individual is

capable of producing only one type of gamete. This is sometimes the only difference between males and females. An example of this situation is found in animals that engage in external fertilization. This is common among the aquatic
invertebrates, many of which reproduce by shedding both eggs
and sperm into the water, where fertilization occurs. The sex of
a clam, oyster, or starfish, is not an easy thing to determine.

Some organisms have developed internal fertilization in
which union of gametes takes place within the body of the female. In these organisms anatomical differences between adult
female and male individuals have evolved. In mammals, females have evolved a complex arrangement of structures and
processes which together provide for the prenatal and postnatal
development of offspring. All mammalian females contain a
structural system that allows for the internal fertilization of eggs
(Fig. 2-2). This consists of an internal apparatus that allows the
introduction of male sperm and a transportation system that
moves the ripening eggs toward the sperm. Mammalian females
have also evolved a complicated arrangement for the protection
and nutrition of the fertilized egg. There is also an arrangement
for the expulsion of the new organisms which have been internally developed. And finally, there is an apparatus for the postpartum nutrition of the developing organisms. Mammalian male
evolution has led to the development of organs which allow the
production of sperm and its introduction into the bodies of females (Fig. 2-3).

Organisms most familiar to us have female and male types.
Femaleness and maleness appear to be the result of two separate but related processes which have come together during the
course of evolutionary development: first, the unique nature of
the physiological process of reproduction among sexually reproducing organisms, which usually requires *two* individuals of
the same species for its operation and completion; second, the
factor of internal fertilization, which requires sexually differentiated and specialized structures for the embryonic and neonatal
development of young.

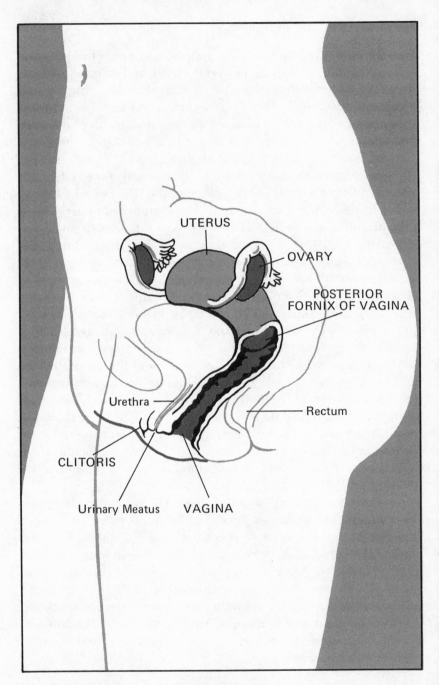

Figure 2–2. A woman's reproductive system.

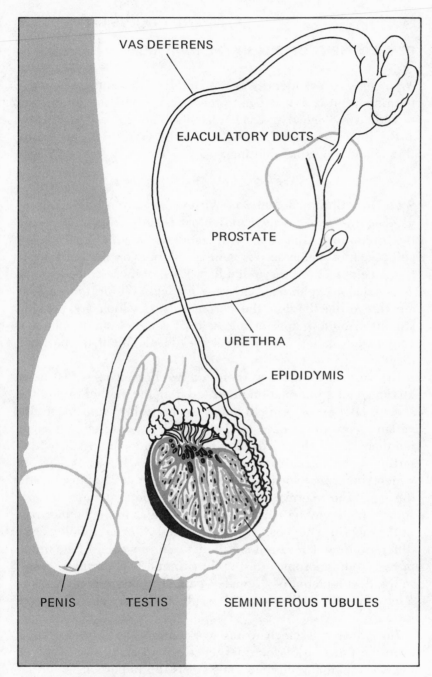

Figure 2–3. A man's reproductive system.

DEVELOPMENT OF SEX IN THE INDIVIDUAL

A person's sexual identity is not simply or instantaneously determined, but is a prolonged process caused by the interaction
of various biological and social factors. This process is initiated
at the time of conception and should be viewed as continuing
throughout a person's lifetime.

Step One: Chromosomal Sex. Among sexually reproducing organisms the sex of a new individual is ordinarily indicated at
the instant of fertilization. Fertilization is the joining of two sex
cells, each of which carries genetic information that will direct
the development of the individual. Each of these cells contains
a conspicuous spherical body, the *nucleus*. Within the nucleus
are thread-like bodies, the *chromosomes*, which are actually
strands of protein and nucleic acid. It is the chromosomes that
contain the genes which direct the development of the organism.

In a normal human egg there are 22 chromosomes that carry
all the genetic information inherited from the mother except the
individual's sex. These chromosomes are called *autosomes*. Invariably they are accompanied by a 23rd, sex-determinant, chromosome called the X *chromosome*. The human sperm, which
fertilizes the egg, also bears 22 autosomes (Fig. 2-4), each of
which is morphologically similar to one of the 22 autosomes in
the egg. The sperm also contains a sex-determinant chromosome which may be morphologically similar to the counterpart
in the egg (in which case it is also called X) or morphologically
different (in which case it is called a Y *chromosome*). The union
of two X chromosomes during fertilization will normally result
in the development of a female infant. The union of an X and a
Y chromosome will normally result in the development of a
male.

How does this mechanisms work? Does the Y chromosome
have the function of determining sex by masking the effects of
the accompanying chromosomes, or is the important feature of

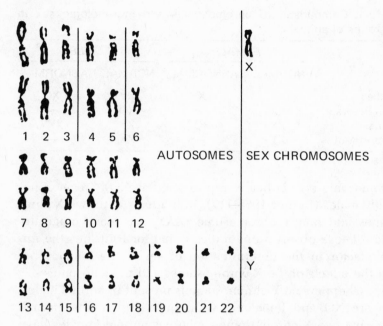

AUTOSOMES | SEX CHROMOSOMES

Figure 2–4. The human chromosomes from a male cell.

sex determination the balance between the effects of X chromosomes and the autosomes?

Interestingly, the mechanism for the determination of sex in animals appears to vary widely, which suggests that it can be easily altered during the course of evolution. One of the easiest ways to investigate the mechanism of sex determination in an animal species is to determine the exact nature of chromosomal abnormalities and the effect they have on the appearance of an individual. When the abnormality concerns sex chromosomes, as when there are either too many or two few sex chromosomes, it is possible to determine how these errors affect the appearance of the organism's sex organs. For example, consider the determination of sex in fruit flies (*Drosophila*). Sex types in fruit flies are similar to those in humans in that normal females have two X chromosomes (Table 2-1), and normal males an X and a Y chromosome. Chromosomally abnormal flies with only a single

Table 2-1. Comparison of chromosomes and morphologic sex in four groups of animals

	FEMALE		MALE	
	NORMAL	ABNORMAL	NORMAL	ABNORMAL
Fruit flies	XX	XXY	XY	XO
Grasshoppers	XX	—	XO	—
Humans	XX	XO	XY	XXY
Birds and Moths	XY	—	XX	—

X chromosome (symbolically represented as XO), are morphologically males (Lerner 1968:117). Individuals with two X chromosomes and one Y chromosome (XXY) are morphologically females. These observations indicate that for fruit flies the important factor in the determination of sex is the balance between the effects of the X chromosomes and the autosomes.

In grasshoppers no Y chromosome is present in normal males. Males are XO and females XX. In birds and moths, normal males have two X chromosomes, whereas normal females have one X and one Y.

In mammals, despite the formal similarities with sex chromosomes of fruit flies, a very different conclusion is reached about the role of the Y chromosome. This can be demonstrated by again observing the effects of chromosomal abnormalities. XO mammals are morphologically females; that is, they have external sex organs like those of normal females. XXY individuals have male external sex organs. This shows that the Y chromosome in humans and other mammals plays a vital role in the determination of sex.

It is also significant that the Y chromosome carries very little additional genetic information. The evidence is strong that only one trait, the characteristic of hairy ears, is inherited in this fashion (Lerner 1968:114–15). Thus, although men and women differ fundamentally in every cell in their bodies, this difference has limited and specific, rather than general, genetic effects.

Subsequent Processes. A person's sexual identity is not completely settled as a result of a union between an egg and sperm cell. At this time, of course, a person's chromosomal sex is irrevocably determined, but the single cell must be smoothly transformed into a normal man or woman. During this transformation several critical variables in the development of adult sex are involved. Hampson and Hampson (1961) have clearly shown that sexual identity is not simply determined by a single factor. They identify seven variables of sex: chromosomal sex (already discussed), gonadal sex, sex of internal reproductive structures, sex of external reproductive structures, hormonal sex (to be discussed below), sex of assignment and rearing, and psychologic sex. (Sex of assignment and rearing refers to the sex ascribed to a person by society; psychologic sex is the person's own view of his sexual identity. In subsequent chapters we shall discuss the role of society in sex-typing.)

After an egg has been fertilized, only the chromosomal sex of the developing person has been determined. All other information, including programmed instructions for sexual development, is coded and contained in the chromosomes. Certainly, the mechanism that directs the formation of sexual organs must be powerful if it is to prevent the development of ambiguously sexed infants. The mechanism responsible for the development of the sexual organs appears to be dormant during the first two months of fetal life. During this period the prototypic structures for female and male sex organs are identical, regardless of the chromosomal sex of the infant. Thus a human fetus with a two-month gestation can only be sexed by means of chromosomal studies. During the third to fourth month of fetal life the powerful switching mechanism that directs the differentiation and development of male and female reproductive systems begins to operate. It is during this developmental period that sexual differentiation of gonads, and internal and external reproductive structures, takes place.

Structures in a two-month-old fetus that will later develop into internal reproductive organs include a pair of sexually undifferentiated sex glands (Fig. 2-5), and two additional struc-

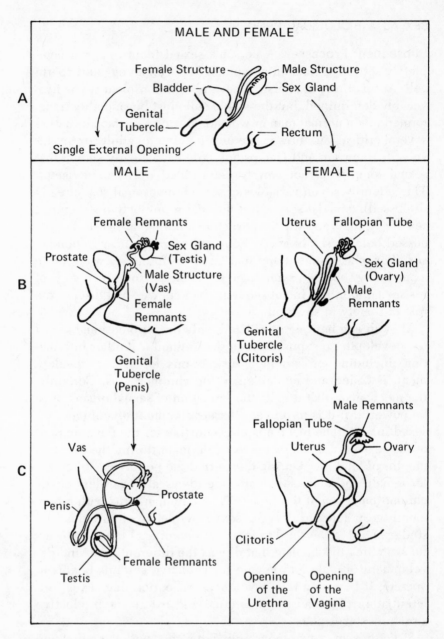

Figure 2–5. Internal genital differentiation in the human fetus.
A. Sexual organs of baby at 2nd to 3rd month of pregnancy.
B. Sexual organs of babies at 3rd to 4th month of pregnancy.
C. Sexual organs of babies at time of birth (after Money 1965:4).

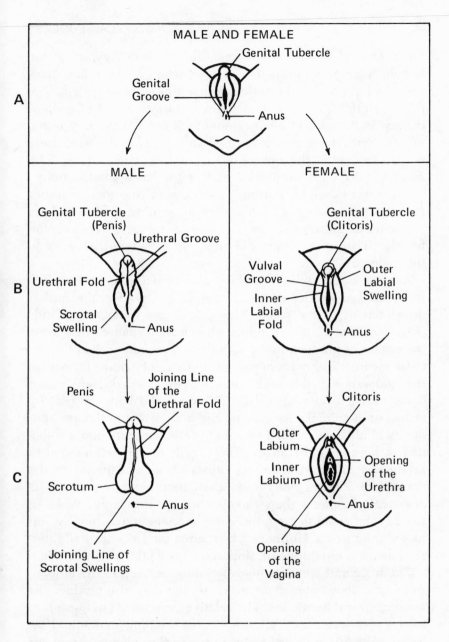

Figure 2–6. External genital differentiation in the human fetus.
A. Sexual appearance of baby at 2nd to 3rd month of pregnancy.
B. Sexual appearance of babies at 3rd to 4th month of pregnancy.
C. Sexual appearance of babies at time of birth (After Money 1965:5).

tures. One of these has the capability of forming part of the female internal reproductive system, whereas the other structure can form part of the male internal reproductive system. The pair of rudimentary sex organs develops into a pair of gonads, ovaries in the case of a female and testes in the male. Simultaneously with these changes in the body cavity of the fetus there occur changes in the region of external sex organs (Fig. 2-6). The sexually undifferentiated early fetus has a genital groove and genital tubercle. During development, the groove either enlarges to become the female vaginal opening or fuses to form the seam of the scrotal sac. The genital tubercle becomes the female clitoris or enlarges and undergoes changes that result in the male penis.

As soon as the rudimentary sex glands of a fetus become differentiated as ovaries or testes, they begin to affect the further development of the fetus. The gonads are endocrine glands (Fig. 2-7); that is, they produce chemical substances that leave the organs of production through the tissues rather than by vascular means. These chemical substances, which are formed in the endocrine glands and produce special effects, are called *hormones.* All hormones diffuse through the body, in part by means of the circulatory system, and are present in the environments of all body cells. Some body cells are particularly sensitive to hormonal chemicals. These cells may be stimulated to produce a different chemical substance as a response to the amount of a particular hormone in their environments. The chemical produced then travels through the body. When it reaches the gland that produces the hormone it may modify hormonal production. Hormones, by maintaining a controlled internal chemical environment, thus coordinate all body functions.

The male and female gonads not only develop in the embryo from a common antecedent structure, but they also produce the same chemical hormones. The relative proportions of these hormones, however, are different for developing males and females, which is a critical factor in the further elaboration of sex differences. The dominant male hormones are called *androgens;* the female-inducing hormones are called *estrogens* and *progesterone.* Before the gonads begin differential produc-

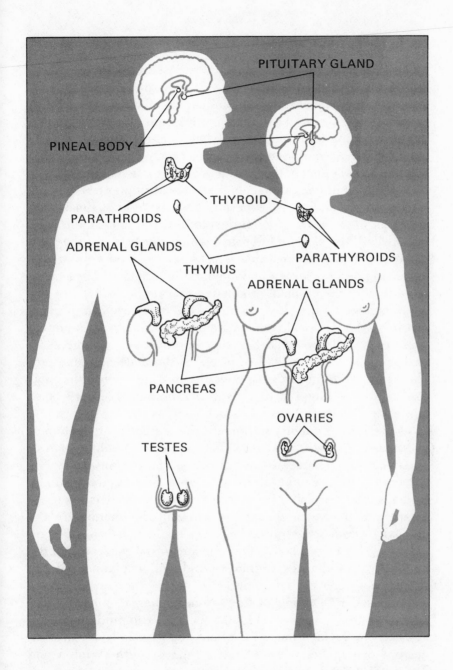

Figure 2–7. Location of human endocrine glands. The left figure shows the gonads (testes) characteristic of the male, and the right figure shows the gonads (ovaries) characteristic of the female.

tion of hormones, a human fetus is exposed to a female mix of hormones, which is transmitted to it through the mother's placenta. Unless the feminizing influence of the mother's hormones is counteracted by a massive infusion of male hormones, the developing fetus, no matter what its chromosomal sex, will develop female reproductive organs.

The critical effect of the presence of the male hormone for the development of normal mammalian male attributes can be demonstrated by laboratory experiment. Laboratory animals castrated *in utero* at the time of development of female and male gonads will develop into females, which suggests that the presence of a male hormonal mix is necessary to produce a normal male from a fetus with a male genetic inheritance. The powerful effects of the prenatal production of male hormones can also be illustrated by the phenomenon of the freemartin, a reproductively abnormal female calf. A freemartin always has a normal male twin. It is believed that the reproductively abnormal female results from prenatal exposure to the male hormone produced by her twin. This happens because the twins' placentas are so closely joined in the womb that hormonal leakage takes place through the vascular interconnections.

At the time of puberty in humans the hormonal production of the gonads is vastly increased. This results in the formation of secondary sex characteristics. In girls, changes in the pelvic structure, enlargement of breasts, and deposition of subcutaneous fat take place. In boys (Fig. 2-8), facial hair often appears, and the voice changes as a result of alterations in the larynx. In both sexes pubic hair and auxiliary hair appears on various parts of the body. These changes are governed by the production of the sex hormones and will not appear if the gonads are removed before puberty.

Increased production of the sex hormones at puberty coincides with the gonads' developing the ability to produce mature sex cells. A female human infant has approximately 400,000 immature ova in her ovaries at the time of birth (Winton and Bayliss 1962:281). In fact, the primordial ova are more numerous at this time than at any other time of her life. Many of these potential egg cells atrophy before puberty, whereas others do so after the onset of ovulation. Approximately 400 of the primordial egg cells can actually mature during a woman's life. In the human male, primordial sex cells are also present in the testes at the time of birth. These do not mature into sperm until the hormonal environment of the cells at puberty signals this process to begin.

These changes at puberty are directed by the presence of hormones produced by the pituitary gland, located at the base of

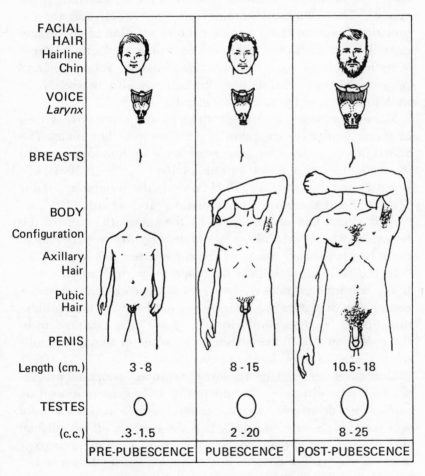

Figure 2–8. Stages of sexual development and maturation in the human male (After Schonfeld 1943:544).

the brain (Fig. 2-7). This tiny gland produces at least fifteen different hormones instrumental in the regulation of a wide variety
of body functions. The pituitary serves as a master chemical
coordinator of the activities of other endocrine glands. At least
four of the pituitary hormones act in different ways on the sex
glands. One of these is called the growth hormone because it
directs somatic growth of the entire body, including the sex
glands. Three of the hormones of the pituitary are called *gonadotrophic hormones* because they affect the functioning of the
gonads. The follicle-stimulating hormone (FSH) and the lu-
teinizing hormone (LH) maintain the production of sperm and
eggs. Together with the third gonadotrophin, prolactin, internal
secretions of the sex hormones (androgens, estrogens, and
progesterone) are maintained. Prolactin is also necessary for
milk formation in the mammary glands.

Mammalian testes produce androgens and estrogens, as well
as sperm, under the direction of gonadotrophic hormones. The
actual processes by which the gonadotrophic hormones control
the testicular action is not well understood (A. Albert 1961:306).
It has been suggested that FSH controls the tubular apparatus
(Fig. 2-3) and therefore sperm manufacture, whereas LH controls the secretion of androgens by the interstitial cells of the
testes. However, difficulties in obtaining pure preparations of
these hormones have made it impossible to test this hypothesis.

In the fully adult human male sperm production is a relatively continuous process. The sperm leave the testes before
completion of maturation which is accomplished in the epididymis. Sperm become motile in this organ. They accumulate in
the epididymis until ejaculation takes place or the sperm cells
die and are absorbed by the body.

Hormones secreted by the ovary include estrogens, progesterone, and androgens. The amount of androgens produced by
normal female ovaries and the nature of their actions are not
well known (Young 1961:465). It is, however, well established
that ovaries have the capacity for production of androgens
under abnormal conditions. For example, ovaries transplanted
into castrated male laboratory animals can maintain some male
physiological processes. The ovarian hormones, estrogens and

progesterone, have been studied more intensively than ovarian androgen and their action in the female is relatively well understood.

At the start of a female periodic cycle the pituitary gland secretes gonadotrophins (Fig. 2-9), which activate the maturation process of several follicle cells surrounding an immature egg. The ovaries begin to secrete estrogens, which stimulate the further maturation of the follicles and make them more receptive to the gonadotrophins. Estrogens also flow into the bloodstream, where their accumulation stimulates the lining of the uterus to become enriched with blood vessels in anticipation of the arrival of a fertilized egg. At the same time, when the amount of estrogens in the bloodstream reaches a critical level, it signals the pituitary to decrease FSH and to secrete LH. The function of LH is to stimulate ovulation. This is accomplished by the release of the egg from the surrounding follicles, at which time it bursts from the ovary. The ovum passes into the oviduct which connects with the uterus. The follicle cells remaining in the ovary collapse and form a new body, the corpus luteum. Under the direction of prolactin, the corpus luteum manufactures progesterone. If fertilization of an egg occurs, the corpus luteum maintains a stable level of progesterone which, in turn, maintains pregnancy. At the termination of pregnancy, or when fertilization does not occur, the corpus luteum continues to secrete progesterone until high levels cause two effects: (1) inhibition of the pituitary production of LH and thus ovulation, and (2) stimulation of the pituitary to produce FSH, which begins to activate some follicles for a new cycle. Degeneration of both the corpus luteum and the unfertilized egg occurs. Secretion of progesterone then drops, which causes the uterine lining to slough off, resulting in menstrual bleeding.

Permanent cessation of menstruation (*menopause*) normally occurs between the ages of 46 and 50 (Katchadourian and Lunde 1972:91). Menopause does not happen abruptly, but is usually preceded by several years of irregular menstrual periods and reduced fertility. Menopause is not caused by changes in the pituitary gland but rather in the ovaries, which gradually discontinue the production of estrogen.

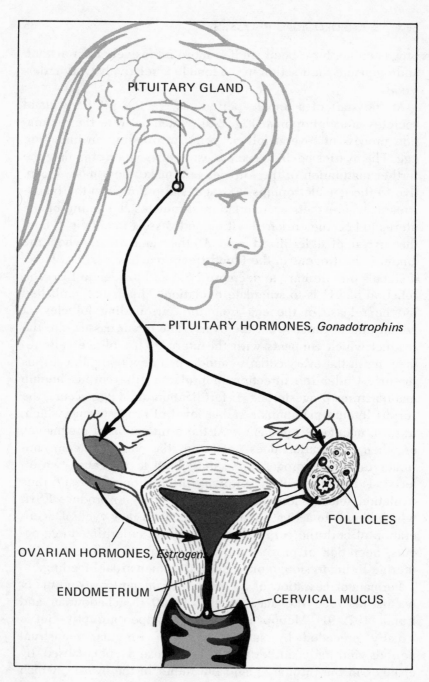

Figure 2–9. A woman's periodic cycle.

Approximately 10 percent of women in industrialized countries are inconvenienced by this transition between reproductive and postreproductive stages. These people variously suffer from headaches, dizziness, hot flashes, and severe depressions. Menopausal women also experience atrophy of the uterus and shrinking of the vaginal lining. All of these symptoms can often be relieved by treatment with estrogens.

It is not yet known whether similar inconveniences are experienced by women in non-Western societies. We suspect that this period of physiologic change is especially difficult for women who live in societies that place a high value on youth, physical beauty, and sexual attractiveness. The transitional stage, or *climacteric,* can be traumatic under these circumstances, because a woman feels herself losing the attributes that formerly guaranteed her social acceptance and self-esteem. We wonder if in societies where elderly women are valued for their knowledge and wisdom the climacteric is relatively less traumatic than in America.

Men do not undergo an exact equivalent of menopause. Testes continue to produce sperm indefinitely, although some decline in testosterone secretion and sperm production can occur. Hormonal changes in middle-aged men are thought to be responsible for the common problem of prostate enlargement. The prostate is a gland which encircles the urethra and, when enlarged, interferes with the flow of urine. This condition can be treated surgically by removing that part of the prostate which is pressing upon the urethra. Aging men often experience depression and irritability with increasing frequency. These behavioral changes have not as yet been correlated with hormonal changes.

We have seen that human physical sex is the result of the coordinated interaction of several processes. Chromosomal sex is established at conception. The reproductive organs—which consist of gonads, internal, and external reproductive structures—are developed during fetal life. At this time the sex hormones are also produced by the gonads. If no genetic mishap occurs, a boy or girl infant is born. The sex hormones sharply increase at puberty, at which time changes also occur in other parts of the body. These hormones serve important regulatory functions throughout the reproductive life of the mature adult.

DISCUSSION

We have been examining human sex differences from two perspectives. The evolutionary perspective permits an appreciation of the adaptive significance of anatomically different sexes. Organisms with this characteristic reproduce sexually, and the union of gametes takes place within the body of the female. Sexual reproduction ensures genetic variation, which can in turn improve the survival chances of the population as a whole. Internal fertilization improves the chances that gametes will unite and that the union will result in the development of a new individual. Humans are among the many organisms that share these reproductive patterns.

We also discussed human sex differences from a developmental perspective. The development of anatomically different human males and females is a long and complex process. This process begins at conception when the chromosomal pattern is established. The pattern is then endlessly replicated so that ultimately every single cell within a person's body carries the imprint of that person's sex. This fundamental difference between males and females is probably related only to the development and maintenance of the sex organs themselves. Male-female chromosomal differences are not believed to be fundamentally related to behavioral differences between the sexes.

The development of sex organs, which is directed by the sex chromosomes, may have pervasive effects on behavior. At least this is a debated contention we shall examine in detail in chapter 3. The sex organs consist of the gonads, the genitalia, and internal reproductive structures. These organs have been found to develop from common structures that arise in early fetal life.

The gonads, ovaries in females and testes in males, produce the sex cells and sex hormones. Each sex cell is genetically incomplete and must unite with another cell of the opposite type in order to develop.

The sex hormones are critically important in the regulation of the reproductive system. The same hormones are found in both females and males but their proportions are significantly different in each sex. These differences have been especially cited as important in the determination of behavioral differences between men and women.

Origins of Some Sex-Linked Traits

CHAPTER THREE

INTRODUCTION

Most of us have well-defined but perhaps largely unconscious ideas about what personality traits are typical of women and men. These ideas tend to be remarkably similar from person to person, although the total constellation of traits believed typical of each sex may not be exactly alike in any two people's minds. Even social scientists are not immune to these biases. The similarity in ideas about behavior and sex is nicely illustrated by responses to a questionnaire we distributed to students in a course on the anthropology of women (see also Travis 1972). The questionnaire, modified from one that appeared in *Psychology Today* (Travis 1971), in part sampled opinions concerning sex differences in personality traits. The students were asked whether they thought a particular trait was more characteristic of men or women or equally characteristic of both. The results (Table 3-1) show that most of the traits which appeared on the test were generally believed to be expressed differentially by the sexes. In only three cases (two concerning types of intelligence and one on objectivity) was the majority of respon-

Table 3-1. Attitudes of college students concerning the association of some personality traits and sex

TRAIT	PERCENTAGE OF RESPONDENTS		
	ASSOCIATED WITH MALES, %	ASSOCIATED WITH NEITHER SEX, %	ASSOCIATED WITH FEMALES, %
Aggressiveness	85	14	—
Emotionality	—	13	87
Independence	72	27	—
Objectivity	32	62	3
Nurturance	—	16	83
Intelligence			
Abstract Reasoning	35	64	—
Verbal Ability	9	71	18
Ambitiousness	56	42	—
Empathy/Intuition	—	40	58

dents convinced that the traits were *independent* of sex. Even in these exceptional cases a significantly large number of respondents disagreed with the majority.

The data provided by the tested students can be used to construct ideal models of the typical American woman and man, at least as they are conceived by a group of college students in California. These hypothetical sketches represent a kind of collective consciousness of the examined group. According to the composite model, the typical woman is emotional, nurturant, empathetic, and intuitive; whereas the typical man is aggressive, independent, and ambitious. Furthermore, on the average, men are believed to be more objective than women and have a knack for abstract thinking. Women are considered to be more verbal than men.

As we show in the following discussions of selected traits, the class's stereotypes are often consistent with the results of elegant behavioral studies. For example, 85 percent of our class thought that aggression was characteristic of males. Many tests run on Americans show that men *do* tend to be more aggressive than women. One such test allowed the subject to give an electric shock to another individual who was visible, but separated from the subject in a soundproofed room. The results show that men shock the victim more freely and with less consequent guilt than women (Buss 1963, and Buss and Brock 1963). In this experiment the expected behavior that men are more aggressive than women was confirmed.

Such observations raise the question of the origin of aggression and similar traits. Nineteenth-century scientists posed a simple dichotomy between genetic and environmental factors. This became known as the nature-nurture dichotomy. Much ink has been expended in attempts to resolve this dichotomy for a number of different human characteristics. The general result has been that the original formulation of the problem was too simplistic, and as such has resulted in distorted conclusions. This was best shown in a series of experiments on identical twins raised in separate homes. (Identical twins are genetically alike because they both develop from the same fertilized egg.) If separately reared identical twins show similar traits, these must be due to the shared genetic inheritance. Observed differences must be due to the different environments of each twin. The studies show that inheritance and environment *always* interact in the formation of any particular trait. If one twin is found to have an unusually low level of intelligence, so will the other. However, there is often a significant difference between the measured I.Q.'s of the two twins. One individual may score so low that he is institutionalized as an incurable mental defective. His twin may score at the low end of the normal range and be an active member of society, capable of earning his own living and caring for himself. These important differences stem from the twins' differing social environments.

However, when we wish to investigate trait differences and sex, twin studies cannot be used: identical twins are always the same sex. The sexes *are* genetically different, although this should not be taken to mean that all observed differences between the sexes are caused by these genetic differences. One useful way to investigate the origins of human behavioral differences between the sexes is to observe female-male behavior in a large number of different societies. This is a less precise and controlled duplication of twin studies, in that the genetic factor is believed to be relatively constant in comparison with the high degree of environmental variation. Thus, in anthropological studies dealing with sex differences there is an underlying assumption that women and men are genetically similar all over the world, whereas cultures are strikingly different. Unfortunately, there is not enough evidence on human genetics to confirm this assumption unambiguously. Nevertheless, the consistency of the findings gives strong support to the approach.

We shall now probe into various implications and ramifications of differential sexual behavior for certain traits: aggression, intelligence, dependency, ambitiousness, and nurturance. We shall examine each trait in a number of societies in order to determine the extent to which it is linked to a particular sex. This will enable us better to evaluate whether the correspondence between trait and sex is unique to our society. After determining the pervasiveness of correlations between sex type and trait manifestation, we shall explore various other lines of evidence that bear on the question of trait origin.

AGGRESSION

Recently much has been written about human aggression, apparently in response to a worldwide political situation in which aggression plays a central theme. It is small comfort to conclude, along with Konrad Lorenz (1966) and others, that human aggression is genetically determined. This conclusion is somehow taken to mean that aggression is not amenable to control. On the other hand, it is simplistic and naive to maintain that humans are basically pacifists who have become enraged and berserk en masse because of technological torments of the modern world. Moreover, whether it is attributed to innate factors or to social factors, aggression appears to be equated by everyone with masculinity. Some feminists have taken up this standard by arguing that war, a social evil, is caused by the inherent aggressive nature of men. They imply that war cannot be ended until women are the world's political leaders.

It is thus important for us to determine whether Western societies' strong feeling about the correlation between masculinity and aggression seems to hold widely for non-Western societies as well. However, we must first look at what is meant by aggression.

Aggression actually has several different meanings (see Kaufmann 1970), and it is important to know which meaning an author who deals with the subject is using. In the literature on animal behavior, aggression is strictly defined as the intent to do *bodily* harm. In this sense, physical assault is the primary factor in the definition. Thus the aggressiveness of an animal is judged by observers solely on the basis of the attacks or threats he makes on others.

In some literature—for example that of the social sciences—aggression is often a synonym for hostility. Judith Bardwick argues that to get a true measurement of levels of aggression one must examine "verbal aggression, interpersonal rejection, academic competitiveness, gossip, . . . deviation from sexual standards, passive aggression, the manipulation of adults with power, withdrawal, tears and somatic complaints—as well as fighting, hitting, and biting" (Bardwick 1971:134). Bardwick's conception of aggression is so broad that it becomes almost meaningless. At the very best, aggression as she defines it is difficult to observe and evaluate.

Bardwick does argue convincingly that in our society physical aggression is linked with males, whereas psychological aggression is associated with females. If men and women manifest their hostile feelings in very different ways, we cannot determine which sex is more aggressive because such a comparison requires a value judgment on the effectiveness of each aggressive pattern. Perhaps someday in the future we shall know if these sex-linked patterns of aggression occur widely in human societies; at present this possibility has not been fully investigated.

More is currently known about the origins and expression of physical aggression than psychological aggression. Physical aggression has a firm and regular correlation with males. In our society this sex difference is discernible at the nursery school age—that is, as soon as children are old enough to engage in prolonged interpersonal interactions—and continues into adulthood. In six studied societies Whiting and Whiting (cited in Bardwick 1971:128) also found that boys aged three to six were always more physically aggressive than their female age mates. This sex difference was found to be most pronounced in younger children. These data seem to indicate that physical aggression has a genetic basis because it is expressed by very young boys.

Aggression in Non-Western Societies. It is inappropriate to draw conclusions about human nature on the basis of observations made on a handful of societies. Unfortunately, only a small portion of the total number of human societies has been studied for sex differences in aggression. It is possible, however, to use indirect data in order to generalize as widely as possible about the human condition. For example, in all known societies in which warfare is a regular way of life, males are the combatants. In the majority of these societies only males fight, although in some societies the women also play an active part. Despite pervasive legends of Amazons, there are no known societies in which females *exclusively* assume the role of warriors. Even weapon-making, which is related to hunting as well as warfare, is reserved for males in most known societies. George Murdock (1937) found in his study of 224 societies that weapons were made by males in 99.8 percent of the cases studied. In only one society (0.2 percent) did women sometimes make weapons. This is true of Tiwi women (discussed in chapter 6) who make the weapons they use in hunting activities.

If men appear to be universally more physically aggressive than women, does this mean that all groups of men are equally fond of fighting? Margaret Mead tackles this problem in her book *Sex and Temperament* (1963). Mead's study contrasts the behavior of the gentle Arapesh from Northeast New Guinea with that of their aggressive neighbors, the Mundugumor.

The mountain dwelling Arapesh believe that both men and women are "inherently gentle, responsible, and cooperative, able and willing to subordinate the self to the needs of those who are younger or weaker, and to derive a major satisfaction from doing so" (Mead 1963:134). In their opinion all evil derives from the people who live in the adjacent interior plains of the Sepik River. The mountain Arapesh themselves consider each other equally "brothers and sisters" who live in a gentle, nonthreatening world in which the major human task is to promote growth of all living things. These people are primarily concerned with the growth and development of pigs, yams, and especially children. Human nature, as it is conceived by the Arapesh, is not basically grasping, aggressive, or difficult to train to peace. Instead it is basically gentle, but can be trained to be aggressive when defense of another person requires such action. When quarrels do arise among the Arapesh, any expressed aggression is always in behalf of a third party who may be the aggressor's friend or relative. In the Arapesh society aggression is permitted only when someone who is not permitted to defend himself needs defense. As Mead points out, in our society this type of behavior is considered typically feminine.

The surprisingly peaceful Arapesh present a challenge to the popular notion that humans are inherently aggressive. Mead asks whether this underdeveloped trait is due to dietary deficiencies, genetic inbreeding, or cultural factors. She concludes that diet cannot explain this observed behavior because the plains-dwelling Arapesh, who are very bellicose, have a more limited protein intake than their peaceful mountain-dwelling relatives. The idea that inbreeding may have favored docile people has no support because the level of expressed aggression varies widely within the Arapesh community. In addition, Mead observes that the Arapesh men are not physically different from their fiercely aggressive neighbors as would be expected if differential genetic evolution had taken place.

Mead concludes that the best explanation for Arapesh docility is that it is a highly valued personality trait which is vigorously taught to children of each new generation. Her observations on Arapesh child-rearing demonstrate that from the time of birth the child is continuously held and nurtured in such a way that aggressive behavior is seldom expressed.

We suspect that the encouragement of pacificity has an adaptive advantage for the Arapesh society as a whole. These people live in a part of the world where chronic warfare is the norm. Perhaps their obvious disinterest in fighting shields them from some attacks by other groups who prefer more zealous enemies. Analytically the Arapesh may be seen to occupy a cultural niche which permits them to survive in the hostile social environment of New Guinea.

Despite a cultural deemphasis on aggression, slightly more aggression is tolerated in males than in females. This is due, in part, to differences in child rearing. An Arapesh girl, who is married at an early age, usually goes to her husband's home to be raised. Boys, however, remain in their own family homes. Mead reports that parents are more tolerant of a child's anger than are in-laws. This means that boys are permitted to express anger more easily than girls in Arapesh society. In addition, some boys who show promise as future community leaders are groomed for that role by being permitted to be more aggressive than other boys. This is because Arapesh leaders are expected to represent the community in an arrogant and aggressive way.

People who are exceptionally aggressive often become partial social dropouts. Mead describes one such individual "who approached most strongly to a Western-European ideal of the male, well built, with a handsome face with fine lines, a well-integrated body, violent, possessive, arbitrary, dictatorial, positively and aggressively sexed. Among the Arapesh he was a pathetic figure" (Mead 1963:149). In fact, at the age of 25 this man "had retired from taking any active interest in his culture" (Mead 1963:148).

This man's female counterpart, a woman named Amitoa, is described as an even more tragic figure.

> Raw-boned, with a hawklike face and a sinewy body that lacked all the softer signs of femininity, her small high breasts already shrunken although she was a scant thirty-five, Amitoa had found her life a stormy one. Her mother before her had been a violent, tempestuous person, and both Amitoa and

her sister showed the same characteristics.
She was betrothed at an early age to a youth
who died, and she was inherited by a man
much older than she, a man enfeebled by illness. Now although Arapesh girls prefer
young men, this is not on grounds of physiological potency, but rather because they are
less grave and decorous, and less exacting
in the matter of household duties. Amitoa
alone, of all of the Arapesh women whom I
knew well, was articulately conscious of sexual desire and critical of a husband in terms
of his ability to satisfy it. She alone knew the
meaning of climax after intercourse, while
the other women to whose canons she had
to adjust did not even recognize a marked
relaxation, but instead described their post-
intercourse sensations as diffused warmth
and ease. Amitoa despised her timid, ailing
husband. She mocked her husband's orders,
she flew out at him savagely when he re-
buked her. Finally, enraged at her insubordi-
nation—she who was a mere child whose
breasts had not fallen down, while he was an
older man—he tried to beat her, seizing a
fire-brand from the fire. She wrested it from
him, and instead of giving blows he received
them. He took up an adze and this also she
seized. He screamed for help, and his
younger brother had to rescue him. This was
a scene which was to be repeated again and
again in Amitoa's life (Mead 1963:149–50).

Mead found the gentle, nonaggressive life of the Arapesh in
sharp contrast to that of the Mundugumor, another group in
Northeast New Guinea. The Mundugumor live only about 100
miles from the Arapesh but contact between them is restricted
to indirect trade connections. The two groups are known to
each other only in a vague way. The Arapesh men summed this
situation up when they counseled Dr. Mead as she was prepar-
ing to leave for Mundugumor country: "We are another kind,
they are another kind. So you will find it" (Mead 1963:167).

The Mundugumor are river-dwelling people who have a tradition of head-hunting and cannibalism. Men spend much of

their time organizing themselves into raiding parties, the primary purpose of which is to return with a human trophy. A Mundugumor group is always vulnerable to predator attacks by neighbors seeking retribution for recent homicides and maintains uneasy alliances with other neighbors, who may suddenly become treacherous.

Hostility and distrust are not only characteristic of external relations but are also typical of interpersonal relations within a community. Symptomatic of this condition, the Mundugumor have no permanent residence groups, but only temporary associations of families linked together by the presence of male kin or male in-laws. These associations break up when serious quarrels necessitate moving in order to pacify someone's injured pride. The touchiest members of the residential group are often the male relatives who, according to Mundugumor beliefs, share a natural hostility toward each other as members of the same sex. This belief is reflected in Mundugumor social organization. Social group membership, rather than passing from the mother or father to *both* male and female children as in the typical unilineal system, is reckoned through opposite sex-links only. That is, a father may pass on his kinship affiliation only to his daughter, and she in turn only to her sons. People in a single group respect the same supernatural beings and are bound by certain responsibilities and obligations to each other. Property is also inherited within this group so that a man leaves all his important goods, including his weapons, to his daughters. Mundugumor social organization thus fragments a family by allying the mother with her sons and the father with his daughters.

The structural antagonism within the family is compounded by several other factors. For example, brothers are taught to be formal with each other and become rivals for their mother's affection. Later on in life this rivalry is exacerbated by the custom of marriage arrangements, in which a boy with his eye on a future bride must arrange for his sister to marry the girl's brother. This is hard enough to accomplish without the further complication that several brothers may each be trying to use their only, or most popular, sister in their marriage arrangements. Even their father may be simultaneously trying to use the same girl in his attempts to win a new wife. So the practice of sister exchange, combined with that of polygyny (which allows a powerful man to have many wives), puts brothers and fathers at constant odds with one another. Sisters also actively compete with each other in trying to better their positions. This competition begins when they are children vying for their father's affection, and continues later when they vie for influence over the man who is likely to arrange the most desirable marriage.

Social alienation in Mundugumor society is even reflected in sexual relations. Young lovers express their affection by biting, scratching, tearing clothing, and destroying ornaments and other objects of their beloved.

In this ruthless world created by the Mundugumor, a premium is placed on rugged individualism, self-assertion, passionate sexuality, and physical aggression. These traits are equally desirable in men and women. Mead (1963:210) reports that the women "are believed to be just as violent, just as aggressive, just as jealous" as men. Despite this quote, Mead's study makes it clear that men engage more often than women in physical aggression. For example, she says "although women choose men as often as men choose women, society is constructed so that men fight about women, and women elude, defy and complicate this fighting to the limit of their abilities. So little girls grow up as aggressive as little boys and with no expectation of docilely accepting their role in life" (Mead 1963:210). These remarks indicate that aggression is high in Mundugumor society and that it is expressed differently by women and men. Physical aggression is practiced regularly by the men, whereas the women often resort to other means of expressing their hostilities.

Biological Basis of Aggression. It has now been amply demonstrated that aggression among humans is a trait that a particular society may treat as either desirable or undesirable for all or some of its members (see Kardiner 1939 for a general cross-cultural comparison). Physical aggression, nevertheless, seems to be expressed more extensively by males than by females in any given group. In addition, this correlation between maleness and physical aggression holds true for many vertebrates, including most monkeys and apes. This indicates that a factor common to male vertebrates may be involved in the expression of physical aggression.

Hormones are one such common factor. Sex hormones are being studied to determine their role in behavior (see Beach 1965) including aggressive behavior. For example Young and his associates (1964:216) found that female rhesus monkeys which had been masculinized by prenatal treatment of androgen behaved more like normal male than normal female rhesus monkeys. The altered females exhibited more threat behavior and less withdrawal from other individuals than normal females. The behavioral changes were not only restricted to aggression but also were observed in play behavior. This study shows that the sex hormones influence behavior which is not directly sexual and that the expression of aggression may be induced by sex hormones.

Another study on rhesus monkeys shows that no matter what the biological basis of aggression, social learning greatly affects its expression (Delgado 1967). In Delgado's study monkeys were stimulated by means of electrodes implanted in their brains (the hypothalamus). This stimulation caused a response that varied depending on the social rank of the stimulated animals. For example, normally dominant monkeys attacked others when artificially stimulated by an electrical impulse. Subordinate monkeys, in contrast, cowered and were themselves attacked more frequently as a result of the same stimulus. This shows that for monkeys social learning is significantly involved in the expression of aggression. Even when stimulated the hypothalamus is monitored by other parts of the brain concerned with learning and other behaviors. This network of communications allows for the hormone-hypothalamus response to be modified by learning in a social environment.

Discussion. Before leaving the subject of sex and aggression we shall review some general points. It has often been observed that humans are the only known animals that systematically attempt to exterminate their own kind. It has also been speculated that this gruesome tendency is due to a genetically based need to be aggressive. This is as if people in general and males in particular have basic urges to damage other people. According to this theory, these urges, which are infinitely renewable, can be controlled only by periodic blowouts which serve to temporarily discharge these needs. Thus, aggressive needs are mentioned in the same breath with physiological needs for nourishment, or psychophysical needs for sex.

This concept of aggression is sharply at variance with our own. We believe that humans are born with the capability of being aggressive and that this capability is closely akin to other defensive mechanisms found in animals. All animals have means to allow them to compete successfully for various resources needed for their survival. Among humans, of course, the only serious competitors that have to be dealt with by one group are those of another group. Thus, physical aggression is one possible response to these conditions. It should be noted immediately that another very appropriate response, mutualism or cooperation, is also highly developed among humans. In other words, humans are faced with the same general problems as are other organisms. The human solutions to these common problems are unique in their intensities. Humans not only fight each other harder than do other animals, but they are also more intensely cooperative.

If the potentiality for aggression is in us all, this is only half the story. It seems also true that the potentiality for the *control* of the expression of aggression is equally present in us all. Coevolving with human aggression was the mechanism for its control. Without this control human social life would not be possible. Strongly aggressive people are asocial and hence maladaptive to the group unless they are able to control and direct their aggressive tendencies in appropriate ways. Hence, to admit that all people *can* always respond aggressively to a situation is certainly not saying that it is necessary and sufficient for them to do so.

When we examine the question of sex differences in aggression we must consider several aspects. If we attempt to consider aggression in all its manifestations, we run into considerable difficulty. How can we compare the relative intensities of physical and psychological aggression? These traits cannot be directly compared without placing a value judgment on their relative effects. In our own society there is good evidence to suggest that females usually manifest one type of aggression and males the other. If we cannot rigorously compare these differences of expressed aggression, how can we argue that one sex is actually more aggressive than the other? At present very little is known about nonphysical aggressive acts cross-culturally. We cannot say if women generally are psychologically more aggressive than men, but at least this possibility should be acknowledged.

If we consider the expression of physical aggression, we see that males are consistently more aggressive than females in most human societies and in closely related animal groups. This commonality is clearly related to effects of the male hormones, common to these animals. Social learning, in contrast, can greatly modify the hormonal effects in monkeys as well as humans. Thus it appears that learning factors are more important than genetic factors in the expression of aggression in humans and closely related species.

INTELLIGENCE

Is there any correlation between sex and intelligence? Judging from the responses to our questionnaire (Table 3-1), most people would answer that no such correlation exists. Some respondents disagreed with the majority and the patterning of their answers is noteworthy. For example, abstract thinking was frequently associated with males, whereas verbal ability was linked with females. Is there any evidence for these beliefs, and if so, what is the cause of sex-linked intelligence differences?

Intelligence and Intelligence Tests. We must first attempt to define intelligence. Most of us think we can recognize an intelligent person when we meet one, but it is difficult to precisely define this trait. Even Alfred Binet, one of the founding fathers of intelligence testing, avoided formulating a definition of this concept. Instead, he described intelligence as the ability "to judge well, to comprehend well, to reason well" (cited in Heim 1971:349). Others have said that intelligence is that characteristic which is measured by intelligence tests. This humorous statement has the merit as well of suggesting there may be more to "intelligence" than what is ordinarily tested. Despite a growing recognition of this fact, many people continue to believe that intelligence tests are an accurate measure of a person's mental abilities. We need to examine this idea carefully before discussing sex differences in intelligence.

Intelligence tests were developed in large, complex, industrial societies in which it had become necessary to predict a person's relative ability to perform special tasks. It was important for planning purposes to be able to predict the percentage of fourth graders that would continue to college, or which of the men inducted into the army would have an aptitude for electronics. Intelligence tests have therefore evolved as measures of a person's probable success in the area of performance under evaluation. When a particular test is being created, the tester has a particular goal in mind. If the tester wishes to predict the future academic success of a fourth grader, he writes some sample questions and uses them on a test group of fourth graders. The academic success of these tested children is then monitored over the years. The tester uses his results to revise the test so that questions that seem to discriminate well on the parameter of academic achievement are retained in his test, and unuseful questions are discarded.

When we consider the results of intelligence tests it is important to keep two points in mind. First, they are standardized by examining a sample of the population for which the test is intended. Traditionally in America this sample has consisted of white, middle-class individuals of both sexes. This means that the tests are invalid when applied to population segments not represented in the group used for standardization. Second, intelligence tests are designed for specific purposes and they are not useful in making other types of discriminations.

For example, men and women show no overall differences in
general intelligence on most tests. Differences do exist, but
most tests are not designed to reflect them; the kinds of tasks in
which each sex excels are given equal weight on the final score
(Maccoby 1966). The exams are created in this way because the
testers are not interested in differentiating males from females.
This differentiation can be done much more expedititously by
other means. Therefore, questions that discriminate the sex of
the respondent well but do not discriminate well on the future
of academic achievement are promptly removed from the questionnaire.

Despite the attempt to minimize the effect of a person's sex
on the final score, intelligence differences between the sexes do
show up on most examinations. These are real, measurable differences between two subgroups of the population. The nature
of the differences tells us something about how these subgroups
are unlike.

The results of intelligence tests confirm the impressions of
those students who related various attributes of intelligence to a
specific sex. Generally speaking, females tend to excel in verbal
ability, when compared as a group with males (Anastasi
1958:472–74). This differential ability is first manifested in very
young children; little girls learn to talk and to formulate complete sentences sooner than do little boys. In fact, throughout
the preschool years girls are more fluent than boys. This greater
verbal skill continues to be evident during the early school
years, when girls excel in reading ability, grammar, spelling,
and word fluency (Bardwick 1971:109). During the later school
years differences in verbal ability between boys and girls tend
to become less pronounced, but even in adulthood women appear to be slightly superior in verbal skills (Oetzel 1962:128).
For example, women perform better than men in the verbal aptitude subtest of the Graduate Record Examinations (Garcia
1972:43).

Males, in contrast, tend to excel in measures of abstract thinking (see Anastasi 1958:477). This trait refers to the ability to
draw inferences, or elicit relationships, between theoretical
facts or symbols. If mathematical reasoning is accepted as being

indicative of abstract thinking, the tests indicate that boys become more skilled than girls in late adolescence. In the earlier years no significant differences are correlated with sex. Once they appear, however, they continue into adulthood. Men do better than women, for example, in the quantitative subtest of the Graduate Record Examination.

These measurably different expressions of intelligence have led to considerable literature dealing with this subject. This literature seeks to explain the observed differences in terms of biological or social factors. Thus, some argue that woman's reproductive role has required her to develop abilities consistent with her child-bearing and -rearing tasks, whereas men, as group defenders, have been required to hone their wits differently. Others argue that the major factor in these observed differences is the different training given to boys and girls. Personality traits that are thought to be feminine are encouraged in female children, whereas those believed typically masculine are inculcated in boys. It is necessary to review the evidence backing each position in order to evaluate their relative validity.

It is generally agreed nowadays that both environmental and genetic factors interact in the determination of a person's intelligence. This fact can best be demonstrated by considering the relative intelligence of twins. Fig. 3-1 shows that among pairs of children, identical twins reared together have the closest I.Q.'s. These twins are genetically alike and reared in similar environments. The fact that such co-twins do not show exactly identical I.Q.'s, or for that matter personalities, can be explained by their slightly different social environments. For example, parents and other people relate differently to each twin. In contrast, identical twins reared separately show a greater average disparity between their I.Q.'s than identicals reared together. This clearly shows that different environments do affect the expressed intelligence of children. Compared with identical twins, however, pairs of fraternal twins and other pairs of siblings show greater differences in I.Q.'s when reared in the same household. This comparison shows the role of genetic factors in determining intelligence.

Generalizing from these data we conclude that genetic and

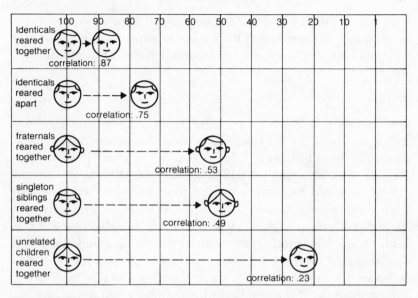

Figure 3–1. I.Q. correlations (degrees of closeness) between pairs of twins of different kinds, as compared with those of other paired children (after Garcia 1972:92). (Reprinted from *Psychology Today* Magazine, June 1972.)

environmental factors jointly determine intelligence, and that environmental differences can produce at least as much differentiation in I.Q. as is produced by genetic differences (Dobzhansky 1962). It is expected that if environmental differences were truly maximized by raising identical twins in totally different cultural settings, their intelligence could not be compared by means of a single test.

As important as twin studies are for demonstrating the roles of genetic and environmental factors in the general determination of intelligence, we have pointed out that they are not useful in investigating sex differences in this trait. The lack of closely controlled studies does not prevent the examination of factors involved in the determination of sex-linked intelligence differences. It does mean, however, that this examination must draw together evidence gleaned from various approaches to the study of humans.

To begin this examination we shall consider the evidence that supports the idea that *genetic* factors are related to male-female intelligence differences. This idea was especially popular 100 years ago and has continued to have advocates until the present time.

Intelligence and Brain Size. Approximately a century ago there was a scholarly consensus that males and females differed significantly in intelligence. Some scholars argued that the difference was in a quality called general intelligence, whereas others believed females were deficient only in the powers of higher reasoning. In other words, some felt females were just plain dumb, whereas others felt that female intelligence was different from male intelligence and lacked the faculties touted by the scholars themselves. The evidence for intelligence differences between the sexes came from personal observations, including general impressions plus the observation that women rarely excelled in professions, and from sex differences in skull size, which were believed to be a direct indicator of intelligence. Women, with demonstrably smaller heads and brain cavities than men, were believed to be less intelligent.

The observed differences were invariably attributed to constitutional differences between males and females. For example, in 1874 W. L. Distant delivered a talk on this subject to members of the Royal Anthropological Institute of Great Britain and Ireland, in which he argued for a partially different evolution for each sex. According to Distant's formulation of early human social life, there was once a time when men and women were nearly equal and very bestial in mentality. These early people were believed to have lived in groups that were sexually promiscuous and chaotic. The males were responsible for maintaining whatever social order was present by means of sheer physical force. Somehow, men gradually came to depend more on brain power than brawn. According to Distant this had important implications for male-female relations: "Now in the possession of the female, other things being equal, the man with the larger brain has the advantage" (Distant 1874:81). Male braininess, the argument continues, was enhanced through the course of evolution by means of selective factors involved in the male-male political power struggle. Apparently no one suggested that females preferred brainy men. Men were, therefore, self-selected for mental ability. The women, in contrast, were selected by these men for their beauty. "The course of sexual selection thus tends to mentally strengthen the males, but applies in an inverse ratio to females" (Distant 1874:81). Distant argued, then, that during the course of evolution men become more intelligent but women became less so.

The bases for Distant's ideas were derived from several sources. First, he believed that sexual differences in mental ability were greater in the European population than in primitive races. This belief was based on the study of skulls from various populations. At that time sexually dimorphic skull differences were believed to be less pronounced among primitive peoples than among Europeans. In other words, Distant believed that male Europeans were selectively favored over other people in the inheritance of mental capability. Second, Distant believed—along with many of his contemporaries—that beauty and intelligence were incompatible and perhaps inversely related traits. Alexander Walker expressed this idea in 1837 in a treatise on beauty in which he suggested that the ideally beautiful woman should have a small-sized head "because the mental system in the female ought to be subordinate to the vital . . . [that is, to life forces allowing a cheerful temperament] sensibility should exceed reasoning power" (Stannard 1971:198). According to this logic, if women were selected for their beauty, their intelligence would be selectively decreased.

The idea that males benefited more than females from the evolution of mental faculties was even expressed by Charles Darwin. "These latter faculties [imagination and reason], as well as the former [perseverance] will have been developed in man, partly through sexual selection—that is, *through the contest of rival males,* and partly through natural selection—that is from success in the general struggle for life" (Darwin 1874:588, emphasis ours). Darwin suggested that these traits, which are gained after maturity in a man's life, would be differentially transmitted to male offspring. This he felt was in accord with the general tendency for physical characteristics acquired by either sex late in life to be transmitted only to children of the same sex.

Darwin thus suggested that the quality he called genius was selected for by natural selection (in which case both sexes were subject to the same evolutionary pressures) and sexual selection (applicable only to males). Darwin did not agree with Distant's interpretation that women became less intelligent with evolutionary development, but he did believe that men became brighter at a faster rate, because of increased selection pressures. Despite his belief that men were favored for brightness by evolution, Darwin was perplexed by the observation that the sexes did not manifest greater differences in mentality. "It is, indeed, fortunate that the law of equal transmission of characters to both sexes *prevails* with mammals; otherwise it is probable that man would have become as superior in mental endowment to woman as the peacock is in ornamental plummage to the peahen" (Darwin 1874:588; emphasis ours).

For a man of his time Darwin was cautious in his treatment of sex differences in mental ability. He believed differences actually existed, and he attributed them to evolutionary forces. At the same time he recognized that the intelligence differences between the sexes were not great and pervasive, and that the mental abilities of the sexes were more alike than different.

In the years intervening between us and Darwin and Distant, much new information has accumulated on this topic: the mode of inheritance of characteristics was worked out by Mendel; skull size among humans was found *not* to be an indicator of intelligence; intelligence was discovered to be a complex trait dependent on multiple modes of inheritance as well as environmental factors; and intelligence tests were invented. These and other factors led the scholarly community's interest away from male-female differences in intelligence. Indeed the topic was not particularly popular for some time.

Intelligence, Brains, and Hormones. Currently genetic factors are again being advocated to explain observed differences in intelligence styles between men and women. This renewed interest is based on an improved understanding of the effects of sex hormones on organs other than those associated with reproduction. Researchers are now exploring the possibility that even brains may be affected by sex hormones during fetal development.

The mammalian brain is known to undergo a period of development during which critical changes occur in brain chemistry and cell organization. The time of these changes varies for each species but is always simultaneous with the earliest signs of brain function. Recent studies have led some investigators to conclude that behavioral patterns related to sex are indelibly stamped on an animal's brain during this period. No amount of later manipulation of the internal hormonal environment of the animal will permit behavioral reversal.

These studies have been carried out on rats (Levine 1966), guinea pigs, and rhesus monkeys. Some of these animals were subjected to hormones typical of the opposite sex during the critical period of brain development. This was done either by castration of gonads (ovaries and testes) and their replacement by gonads of the opposite sex, or by castration and injection with hormones of the opposite sex. The startling results were that the young animals tended to behave like animals opposite to their own chromosomal sex. This behavior change was most noticeable after puberty when the animals responded in the sexually appropriate manner to hormones that were similar to those present during the critical period of brain development. Sex hormones opposite to those present during the critical period had little or no behavioral effects. Yet these hormones were congruent with the animal's chromosomal sex.

These observations led to the hypothesis that changes in an animal's organs take place as a result of exposure to sex hormones in early life. What organs are affected? At first, the pituitary seemed a likely possibility because hormones emanating from it regulate the production of the sex hormones by the gonads. Until recently it was also thought that these sex hormones in turn regulated the pituitary's hormonal production. It was later discovered that transplants of pituitaries across the sexes had no effect whatsoever on the recipient's behavior. This clearly showed that the pituitary was not modified by exposure to sex hormones. Now it is known that the hypothalamus, a part of the brain, is also integrally involved in the process of sex hormone regulation. This structure appears to be altered by the sex hormones during early development. So far, however, it has not been possible to perform cross-sex transplants of hypothalamus glands in order to determine whether behavioral changes result.

If brains are sex typed in some animals does this also apply to humans? Sexual behavior in the animals studied is, of course, much more closely tied to hormonal changes than is human sexual behavior. It could be argued that for this reason conclusions based on animal studies cannot be applied to humans. It is important to note, however, that the behavioral changes observed in the studied animals were not restricted to sexual activity. General behavioral patterns relating to play, threat, and mounting (Bardwick 1971:85) were also altered. This pervasiveness of behavioral alteration makes it imperative to consider the implication of these studies for humans.

Fortunately direct experimentation is not allowed on human subjects. This means that indirect evidence must be accumulated and evaluated in light of the animal studies just discussed. Some indirect evidence comes from research carried out by John Hampson. Hampson was interested in studying the development of sexual identity in human beings. In order to do this he collected case material on individuals whose sexual development was inconsistent. These inconsistencies concerned contradictions between one of the six variables of sex outlined by Hampson and Hampson (see chapter 2) and the sex of assignment and rearing. Hampson and Hampson discovered that overwhelmingly the patients identified with the sex of their rearing. The implication was that sexual roles are learned and are remarkably free from genetic influences. The researchers thus believed that their data supported the idea of psychosexual neutrality at birth.

This extreme position may need modification. For example, Hampson and Hampson's work may in fact be consistent with the idea of prenatal alteration of the central nervous system. Infant girls who are born with masculinized genitals are often misidentified as boys and are raised accordingly. Their masculinized genitals are probably the result of excess androgens during prenatal development. Therefore, the possibility exists that these hormones have affected other organs, conceivably including the brain.

The idea that sex hormones affect the human brain in a sex specific way is not found to be compelling by John Money (1971), who has studied the effects of prenatal excess androgens. Money points out that if human brains are sex-typed during prenatal development, then people who have been subjected to more than the normal amounts of male hormones while in the womb should score in a male pattern on intelligence tests. His patients, who are both male and female, showed no such pattern of scoring.

Money did make a startling discovery. He found that his patients uniformly excelled in intelligence tests. Thus, these people whose adrenal glands malfunctioned while they were carried in their mothers' wombs proved to be exceptionally bright in later life. Does this mean that male sex hormones can be linked directly to mental ability? At present there is no pat answer because follow-up studies have not yet been made. Nevertheless, the possibility is strengthened by the fact that prenatal excess of a synthetic hormone, progestin, which is chemically similar to androgen, was found to have the same effects on morphology, physiology, and the performance of affected individuals on intelligence tests as did androgen excess. The results of these interesting studies remain to be fully explored. Unfortunately no comparable data are available on the effects of prenatal excess of *female* hormones.

Intelligence and Other Personality Traits. Some investigators have pointed out that sex differences in intelligence relate to general personality characteristics which are typical of males and females in this society. There is considerable evidence to suggest that these characteristics are largely learned rather than inherited.

Maccoby (1966) summarizes several tests that investigate the relationship between dependency and intelligence in children. There is a tendency for independent children of *both* sexes to excel on a variety of intellectual tasks, whereas dependent children do less well. Dependent children score lower on tasks that require restructuring a problem or ignoring background information. These children are thus not good at tasks that require abstract thinking.

Maccoby suggests two possible reasons why there should be a correlation between dependency and analytical thinking. One is that an individual who is dependent is oriented toward stimuli emanating from others. This may make it difficult to ignore external stimuli in favor of internal thought processes. Another reason is that dependent people tend to be passive. Some intellectual tasks, such as those solved by trial and error, require considerable initiative, a characteristic of independent rather than dependent people.

There seems to be a clear-cut relationship between certain types of mental activity and an individual's emotional and social self-sufficiency. This holds true for people of both sexes. In general, however, females in American society tend to be both more dependent and less analytical than males. The question thus arises whether this pattern of associated traits is derived from physiological features or is primarily due to the American conception of appropriate behavior for females.

DEPENDENCY

Dependency refers to an individual's need to rely for support on someone or something. Psychologists recognize that a moderate amount of dependency is one component of the personality of a normal healthy adult; excessive, dependency is considered to be symptomatic of emotional or mental illness.

Dependency Patterns in American Society. Americans generally believe that women are more dependent than men. This trait

was not sampled in the reported study (Table 3-1), but the results do show that 72 percent of the respondents believe that
men are more *independent* than women. Psychologists have
devised several tests that measure dependency and independence. When they are given to groups of middle-class adults,
the results consistently show that women do indeed score
higher in dependency and men in self-reliance (Goldin et al.
1972).

In order to examine this situation in more detail it is instructive to explore the developmental origins of dependence and
independence. All human infants begin their lives in a state of
unconditional dependence on others. At this stage of development there are no differences between boys and girls.

During the course of individual development a child must
gradually learn to become ever more self-reliant. Slowly the
dependency on his-her parents is reduced in scope and intensity. As the child becomes more self-reliant, dependency is
directed at a wider circle of individuals. This usually occurs at
the age when children form play groups of same-aged individuals (see Parens and Saul 1971). The transition from dependence to independence is made easier by parents who are
warm, supportive, and who have the patience to allow the child
to work out tasks that are within his abilities—parents who actively encourage this trait by allowing their children to explore
the limits of their abilities. This is a difficult task for parents
because a child's abilities are continually expanding with his
growth.

Although parental interest and support is important in the development of self-reliance in both boys and girls, it is found that
the behavioral dynamics within individual families differs depending on the sex of the self-reliant child. Self-reliant boys
come from homes in which the father frequently interacts with
the child but does not impose overly strict standards of behavior. Self-reliant girls also have fathers who are available and interested in their development (see Goldin et al. 1972:41). Their
mothers, however, tend to be either rejecting or excessively
permissive. This shows that when men are actively involved in
the rearing of their children there is a tendency for the young-

sters to develop self-reliance. Often, however, fathers are more involved with their sons than with their daughters, so that the perpetuation of self-reliant behavior is greater in the male line. Under special circumstances, when a mother is not active in the rearing of her daughter, the father may be atypically involved in her development. This can provide the girl with an available model of self-reliant adult behavior as well as the paternal encouragement to develop this trait.

An examination of patterns of dependency aids in assessing these sex differences. Researchers have found that children under the age of eight differ measurably in their expressed dependency, but that this does not correlate significantly with sex (Bardwick 1971:117). Instead, the most significant correlation is with child-rearing practices of parents. These findings indicate that dependency is found in children who have nonaffectionate and nonsupportive parents. These parents do not satisfy their infant's psychobiological needs. The child apparently learns to mistrust parents who fail to provide him with his desired gratifications. This, in turn, causes the child to be insecure and constantly in need of reaffirmation of the relationship. Judging from the available data there is an equal probability for the development of excessive dependency for boys and girls at this age.

In school-age children sex correlates with dependency. Girls are more dependent than boys and this association holds true to adulthood. In fact, a long-term study of people over a 25-year period (Kagan and Moss 1962) showed some interesting contrasts between patterns of dependency in males and females. In females it was found that patterns of dependency tend to be consistent throughout life. Highly dependent girls became highly dependent adolescents, and later highly dependent women. Males, in contrast, did not follow the same trend. Often, highly dependent boys became independent men.

These results suggest that the social pressures for independence in males continue unabated during development. Thus, some boys can learn independent behavior in later years, whereas females who have not learned independent behavior as children are not continuously encouraged to do so in their later years.

Adult men and women also differ significantly in the foci of their dependencies. It has been found that dependent adult women tend to focus their needs for gratification on a single individual who is the object of their love. These are often the husbands or male friends of the women. Highly dependent men direct their dependency needs at several individuals. These often include some of their male friends, as well as their love-objects.

These observations indicate that male dependency and female dependency are qualitatively different. It appears that even the most dependent men in our society have managed to become relatively more self-reliant than their female counterparts. It is as though the development of self-reliance is arrested at a later stage for dependent men. Just how these expected behaviors are communicated to children remains an interesting and poorly unexplored area of research. In fact so little is actually known that some people remain convinced that biological factors are involved significantly (see Maccoby 1966).

Curiously, we know more about how some monkey mothers actively encourage independence than we know about human mothers. Jensen and associates (1968) found that monkey mothers encourage independent behavior in their male offspring to a greater degree than in their female offspring. The monkeys do this by punishing the males more frequently, and denying them less positive physical contact than females. This differential treatment does not start at birth but later on, during the initial stages of weaning.

In humans many factors in addition to the mother-infant interaction are involved in the development of independence. The father's role has already been discussed. Factors other than interpersonal relations may also play a significant part. Bardwick (1971:117) suggests that even toys may contribute to this difference. She observes that boys often play with toys that work only when they are properly constructed. The child is able to judge for himself whether or not his efforts have been successful. Girls play with toys that often do not foster independent judgment of success. The decoration of a doll's house requires the opinion of others for a child to judge whether her efforts have yielded pleasing results.

We do not know of any rigorous studies that examine the relationship between toys and the dependency-independency variable. A number of studies are more generally concerned with sex typing—the socialization process that leads to gender role behavior. Ball (1967), for example, has argued that toys are part of the social environment impinging upon a child, and as such affect the child's behavior. Weitzman and her associates (1972) have investigated the sex-role socialization effects of picture books designed for preschoolers. Goodman and Lever (1972) have examined attitudes about toys and discovered that in general boys' toys are considered to be more complex and to encourage more active and social play than girls' toys. Girls' toys were rated as less complex, less active, and less social than boys' toys. Interestingly the youngest group of respondents, fifth graders, preferred boys' toys. The authors conclude that girls' toys in general encourage more solitary, passive, and simple play.

Dependency in Non-Western Societies. The above observations indicate to us that in American society males are socialized to be independent, whereas females who maintain childlike dependency patterns are acceptable. These differences in socialization for independence seem to be characteristic of a great many societies.

Barry, Bacon, and Child (1957) compared the socialization practices of the sexes in a number of societies for which such information has been reported by anthropologists. One of these traits was self-reliance. In the study two judges read each field report and decided whether a particular trait was taught equally to children of both sexes or differentially to one or the other sex. When the judgments differed the trait was considered not related to either sex.

The investigators found that in 85 percent of the 82 societies studied boys were taught self-reliance to a greater extent than girls. In the remaining 15 percent one judge believed the sexes were equally socialized in the development of this trait, whereas the other judge felt boys were encouraged to be more self-reliant than girls.

This result is striking, particularly because of the difficulties in comparing reports written by different authors. We believe that these results do not indicate that women have a greater inherent tendency for dependence than do men. Instead, it appears that independence must be taught to children, and that this lesson is directed at males more than at females in a large number of societies. This situation needs to be explained, and one way to do so would be to study societies in which high female dependency is found. Perhaps these societies all share certain features that combine to create a social organization conducive to female dependency. Before we tackle this issue it is instructive to examine one society that does not conform to American expectations concerning dependency and sex roles.

The Tchambuli are a group of people in central New Guinea whose sex roles have been studied by Margaret Mead (1963). They live near the shores of a lake; fishing is their primary economic activity, but it is supplemented by the manufacture of trade items, and produce from household gardens. Most of their food not derived from the lake is obtained from horticultural people in exchange for fish and manufactured items.

Tchambuli women are the providers in this society. They do the bulk of the fishing, farming, and manufacturing. They also raise the children and maintain the houses where they and the children live apart from the men. Mead describes Tchambuli women as cheerful, industrious, and energetic. Their activities are shared in an atmosphere of group solidarity, friendly activity, and firm cooperation (Mead 1963:239).

Mead describes the men's life in much less glowing terms. The men live in ceremonial clan houses close to the lake shore. They cook and collect firewood for themselves. They also are skilled artists who spend a great deal of time creating elaborate masks, lime gourds, and personal ornaments, as well as learning to play the sacred music of the society. Mead describes the atmosphere in the men's houses as being one of mutual suspicion, competition, and petty jealousies. Interpersonal alliances between men are shifting, insubstantial, and briefly intense. "The membership in the men's houses varies, and quarrels are frequent. Upon the merest slight—a claim of precedence that is not justified, a failure of the wife of one man to feed the pigs of another, a failure to return a borrowed article—the person who cherishes a sense of hurt will move away, and go live with some other clan group to which he can claim relationship" (Mead 1963:246).

These differences relate in part to features of the social organization. Although both men and women have clan affiliations, the men are active in other associations with memberships that cut across clan lines. These formal alliances between men depend on the situation; men who are allied on an issue one day may find themselves shortly thereafter on opposing sides of another issue. Women, in contrast, are primarily active in clan functions and their daily lives are usually spent in close association with female clanmates. This is because a woman's co-wives are often her sisters, and her mother-in-law is her paternal aunt. All of these women have known each other for much of their lives, and their association is stable, long-lasting, and congruent with the formal affiliations. Men, then, have conflicting demands placed on their allegiance, whereas women do not.

Another aspect of the differences in the interrelationships between same-sexed individuals is that courtship tends to be divisive in male-male interpersonal relations. Although ideally men arrange for bride-price exchanges in the obtainment of spouses, in practice women chose their mates. "No one knows where a woman's choice will fall, each youth holds his breath and hopes, and no young man is willing to trust another" (Mead 1963:258). The mistrust characteristic of male-male relations often is exacerbated by marriage. Often a young boy is married to an older girl. The girl not infrequently becomes impatient with her husband's awkwardness in sex and resorts to an affair with one of his clanmates. This is consistent with the sex roles among the Tchambuli, where female sexuality is believed stronger than male sexuality. The cuckolded husband is publicly ridiculed and berated for his failure to satisfy his wife. This causes him to be withdrawn, jealous, and suspicious of his clanmates.

The relationship between the sexes is embedded in the larger societal context. A man relates to his female relatives as "a solid group upon whom he depends for support, for food, for affection" (Mead 1963:251). The women, in contrast, treat the men "with kindly tolerance and appreciation" (Mead 1963:255). Mead's description of sex roles in Tchambuli tell us that men, who are legally dominant in a patrilineally organized society, can be both economically and emotionally dependent on women.

Tchambuli children are raised in a way that prepares them for their future sex roles. Boys and girls are treated very much alike until they reach the age of six or seven. Infants and young children are constantly with their mothers and female clanmates. These women are nurturant and supportive towards the children. Six- or seven-year old girls continue their associations with these same women. They are rapidly taught the tasks of womanhood and are given responsibilities within the household.

Boys who reach the age of six or seven begin to spend less time in the women's houses than when they were younger. Unlike their female agemates they do not have the opportunity to participate in adult life to their fullest capacities. When young they are rarely allowed to enter the men's houses. Gradually these vague prohibitions are relaxed, but the boy is often unsure about his rights. In fact, for three or four years of a boy's life he has no certain place with either the men or women. This causes him to be resentful and mistrustful—characteristics he retains for the rest of his life. Sometime during this difficult developmental period each boy must undergo ritual scarification. This painful event does not mark the boy's full attainment of manhood. It is not even shared by several boys simultaneously. A boy is simply scarified by his male clansmen at their convenience. The boy's recovery is lonely and unrewarding.

Discussion. There are some interesting parallels between the sex roles in America and Tchambuli. In each of these societies one sex is emotionally dependent on the other. In America women are dependent but in Tchambuli the men show this trait.

These people are not only emotionally dependent but also economically dependent on the members of the opposite sex. Thus, in both societies emotional and economic dependency are sex-linked and follow the same sex lines.

In each society children of the sex that has the economic power are taught the skills necessary for their future well-being. They are encouraged to become independent as they grow older. The children who, because of their sex, will have little economic power are not equally encouraged to be self-reliant. In fact, ambiguities involved with the attainment of adult status lead to personal insecurities and lack of confidence.

Is emotional dependency related to economic dependency in societies other than the two just discussed? This question cannot be satisfactorily answered because of limited information. We have found that in a number of societies, greater than would be expected by chance, boys are taught self-reliance more than girls. In later chapters we shall show that economic power is also concentrated in male lines in a disproportionate number of societies. This gives some support to the idea that these factors are correlated. What is needed is a cross-cultural study of the relationship between sex-linked economic and emotional dependencies.

We hypothesize that in societies where economic power is unequally distributed between the sexes, emotional dependency will also be sex-linked. These two types of dependencies will tend to follow the same sex lines. If this hypothesis is confirmed, we can expect to find that there is some adaptive significance in such a social organization. Perhaps excessive dependency on the part of one sex ensures that the sexes are bound together tightly in a single societal fabric. The bonds, instead of being forged on a basis of mutual interdependence, are based on the principle of asymmetrical dependence.

AMBITIOUSNESS

Returning once again to our sample (Table 3-1) we see that ambitiousness is a characteristic that is attributed to males rather than females when correlated with either sex. Slightly less than half the sampled students felt that this trait was sexually neutral.

Ambitiousness indicates a strong desire to achieve a goal. People, of course, set an infinite variety of goals for themselves. Some of these, like the desire to surpass existing records for goldfish swallowing or marathon dancing, fall within the realm of stunts, and are not ordinarily regarded as evidence of ambition. Nevertheless, desire for success has to be well-developed in people with such professed goals. Other, more long-term goals that are related to career aspirations are more generally associated with the word ambition.

It seems clear that the goals for which men and women strive are widely different. In general, men are oriented toward achieving goals associated with careers or the exhibition of physical prowess or skill. In these areas, standards of excellence are applicable, and precise measurements are therefore easily made. Women in American society do not appear to participate in a significant manner in fields that have these characteristics, except in a derivative way. In fact, ambition in women is very related to interpersonal relations, an area that is not characterized by standards of excellence. Therefore, women as a group may well manifest the same amount of ambition or motivation to succeed as men, but because the goals are different for each group they cannot be directly compared.

Psychologists employ testing techniques to measure a quality they call achievement motivation. This trait has long been suspected as one of several factors determining people's ultimate academic or economic success (see Heckhausen 1967). The tests are devised in such a way that male-oriented goals are the only ones included, so females predictably show less achievement motivation.

Recognizing the existence of sex differences in goals does not, however, help to explain why these differences exist. Is it true that women lack the drive to excel in nonpersonal activities because their creative urges are fulfilled by their child-bearing and -rearing roles? Certainly, this explanation is frequently offered. Conversely, are boys born with forces, perhaps related to

womb-envying patterns, that relentlessly drive them ever closer
to their goals? Why don't women seek to achieve in the same
way men do, and vice versa?

According to the literature summarized by Bardwick
(1971:172–77; also Heckhausen 1967:141–62), achievement in
young children is not sex-linked, although differences do occur.
In other words, this situation is similar to that found in our analysis of dependency—at the time when these differences are first
manifest in children, they show no correlation with sex. We
think that this observation is very important for the final assessment of the origin of these differences because it supports the
idea that sex role socialization is needed to mold personality
differences in the socially sanctioned manner correlated with
each sex.

Even though young school children do not show differences
in achievement motives according to sex, there are discernible
differences in association with other personality variables. Boys
who are high achievers are relatively independent, and able to
evaluate their success accurately. Their expectations of their
own performance and the actual performances are closely similar. Girls who are high in achievement motives are relatively
dependent, low in self-esteem, and use achievement as a means
for seeking approval. The higher the girl's intelligence the less
accurately she is able to predict her own success in intellectual
tasks.

Differences in rearing are associated with these sex differences in personality. A boy who has a well-developed drive
for achievement typically has a father who pressures his son in
this direction, and a mother who is nurturant and supportive.
Girls who are achievement oriented often have fathers who are
also achievement oriented, and alienated or hostile mothers.
Apparently during their childhood these girls try to win affection from their fathers by behaving in a way the fathers admire.
At the same time the lack of parental support leads to low esteem and lack of independence. In short, the development of
achievement closely follows the pattern of self-reliance discussed earlier.

In adolescence, patterns of achievement undergo alteration
for girls but are strengthened for boys. Before this period,

middle-class boys and girls in America win social approval for the same kinds of achievements. Primarily, these are demonstrated excellence in academic and athletic spheres. After puberty girls find that success in the former areas of achievement no longer wins social approval from others. During high school, social approval for girls becomes ever more related to success in interpersonal relations. In fact, success in academics seems to threaten a girl's popularity. These conflicts between academic and social success do not arise for boys. Bardwick (1971:178) points out that women who never develop high motives to achieve are not motivated to succeed in the work force. They are happiest in traditional roles. Women who have been successful in fusing achievement and affiliation needs often desire to return to the work force after 10 to 15 years of marriage—in other words, after they have achieved success in traditional roles. Women who develop high autonomous achievement needs upon which their own self-esteem rests show traits like competition, aggressiveness, and independence. These are traits necessary for success in the work force but thought of as unfeminine. These women experience the greatest conflict between sex-role identity and their achievement efforts. This conflict may force them to drop out of their professions or alternatively out of their sex roles. We think this conflict also helps explain why, for example, women who are unmarried Ph.D's working full-time are generally less productive than men (Bardwick 1971:168).

So far we have been discussing sex differences in achievement in this society. These differences appear to be the result of different social forces operating on each of the two sexes. If this is the most powerful explanation we should expect to find evidence of similar processes leading to similar results in other societies.

It is disappointing to find that anthropologists have not studied non-Western societies to see if achievement correlates with sex. Available studies of achievement in other societies are insufficient for our purpose in that they are based on content analysis of folktales (Child, Storm and Veroff 1958), studies of males only (McClelland 1961:336–90), individuals whose sex is not identified (Mischel 1961), and samples which are not directly comparable (Kardiner 1945:218–38). Dennis (1955) has found that Hopi children, while noncompetitive by standards of Anglo-Americans, exhibit competition when their behavior is not visible to other Hopi. Competitiveness between boys and girls differed according to the goal; girls were more competitive academically, whereas boys were more competitive athletically.

An outstanding study is that of Barry, Bacon, and Child (1957), which we cited in the section on dependency. These investigators also analyzed the socialization of achievement in their cross-cultural sample. They define this process as "training the child to orient his behavior towards standards of excellence in performance, and to seek to achieve as excellent a performance as possible" (Barry, Bacon and Child 1957:327). They found 82 societies with information on the socialization of achievement. Of these, 85 percent socialized only boys to be achievers, and fifteen percent showed no significant differences in the treatment of boys and girls. No society in the sample taught achievement to girls only. It is of course possible that societies do exist where achievement is taught to girls but not to boys, although the reported data suggest that such societies are relatively uncommon.

We wonder why this should be true. Our preliminary conclusion is that sex role socialization is fundamentally related to aspects of social organization. In particular, high achievement motivation appears to be encouraged in societal members who will benefit by this trait in their adult economic roles. In many societies the masculine role requires drive and initiative whereas the feminine role does not. In fact, it is possible that if females were high achievers the entire economic structure of many societies would be undermined. The relationship between women's social and economic roles in a large sample of societies will be discussed in later chapters.

NURTURANCE

The last personality trait to be discussed is nurturance, the quality of protecting and promoting the growth of others. Our sample (Table 3-1) shows this trait is associated most often with females, but some respondents felt that the trait is not sex-linked. Even the etymology of the word suggests an unambiguous female orientation because it is derived from the Latin *nūtrire*, to suckle.

Psychological tests generally confirm the popular impression that, in our society, females are more nurturant than males. This sex difference first appears in nursery school children and continues through life (Anatasi 1958:481).

As in most of the sex-linked traits we have been discussing, the difference in nurturance between the sexes is popularly explained as having a biological basis. This, in turn, seems to indicate to many people that the differences cannot be modified by other influences. The biological basis for female nurturant qualities is attributed either to general genetics or specifically to physiological changes associated with the birth process.

Let us first examine the idea that female nurturance is associated with physiological changes attendant upon childbirth. It is well known that dramatic physiological changes occur in a female during pregnancy, delivery, and lactation. We also know that in some mammals there is a short postpartum phase during which the mother becomes strongly attracted to her young (see Klopfer 1971). If young are not available to the mother during this period she will not exhibit normal rearing activities. The mechanism that regulates this behavior has not yet been identified, but it is clearly within the female's body.

If a similar mechanism exists for humans, it plays a minor role in explaining male-female differences in nurturance. Many women claim to be strongly attracted to their children at first sight. This is intriguing, and should be investigated; there is a possibility that physiological factors are involved. Despite this, however, female nurturance patterns are not restricted to feelings about their own children. Girls become more nurturant than boys as early as nursery school. Nurturant people are usually kind and supportive to all kinds of weak, defenseless creatures other than their own children. Women who have never borne children are often strongly nurturant, and even women who have a male chromosomal pattern and can never

have their own children exhibit normal nurturant patterns
(Money et al. 1968). It seems obvious that the birth process can
only strengthen any existing nurturant pattern already present
in a woman.

But what about the possibility that women are more nurturant
than men because of biological sex differences more fundamental than those associated with reproduction? Because of
Money's study, we can eliminate the possibility that chromosomal differences are relevant. Hormonal differences may possibly be a factor, because of their relative rather than absolute
differences in males and females and because of their possible
effect on neural organization in fetal life. At present, however,
there are no data that unequivocally link the trait of nurturance
with hormones. Thus we can say that the evidence for a biological basis for sex differences in nurturance is neither significant
nor compelling. In contrast, there is substantial evidence that illustrates the importance of environmental conditioning.

One of the most compelling pieces of evidence has come
from studies on primates under the direction of Harry Harlow.
Harlow and his associates (1971) raised rhesus monkeys in isolation. These monkeys were physically normal at birth so that
behavioral differences compared with normally socialized
rhesus monkeys cannot be attributed to aberrant physiology.
The observed behavioral differences were enormous. Monkeys
reared in isolation manifested symptoms best described as psy-
chopathic. When adult, these monkeys were incapable of normal heterosexual behavior (which shows, incidentally, that this
behavior is not "instinctive" in rhesus monkeys). Some of the
females who were reared in isolation were eventually impreg-
nated by experienced males or by artificial insemination. These
monkeys became the now famous motherless mothers: All were
totally inadequate mothers; most ignored their infants; some
engaged in what humans euphemistically call "child
abuse"—they physically maimed and occasionally killed their
infants. Harlow's study clearly shows the great importance of
social factors in the determination of nurturant behavior in a
species closely related to humans.

The data from human societies contain a smattering of evi-

dence that illustrates the importance of learning in the development of nurturance. Out of the 110 ethnographies studied by
Barry, Bacon, and Child (1957), only 33 contained information
concerning socialization for nurturance. Of these, 82 percent
showed socialization of the trait stronger for girls than boys,
while 18 percent of the societies showed no sex difference in
this socialization practice.

The Arapesh, whom we have already discussed in some detail, are an example of a society in which nurturance is not sex-
linked.

> We found the Arapesh—both men and
> women—displaying a personality that, out of
> our historically limited preoccupations, we
> would call maternal in its parental aspects,
> and feminine in its sexual aspects. We found
> men, as well as women, trained to be co-
> operative, unaggressive, responsive to the
> needs and demands of others (Mead
> 1963:279).

In contrast, Mead has described one society in which males
are *more* nurturant than females. This society is Manus, located
on a small island off the coast of New Guinea. Here the societal
assumption is that only males enjoy playing with babies and
when dolls were introduced by Mead, the boys, not the girls,
treated them like babies.

Our survey of information on the personality trait of nurturance indicates that this trait is based primarily in social
rather than biological factors. In a survey of all known societies
we would probably find that the majority differentially social-
izes females to be more nurturant than males. This is consistent
with the observations that in most societies women have the
major responsibility of rearing small children. Such a task is obviously one in which nurturant behavior is an asset. Other societies are organized in such a way that child rearing is shared
by both men and women, and in these societies there is no sex
bias in nurturance. In a few societies child rearing becomes a
task for men and thus nurturance is encouraged in males more
than in females.

DISCUSSION

At the beginning of this chapter we observed that middle-class Americans tend to share certain ideas about the behavior of men and women. These two groups of people, fundamentally distinguished on the basis of sex, are also believed to exhibit some different behaviors. This means that certain behavioral traits are thought to be sex-linked, that is more characteristic of one sex as compared with the other. One survey found that the traits associated with the masculine role include aggressiveness, independence, objectivity, ambitiousness, and abstract reasoning. The feminine traits were identified as emotionality, nurturance, empathy, and verbal ability. These traits probably do not exhaust the ones differentially associated with the sexes in this society but do provide two trait clusters that can be examined.

We have examined only five of the sex-linked traits. For each trait we first determined whether the expected linkage with one or the other sex matched actual behavior in American society. For example, after discovering that men are expected to be more aggressive than women, we examined whether this is indeed the case. Consistently it was found that the stereotypes and observed behaviors were closely congruent.

These findings led to other questions: Do attitudes regarding appropriate behavior for each sex primarily determine that behavior? Or, conversely, are the attitudes merely a reflection of the realities of behavioral differences which have a fundamental basis in the genetic differences between the sexes?

In order to examine these problems critically it was necessary to draw upon data collected within the frameworks of several disciplines. One approach was to use developmental psychology. In this field the development of traits in children is studied. If male-female behavioral differences are primarily biological in origin, these differences should show up in the behavior of young children and be correlated with their sex. Also the correlations should be consistent at every stage in the life cycle. With the exception of aggression, the examined traits did not meet these criteria. In the other traits for which information is available, correlations with expected sex did not occur in young children. The correlations with sex appeared in somewhat older children and were found to be regularly present into later life. These observations suggest that learning is a primary factor in the development of most sex-linked behavioral differences. This conclusion can be challenged, however, on the basis of physiological changes that sometimes occur at the same developmental time as observed behavioral differences. Nevertheless, correlations between parental behavior and their children's personalities strongly support the socialization theory regarding the specified sex-linked traits.

A second approach used, whenever possible, is anthropological. Basically we asked whether each of the sex-linked traits being examined showed a regular association with the same sex in most or all known societies. Random or no sex linkages would indicate that there is no connection between specific behavior and genetic sex differences. Regular associations between a trait and a particular sex would suggest that a biological basis is involved. This anthropological approach is founded on a basic assumption about men and women—that the genetic processes of differentiation (discussed in chapter 1), are alike for all human groups.

The examination of specific traits cross-culturally demonstrated that no absolutely fixed correlations with sex occurred. It was found that traits for which cross-cultural information is available could be assigned to either sex or both, depending on the society studied. This, of course, supports the theory of cultural rather than biological determinants. Nevertheless, some traits were associated with a specific sex to a much greater extent than would have been predicted by chance. Obviously one possible interpretation is that some biological factor is involved.

One important cross-cultural study on socialization practices, however, weakens the biological argument. The findings show that certain cross-culturally sex-linked traits are actually *taught* differentially to children of different sexes. This observation makes it necessary to shift the level of analysis from the individual to the society. What broad social factors make it advantageous for a society to inculcate dependence in women and independence in men, for example? This type of analysis will be the concern of later chapters.

It is now time to evaluate each of the examined traits to see which factor—social or genetic—contributes most to their unequal expression by the sexes. Of all the traits considered, the one with the most clear-cut sex-linked biological basis is aggression. This has been traced to the effects of male hormones on the hypothalamus. In light of this finding it is perhaps surprising to discover that males and females vary greatly in aggression if we compare people from many societies. This shows that the biological capacity of males for physical aggression is as amenable to cultural factors as, for example, the human capacity for language. Both have a biological basis which depends on learning for actual expression. It was also speculated that physical aggression against others may have the same motivational basis as other more self-damaging behaviors which are found frequently among women. In short, despite a demonstrated biological base for aggression, social learning greatly affects its expression and perhaps whether it is directed inwardly or outwardly by an individual.

In general, intelligence is known to be related to both genetic and social factors. It is difficult to evaluate how these two influences combine in the determination of sex differences in intelligence. One reason for this is that measurements of intelligence are so bound up in assessing knowledge specific to each society that it is impossible to measure intelligence so that culturally different groups can be compared. In Western societies sex differences in intelligence develop late, which leads us to conclude the primary factor is social rather than biological.

Dependence and achievement can be assessed together because they appear to be related traits. There is no strong evidence supporting the contention of a biological base for sex differences in the expression of these two traits. Considerable data point up the role of social learning in the development of these characteristics. In addition, these traits show an important relationship to differential aptitudes of males and females on I.Q. tests.

Nurturance is also a characteristic which can be thought typical of either men or women, or neither sex, in any given society. Nevertheless, nurturance is most often found in females in a large number of societies. Here the biological connection is perhaps indirectly causal. Since the woman is necessarily closely associated with a child because of the requirements of nursing, it is beneficial if she has been taught nurturant attitudes toward infants. Physiological changes associated with childbirth, which might predispose females for nurturance, are comparatively limited in scope and time. Learning is clearly the most powerful force in the development of this trait.

CHAPTER FOUR

Supernumerary Sexes

To begin with you must grasp the true nature of mankind and its sufferings. Our nature wasn't originally what it is now. No, it was quite different. First of all, there were three kinds of men, not two as now, the male and the female, but also a third kind combining both. We have the name still, but the thing itself has disappeared. The androgyne, separate in name and nature, partook of man and woman both. But the name is used now only as a reproach. Then also people were shaped like complete spheres. Their backs and sides made a circle. They had four hands, with the same number of legs and two faces—completely the same—on top of a circular neck. These two faces were set on opposite sides of the head, with four ears. And there were two sets of sexual parts, and whatever else one imagines goes along with this arrangement.

They walked around quite upright, just as we do today, but in whichever direction they chose, and whenever they got running fast, it was just like acrobats revolving in a circle— legs straight out and somersaulting! But then they had eight limbs to use for support when they were rolling swiftly around in circles! The three sexes were like this: the male was descended, in the beginning, from the sun, and the female from the earth, and the

one that partook of both of them came from
the moon, because the moon itself partakes
of the natures of those two. So these things
were globes themselves, you know, and took
after their ancestors in the way they got
around. In fact, they had terrific power and
energy, were arrogant, and assaulted the
gods.

Aristophanes's speech
in Plato's *Symposium*

INTRODUCTION

Aristophanes's discourse, delivered with great bravado at a din-
ner party described in Plato's *Symposium,* is obviously intended to satirize the improbable theories of pretentious Greek
philosophers. While any attempt to investigate the idea of three
sexes may align the present writers with those nebulous Greek
thinkers, a fair examination of this concept offers a new perspective on human sexual identity.

In previous chapters we have discussed the basis for physical
sex differences and sex-linked behaviors in humans. It should
be clear by now that many factors interact in the determination
of phenotypic sex and gender roles. The previous discussion
has nevertheless been implicitly based on the assumption that
there are invariably *two* phenotypic sexes and *two* gender statuses in every human society. In this chapter we shall examine
whether, in fact, it is correct to assume universal duality of
phenotypic sex and gender roles.

The fact that more than two physical sexes can coexist has seldom been recognized by investigators concerned with the interrelationship between physical sex and culture. Social scientists usually assume that human sexual attributes are perceived
by all societies as exclusively dichotomous (Edgerton 1964;
Trager 1962). According to prevailing thought, people in every
society determine a child's sex on an either-or basis, which
derives from a judgment about the appearance of the child's
genitals. This perception of physical sex as bipolar persists, it is

said, even though a large number of societies are aware that occasionally a person is born with sex organs neither clearly female nor male (Edgerton 1964:1288). Most of the available literature thus gives the impression that physical sex is universally
perceived as exclusively dichotomous.

Trager, for example, has published a paper that outlines an
analytical framework for the systematic study of all activities
pertaining to the broad concept of sex. This framework is explicitly designed as a "systematic map or guide book" for the
"anthropologist who would do something anthropological about
sex" (Trager 1962:114). According to Trager the starting point
for the study of sex in any society is the recognition of the bisexual nature of human populations:

> I propose to elaborate the focus I call bisex-
> uality. I hold, with many other present-day
> anthropological theorists, that culture is
> firmly rooted in the biological nature of man.
> And I believe that this biological nature is in
> essence the fact that man is a mammal and,
> like nearly all other living things on our
> earth, is of two sexes. This means that the
> examination of human biology must be in
> terms always of the two sexes, that it is
> through and by virtue of sex that man ex-
> presses his biological nature (Trager
> 1962:115).

We, of course, agree completely with Trager that the reproductive aspect of sex is bipolar and that this aspect pervades
human social life. But, in addition, we believe that Trager has
underrated the fact that humans infuse their physical sex differences with cultural meaning. Because of this, physical sex
differences need not necessarily be perceived as bipolar. It
seems possible that human reproductive bisexuality establishes
a minimal number of socially recognized physical sexes, but
these need not be limited to two.

Before turning to the evidence supporting the argument that
more than two physical sexes may be recognized by a society,
we must discuss the background upon which this argument is
based. The idea that cultural interpretations of sex may vary in

number as well as content seems plausible because of recent studies in anthropology, which demonstrate cross-cultural variation in many types of folk classifications (see Sturtevant 1964).

The growing evidence indicates that environmentally uniform physical elements are classified differently by societies. For example, a color spectrum, which consists of a range of visible light, is probably perceived as having the same color properties by all normal humans (Conklin 1955). The categorization of named color units, however, is highly variable from one society to another. For example, English speakers (Fig. 4-1) recognize six major named categories (purple, blue, green, yellow, orange, and red), whereas Bassa speakers recognize two (*hui* and *zĩza;* Gleason 1955:4). Both languages have minor named categories that permit them to make finer color distinctions than is possible with the major categories alone. It is important to recognize that neither of these systems is inherently superior, although either may be more useful for a particular purpose. Gleason (1955:5) illustrates this by citing the shortcomings of English encountered by botanists wishing to generalize about flower colors. The botanists wished to distinguish blues, purples, and purplish-reds from yellows, oranges, and reds. They were forced to coin new technical words since the desired distinction is not made in ordinary English. Bassa speakers, in contrast, would have this particular distinction ready-made in their language.

Variations in folk classifications have been demonstrated for a significant number of cultural domains, in addition to the domain of color. The domains of soils, plants, firewood, diseases, and kin types (Sturtevant 1964), as well as perceptions of historic time (Hudson 1966), have been studied in a few different societies. It seems theoretically possible that the domain of phenotypic sex could also be variously classified by societies.

We readily admit that physical sexual characteristics are much less variable, in an objective sense, than previously studied areas of folk classification. Nevertheless, actual variation does occur. Some individuals are born with genitals that are neither typically male nor female in appearance (see Katchadourian and Lunde 1972:95–97; Money and Ehrhardt 1972 for discussions of anomalies in the human reproductive system). The estimated frequency of this occurrence in human populations is between 2 and 3 percent (Overzier cited in Edgerton 1964:1289). Intersexes, although rare, apparently occur frequently enough for many societies to be aware of their existence (Edgerton 1964:1289; Ford and Beach 1951:134). It seems possible that the existence of such people could be accepted by a society as indicative of a third sex. This possibility will be examined in the following section.

Purple	Blue	Green	Yellow	Orange	Red	ENGLISH
Hui			Ziza			BASSA

Figure 4–1. Schematic representation of the color spectrum and its classification by English and Bassa speakers.

FOLK CLASSIFICATIONS OF SEX

As we indicated earlier, anthropologists have generally assumed that physical sex is everywhere viewed as dichotomous. This means that there are very few societies for which the classification of sex has been reported. Fortunately, there are available three studies of societies which illustrate some social possibilities in the classification of phenotypic sex. In one of these societies the folk classification of sex has two categories, but there are three categories in the other two.

The Pokot of Kenya (Fig. 4-2) are an example of a society that recognizes two phenotypic sexes (Edgerton 1964). Affiliation with either of these physical classes of sex qualifies an individual for either a masculine or feminine status in that society. The transition from child to adult is heralded by a rite of circumcision. Both gender roles place an emphasis on physical beauty, amorous achievement, and sexual skill.

Edgerton has reported the Pokot's treatment of intersexes. Such individuals, called *sererr,* are considered to be neither male nor female. Their genitals are too underdeveloped to be

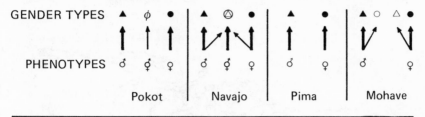

SYMBOLS

♀ female sex	● feminine gender status	○ feminine-like gender status
♂ male sex	▲ masculine gender status	△ masculine-like gender status
⚲ intersex	⌀ no gender status	⊘ intersexual gender status

Figure 4–2. Schematic representation of the relationship between categories of biologic sex and those of gender in four societies.

circumcised either in the male or female fashion. A Pokot's failure to be circumcised is equivalent to the denial of any adult gender status.

Some parents respond to the birth of a *sererr* by immediately killing it. This reaction is acceptable among the Pokot, who resort to infanticide whenever a malformed child is born. *Sererr* are thus one type of physical deviant who are diagnosed by that society as defective and undesirable.

Sometimes, however, *sererr* are permitted to live. Surviving *sererr* can never pass as legitimate males or females and their ambiguous condition is public knowledge. They live on the fringes of their society without a mandate for either gender status. Often they win some social approval by excelling in economic activities, yet their lives are ruthlessly limited in other respects.

The Pokot thus recognize two mutually exclusive sexes. The identification with one of these is the primary criterion for the attainment of one of two gender statuses.

The Navajo (Fig. 4-2) react very differently to the birth of an intersex (Hill 1935). Such infants are called *nadle*. "Real *nadle*" are recognized at birth. Their genital appearance sets them

Societies mentioned in text.

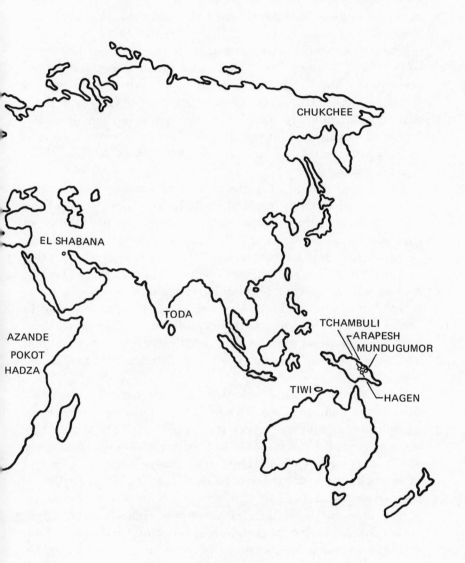

apart from either males or females and, in addition, provides them with a clear mandate for a gender status which we can also call *nadle*. This status also contrasts with masculine and feminine statuses.

The gender status of *nadle* is actually composed of two types of people: real *nadle*, and "those who pretend they are *nadle*" (Hill 1935:273). The pretenders are people with either male or female genitals. Hill reports that at the time of his study there was an approximately equal number of male and female *nadle*. These observations indicate that the Navajo have three recognizably different categories for physical sex as well as three gender statuses.

This interpretation of *nadle* as a third gender status is supported by other data provided by Hill. The dress code of the *nadle* is apparently variable, depending on the proclivities of the individual. Some wear either male or female clothing depending on specific circumstances. Hill's data suggest to us that in these cases the *nadle* matches behavior and clothing. That is, a *nadle* will wear women's clothing when doing women's work, male clothing when doing men's work. Real *nadle* are said to prefer the dress of women. Changeability of clothing and allowance for individual preference symbolically reflect the fact that *nadle* can perform the functions and duties of both men and women.

In an economic sense enterprising *nadle* have an advantage over either men or women. They may perform all Navajo tasks except hunting and war, which means their chances of discovering a special skill are enhanced compared with men or women. *Nadle* also have special rights over the personal property of other members of their households. They can even dispose of the private property of their relatives without their permission. Navajo men and women never have these rights.

Hill mentions that in certain respects *nadle* behave and are treated as women. They assume the women's role at dances, are addressed by appropriate female kin terms, and have the social and legal status of a woman, which is greater than that of a man. These circumstances, in addition to the fact that real *nadle* are said to prefer women's clothing, are possibly an example of partial "passing" in a primitive society (see Goffman 1966).

In other respects the status of *nadle* is clearly apart from that of either men or women. For example, these people act as mediators in disputes between a man and a woman, have unusual sexual license, and may marry a spouse of either biologic sex. According to informants, real *nadle* never marry.

The well defined and respected social status of *nadle* is possible because it is sanctioned by social ideology. One important figure in Navajo mythology is *May-des-tizhi,* who is described as having been both man and woman. This mythic person was especially rich and had the responsibility of caring for all paired creatures on earth. During a time in the mythological past when the sexes quarrelled and separated, *May-des-tizhi* was instrumental in tipping the balance in favor of the men because of his/her ability to perform women's tasks (Klah 1942).

There is yet another society that may recognize three sexes, but lack of information makes the issue unclear. The possibility arises in the study of a group of people called *hijarā,* who live in India. These are troupes of entertainers who perform at religious festivals and celebrations in honor of newborn children. The *hijarā* live and work together and each troupe has a territory in which it operates. In Allahabad the troupes have an assembly that formally allocates the individual territories (Opler 1960:507).

Three *hijarā* interviewed by Opler describe themselves as intersexes: they claim all *hijarā* "are born that way" (Opler 1960:506). Although these people wear women's clothing and adopt feminine names they consider themselves neither female nor male. Opler's informants distinguished themselves from female impersonators who wear women's clothing only while entertaining. Thevenot, who wrote in the seventeenth century, noted that hermaphrodites in Surat were forced by authorities to wear men's turbans in addition to their female clothing (Laufer 1920:262).

According to Opler's informants, intersexed children voluntarily join *hijarā* groups after living their earliest years in their own households. They retain only religious affiliations but not caste distinctions when they become *hijarā*. They say that they cannot carry on sexual activities and never marry.

Carstairs (1958:59), in contrast to Opler, reports that *hijarā* are male prostitutes. This conclusion was reached on the basis of information collected from informants who were not themselves *hijarā*.

The lack of agreement in the literature concerning the genital morphology, social functions, and sexual functions of *hijarā* makes it impossible to accurately assess this situation at the present time. Are some of these people intersexes, as they claim to be? If so, is the condition recognized at birth as a distinct type of sex and thus a validation of the subsequent attainment of *hijarā* status? Or perhaps intersexes are considered malformed individuals who cannot function normally in Indian society and thus are driven together for economic security. Additional research is necessary before these questions can be answered.

Our analysis of folk classifications of sex has been limited to only three societies, perhaps primarily because most field workers have not been sensitive to this type of study. We have learned from this extremely small sample that physical sex can be categorized differently by different social groups. Probably, most societies recognize only two sexes; some recognize more. A minimal number of sexes is thus established by the dichotomous aspect of human sexual reproduction, but sometimes a third sex can be recognized. This can be called supernumerary because it exceeds the minimal number of two physical sexes.

In this discussion we have been careful to separate physical sex from gender status. We have found that, at least among the Navajo, there is a supernumerary gender status that corresponds to the supernumerary sex category. In the following section other examples of supernumerary gender will be discussed.

SUPERNUMERARY GENDERS

Anthropologists have been more attuned to variations in gender than to the classifications of physical sex. Cross-cultural variations in the content of gender, for example, are recognized by almost all anthropologists as proof of the importance of learning in human life. Fewer investigators have been concerned with variations in the numbers of genders found in each society. Margaret Mead is exceptional in this respect.

> All known human societies recognize the anatomic and functional differences between males and females in intricate and complex ways; through insistence on small nuances of behavior in posture, stance, gait, through language, ornamentation and dress, division of labor, legal social status, religious role, etc. In all known societies sexual dimorphism is treated as a major differentiating factor of any human being, of the same order as difference in age, the other universal of the same kind. However, where in contemporary America only two approved sex roles are offered to children in many societies there are more (Mead 1961:1451).

Mead clearly states her view that societies may have more than two sexual statuses. In this same work she continues with a discussion of what she terms "sex careers." In many of these cases the sex careers are so like gender statuses that we feel confident in calling them supernumerary genders.

The supernumerary genders we shall explore here have been selected from the Pima, Mohave, Siouan-speaking Plains Indians, North Piegan, Chukchee, and Azande societies.

The Pima, an American Indian group of the Southwest, apparently recognized two sex phenotypes and two genders in precontact times (Fig. 4-2). The evidence for this comes from a report (Hill 1938:339) on Pima attitudes toward transvestism, which is often practiced by people who take on many behaviors of the contrasex in addition to the clothing change (see Angelino and Shedd 1965). It thus involves the adoption of the gender role not congruent with a person's physical sex. The Pima prohibition against transvestism was therefore a prohibition against gender change.

This absence of Pima transvestism is explained in one of their myths (Hill 1938:339). Transvestites, it is said, originated among the neighboring Papago as a result of a shortage of raw materials in Pima territory. The Pima, finding they lacked materials for making bows and arrows (symbolic of maleness), requested material from the Papago. The Papago sent two boys to deliver the items, which they carried in net frames (symbolic of femaleness). The boys became transvestites when they returned to Papago country. The Pima did not suffer such a fate.

Pima raised their children in a way that prepared them for their future adult roles. Sexes were separated during early childhood and children were not allowed to play with toys of the opposite sex. If a boy began to adopt behaviors that were considered feminine, he was given a test to determine his future. The boy was put into a brush hut, which contained a bow and arrow, and a basket. The hut was set on fire and the object grasped by the boy as he fled was taken to be symbolic of his future role. If he chose the basket he was destined to become a *wi·kovat*. This can be translated as "like a girl." Such people used mannerisms that were considered feminine, but they had no special status within the society. *Wi·kovat* were ridiculed and treated as inferiors. *Wi·kovats* who committed crimes were treated with special leniency because they were considered "not normal" (Hill 1938:340).

Gender transformations were thus not encouraged by the Pima. Phenotypic males adopted feminine behaviors, but such individuals were believed to be not responsible for their social actions because of their condition. Pima probably considered this condition as a type of mental illness rather than a third gender type.

There is compelling evidence (Devereux 1937) for the existence of two supernumerary gender roles among the Mohave, a group of Indians who lived in California and adjacent states at the time of contact (Fig. 4-2). The two alternate status positions exist for phenotypic females adopting a masculine-like role, and phenotypic males adopting a feminine-like role. They are called *hwame·* and *alyha·* respectively. The change from a status congruent with phenotypic sex to one contrastive with physical sex is described (Devereux 1937:500) predominately in terms of sexual behavior, but it is clear that homosexual activity per se is not diagnostic of this role change. Sex partners, for example, of people with these supernumerary gender statuses are not considered either *hwame·* or *alyha·*. The sexual activity of individuals with alternate sex status is clearly a part of the total role change commensurate with that status.

Boys who desire toys and clothing of the opposite sex formally undergo an initiation ceremony which serves the function of legitimatizing change in status. Phenotypic males in the process of becoming *alyha·* behave like women during the ceremony and are presented with a bark skirt which they subsequently wear in the manner of women. These boys undergo the *alyha·* ceremony in lieu of the male puberty ritual. They therefore do not have their noses pierced and always paint themselves according to the fashion of adult women. They also adopt feminine names.

Phenotypic females apparently undergo a similar ceremonial initiation into their new status of *hwame·*. Although some conflicting reports are available (Devereux 1937:508) concerning whether or not such a ceremony existed, they probably result from the fact that the status of *hwame·* was collapsing during acculturation to European-derived American society. The *hwame·* traditionally wears paint according to male fashion, a breechclout, and adopts a new name. The activities of *hwame·* are closely similar to Mohave men. One such individual, described by a Mohave informant, was a good provider who earned a living not only by practicing shamanism, but also by farming and hunting (Devereux 1961:416). *Hwame·* are, however, restricted in their role adoption by being ineligible for tribal or war leadership positions (Devereux 1937:502).

The institutionalization of the two supernumerary gender statuses are sufficiently developed so that individuals of each can marry persons of the same phenotypic sex. An *alyha·* upon marriage fictively creates first menstrual flow by drawing blood from "her" upper legs. Both husband and "wife" are thus required to observe puberty taboos in the customary fashion. Pregnancy is also acted out in an elaborate fashion. Labor pains, induced by drinking a severely constipating drug, culminate in the birth of a fictitious stillborn child. Stillborn Mohave infants are customarily buried by the mother, so that an *alyha·*'s failure to return to "her" home with a living infant is explained in a culturally acceptable manner.

Hwame· are able to assume paternity of children quite easily because of the Mohave belief that intercourse with a pregnant woman can alter the paternity of the child (Devereux 1937:515). They do not observe their own menses but only those of their wives (Devereux 1937:515). Some women are reported to have become *hwame·* after having borne children.

Devereux's study suggests that the status of *hwame·* was regarded as socially less desirable than that of *alyha·*. *Hwame·* had restrictions on their adoption of male leadership roles, whereas no restrictions are mentioned for the *alyha·* role. Girls were discouraged from becoming *hwame·*, and, once the status was accepted, may have had more difficulty in finding spouses than their *alyha·* counterparts.

Validation for the Mohave supernumerary gender statuses is present in their mythology. Devereux cites two accounts, given by an old Mohave informant, which state that "homosexuals" and "transvestites" have been present since the beginning of the world (Devereux 1937:501, 503). The Mohave also believe that in the early periods of the mythical era sexes were undifferentiated. This is particularly significant in view of the fact that "it is a basic principle of the Mohave philosophy of life that everything on earth happens in accordance with rules and precedents dating back to the time of creation" (Devereux 1961:12).

Devereux's outstanding studies do not refer to the fate of Mohave intersexes. There is no available information concerning Mohave attitudes and treatments for this situation. If a phenotypically intersexed child is permitted to live by the Mohave, then theoretically four adult gender positions are open to it. Phenotypically male and female individuals each have a choice of two gender roles, one of which is ascribed at birth. If an individual wishes to renounce that status he or she does so publicly and thus achieves an alternate status position.

The available data make it reasonable to question whether the status positions of *alyha·* and *hwame·* are actually alternate to those of feminine and masculine statuses respectively, or if they are identical to them. In our opinion, the best interpretation is to consider these alternate statuses because, in addition to the different procedure in role assignment, the behaviors appropriate to the *alyha·* and *hwame·* statuses differ from those of feminine and masculine statuses respectively. These differences relate primarily to sexual activity. In addition, social reaction to people of these alternate gender positions differs from that elicited by others. Such people are the focus of much teasing, especially of a sexual nature. Nevertheless, the statuses of *hwame·* and *alyha·* closely approximate those of Mohave men and women respectively, and they provide a good example of people of different sexes occupying nearly identical gender statuses.

Another example of an achieved supernumerary gender status is that of the *berdache*. The term has been applied widely to certain individuals in aboriginal groups in northern Asia and North America. It is an Anglicized version of the French *bardash*, the etymology of which traces back to a Persian word meaning "male prostitute" (Angelino and Shedd 1955:121). It was first applied by early French explorers to individuals who were believed to play passive roles in male homosexual activities. These people did not restrict their unusual behavior to sexual activity; they also dressed and behaved like women. As Kroeber (1940:209–10) pointed out, there is very little reliable information available about the sexual activity of these people. ". . . At any rate, the North American attitude toward the berdache stresses not his erotic life, but his social status; born a male he became accepted as a woman socially" (Kroeber 1940:209–10).

The institution of berdache, because it was so widespread in aboriginal America, must have had different attributes in different societies. Recruitment in general came from two distinct sources: (1) war captives (Angelino and Shedd 1955:122; Lurie 1953:710) and possibly disgraced warriors (Lurie 1953:711); and (2) individuals "chosen" for this role by some supernatural power. These latter recruits tended to be highly proficient in dealing with the supernatural as shamans, and accordingly were highly respected by other members of their communities.

The scattered information available for the berdache is most complete for Plains Indian groups of the Siouan language family. This family includes the Omaha, Crow, Mandan, and Winnebago tribes.

Only meager information is available concerning the phenotypic sex characteristics of berdaches. The Omaha say that a
berdache is "indistinguishable from male infants at birth, but as
he grows up his weak voice sets him off from other boys" (Lowie
1935:48). This situation could be due either to hormonal malfunc-
tion at puberty or to social learning. An individual Crow berdache
examined by a doctor was found to be a morphologic male (Holder
1889). It is not possible to determine from available evidence
whether intersexes could also become berdaches.

A Plains Indian man often became a berdache after having
received a vision (Bowers 1950; Flecher and La Flesche
1905–6:132; Lurie 1953:708). The vision usually involved a
female spirit who in some way guided (or tricked) the visionary
into contact with objects symbolic of the female role.

In at least some of these societies role transformation included change in clothing style, speech habits, hairstyle
(Flecher and La Flesche 1905–6:132), and permitted marriage
(Lurie 1953:708). In every case known to us gender transformation also involved spiritualization. All berdaches were shamans
who had increased access to the supernatural compared with
non-shamans. Lowie (1935:48) notes the Crow berdache's special function in cutting down the first tree for the Sun Dance
Lodge. He concludes that berdaches must have been relatively
common because of this special task reserved for them.

Simms, who visited the Crow reservation in the early twentieth century, was informed of three people described as "half
man and half woman." These people, referred to as "she," were
apparently very well off economically by Crow standards.
"They are also generally considered to be experts with the
needle and the most efficient cooks in the tribe, and they are
highly regarded for their many charitable acts" (Simms
1903:580).

Mead refers to berdache as combining the features of role
change and ceremonialism. Her view is that the berdache role
cannot be fully understood unless both principles of role definition are recognized. A berdache had rights and duties that over-
lapped with those of women and of shamans. Nevertheless, for
each of these three roles the constellation of behavioral traits is
unique.

Some alteration of gender role was possible for North Piegan women. The North Piegan are Blackfoot speakers who live in Canada. In their society the masculine role involves aggressive and bold behavior, whereas the feminine role requires submission, kindness, loyalty, decorum, and faithfulness (Lewis 1941:176). The society is male-dominated, and a higher social value is placed on male as compared with female traits. This is also true of most other Plains Indian groups. Lewis (1941:173) states that the North Piegan contrast with other Plains Indians in their emphasis on "ownership, manipulation and disposition of property." This social emphasis on wealth provides an opportunity for women to excel because they are able to accumulate property through inheritance and by means of their own personal endeavors.

Some North Piegan women become *ninauposkitzipxpe,* which is translated as manly-hearted women. The manly-hearts are women who share behavioral traits such as aggression, independence, ambition, boldness, and sexuality—traits that contrast strongly with the ideal behavior of the non-manly-hearted women. Moreover, these characteristics are precisely those held to be desirable in men. Lewis makes it clear, however, that the mere presence of these traits is not sufficient for a woman to attain this status. She also must be married, wealthy, mature, and have a high social position.

The behavior of manly-hearts differs from that of other women in property ownership, public deportment, domestic and sex life, and participation in religious affairs. Manly-hearts have more individual wealth than do all other wives. They are industrious workers and excel in both men's and women's tasks. This advantage provides them with considerable economic independence. Because they can be economically self-sufficient, they do not need to immediately remarry if deserted or widowed. They also often earn income by practicing medicine. In public, manly-hearted women, according to one informant, "act as though they were men" (Lewis 1941:180). They talk freely, expressing opinions and disagreements, act at ease, and do not hesitate to make speeches. At dances they choose partners without hesitation. In the home, manly-hearted wives share the decision making with their husbands—a custom not typical of most Piegan households. Manly-hearts are reported to be sexually more aggressive and demanding than other women, and also to engage in a wide range of sexual activity.

Manly-hearts are particularly important in the Sun Dance ceremony, which is sponsored by individuals who purchase medicine bundles. Any man or woman can make this purchase, but manly-hearts participate more than other women, probably because their personality characteristics are well suited for the responsibility. Also, manly-hearts, who are usually wealthy, are able to afford the bundles.

The role of manly-hearts is clearly different from the gender roles discussed previously. Manly-hearts remain women after achieving their new status, but they are women who act like men in many contexts. Thus the configuration of feminine traits and activities is repudiated by some select women in favor of masculine traits. This decision allows the manly-hearts to gain more respect and responsibility from their community than would be otherwise possible. At the same time they retain many characteristics of their feminine status.

It seems best to consider the North Piegan manly-hearts as having a gender status that combines features of both feminine and masculine statuses in their society. This status is available only to phenotypic women; there is no information regarding status positions, if any, for intersexes. All manly-hearts have previously demonstrated their abilities in the more common feminine role. The change in status is made only by women who possess certain manlike characteristics and are skillful in economic matters.

The Chukchee of Siberia also have a supernumerary gender status, which involves partial as well as total transformation of gender roles. Chukchee of both phenotypic sexes can transform their gender roles. A transformed male is called *yIrka-E-la'ul* (soft-man) or *ñe'učhičä* (similar to a woman), whereas a transformed woman is called *ga'čIkIčheča* (similar to a man) (Bogoras 1904–9:449). Male transformation is reported as more frequent than the reverse, and consequently this phenomenon is better documented than its female counterpart.

Transformation of gender for phenotypic males has three

levels of intensity. An individual who is transforming may stabi-
lize his behavior at one of these levels and he may or may not
later alter his behavior, either to conform with the traditional
masculine role or to become more closely congruent with the
traditional feminine role. The least intense behavioral change
involves hair arrangement, which is simply styled according to
female patterns. This is either done during the first stages of
shamanistic inspiration or by a sick person for medical reasons.
In the latter case the prescription has been given by a shaman
with the intention of disguising the patient so that the malinten-
tioned spirits will not recognize him. The data are not explicit
on this point, but presumably after all danger is past the prescription is discontinued.

On the second level, a man adopts female clothing. This is
also done either as a part of the process of shamanization or for
magico-medical purposes. In either case the man can marry,
have children, and carry on other traditional masculine activities.

The third stage of transformation is affiliated with shamanization exclusively, and is never prescribed for a patient. This
stage involves complete role alteration. Economic tasks, speech
characteristics, physical attributes culturally associated with
masculinity, personal interests, and sexual activity are all femi-
nized. The transformed shaman will take a male lover and eventually marry. The marriage union resembles that of heterosexual
couples in most respects. However, the transformed "wife" is
supposed to have a supernatural husband who is the real head
of the household. This is an example of a *menage à trois*, in
which one of the partners is supernatural. This partner's
thoughts are known only to his "wife," who relays them to the
mortal husband. Thus, in this type of household the "wife" has
the primary voice in decision-making. Name changes do not accompany gender transformation, but many Chukchee men and
women have contrasex names. These are given to them by shamans to protect them from evil spirits.

Transformed shamans are considered more powerful than ordinary shamans (Bogoras 1904–9:453). This belief is in accord
with a popular folktale that attributes power, wealth, and pres-

tige to a legendary soft-man who triumphed when assaulted by a foreign tribe.

Female transformation is reported as being less frequent than the male counterpart and was never directly witnessed by Bogoras. He was told of a widow with three children who was inspired by the supernatural to become a *ga'čIkIčheča*. Total transformation, including marriage to a young girl, eventually resulted. When the female "husband" wanted children, the couple entered into a mutual marriage agreement with a young man who fathered children with the "wife." The "husband" retained rights of paternity over the family's children.

In Chukchee society phenotypic males have the option of choosing between four gender statuses that are in some ways mutually exclusive. Two of these are mirror images of each other. One, the masculine status, can be replaced by a second status which is much like the feminine one in that society. In addition to gender status reversal, it involves supernatural sanctions so that the transformed individual is also a shaman. The two other statuses involve less complete changes from the behaviors associated with the masculine role. These statuses can also be held for a short time, after which a different gender status can be achieved.

Phenotypic females have at least two gender statuses from which to choose. A woman with a feminine status can adopt an alternate status, which is possibly very much like the masculine status in that society but is simultaneously based on the acceptance of the status of shaman.

The Azande of East Africa traditionally had a custom that allowed the regular alternation of feminine and masculine roles during the lifetimes of certain individuals. The Azande had a chiefdom form of political organization—they were governed by a paramount leader. The Azande chief required the attendance of many young men at his court, who functioned as a residential labor force in time of peace and a military force during war (Seligman and Seligman 1932:506). These young men, between the ages of 20 and 35, lived in large houses outside the palace grounds and far from their own homes. The men were not able to marry because eligible females were usually unavailable.

This is because mature, wealthy men—who were permitted to have several wives—would often marry girls just after they were born. Thus young men were separated from their kin groups before the age at which it was socially possible for them to marry. This meant that they were separated from womenfolk, who, of course, provided important economic duties necessary for survival.

The Azande solution to this dilemma was to allow warriors at court to take young boys as wives. These boy-wives fulfilled most of the usual functions of female wives, such as providing food, water carrying, spear carrying, and sexual activities. The boys were addressed as women, were referred to by their individual partners as "my wife" and called them "my husband." Men paid spears for their wives, similar to the custom of providing bride payments for female wives. The bond between a young man and his boy wife was publicly recognized and accepted. When a warrior earned enough wealth to make a second bride payment he obtained a female wife while the boy wife, by then a young man, would assume the role of warrior.

This solution is nicely congruent with other aspects of Azande society. Warriors were able to perform their tasks without simultaneously being responsible for their own personal comforts. Boy wives were indoctrinated into the lives of warriors by witnessing first-hand what such a life was like.

In this example, men, during the course of a normal lifetime, performed first the duties and responsibilities of Azande women and later assumed those of Azande men.

DISCUSSION

One major conclusion that can be drawn from this review of supernumerary sexes is that the relationship between biological sex and social gender categories is neither simple nor direct. The biology of human reproduction requires two anatomically differentiated classes of persons, male and female. As we discussed in chapter 2, however, physical sex differences are the result of highly similar developmental processes. Because of this, persons can be born with genitalia intermediate in form between male and female types.

Folk classifications of sex demonstrate the various social responses to these attributes of human bodies. Some societies, exemplified by the Pokot, recognize only two phenotypic sexes. Biological identification with one or the other of these is a necessary prerequisite for attaining adult gender status.

Other societies recognize three anatomically distinct sexes. This situation was exemplified by the Navajo and possibly India. The recognition of three sexes permits societies to create a gender status for each of the recognized biological categories.

We do not know how many societies perceive three classes of human sexes. One difficulty is that ethnographers, believing in the immutability of sex types, rarely examine this aspect of their study groups. Initial research has led us to believe that folk classifications that recognize three sexes are found more frequently in Asia than in other areas, but further research is needed.

Some societies that apparently recognize only two phenotypic sexes manage to use the principle of biological sex to generate four rather than two gender statuses. This is done by the social device of allowing cross-sex transformations. Both the Mohave and the Chukchee permit transformations between biological and social sex categories.

The Plains Indian berdache is similar in that phenotypic males were permitted to attain a feminine-like gender status. A reverse option does not seem to have been permitted for Plains Indian females, however. In the case of the berdache and other cross-sex transformations the process of sex change infused the transformed individual with great supernatural power. This device seems to permit a rudimentary form of social ranking in societies that are essentially egalitarian in nature. Ranking is generated by combining principles of sex and religious identity.

The Chukchee, North Piegan, and Azande societies permitted cross-sex transformations that are either partial or reversible. In the Chukchee case these transformations are linked with magico-religious attributes. The Azande and North Piegan cases are more mundane and associated with the segmentary principle of age. In the Azande case a feminine-like status is permitted for young boys, whereas in the North Piegan situation a masculine-like status is permitted for old women.

In all these cases, however, the lesson is clear. Biological sex is used by societies to build social categories, and human ingenuity permits more elaborations on the biological theme than at first seems possible. We are not yet ready to predict what governs the occurrence of supernumerary sexes in some societies and their absence in others. For the moment it is sufficient to recognize the range of possible variations in sex types and gender types. In the following chapter we shall turn our attention to variations in social roles in animals, which are of course more closely tied to their biological natures than are those of humans. We shall discover that even among these animals variations in the nature, but not the number, of social roles based on sex do occur.

The Biosocial World of Nonhuman Primates

CHAPTER FIVE

INTRODUCTION

Social scientists have recently been turning to studies of animal behavior to learn something about the basis of human sex differences. It was once thought that humans were so unlike animals that it was pointless to attempt to learn about humans by investigating other species. For example, in the eighteenth and early nineteenth centuries the prevailing viewpoint was that humans depended so greatly on learning that they had little in common with animals, which were characterized as behaving in ways that were automatically determined by genetic inheritance. As scientists have learned more about both humans and animals, this simple distinction appears less compelling.

Many species have been shown to have a much greater capacity for learned behavior than was formerly recognized. Tool use, once thought to be exclusively human, is now known to occur in, for example, several kinds of birds and apes. Likewise social inventions and their spread have been observed in a group of monkeys, and the effects of social deprivation have been shown to be extreme in other simian groups. In addition, field studies of animals in the wild have shown that the social organization of many species is more complex than was previously surmised. The earlier view that animals were totally unlike humans was based in part on observations of caged and isolated animals. Such animals tend to exhibit rigid, stereotyped behavior which hardly resembles that of normal human beings (but is not unlike behavior of caged and isolated humans). Ecological studies of wild primates are demonstrating variations in forms of behavior within a single species. These variations correlate with different environments and are now understood to be means of group adaptation.

The thrust of these developments has broken down the simple dichotomous view that animal behavior is predetermined and inflexible whereas human behavior is learned and completely flexible. It is now evident that behavior in the higher vertebrates is invariably due to a combination of learning and genetic factors.

The group of animals having the most relevancy for human studies are those which are most like *Homo sapiens.* These are the prosimians, monkeys and apes (also called simians), which together with humans constitute the primates (Fig. 5-1). The primates share certain morphological similarities: similar tooth patterns; hands or feet that can grasp; nails rather than claws; a partly opposable thumb or big toe; and a relatively greater reliance on vision than on smell (Napier and Napier 1967:6).

Many of the recent attempts to unravel the issues associated with human sex differences have relied heavily on evidence from primate studies. There is a very good reason for this approach; all primates share a basic pattern of reproduction. The behavioral differences between men and women are grounded in their different reproductive roles. Any assessment of the impact of biology on sex-linked behavior can benefit from comparative studies of sex roles of animals with the same reproductive pattern.

Comparative studies of primates, while extraordinarily useful, must be carried out with considerable caution. Each species has evolved in response to a unique set of conditions so that observations made on one group cannot be uncritically extended to another. Apes or monkeys are not proto-humans, nor are humans simply naked apes. Nevertheless, an understanding of the processes which result in ape, as well as human, behavior greatly enriches analytical understanding of the course of evolution as well as its current state of affairs.

In this chapter we shall assess the validity of various primate studies to the study of human sex differences. We shall first

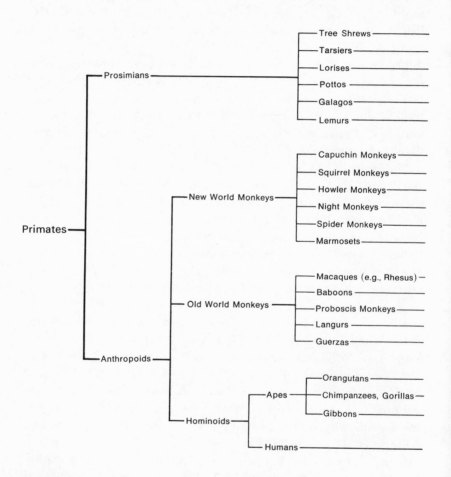

Figure 5–1. Schematic diagram of the classification of some living primates.

discuss the primate pattern of reproduction in order to highlight both the similarities and differences between the human and nonhuman primate systems. We shall next consider the ways in which primate studies have been used in studies of human sex differences. We shall distinguish the comparative and case study approaches, illustrate each with one example, and judge the validity and utility of each of these studies.

PRIMATE REPRODUCTION

Some people are under the impression that the human reproductive system is unique when in fact most human reproductive traits are also found in other primates. These shared characteristics not only substantiate the conclusion of genetic affinity among primate groups, but also indicate the nature of the reproductive system of the common ancestral group.

Primates mature slowly, produce relatively few young, and have long lifespans. These features of the primate pattern of reproduction were most likely present in the ancient common ancestor of all living primates. This pattern, which proved to be adaptive for the common ancestor, has continued to be so during the evolution of diverse descendent forms. Each evolving species recasts the pattern in line with other evolutionary changes, but cross-specific similarities attest to the biological success this system has conferred upon many species.

The primate reproductive pattern is a variation on the basic mammalian reproductive system. The traits just mentioned as typical of primate reproduction are somewhat typical of all large-sized mammals. The uniqueness of the reproduction system of primates is that these traits are more highly developed than in other mammals of comparable size. For example, large-sized mammals tend to have long pregnancy periods, but the length of human pregnancy is closer to that of cattle than to that of similar sized mammals. Just as the primate system is a variation of the mammalian system, so also is the human system a variation on the primate one.

In the following discussion we examine some significant

Table 5-1. Comparative data of reproductive patterns of some primates and comparably sized nonprimates

ANIMAL	MATERNAL WEIGHT	GESTATION PERIOD (DAYS)
Tarsier *Tarsius* spp.	87–154 g.	c. 180
Eastern chipmunk *Tamias striatus*	70–142 g.	31
Galago (Bush baby) *Galago senegalensis*	229 g.	144
Rat *Rattus* spp.	115–350 g.	21–30
Rhesus monkey *Macaca mulatta*	8.0 kg.	168
Dog (Beagle) *Canis familiaris*	8.4 kg.	59
Chacma baboon *Papio ursinus*	11.0–15.0 kg.	170
Lynx *Lynx* spp.	5.4–11.3 kg.	c. 60
Chimpanzee *Pan troglodytes*	40.6 kg.	225
Wild hog *Sus* spp.	35–150 kg.	112–115
Human *Homo sapiens*	56 kg.	243–298 280 (av.)
Laughing hyena *Crocuta crocuta*	59–82 kg.	90–110
Gorilla *Pan gorilla*	75–110 kg.	251–289
Sheep (Hampshire) *Ovis aries*	70 kg.	147

Table 5-1. (*Continued*) Comparative data of reproductive patterns of some primates and comparably sized nonprimates

ANIMAL	AGE AT PUBERTY	LIFESPAN (YEARS)	USUAL NO. OF YOUNG
Tarsier *Tarsius* spp.	—	12 [a]	1
Eastern chipmunk *Tamias striatus*	—	5 8 [a]	2–8
Galago (Bush baby) *Galago senegalensis*	52 wk.	3.25 [a]	1
Rat *Rattus* spp.	6–9 wk.	2–3 (av.) 4 (max.)	7
Rhesus monkey *Macaca mulatta*	3–4.5 yr.	c. 30	1
Dog (Beagle) *Canis familiaris*	6–8 mo.	c. 34 max.[a]	5
Chacma baboon *Papio ursinus*	F: 3.5–4 yr. M: 5 yr.	c. 30	1
Lynx *Lynx* spp.	1 yr.	10–20	1–4
Chimpanzee *Pan troglodytes*	8 yr.	41 (av.) 60 (max.)	1
Wild hog *Sus* spp.	1.5 yr.	15–20	3–12
Human *Homo sapiens*	12–14 yr.	20–60	1
Laughing hyena *Crocuta crocuta*	—	25	1
Gorilla *Pan gorilla*	9 yr.	33	1
Sheep (Hampshire) *Ovis aries*	28–35 wk.	15–20	2

[a] In captivity.

aspects of primate reproduction with special emphasis on the human system.

Fecundity Rate. The fecundity rate refers to the maximum frequency of births that can be produced by a species. It is the combined result of the number of infants normally born at one time and the minimum length of time possible between conceptions. Fecundity rate does not refer to the number of infants actually born over time, but instead those that could have been born if the reproductive system were in full operation.

The fecundity rates of primates are slow compared with those of other mammals. For one reason, the majority of primate females produce single births (Table 5-1). Among these animals, an infant is constantly carried by its very mobile mother, who presumably could not manage to care for twins in the same fashion. The characteristic pattern of single births was probably established in the primates' mutual ancestors, which lived mobile lives in the trees. Some prosimians—the lemurs, and a group of New World monkeys, the marmosets—normally produce twins, but these animals keep their young in nests and are atypical of primates.

In addition to the small number of offspring per birth, a primate female is usually able to produce less than one birth per year, as a result of pregnancy and lactation, which respectively eliminate and suppress ovulation. In prosimians it takes about a year for the development of an offspring from a fertilized egg to a weaned juvenile. This process takes even longer in monkeys and apes. In some of the simians pregnancy and lactation associated with a single birth may last more than two years.

The fecundity rate of humans is integrally dependent on cultural factors, because each society has a set of customs that guide individuals in their sexual activity and childbirth. The closeness between biological and cultural factors makes it necessary to study reproduction in many societies before accurate generalizations can be made about the entire species.

In industrial nations pregnancy lasts an average of 41 weeks. A woman typically resumes menstruation five months after childbirth. This period may be as long as 18 months (Katchadourian and Lunde 1972:125) or as short as two to three months. Assuming that a woman conceives during her first ovulation after childbirth, her children would ordinarily be spaced every two and a half years, but could be as much as four or as little as two years apart. This theoretical rate is only rarely obtained by individual women in industrial societies. The actual birth rate for populations as a whole is strikingly slower.

It is difficult to assess whether the fecundity rate of women in industrial nations is similar to that of women in all other societies. One possible factor is that differences in adult nutrition may affect fecundity rate. A second important factor concerns the length of time a mother nurses her baby. It is probable that lactation in humans suppresses ovulation when whole populations (not individuals) are considered. In primitive societies women typically nurse children longer than do women in industrial societies. This practice may depress the theoretical fecundity rate in the former group. Until careful studies have been made this assertion must remain speculative.

Maturation Rate. Gestation and maturation rates in primates are characteristically slow. This is especially obvious when comparisons between primates and other mammals of equal size are made, in consideration that gestation periods reflect the body size of the infant. The gestation period of a tarsier, a prosimian about the size of a chipmunk (Table 5-1) is approximately 180 days (Napier and Napier 1967:324), whereas that of chipmunks is only 31 days. Predictably, the largest sized primates have the longest gestation periods. For example, the gestation periods of humans and gorillas are approximately 280 days long; the gestation periods of laughing hyenas and sheep, which are paired for size respectively with humans and gorillas, are approximately one half of those of the primates. In fact, the 278-day gestation period of the Jersey cow (Harrison 1971:21) is very close to that of these much smaller primates.

The lengthy development of the prenatal period in primates continues in the postnatal development of young. Infant dependency lasts longer in primates than in comparably sized nonprimates, as does the interval between birth and sexual maturity.

The lengths of these developmental periods progressively increase from the lower to higher primates. Galagos reach puberty at 52 weeks of age, compared with six to nine weeks for similar sized rats (Table 5-1). Humans reach the age of puberty between 12 and 14 years (Ford and Beach 1951:168). Even the massive Indian elephant matures more rapidly; it reaches puberty between the ages of 9 and 14 years (Harrison 1971:23).

The primate tendency for slow maturation rates is directly associated with capacity for social learning. Long developmental periods permit the formation of complex brains and for increased information to be stored in them.

Lifespan. Longevity is also typical of the primates. In general, smaller animals have shorter lifespans than larger animals. It is difficult to determine with accuracy the average lifespans of long-lived animals in their natural habitats, however, so the data are not very reliable. Nevertheless, comparisons between similar-sized primates and nonprimates (Table 5-1) show the tendency for increasing longevity in the primates.

Humans are the best-studied primates in this respect, and for them lifespans are known to be highly variable within and between populations. The average lifespan for agricultural populations is between 25 and 35 years, whereas for industrial populations it averages over 60 years (Cipolla 1970:83; 86). In the United States the average lifespan for females is 74 years, whereas for males the average is 66 years. The longest life expectancies are currently for Norwegian women, with a lifespan of 79 years, and Swedish men, with an average of 72 years. The maximum verified age reached by an individual is 114 years (McWhirter and McWhirter 1971).

Fertility Cycle. Reproduction in the primates shows a pattern of regular, periodic cycles. Regular changes in frequency occur in fertility, sexual activity, and births (Lancaster and Lee 1965). In general, the periodic nature of these cycles is most marked among primitive primates and least pronounced among the higher primates, including humans.

In all primates each periodic fertility cycle lasts about a month. All primates share the major features of this cycle, with ovulation apparently occurring midway through the cycle. If fertilization does not occur, the lining of the uterus sloughs off, producing menstrual flow in humans, apes, and Old World monkeys. New World monkeys and prosimians do not menstruate; although the uterine lining is replaced in regular periodic cycles, in their case the dead cells are simply absorbed by the body. Primate females who are not pregnant at the end of one cycle will immediately begin another cycle. This phenomenon is difficult to observe, however, because fertilization usually occurs at the time of ovulation. Some lower primates may experience only three or four cycles followed by a period of time when no cycling occurs (A. Jolly 1972:201). Other primates, particularly apes and humans, cycle continuously if pregnancy does not occur. Knowledge is limited concerning the exact nature of female cycles in most primates, but it is certain that they are strongly affected by environmental conditions. Wild rhesus monkeys, for example, ovulate only during a part of the year. In captivity, however, these monkeys cycle continuously. One of the most important characteristics of primate fertility is that it is flexible enough to respond to a wide variety of environmental conditions.

Sexual Activity. There is a distinct progression from prosimians to humans in the degree to which sexual behavior is cyclic and is determined by physiological changes. In some prosimians, such as *Lemur catta*, both males and females undergo physiological changes which allow sexual activity to occur only within distinct seasonal periods (A. Jolly 1967:4). This situation, uncommon among primates, is similar to seasonal ruts in other mammals. In most primate groups the males are potentially sexually active at any time. The females, however, are physiologically capable of copulation during only part of their fertility cycles. This segment of the female cycle, estrous, is controlled by the flux of female hormones.

In apes, sexual activity is primarily controlled by female fertility cycles but some data suggest that other factors are also involved. Captive orangutans, gibbons, and chimpanzees have been observed to copulate when females were infertile (Ford and Beach 1951:204); this also occurs rarely in wild chimpanzees (Van Lawick-Goodall 1968:216). Chimpanzees who have had their ovaries removed do not ordinarily copulate but have been known to do so, particularly in order to avoid injury (Ford and Beach 1951:222). Female apes sometimes show marked preferences for individual males and have been known to reject perfectly willing and able males during a period of maximum estrous. These observations indicate that sexual activity in female apes is not completely dependent on hormones.

Sexual activity in humans is potentially possible for both males and females at all times. This is unique to humans. Nevertheless, cyclic patterns in sexual behavior have also been noted in human populations. In a recent study (Urdy and Morris 1968), the sexual behavior of two groups of women showed an increase in orgasm around day 14 of the cycle, the time when ovulation was most likely to occur. This periodicity did not seem to be affected by periodicity in copulation, which differed in the two groups, apparently in response to cultural factors.

A very small amount of time is actually spent by nonhuman primates in sexual activity. The Indian langur is believed to be in estrous only 5 percent of her adult life and sexually active for even less time (Jay 1963:6). The majority of her adult life is spent in such activities relating to motherhood as pregnancy, nursing, and weaning. The same general pattern is true for another Old World monkey, the rhesus macaque. Female rhesus monkeys are in estrous for 3 to 5 percent of their adult lives; again, the rest of their reproductive lives is occupied by maternal activities. Female macaques give birth once a year, and because the previous offspring is not fully weaned at the time of the sibling's birth, the females are usually associated with several offspring of different ages.

Van Lawick-Goodall (1968:219) noted only 93 copulations during her first two and one-half years observing a chimpanzee population. Using her data on minimum interval between births, cycle length, mean length of genital swelling, and normal number of cycles between infants, it can be shown that a female chimp is potentially sexually active only 1.1 percent of the time. This figure does not take into account that chimps have occasionally been observed to copulate while pregnant or while not in estrous. Nevertheless, it is probable that we can accept this figure as a rough estimate of time spent by adult females in sexual behavior.

Among human societies the amount of time spent in sexual activities varies greatly (Mead 1961:1455–56). The events associated with sexual activities are so diversified that it is very difficult to generalize about this topic. In some societies sexual activity is allowed under a wide variety of circumstances, whereas in others it is regulated by various conditions such as the female reproductive cycle, as well as demographic, economic, political, or religious events (Ford and Beach 1951:75–77). Cross-cultural information on the frequency of intercourse is limited, and usually derived from statements made by a few members of each society, who may not be typical of others in their sexual behavior. Direct ethnographic observations of human sexual activity are almost never possible because of a widespread sense of privacy about these activities (Bateson 1947).

Societies reported to have low frequencies of intercourse include the Keraki of New Guinea and Americans of the United States. The Keraki reportedly copulate on the average of once a week, whereas Americans average between once and four times a week, depending significantly on the husband's age (Ford and Beach 1951:78). In contrast, in other societies multiple intercourse commonly occurs nightly. Ford and Beach (1951:78) report that in the majority of societies for which some information is available, adults engage in intercourse on the average of once a day when they are permitted to do so by social conditions.

Birth. Variations in the patterns of births are observed in most primate populations. Lancaster and Lee (1965) describe three types of birth cycles. Some animals give birth only within distinct time periods, or birth seasons, in the annual cycle. Some animal populations have birth peaks—births occur all year round but frequency increase markedly at particular times of the year. Some animals give birth all year round with no significant seasonal variations.

Periodicity in primate births is most pronounced in the prosimians, which usually have distinct birth seasons, with no births occurring during other times of the year. This is true also of some Old World monkeys, such as the Japanese macaque. Other Old World monkeys—the baboon and Indian langur for example—show birth peaks rather than true birth seasons. These animals live in environments where climatic seasonality is not pronounced. This is an important point, because most primate species that have been studied show a high degree of interspecific variability in frequency of births. This variation apparently correlates with environmental factors. Natural populations of rhesus monkeys have birth peaks, but those kept artificially on Puerto Rico have distinct birth seasons, and those in captivity show little cyclic fluctuation in births, much like human populations.

Seasonality in births is present in human populations and is more noticeable in primitive than in urban industrial populations. Ursula Cowgill's (1970) study of births in York, England, showed pronounced birth peaks in the summer and fall seasons of the sixteenth and seventeenth centuries. Since then the seasonality of births in the York population has gradually and progressively decreased, but is slightly present in the birth records for the period 1939–1961.

In another study of seasonal variations in conception and birth (Thompson and Robbins 1973) the authors compared rural populations in Uganda and Mexico. In both populations births and inferred conceptions showed patterns of variation throughout the calendar year. In the Uganda population the patterns showed highest statistical correlations with rainfall patterns. Ethnographic observations showed that during the rainy season husbands and wives spent more time together in their homes than at other times of the year. The Mexican population, in contrast, had strongest statistical correlations between births and urban migration. The ethnographic observations show that many migrants are young married men who leave their wives in the rural areas during their sojourns in the city.

This study clearly illustrates that seasonal variations in frequency of human conception and birth depends on the multiple effects of cultural and climatic variables. Human patterns of reproduction, like those of nonhuman primates, are dynamically in equilibrium with socioenvironmental variables.

SIMIAN MODELS FOR HUMAN BEHAVIOR

It was once thought that activities of nonhuman primates had no relevance to the study of humans; however, it is now in vogue to discern the glimmerings of human idiosyncrasies in monkeys and apes. Today, authors of popular books frequently assert that similar behavioral traits observed in humans and a simian group have common origins. Often the inferred common factor is declared to be genetic. Primates, in fact, differ greatly among themselves and in their resemblances to humans. These differences pose analytical problems for investigators who are interested in generalizing about human behavior on the basis of studies of nonhuman primates.

Primate variations are both phylogenetic and ecological. Phylogenetic relationships are constructed by biologists on the basis of observed morphological and physiological similarities between species. The primates are not uniformly related to each other, but can be classed along gradients according to their relative similarities. These relationships are shown in a very general way in Fig. 5-1. Humans, for example, are biochemically and anatomically more like the apes than like either monkeys or prosimians. Furthermore, humans are more like chimpanzees and gorillas than like either the orangutans or gibbons. The graded nature of genetic relationships is important because it indicates variations in the time depth of common evolution. A possible approach to the study of human sex differences is to utilize data from closely related species, recognizing, of course, the separateness, in the recent past, of each group's evolutionary history.

Living primates are not only the result of unique evolutionary developments; they also each manifest unique ecologies. Therefore, each species has a unique physical, chemical, and biological function within a community of organisms. Kormondy (1969:5) expresses this basic biological concept when he maintains that "each species has not only morphological, physiological, and behavioral attributes, but, because of them, unique ecological attributes as well."

Despite the specificity of ecological adaptations of each primate species, it is possible to distinguish broad similarities among them. These similarities form patterns of affinity not always congruent with those based on genetic kinship. Therefore, the primate group genetically most like early humans may not be the group ecologically most like them. This poses a problem if one primate group is selected for its great relevancy to the study of human behavior. Should the model group be the one most alike on the genetic or ecological gradient? Either choice weights the conclusions. This and other difficulties encountered by investigators who look for insights concerning human behavior in the activities of a single primate group will be discussed in the section on Case Study Approach. Some students of primate behavior who feel that primatology has relevance to the study of human sex-linked behavior avoid the pitfalls inherent in the case study approach by using the comparative method. This approach usually focuses on general patterns of primate ecology. Human analogs are then sought to explain the diversity of human behavior.

The choice of the method of relating nonhuman to human data greatly affects the outcome of the study. This observation applies to many aspects of human behavior including sex differences. In order to illustrate this we shall first consider variations in primate ecology with regard to the comparison of many primate species. We shall also show how this comparative approach has been used to provide analogs for human behavior. Second, we shall review the case-study approach to human behavior and illustrate how it has been utilized.

The Comparative Approach. Some people who are interested in the significance of human sex roles look for regular patterns among the sex roles of all living primates. The identified patterns are then commonly correlated with two variables. One of these is ecological. Another variable is physical dimorphism between the sexes. This refers to a situation in which females differ significantly from males of the same species in their secondary sex characteristics. In primates, sexual dimorphism is commonly found in body size (height and weight), canine tooth size, various attributes of body fur and hair and certain other characteristics. The correlations between behavior, morphology, and ecology among nonhuman primates are used to provide analogies for human life.

The comparative approach is illustrated by the work of Claire and W. M. S. Russell (1968:1971). These authors point out behavioral and morphological regularities in groups of primates that have basically similar ways of life. The Russells distinguish three major primate life patterns: *arboreal, semi-terrestrial,* and *terrestrial.* Primate populations in each of these categories differ significantly in the spatial positions of their activities, as indicated by the terms.

According to the Russells, it is possible to generalize about the differences between the sexes in groups of primates with these contrasting ways of life. For example, arboreal primates show very little sexual differentiation. Males and females are alike in size, markings, and behavior.

> The female takes part in finding food sources and in maintaining the band or family territory against other bands or families; the male takes part in carrying and rearing the young and in all aspects of their care except suckling. There is little or no status difference between male and females who are essentially equal in rank (Russell and Russell 1971:64).

Semi-terrestrial primates, in contrast, are more sexually differentiated in body size and behavior than their tree-living relatives.

> To some extent, they have specialized their males for functions of leadership and defence against predators. Though the sexes

> look somewhat alike, the males are bigger,
> more powerful, and armed with enlarged ca-
> nine teeth (Russell and Russell 1971:64).

The greatest difference between sexes, however, is found in terrestrial monkeys in open savanna country.

> There is an imperative need for powerful
> males for defence against predators. The re-
> sult is a society ruled by an establishment of
> leading males, in which females have vir-
> tually no influence and are only kept in the
> centre of the band when they are nursing
> mothers. Division of labour is sharp, and the
> male and female look very different (Russell
> and Russell 1971:66).

The Russells' review of primate societies leads them to the conclusion that sex differentiation is directly correlated with danger. Thus arboreal primates, with few predators to threaten them, have not evolved strongly differentiated sexes. Terrestrial primates, in contrast, live in dangerous environments. Their evolutionary response has been the development of sexes that are strongly differentiated. Males have assumed a protector role, thus leaving the parental role exclusively to the females.

Before we discuss how the Russells extend their findings about nonhuman primate sex differences to human ones, it will be useful to examine some primate groups in more detail. We shall do this within the ecological framework utilized in the Russells' study. The primate profiles permit the reader to evaluate the Russells' generalizations as well as to appreciate the range of biosocial differences between the sexes within each of these categories.

Arboreal Primates Arboreal apes and monkeys (except orangutans) are agile and lithe and spend most of their time in trees. They are almost exclusively vegetarian, often consuming only fruits or leaves. Insects provide occasional condiments in their diets. Each adult animal feeds only himself; food sharing between adults has never been observed among arboreal primates. Many of these animals are nocturnal and some members of all species live in social groups consisting of two or more adult individuals with several subadults. However, there are usually less than 50 individuals within a group.

In times of danger arboreal primates usually act individually to avoid capture by a predator, although vocal communication is an important cooperative warning system. Sometimes adults will frighten an intruder by mobbing, which is concerted group threat behavior. Importantly, however, males do not act as protectors of females and young. In fact, it is reported that howler monkey females are more aggressive than the males (Buettner-Janusch 1967:253), although this is an unusual situation. In general, however, there is slight behavioral difference between the sexes in arboreal groups.

There is also a correspondingly slight physical dimorphism between the sexes. In general, adult arboreal females and males tend to be alike in both body size (Table 5-2) and markings, especially in comparison with sex differences in primates with a terrestrial way of life. Sexual swellings and other morphological expressions of sexual readiness are often not observed in female arboreal primates. When females are prepared for sex they actively solicit the attentions of males.

There appears to be very little status ranking within troops of

Table 5-2. Female size as percentage of male size in some primates

PRIMATE	NICHE	FEMALE SIZE IN PERCENTAGE OF MALE SIZE	
		WEIGHT	LENGTH
Gibbon *Hylobates*	Arboreal	94	99
Howler monkey *Alouatta*	Arboreal	81	81
Langur *Presbytis*	Semiterrestrial	89	94
Chimpanzee *Pan troglodytes*	Semiterrestrial	90	94
Baboon *Papio anubis*	Terrestrial	50	81

arboreal primates. Males are not strikingly more aggressive than females and, unlike the more terrestrial primates, are not involved in much activity that pertains to the expression and control of aggressive behavior. Males and females participate in the rearing of young, although in some species the early weeks of infant life may be spent in contact solely with the mother.

In order to illustrate these generalizations, we shall first examine a group of New World monkeys, the howler monkeys, and then the gibbons, a group of apes. Both fully arboreal groups are very unlike humans in their contrasting ecologic niches. Genetically, the gibbons are more closely related to humans than are the howler monkeys.

The howler monkeys (Alouatta palliata) are arboreal primates that live in the tropical rain forests of America. They are named for the adult males' eerie vocalizations. Howlers live in groups that range in size from 2 to 45 individuals. Average troop size is 16 individuals. One island-dwelling howler group studied by Carpenter (1965) consisted of 45 percent adult females, 16 percent adult males, and subadults of both sexes. The sex ratio of this howler group was 2.5 females to one male. It is probable that the sex ratio of the entire island population was more nearly equal because more males than females lived as solitary individuals.

Females and males are similar in height and weight with the males slightly heavier and taller (Table 5-2). The ranges of female and male weights and lengths overlap, however, and the averages for each sex are very close. Males do have longer beards and longer and more extensive mantles than females. Males also have a yellow-colored scrotum which is mirrored by yellow vaginal lips in the females.

Males perform slightly more dominance and leadership functions than females. When a troop is moving through the trees, usually in single-file, the first individual is often, but not always, the largest male. Aggression is rarely expressed, but mild competition for females sometimes occurs. In general, males are not strikingly competitive and dominance ranking is not pronounced. Males cooperate with each other by howling and sometimes by mobbing, with or without adult females, in order to protect a fallen infant.

Female howlers have mutually friendly interactions with each other. Adult females may occupy any position when the group is moving; they are not herded together by the males for protection. Females may have a slight dominance hierarchy among themselves, and sometimes have been observed to assert majority leadership.

The gibbons, apes that live in Southeast Asia, are another example of arboreal primates. Gibbons *(Hylobates lar)* are the aerialists par excellence of all the primates. When gibbons need to walk on the ground, which is seldom, they stand on their hind legs; but they are rather inefficient at this form of locomotion. Gibbons are predominately fruit- and leaf-eaters, but they also eat birds' eggs, nestlings, and insects (Carpenter 1964:195–96). They live in groups that range in size from two to six individuals. The groups usually consist of a pair of adults with or without subadults. Lone males and lone females have been observed. These extra-group individuals are often young adults that are probably in transition from membership in natal groups to groups of procreation. Thus it appears that gibbon groups are cohesive and relatively stable in composition, except that offspring are driven off when they reach sexual maturity. Sexual dimorphism is very low (Table 5-2). The ranges of sexual differences in weight and length overlap. There is no sexual swelling in the females and copulation is believed to occur throughout the menstrual cycle and even during pregnancy (Carpenter 1964:223). Typical female and male behavior is very similar. Carpenter describes the situation in the following manner:

> As far as could be learned by observations, adult male and female gibbons show no striking sex difference in dominance. This may relate to their lack of anatomical secondary sex differences. It may be concluded that in this primate, though the adults are very aggressive, there is an *equivalence of*

dominance in the sexes. However, among individuals there is a wide variation in dominance which may vary also from one type of
behavior to another, e.g., the animal most
dominant in feeding may not be the most
dominant in play or sexual behavior (Carpenter 1964:266).

Adult male and female gibbons are dominant to young adults
and subadults in the family-like group. Male-male and female-
female interactions are difficult to describe because no group
with two same-sexed adults in their prime was observed. When
two same-sexed adults were found within one group, one was
always in his prime, whereas the other was a young adult or senile. In captive situations, same-sexed adults are intolerant of
each other and fiercely aggressive. Both males and females are
involved with rearing of offspring. Because group size is small,
infants lack age mates; but they often play with siblings and
adult males. Adult males and females both guard the young of
their group whenever the need arises.

Semi-terrestrial Primates Devore (1963:302) mentions the Indian langur *(Presbytis entellus)* and the chimpanzee *(Pan troglodytes)* as examples of semi-terrestrial primates. In both species, sexual dimorphism is present but not pronounced.

The common Indian langur, studied by Phyllis Jay (1965), appears to be at home both in the trees and on the ground. Groups
of langurs may spend as much as 80 percent of the day on the
ground, but they never move far from the vicinity of trees. In
times of danger the animals make warning calls which alert the
group, but it is every langur for himself as each individual seeks
safety in the trees. No cooperative defense action is taken by
group members. The principal food sources of langurs are
leaves and other vegetation, including cultivated crops.

A regional population of langurs consists of groups containing
both males and females (called bisexual groups), and males that
are either solitary or part of all-male groups. Average size of
bisexual groups is between 20 and 25 individuals, although
group size ranges between 5 and 120. Large aggregations form
as a temporary response to dry season conditions when groups

cluster around scarce water holes (Jay 1965:206). The sex ratio among adults in the group is 1.5–2 females per 1 male. In addition to the main bisexual groups, some males are solitary or form all-male groups ranging in size from 2 to 10 individuals. The ages of these males are not given but we suspect that these are animals which either have not yet achieved dominance or are senile.

Adult females and males show some behavioral differences. Adult females have exclusive access to infants from their birth until they are approximately five months old. Thus, adult females and subadult females form the social unit that protects and cares for young infants. Males do not respond to the squeals of infants, and if a male frightens an infant, the mother instantly threatens the male—a temporary but predictable reversal of dominance relations.

At about 10 months, male infants begin to approach adult males, which they embrace or mount. The male adults presumably aid the socialization process by permitting these activities. Female infants of the same age do not interact with adult males. According to Jay, male langurs have a linear dominance hierarchy, but it is a subtle pattern, which is apparent only after a long period of field observation. One reason is that aggressive interactions are rare; so dominance must therefore be judged by observations on preferential access to food, leadership positions, and estrous females.

Female langurs also show variations in dominance status, but Jay feels these are best considered as a series of levels of dominance. In female dominance interactions, physical aggression is less frequent than that of males and is limited to slapping. The dominance structure of females is less stable than that of the male hierarchy because a female's position fluctuates with different stages in her reproductive cycle.

Adult females and males both dominate juveniles. Female subadults are subordinate to adult males or females, but subadult males sometimes dominate adult females. Male subadults are always subordinate to all adult males and spend much time on the periphery of the group.

According to Jay (1965:248), "Sexual dimorphism is not pronounced among the north Indian langurs, but adult males can be distinguished from adult females by the male's slightly larger size and more robust body build." Shultz (1956) gives a figure of 88.7 as the average weight of females as percentage weight of males for the genus *Presbytis.*

Chimpanzees *(Pan troglodytes)* are another example of forest-dwelling semi-terrestrial primates. These animals are especially interesting to humans because of the very close genetic relationship between the two species. Jane Van Lawick-Goodall (1968) has studied a group of chimps in an African forest. The chimps normally spend much of their daylight hours feeding or engaging in social interactions on the ground; they almost always travel through the forest along trails. At night, they sleep in the trees and during the rainy season the Gombe Forest population spends as much as 80 percent of the daytime in trees. Chimps are omnivorous. Their primary foods are a wide variety of vegetables. Additional foods are honey, insects, eggs, and meat (Van Lawick-Goodall 1968:169).

Chimpanzees live in nonpermanent social groups, which vary in size and composition. In the Gombe forest study, group size ranged from 2 to 20, with most chimps in groups of 2 to 4 members. Many solitary animals of both sexes were also present. Half of the groups consisted of almost all possible combinations of age-sex classes, except for mature-male–infant associations. The other half of the groups were composed either of adults of both sexes and subadults, or of mothers and offspring. The mother-offspring associations are the only chimp groupings which endure for significant amounts of time. The sex ratios of various chimp age classes indicate that females slightly outnumber males in all classes.

Chimp social structure is loose because of the fluidity of group membership (Goodall 1965:453). Aggressive behavior is very infrequent. Goodall finds that the concept of dominance cannot usefully be applied to the population as a whole, but that it is useful in describing some interactions between individuals. Such interactions involve a situation in which one animal clearly supplants another. Most of these situations involve two mature males. In such instances mature males are always dominant to females, adolescents, and juveniles. Mature females are always dominant to adolescents. Goodall notes that these animals are not continuously in each other's company so that the stability of these relationships is difficult to judge. There is some evidence, however, to suggest that dominance behavior between two individuals is dependent on situational factors.

Female-male dimorphism is low in both length and weight indices (Table 5-2). Behavioral differences between the sexes are not pronounced but do occur. For example, there appear to be sex differences in greeting behavior (Van Lawick-Goodall 1968:284) although most greeting and other gestures are shared by both sexes. Mature males and females spend approximately the same amount of time in grooming activity but partners differ for each sex. Females most frequently groom their offspring, whereas males groom each other (Van Lawick-Goodall 1968:266). Also males receive more grooming than do adult females. Males and females are involved in the rearing of offspring, but each has a different role in this activity. Females feed, carry, and protect very young infants. Mature males play with infants and prevent them from playing too roughly with other infants. Older infants who are learning to move away from their mothers begin to interact with males. Mature males, for example, groom juveniles more than do mature females. It appears that mature females play a critical and intense role in the early stages of infant rearing and that males perform a less intense, but significant function in the latter stages of development of the subadult chimpanzee.

Terrestrial Primates Very few primates can be described as being fully terrestrial. Humans are, and some baboons and macaques have also adjusted to this way of life. Terrestrial nonhuman primates show great differences between the sexes. Males and females look and behave very differently from each other. They are found in a wide range of habitats including treeless savannas. Among all nonhuman primates savanna-dwelling monkeys spend the greatest amount of time on the ground. They are also more terrestrial than populations of the same species living in other environments. Most of what is known about terrestrial primates is based on studies of savanna-dwelling baboons (*Papio ursinus*). They have been studied by Irven DeVore and K. R. L. Hall (1965).

Savanna baboons travel in troops the size of which widely varies within and between areas. Troop size tends to be between 30 and 50 individuals. Baboon troops are described as closed because membership is fixed in the group of the individual's birth. Baboons rarely change group affiliation and there are no solitary animals. The adult sex ratio varies widely among the groups, from as little as 1 male to 1.2 females to as much as 1:10, although a ratio of 1:2–3 is most common. It is possible that groups with high sex ratios have been newly formed when one male and several females split off from a parent group, but this process has not been observed. The uneven sex ratio of adult baboons may result from a combination of sex differences in mortality and maturation rates. In some groups the sex ratio for the entire population of animals of all ages is approximately equal.

Savanna baboons are potential prey for a variety of animals including lions, cheetahs, hyenas, wild dogs, leopards, birds, and humans. Much of baboon sexual dimorphism and social organization is related to this fact. For example, males are almost twice the size of females (Table 5-2) and have long canines, which are used primarily for defense. Males act as group protectors, although their roles shift in this regard during the life cycle. Young males fan out from the central part of the group and act as sentinels to warn of imminent danger. Dominant adult males stay near the troop core except when the troop is endangered. They then move toward the predator in advance of the troop.

Dominant males also threaten attacking individuals during intragroup interactions. Savanna baboon males are more aggressive than males of arboreal and semi-terrestrial species and the dominance ranking is therefore more pronounced.

Females are smaller, less aggressive, and have a less straightforward dominance hierarchy than males. Individual female ranking may vary with the reproductive cycle and two females

often coordinate their attacks on another in a form of cooperation not often observed among males. A mother with a young infant will seek out a dominant male and will always stay next to
him until her infant has matured enough so that she need not
decrease her mobility because of it.

Among terrestrial primates living in habitats where refuge
places are scarce and predation is present, there is selective
pressure for strong group cohesion and group defense. Among
the savanna baboons these needs are met by closed social
groups and male defensive behavior. Such behavioral specialization serves to differentiate males and females in ways other
than those of reproduction: body and canine tooth size for example.

Our primate portraits have depicted two important aspects of
primate behavior. First, each species has a unique pattern of
sexual dimorphism and social organization. Second, these patterns of sex-linked biobehaviors correlate with broad ecological
variables.

What then do the Russells conclude about human sex-linked
behavior on the basis of their studies of nonhumans? As noted
earlier, the Russells derived their human analogies from Barry,
Bacon, and Child's (1957) study of socialization practices of 110
societies. In that study the authors found that strong sex role
socialization practices did not occur randomly, but correlated
with some other societal traits. Unfortunately they did not consider environmental danger, which was found to be significant
in the Russell study. The studied correlates indicated to the
Russells that sex role polarization occurs in societies where activities requiring some strength and mobility from the home
base need to be performed. Males are biologically more fit than
females for such tasks because of their greater muscular
strength and less biological attachment to the parental role. The
Russells therefore believe that in some societies the biological
predispositions of the sexes are given much additional social
meaning. We shall explore this interesting idea in later chapters, but first it is instructive to examine another approach to the
study of primate sex differences.

The Case Study Approach. One problem in the reconstruction of early human life concerns the method of gauging the relative degree of dimorphism between the sexes. The solution would be fairly simple if sufficient skeletal remains were available for study. It would then be possible to determine the physical differences between the sexes. Such data would have to be available for each stage of human evolution in order for us to obtain a clear picture of the trends in physical sex differences. The degree of behavioral sexual dimorphism could be inferred from these data on the basis of correlations exhibited by living primates.

Unfortunately, the stages of human evolution are reconstructed from severely limited skeletal material and there is no time period for which there is sufficient evidence to provide a sound basis for the reconstruction of each sex type. This circumstance contributes to the necessity of turning to living primates for additional information.

Investigators who wish to reconstruct the social life of early humans frequently turn to a single specific group of nonhuman primates for behavioral models (see Washburn and DeVore 1961; Tiger 1970a). The animal group which is chosen to provide a model greatly affects the nature of these reconstructions, and in turn beliefs about the course of human evolution. In this section we are particularly interested in why the specific groups are chosen, the nature of their sex differences, and the implications of these choices for human evolution.

Lionel Tiger's book *Men in Groups* (1970a) is a good example of the case study approach. Tiger relies heavily on observations of the social life of savanna baboons in his reconstruction of early human social life. This model, of course, has the effect of generating a hypothetical situation in which early human sexes are seen as strongly differentiated rather than weakly so. He then points out similarities between the behavioral modes of the sexes in early human society and some present-day ones. From this he concludes that these similarities must be due to common genetic factors rather than ecological ones.

Although Tiger does not state clearly his reasons for using savanna baboons as models for early human behavior, several possibilities are implied. First, both baboons and humans are terrestrial. Second, Tiger (1970a:33), in accord with others, postulates that early humans lived in savanna habitats similar to those occupied by baboons. He feels that this environment may have provided the necessary conditions for the development of terrestrial life and cooperative behavior, especially among males.

Two additional reasons may help explain Tiger's choice of models, although neither is directly implied in his writings. First, savanna baboons were the earliest well-studied primates in the wild, and for some time provided the only available information about nonhuman primate behavior in natural settings. Savanna baboons achieved this distinction because the good visibility afforded by open savanna habitats makes them one of the most easily studied primate groups. Second, it seems possible that these baboons exhibit sex differences in behavior consistent with Euramerican ideas concerning the innate nature of human sex differences. This means that from the beginning savanna baboon studies have not challenged existing notions of sex roles, but, by conforming to them, have been uncritically used to raise them to new levels of scientific respectability.

We have several reservations about Tiger's choice of savanna baboons as models for human society. One of these is that baboon and early human ecologies may not be very similar. Although no one, including Tiger, pretends that the niche occupied by savanna baboons is precisely like that of ancient humans, he apparently believes that they are highly similar. Tiger argues that the differences between the two groups are related primarily to the significance of hunting in early human life. But, according to Tiger's analysis, hunting patterns only widen the basic cleavage between male and female behavior found in baboons.

Other investigators stress differences in the ecologies of baboons and early humans. Thelma Rowell (1966:345) has questioned the significance of savanna life in baboon evolution. Rowell believes that the savanna habitat itself may have recently been created in Africa through the agricultural activities of humans. She suggests that baboons evolved in a woodland rather than a savanna environment. If Rowell's thesis is correct, then savanna life could not have had a formative influence on either evolving baboons or humans.

David Pilbeam (1972:88), confident that the African savanna predates agriculture, feels that this habitat has had different significance in the evolution of monkeys and humans. According to him, humans, apes, and monkeys evolved separately before any group ventured out onto the savanna. This would mean that savanna-dwelling monkeys and early humans have little in common besides their common habitat. Pilbeam's view is that the two groups' ecological niches are probably dissimilar despite the adaptation of each to the same habitat.

Thus, both Rowell and Pilbeam raise important questions regarding the similarities of the ecological niches of savanna baboons and early humans. Rowell believes that the common habitat inferred by Tiger for the two groups was not significant in the evolution of either species, whereas Pilbeam argues that despite a similar habitat the ecological niches must have been significantly different.

Another of our reservations about the use of savanna baboons as models of human behavior is that the behavior of these animals is not necessarily typical of baboons. Rowell (1966) has pointed out that much of the range of baboons is actually forested country. The good visibility on savannas accounts for the attraction of these places for baboon watchers. Consequently, baboons are described as savanna animals, and many of their features, including their pronounced sexual dimorphism, are explained as adaptations to this environment. Rowell notes that these ideas have in turn been incorporated into theories of primate evolution.

With this in mind, Rowell chose to study groups of baboons in other habitats. She chose two populations that moved through a mixed habitat of short grass and gallery forest. These animals spent 60 percent of their time in the forest.

The two groups studied were approximately the same size as studied savanna groups. The total membership of one group was 32 individuals, while the other consisted of 58. In the forest groups, the adult sex ratio was approximately equal, although most savanna troops had a preponderance of females. Group cohesion was much more fluid among the forest groups than among savanna baboons. In the forest, some individuals apparently changed groups, and occasionally two troops joined for foraging expeditions. In one large troop small parties would sometimes separate from the larger group for part of the day. Adult females apparently never changed group membership so that they can be said to form the nucleus of a troop.

The behavioral differences between savanna- and forest-dwelling baboons are striking. Rowell never observed the forest dwellers moving in formation like savanna baboons. Instead, she observed two patterns of spatial distribution, both of which are unknown for savanna groups. First, an adult male sometimes waited for the entire troop to pass him on a trail before following them. Second, peripheral animals were most often pregnant females. When frightened all animals fled, with the biggest, strongest males well ahead of the baby-carrying females. The dominance hierarchy of adult males was not rigid like that of savanna baboons. Threats, fights, and supplanting behavior were rare. This scarcity of dominance interactions may have been influenced by the presence of abundant, widely dispersed foods. Disputes were common only when limited and preferred foods, such as seedlings and mushrooms, were encountered.

Rowell's description of forest-dwelling baboons is more like a description of forest-dwelling chimpanzees than of savanna baboons. The forest monkeys seemed to lead an unharried, low-key existence in an environment where food was plentiful and predators were few. Indications of group tension and aggression were very infrequent, and no male dominance hierarchies were observed. Most importantly for this discussion, sex differences in behavior were much less accentuated than in savanna-dwelling baboons.

Rowell's study of a population of forest-dwelling baboons (of the same species as the savanna baboons) illustrates the range of behavior that can occur within a single primate species. The extent of variation in social organization between savanna- and forest-dwelling baboons is particularly striking because baboons appear to be anatomically more highly specialized, and their behavior more genetically limited than some other primates—the apes for example. It points up the fallacy of characterizing the behavior of a species on the basis of observations made on a single population. An analogous fallacy is very frequently encountered concerning humans; biobehavioral traits of *Homo sapiens* are too often based only on observations of Euroamerican populations. In both cases it is more accurate to discuss ranges of variations based on wide and diverse, rather than limited and uniform, samples.

Lionel Tiger's choice of the savanna baboon as a model for early human behavior has colored his view of human evolution and of present-day societies. Savanna baboons are extremely sexually dimorphic in both physical size and behavioral traits. In fact, they exhibit as much sexual dimorphism as any of the living primates. This choice leads Tiger to reconstruct an early human society with sharp behavioral divisions between the sexes. Tiger's basic argument is that as humans evolved, sexual specialization became ever more advantageous. Females became more child-oriented and were occupied increasingly with child-rearing as infant dependency grew. Males became more male-group oriented, and male dominance hierarchies developed along the lines typical of savanna baboons. The males' major contribution to the group was to ensure cohesion by protecting it from predation by other animals and by maintaining social order within the group itself. As human evolution proceeded, males, who were preadapted for a defense role, shifted to the provider role.

The major thrust of Tiger's view of human evolution is that with time sex differences in behavior increased and became genetically fixed. It is possible that if Tiger began with a model of early human society based on observations of some primate group other than savanna baboons he would have been less convinced that genetic differences play a strong rule in determining sexual differences in human behavior.

In addition to Tiger's choice of models, there are several aspects of his view of human evolution that deserve comment. First, Tiger's view of human evolution is speculative and based on little hard data. He cannot be faulted for this because only limited data are available for study. Nevertheless, this situation allows a wide latitude in interpretation of the course of human evolution. When freedom is permitted by the data, Tiger's interpretation is in accord with typical male folk views in his own society.

An example of this bias is the distorted view of the evolution of human parental behavior. As a result of a lengthy evolutionary development, human infants are dependent on adults for an inordinately long period of time. Tiger rightly recognizes that adult female behavior had to have been consistent with these changes. He totally ignores the possibility that males too were becoming more child-oriented and nurturant. This probable increase in male nurturance can as easily be supported as that of increased female nurturance. Like maternal behavior, it is based on comparative observations between human societies and those of nonhuman primates. Human males are much more involved in child-rearing than males of any other primate species. Modern industrialized societies, however, are atypical in that males have a minor parental role as a result of several social changes associated with urban, industrial life. In other words, Tiger may have been misled about a major evolutionary thrust because of an unrecognized but narrow and ethnocentric bias.

Second, Tiger argues for the development of opposing features in the course of human evolution: "*Increased* differentiation of male-female behavior through evolution [occurred] at the same time as there was probably a *decreased* physical differentiation" (Tiger 1970b:31; our emphasis). Tiger fails to discuss how this process could have occurred, but to us it seems based on a misunderstanding of evolutionary processes. Physical and behavioral sexual dimorphism are two manifestations of the same process of adaptation. In the long run of evolution, these manifestations will always be consistent. If there were good skeletal evidence to show greater sexual dimorphism in ancient as compared with modern human populations, the most logical assumption would have to be that behavioral differences between the sexes decreased rather than increased with time.

Third, Tiger makes a set of simplifying assumptions that we

cannot accept. He subscribes to the view that baboon biobehavior evolved in a savanna habitat. He then reasons that if early
humans were savanna-dwellers they must have shared many
characteristics of baboon social life. We feel that the unique
conditions of baboon evolution are not replicated by human
evolution. Although it is certainly true that the same habitat can
pose similar challenges to different populations, the vast differences between modern baboons and humans provide strong
indications that these challenges were met in distinctive ways.
In fact the enormous biobehavioral differences between baboons and humans make either group an unlikely model for the
other's evolution.

Apes are more like humans anatomically, genetically, biochemically, and in susceptibility to particular diseases than are
baboons. On this basis alone it would seem that if one species is
to provide data about our human heritage it should be one of
the apes. Chimpanzees and gorillas are the two apes biologically most like humans. Behaviorally, however, chimpanzees
are more like humans than are gorillas.

Chimps are more like humans in facial expressions and
greeting behavior than are the gorillas. Like humans they eat a
wide range of foods—including insects, small game, and hard
seeds. The diet of gorillas, in contrast, is more narrowly restricted to leaves and fruits. Chimps are inquisitive animals interested in exploratory behavior. They are quicker to learn new
behaviors than gorillas, and exhibit a wider range of tool-using
behavior in the wild than their larger cousins (Itani and Suzuki
1967). Chimps use modified sticks for fishing termites and
honey out of inaccessible places, and unmodified sticks for display attacks. They use leaves as sponges to get water out of
small places and are thought to crack hard fruits with stones.
Gorillas are only known to use unmodified sticks to bring food
into reach.

Food sharing is another trait chimps have been observed to
exhibit. Like tool using it was once thought to be exclusively
human. Food sharing does not occur often in chimpanzee
groups, but it has never been observed to occur in other nonhuman primates.

If a single nonhuman primate group with the greatest relevancy for studies of human evolution is sought, chimpanzees appear to be the most highly qualified. They are less genetically specialized than are baboons. Instead, their particular form of adaptation is strongly behavioral. Chimps show a greater range of almost every kind of behavior than baboons. They eat a wider range of foods, have a greater capacity for learning, use tools, and are more inquisitive than the terrestrial monkeys. These traits are far less developed in chimps than they are in humans, yet there are more similarities in the overall trends of chimp and human evolution than with baboon and human evolution. We feel that these broad similarities between chimps and humans outweigh the similarity of common habitat between baboons and early humans.

Chimpanzee social life affords a model of differences in sexual behavior which is useful in reconstructing modes of sex linked behavior in early human groups. Adult males and females behave in basically similar ways, while exhibiting some behavioral differences. Those relate to (1) stability of associations between individual animals, with the mother-offspring association being the most durable, (2) patterns of interaction with young, with females more intensely involved during early developmental stages and increasing male interaction with increased maturation, (3) age and sex classes of grooming partners, and (4) greeting behavior.

The social organization of forest-dwelling chimp groups has been described as loose, because subgroups of shifting membership are often formed. There is evidence that these subgroupings of virtually every possible arrangement of age and sex classes allow for maximum utilization of dispersed and shifting food resources. These behavioral patterns are most obvious in chimp groups living in *mixed* environments of woodland and savanna. Unfortunately, these groups have not yet been so intensively studied as forest-dwelling chimps. It seems, however, that the flexibility of social organization that allows for group aggregation and dispersal, combined with the wide range of foods that are consumed by these animals, permit them to adapt to a wider range of habitats than many other nonhuman primates. These traits must have also been characteristic of our early ancestors.

Savanna-woodland chimps form tighter groups when they are in open country than when they are foraging in the woodlands. Baboons in comparable environments follow the same pattern. The difference between the two species is that chimps often form subgroups containing adults of both sexes. In times of maximum group dispersal, chimps sometimes move in groups of one adult male and female with her young. These are, of course, the minimal units for reproduction. Itani (1967) has argued that these groups provide models for the origin of the human family. They are the smallest groups that are self-sufficient in economic *and* reproductive activities. There are no real family groupings as such among chimpanzees, but it is possible to see behavior that can be viewed as preadaptive to human organization.

DISCUSSION

What can be reasonably inferred about human sex differences on the basis of studies of nonhuman primates? One inference derives from comparisons of sex differences in all of the living primates. This comparison shows a correlation between the amount of anatomical and behavioral dimorphism between the sexes. In general, these traits covary when all primates are considered. The range of variation is striking. Sexual dimorphisms are small in arboreal groups but large in some terrestrial ones. Contemporary humans are not highly dimorphic in physical sex-linked traits. In addition, there is no skeletal evidence available to demonstrate that a greater degree of morphological disparity between the sexes existed in the evolutionary past. From this we can conclude that genetic differentiation between the sexes has not been a major aspect of the development of *Homo sapiens*.

Detailed studies of individual species of nonhuman primates permit a second inference to be drawn about human sex differences. Primate behavior has been shown to be a biological feature that allows greater ecological flexibility than is permitted by physical adaptation alone. Even among monkeys like the baboons, the relative differences between the sexes vary significantly with environmental settings. Thus the relative differences between the sexes in nonhuman primates are in part the result of capacities to adjust social behavior to changing environmental conditions. The major thrust of human evolution has been the development of the capacity for learned behavior. This is permitted biologically by the humans' longer period of dependency. This trend has had the effect of giving humans superlatively wide latitudes in their ability to survive in many different environments. On this basis it is logical to conclude that human sex differences are more significantly behavioral than are those of other primates. This conclusion rests on the assumption that within an evolving group of organisms there is an overall unity of developmental changes.

The behavioral differences between human sexes should correlate with identifiable ecological variables. This prediction is based on the similar correlations observable in nonhuman primates. Ecological variables significant for humans may not necessarily be the same as those relevant to nonhumans, but similarities in the processes of adaptation are expected.

The study of differences between nonhuman primate sexes allows us to make the following predictions about differences between sexes. First, the range of sex differences in human behavior is greater than that of any other single primate species. Second, these variations correlate with group ecology.

In much of the remainder of the book we shall explore these possibilities. But before embarking on this task we shall devote the following chapter to an examination of some anthropological theories that have been advanced to explain the observed variety of sex differences in human behavior.

CHAPTER SIX

The Science of Man Looks at Woman

EVOLUTION OF MAN AND MEN

We shall begin our investigation of the role of women in cultural evolution with a consideration of anthropological theories about the fundamental nature of the sexes and their respective contributions to the development of early human society.

Mankind has long been fascinated with questions of its origins, both biological and social. In recent decades, contemporary primate communities have been examined to gain a clearer understanding of the necessary prerequisites for the critical leap, unknown millennia ago, from proto-human to human society. As we have seen, all higher primates organize themselves into social groups of varying permanency, and display a high degree of cooperation. Most scholars would agree, however, that there is a *qualitative* difference between the most complex ape organization and human ones. The transition from proto-human to human society required a significant reorientation of subsistence activities from those based upon *individual* foraging to those of *communal* foraging and *food-sharing*—from economic self-sufficiency to group dependency. In order for this communal production and distribution of food to develop, a parallel development of a social network or superstructure, however rudimentary, was necessary. In simple human societies, this network is based upon formal parent-offspring relationships. There is every reason to assume that such primary kin ties provided similar functions in ancient society as well. Both economic and social referents, then, appear crucial to a demarcation of early human communities from those of modern and prehistoric apes.

The present chapter is devoted to a critical examination of prominent nineteenth- and twentieth-century theories on male and female roles in proto-human and early human foraging communities. The focus of anthropological interest in the origin of society has varied greatly among subdisciplines, and from one century to the next. During the nineteenth century, social and ideological aspects of early society were of special interest. Stimulated by incoming data on primitive cultures, scholars at that time studied, for example, the origins of incest taboos, and marriage and kinship systems unlike their own. With the maturity of geological and paleontological sciences, the technoeconomic dimension was taken up by archaeologists. The stone tool was thought, until very recently, to be a milestone for mankind; it was associated with the rise of hunting as a distinctly human subsistence technique.

In social anthropology a more empirical trend developed in the early twentieth century. Previous theories on the social aspects of early human culture were rapidly discredited, and a movement toward the data-oriented, phylogenetic framework of archaeology eventually emerged. Modern evolutionists have attempted to weld together both social and economic referents, i.e., to associate certain levels of technological and economic complexity with a characteristic type or types of sociopolitical institutions. In doing so, they have perhaps taken greater liberties in the interpretation of archaeological data than have the archaeologists themselves.

In the creation of any model of society, regardless of the evolutionary level, certain assumptions are made, implicitly or explicitly, about the economic and social juxtaposition of the sexes. The incest taboo and the establishment of moderately stable communal production and distribution groups among proto-human foragers assumes some form of labor division. Questions concerning its nature have attracted a variety of inconsistent theoretical conclusions. Does, for example, the division of labor in ancient society exist primarily between parent and offspring, or between sexual partners? Is the concept of sex-specific subsistence technologies (i.e., hunting by males) applicable to proto-human communities? If so, are the activities of one sex significantly dominant to color the entire social fabric? What is the origin and function, among fossil humans, of male-female social relationships that extend beyond the simple biological contexts of sexuality and descent? How are these relationships reflected in the social structure of early society?

Answers to some or all of these questions have been offered by theorists in both the past and present centuries. As we shall see, prejudices about the nature of males and females at the earliest levels of cultural development tend to provide the foundation for theoretical biases on sex roles in more complex societies as well. Social philosophers of the nineteenth century generally argued for the pivotal role of females in the origin of incest taboos and the establishment of exclusive kinship groups. This notion is challenged by contemporary theorists, who often cite primate social organization as evidence for their arrival at an opposite conclusion. Innate male dominance, they argue, is the central underlying theme of ancient economic and social life, whereas the female plays an evolutionarily peripheral role radiating around reproduction and domesticity. Recently the latter position has itself been challenged as at best ethnocentric, and at worst a sexist approach to the reconstruction of early society. Adherents ask if these theories are concerned with the evolution of *man* or the evolution of *mankind,* and indeed if these two areas have erroneously become equated.

NINETEENTH-CENTURY MODELS

In a discussion of the nature of foraging communities of whatever vintage, a consideration of nineteenth-century hypotheses is critical to an understanding of modern anthropological thought. The development of a body of theory is not simply a smooth progression, or an unfolding of increasingly elaborate ideas from a previously less integrated, less complex set of assumptions. Within the ideal pyramid of theoretical refinement are found endless retrogressions, and the development of new hypotheses in opposition to current dogma. We feel that twentieth-century anthropology developed to some extent in reaction to nineteenth-century ideas. To explore this assumption, we shall examine and compare the theories of the more prominent social philosophers of the previous century with contemporary theories.

Darwin's Social Hypotheses. Although best known for his pioneer studies in biophysical evolution, Charles Darwin (1874, orig. 1871) also ventured briefly into the nature of early society as a special adaptation of *Homo sapiens*. His ideas were especially influential in nineteenth-century intellectual circles, and some are still accorded a position of respect in modern hypotheses on cultural origins. *The Descent of Man* was Darwin's major work on the biological and social development of the human species. Like many other scientists of his time, he became interested in the evolutionary twilight zone that separated mankind from other primates. Darwin argued, correctly, that the skeleton below the skull assumed its modern proportions long before the brain and head attained their humanlike characteristics. Therefore, pressures of natural selection were for a significant portion of human prehistory focused upon mankind's ability to adapt intellectually and socially to an environment filled with species of greater physical strength. This was accomplished through the invention of what we now call culture.

Darwin stressed both material and social preconditions to human society. Tool-making could not take place until the hands were no longer needed for locomotion. Tool-*using*, in combination with increasing skill and cunning, allowed humans to successfully compete with other animals. But our species' adaptive advantage also depended upon an exaggerated development of what Darwin called the *social instincts*. Many species were recognized as displaying a degree of communality in food-getting or offense-defense, but it was argued that in humans the combination of this trait with intelligence led to the development of a higher level of social responsibility and bonding, namely human morality. It was this so-called moral sense that, according to Darwin, gave early human communities an adaptive advantage through heightened internal cooperation. The nature and content of these moral codes were consequently shaped by natural selection.

For Darwin, then, the social life of early humans is distinguished from that of lower animals by the presence of morality. He traced its development to two primary sources. First is the *sympathy instinct*, which may be equated roughly with a spirit of altruism and interpersonal cooperation. Darwin felt the presence or absence of this trait to be innate because of the adaptive advantage it conferred upon individuals and social groups. He saw it developing first out of a selfish anticipation of individual rewards, but as eventually being underscored on a group level as a valued norm maintained by group sanctions. The second source of moral development centered around sexual behavior and its regulation. It is in this context that fundamental differences in the nature of males and females were stressed. For Darwin, the establishment of stable heterosexual unions, whether monogamous or polygamous, was essential to the development of moral society. Marriage was interpreted as a cultural solution to sexual jealousy among males. Darwin saw the restriction of individuals to one sexual partner as commencing first with married females. Males subsequently demanded chastity of unmarried females as well, and only later extended sexual restrictions to themselves. All restraints upon organic or social drives, such as chastity and temperance, were labeled positively by Darwin as *self-regarding virtues*. Self-discipline, and the corresponding reduction of group tension, was envisioned as a major cornerstone of human society.

Darwin, then, was one of the first scholars to systematically link concepts of man-the-evolving-organism with man-the-toolmaker and, indirectly, man-the-hunter. In *The Descent of Man*, male-female behavioral stereotypes were taken out of the context of philosophy and folklore and given the stamp of scientific authority. Males, we are told, have a greater sex drive, and are naturally more assertive and competitive. In contrast, females are unaggressive and nurturant, and emerge primarily as foci of the male dominance hierarchy. The essentially asexual nature of females, it is argued, accounts for their evolutionarily important role in harnessing and controlling male energy, thereby encouraging in-group cooperation through the lowering of sexual tensions. Darwin's emphasis on the importance of marriage and cooperation always stressed the adaptive advantage that early human populations possessing these characteristics had over those that did not.

Sex, Sexuality, and the Origin of Society. Other social philosophers of the nineteenth century for whom natural selection was not a concept of such overriding importance concentrated their curiosity not only on the structure of early society, but also on its progressive transition from rather modest beginnings to the social conditions of then contemporary Europe. Darwin's social hypotheses on early man, although probably clearly formulated by the 1859 publication of *Origin of Species*, were not to appear in print for over a decade. During that interval there appeared several independent works, which sparked a lively debate over the nature of ancient kinship and marriage systems.

The year 1861, for example, saw the publication of Bachofen's *Das Mutterrecht (Mother-Right)* and Maine's *Ancient Law.* These works were followed by McLennan's *Primitive Marriage* in 1865, Lubbock's *Origins of Civilization* and Morgan's *Systems of Consanguinity and Affinity of the Human Family* in 1870, and Morgan's *Ancient Society* in 1877. All of these treatises offered specific formulas for the social structure of early society, complete with stereotyped biosocial roles for men and women. We shall touch only briefly on each of these landmarks in nineteenth-century anthropology. Although the theories contained therein are interesting, and at times entertaining, a detailed investigation would take us far afield from our primary objective—to indicate the influence of nineteenth-century thinking on twentieth-century scientific and folk images of the sexes.

A common thread linking the above works together is the near agreement of the authors on the way in which culture has developed. With the exception of Henry Maine, these early evolutionists traced the ultimate origin of society back to a state of sexual promiscuity. During this earliest cultural stage, reproduction was achieved through random mating without formalized or exclusive male-female pairing relationships. This phase was thought to be followed by a universal stage of matrilineal descent and, according to some scholars, political rule by women. The third stage in this progression was patrilineal descent, or the patriarchal family. Males were conceived as seizing power over property and children, and often subjugating women. Maine alone rejected the promiscuous and matrilineal stages, and argued for the patriarchal family as the earliest human form. The final evolutionary stage recognized was the monogamous nuclear family of industrial Europe.

The sequence of primitive promiscuity to matriliny to patriliny to the monogamous or nuclear family, then, was widely accepted in the previous century. The majority of these scholars emphasized the important role of females in the development of marriage and early kinship groups, and identified descent through women as a universal stage in human cultural evolution. It was only later that paternity became recognized, and males turned the institution of marriage to their own advantage. Men were characterized as taking multiple wives (a practice called *polygyny*), while simultaneously demanding chastity and obedience from their spouses. On the surface, then, the evolutionary stages identified by nineteenth-century theorists seem to stress the high status of women in ancient times, and the gradual erosion of this position to one of subservience and institutionalized inferiority.

A closer investigation of the actual rationalizations given for the initiation and progression of these stages, however, reveals a set of sexual stereotypes not unlike those offered by Darwin. These are outlined for each scholar and major evolutionary stage in Table 6-1.

Despite major differences in the theories of nineteenth-century scholars, their stereotypes for males and females are amazingly consistent. In the promiscuous stage of cultural development, the sexual freedom in which both sexes indulged was thought to have unequal social consequences. Males were identified as the primary benefactors in the exchange, and females as the unwilling objects. The aggressive, competitive stereotypes of men were counterpointed by the female qualities of submissiveness and dependence. Some investigators, such as Lubbock and McLennan, went so far as to suggest that women were biologically inferior, and that only their periodic elimination at birth made group survival possible. Remaining females in early society functioned largely as receptacles for reproduction. Whereas men regularly cooperated, women remained largely as individuals articulated to others only by marriage, or as the objects of male aggressiveness, to be plucked from neighboring groups at the earliest opportunity. We find in these nineteenth-century writings also an argument for male superiority in subsistence. Sir John Lubbock touches upon some of these themes in the following passage:

> There are some things which women could do better than men, some occupations *which pride and laziness, or both, induced them to leave to the women.* . . . Men for slaves, women for wives, and the thirst for glory, made a weak tribe always a temptation to a strong one. Under these circumstances, female children became a source of weakness in several ways. *They ate, and did not hunt.* They weakened their mothers when young, and, when grown-up, were a temptation to surrounding tribes. Hence female infanticide is very prevalent, and easily accounted for (Lubbock 1873:93, emphasis ours).

In sum, characterizations of the sexes for the promiscuity phase by no means connote equality. Males clearly arise as the champions, with a high aptitude for sex, violence, and food-getting. Females, on the other hand, are somewhat of a luxury to be systematically foregone in time of war, and lavished with

Table 6-1. Behavioral characteristics assigned to males and females by 19th-century evolutionists

CULTURAL STAGE	MALES	FEMALES	SCHOLAR
Promiscuity and Group Marriage	Sexually competitive and tyrannical	Submissive, dominated by males	Bachofen
	Sexually and politically dominant; engaged in constant warfare	Asexual, naturally weak; killed in infancy to promote group survival; war captives	McLennan
	Sex-oriented, warlike, hunters and providers	Drag on group; menial laborers, nonproducers	Lubbock
	Aggressive, but socially equal	Moral, conservative; socially equal	Morgan
	Sexual, but regulated by marriage and religion	Matriarchs; religious leaders; Amazons	Bachofen
	Aggressive, militant, forced to share wives	Weak, numerically inferior to males; had several unrelated husbands	McLennan
Matriliny	Militant; took women by force for exclusive sexual rights	Chattels of males; sacrificed because of weakness; property of individual male	Lubbock

unilateral sex, reproduction, and menial labor in time of peace. Lubbock's passage is one of the earlier statements of hunting as the primary subsistence activity of early man, and of females as essentially *non*producers.

With these basic sexual differences established at the foundation of human society, stereotypes fluctuated only slightly in subsequent evolutionary phases. Surely, however, women were conceived of as achieving their greatest victory during the matrilineal stage, although the keys to heightened status are somewhat bizarre by modern standards. Many Victorian philosophers

Table 6-1. (*Continued*) Behavioral characteristics assigned to males and females by 19th-century evolutionists

CULTURAL STAGE	MALES	FEMALES	SCHOLAR
Matriliny	Social equality with females; absence of paternity concept	Dominant in control of sexuality, descent and property	Morgan
	Sexually and socially dominant; competitive, authoritarian	Innate physiological inferiority; dependent; apolitical	Maine
	Intellectual; spiritual link to offspring; dominant	Inferior socially and politically	Bachofen
	Aggressive, militant; brothers share wives	Weak, minority population; common wife of several brothers	McLennan
Patriliny	Socially and politically dominant; claim rights to property and children	Property of males; main function is reproduction	Lubbock
	An anomalous situation: males seize power over property, family; excessively dominant	Intelligent, moral, unaggressive, subjugated by males	Morgan

felt that the aptitudes for sex and morality or religion were inversely related—especially for women. The matrilineal stage coincided with the origin of marriage and the family, both of which were attributed to the efforts of females. The asexual stereotype for woman made her the logical choice for the termination of sexual anarchy through an insistence upon regularized unions. Descent, we are told, was traced through the mother simply because she shared the most basic and obvious biological relationship with her offspring.

The matrilineal stage, then, did not alter the aggressive behavior of males, but merely suppressed or inhibited its expression. The patrilineal or patriarchal phase, typified by ancient Greece and Rome, represented a reassertion of male dominance in all areas of culture. A spiritual rather than physiological bond between parent and offspring was emphasized, and both women and children were reduced to the status of property manipulated by the eldest male. Henry Maine felt that this type of structure was the cornerstone of human society—that sexual jealousy, universal among males, was displaced in the seizure of power over property and family members. The overall status of women certainly reached its lowest mark at this stage in nineteenth-century models.

Earlier in this chapter we noted that every culture provides its members with a definition of human nature and the nature of men and women. By modern standards the conclusions of nineteenth-century theorists are at times bizarre, but we must be reminded that these scholars, too, were products of their own culture. Euroamerican culture is perhaps unique in its creation of a science out of making judgments on the nature of others. Especially in areas such as male-female differences, where the precise line between biology and culture has not yet been drawn, a veneer of Euroamerican cultural definitions seems to attach itself to all attempts at evolutionary reconstruction. We find, therefore, that the behavioral attributes assigned to ancient men and women do not deviate significantly from ideal role definitions for Victorian Europe. The tendency to isolate and polarize the sexes with opposite and complementary behaviors is attributable largely to the European cultural bias that males and females are essentially different in every social and biological context.

Of the common denominators isolated by Victorian evolutionists, sexuality was certainly the most important. It may well be said that anthropology brought discussions of reproductive activities out of the brothel and into the respectability of scientific discourse. Ancient women were thought to mirror the nineteenth-century Englishwoman, without the protection of a morality grounded in religion and codified in law. Males, thus unrestrained, ordered their entire experience around sexual access to women. All stereotypes in nineteenth-century models seem to be grounded in these unequal aptitudes for sexuality. It is from the virile, potent nature of males that the behavioral attributes of aggressiveness, jealousy, and competition were thought to arise. Inversely, the resisting, restraining sexual posture of females formed the entire basis for assumptions of weakness, submissiveness, dependence, and inactivity. If these stereotypes have survived in the folklore of the present lay public, it is perhaps not so much that nineteenth-century theories were influential, but rather that these role definitions are an important part of Euroamerican cultural heritage. It is their fate in the development of modern theory to which we now turn.

TWENTIETH-CENTURY MODELS

The Fall of Promiscuity and Matriarchy. It often occurs in the development of a science that the entire focus of inquiry and the interpretation of phenomena are at some point redirected or fundamentally revised. In the physical sciences, for example, ideas such as Darwin's natural selection or Einstein's relativity effected significant changes in a large body of theory. So it was with anthropology. By the turn of the century, the social sciences had begun to clearly dissociate themselves from each other and from their common roots in philosophy. Anthropology, especially in the United States, took on an empirical, particularistic flavor in direct opposition to the generalizing, synthesizing trends of Victorian thought.

Dependence upon the reports of explorers, missionaries, adventurers, and other untrained observers in the early nineteenth century had surrounded the social life of primitive populations with an aura of mystery and mythology. The era of philosophizing about these cultures, sometimes referred to as "armchair anthropology," ended with the increasing contact between scholars and non-Western societies. The establishment of colonial empires abroad eventually led to the destruction of indigenous cultures, but, ironically, also helped to eliminate the sideshow effect of foreign customs and populations, and made available a vast laboratory of human behavior for direct anthropological investigation. This was nowhere more immediate than in America. Here the consciousness of anthropology as a developing science and the desire for methodological standardization and rigor coincided with a realization of the sheer vastness of the problem of understanding cultural systems. So overwhelming was the detail of North American Indian society that the father of American anthropology, Franz Boas, was led, and led his students, to set about the task of recording *all* cultural data, and to reject any attempts at evolutionary generalization.

In the early part of the present century, American anthropologists spent much energy in discrediting nineteenth-century theories. The idea of universal stages of cultural development was almost immediately thrown out. The search for societal and institutional origins was thought to be an equally futile exercise. Culture, it was argued, was based in the recognition of kinship and the sexual division of labor. Since the existence of a society without marriage or some type of family structure was unknown in the primitive world, a promiscuity phase was dismissed as being inapplicable to human society. Similarly, matrilineal descent as a once-universal stage was vigorously attacked. Indeed, the legitimacy of matriliny as a descent pattern with an independent status comparable to that of patriliny was itself brought into question. This stand was to have important implications for modern notions on the evolutionary status and role of women.

The question of why the nineteenth-century position of matrilineal priority was so objectionable to early American anthropologists cannot be divorced from the influences of prevailing intellectual and political climates. Of all the scholars who had proposed a universal matrilineal stage, Lewis Henry Morgan was the object of the most concerted attacks. The writings of Morgan served as an inspiration to Frederick Engels in his conclusions on primitive society in *The Origin of the Family, Private Property and the State* (1972, orig. 1884). Although primarily an anthropological work, the latter volume was never accepted in the United States because, as some investigators hold, of its technoeconomic or materialist orientation. Likewise, evaluation of Morgan's original work may have been influenced by its association with the Engels volume, and by its acceptance as a cornerstone of Soviet anthropology. In the words of Marvin Harris:

> With Morgan's scheme incorporated into Communist doctrine, the struggling science of anthropology crossed the threshold of the twentieth century with a clear mandate for its own survival and well-being: expose Morgan's scheme and destroy the method on which it is based (Harris 1968:249).

One of the first American-trained anthropologists, Robert Lowie, devoted an entire book, *Primitive Society* (1920), to criticism of Morgan's *Ancient Society*. In it, he correctly pointed out that matriarchy—actual *rule* by women—was not to be found in the primitive world. He went on, however, not only to deny the priority of matrilineal institutions, but to imply that matrilineal descent itself was rare and somehow anomalous:

> In viewing the phenomena from all parts of the world we cannot fail to note that while definite patrilineal descent is often lacking an asymmetrical stressing of paternal influences is extremely common. In comparison the hypertrophy of matrilineal factors appears as *a highly specialized event superadded to rather than substituted for the paternal traits. . . .* From this point of view we can also comprehend the *instability* of matrilineal institutions. . . . It is not so much that the maternal factors have an inherent tendency to vanish in favor of the paternal ones, but rather that the paternal factors, *never suppressed but merely in abeyance under specific conditions,* reassert themselves when those conditions no longer hold sway (Lowie 1920:184–85, emphasis ours).

In essence, what Lowie was saying is that descent and affiliation through males, at least in principle, are universal. Matriliny, on the other hand, is a curious and temporary form of social organization that inevitably passes back into the more stable and basic patrilineal form.

The impact of such conclusions by the forefathers of American anthropology on the theoretical development of the science is only now being assessed. Although the notion of primitive promiscuity had been reduced to the level of sexual fantasy, the behavioral stereotypes for men and women involved therein were never explicitly denied. In ignoring a discussion of their validity, and by discrediting the reckoning of descent through women, males rose to a position of dominance almost by default. The pronounced illegitimacy of matriliny as an organizing principle, especially at the lowest levels of cultural complexity, removed the only glimpse of favorable stereotypes for women in evolutionary progressions. Certainly with the reemergence of refined general evolutionary models by mid-century, the stage had long been set for a theory of early society embracing both male dominance and the priority of hunting in subsistence.

The Man-the-Hunter Hypothesis. After the first three decades of primarily descriptive, data-gathering anthropology in the United States, interest began to be rekindled in the evolutionism so soundly criticized by its founding fathers. Among the wealth of new data available for a worldwide sample of primitive societies, certain regularities became apparent. They could not be explained away on the basis of chance similarity or the simple spread of ideas. The concept of progressive and dynamic culture change had perhaps never been compromised in archaeology and the related search for fossil man. Here the process of evolution on a small or grand scale had been an obvious fact of archaeological excavation. Its reacceptance in social anthropology or ethnology has been a slower process, but the fact that even original students of Franz Boas now claim adherence to evolutionary principles indicates that anthropology has completed a full circle in theoretical orientation.

The significance of these trends for our investigation of male and female roles lies in the fact that subjects such as promiscuity, the origin of the family, and the nature of early human social organization are once more being raised. Since anthropology has considered these issues before, and since there exists an entire body of literature devoted to an invalidation of original nineteenth-century conclusions, modern answers are greatly influenced by preceding ones. Evolutionism in the twentieth century has often been called *neo*-evolutionism, to distinguish it from the "heresy" of the Victorian era, and to establish it as a scientifically respectable orientation which avoids all of the pitfalls so conscientiously exposed by American anthropology's founding fathers.

The evolution of social organization has once again been scientifically extended beyond the nuclear family. A state of sexual promiscuity is now recognized as being universal at some point in man's prehistory, although probably a subhuman one. To consider this question, modern investigators have tended to explore man's primate nature through the study of his closest living relatives. It is hoped that an understanding of social relations in these troops and communities will provide some basis for the construction of a model for early hominid society.

Central to all such studies of primates in the wild is the recording of male and female behavioral differences. Ironically, the sexual stereotypes thus constructed show a close resemblance to those proposed by nineteenth-century evolutionists. Males are characterized as dominant, competitive, and aggressive, and females as submissive, nurturant, and dependent upon the coordinated protection of males. In the great majority of cases, male-female primate roles are observed primarily from the perspectives of sexuality and reproduction.

The tasks of studying contemporary primates and of constructing models of early human communities have typically fallen to different hands. Both past and modern observers, however, when faced with the problem of transition from subhuman to human society, have clung to sexual intercourse as the universal binding-pin:

> Sex is not an unmitigated social blessing for primates. Competition over partners, for example, can lead to vicious, even fatal, strife. It was this side of primate sexuality that forced early culture to curb and repress it. The emerging human primate, in a life-

> and-death economic struggle with nature, could not afford the luxury of a social struggle. Co-operation, not competition, was essential. Culture thus brought primate sexuality under control. More than that, sex was made subject to regulations, such as the incest tabu, which effectively enlisted it in the service of co-operative kin relations. Among subhuman primates sex had organized society; the customs of hunters and gatherers testify eloquently that now society was to organize sex—in the interest of the economic adaptation of the group (Sahlins 1960:6).

Like nineteenth-century evolutionists and, interestingly, Sigmund Freud (1938, orig. 1913), Sahlins sees the "control of primate urges" (i.e., the cortical and social regulation of sexual competition) as the primary prerequisite to human society. It was through morality, the invention of incest taboos and kinship, and the development of the *nuclear* family, he proposes, that the genesis of culture became possible. Sahlins goes on to argue that a division of labor between males and females as conjugal partners in food-getting is a necessity for survival in early foraging societies:

> The economic aspect of primitive marriage is responsible for many of its specific characteristics. For one thing, it is the normal adult state; one cannot economically afford to remain single. Hence the solitary subhuman primate male has no counterpart in the primitive band. The number of spouses is, however, limited by economic considerations among primitives. A male ape has as many mates as it can *get and defend* for itself; a man, no more than he can *support* (Sahlins 1960:9, emphasis ours).

The juxtaposition of the sexes in early society thus takes on a decidedly male emphasis. Since it is males who are viewed as sexually dominant and competitive, it is *their* cooperation in sexual matters that ushers in human community organization. Similarly, it is *they* who must cooperatively hunt, share their prey, and support the domestic units of *their* creation. In this model, the female role is clearly peripheral. Her activities are primarily reproductive and of only supplementary economic value.

The majority of theories on early foraging societies deal little, if at all, with the origin of culture, except with reference to the advent of hunting. The idealized role of the male as *provider* to a consort and his offspring has been grounded in the assumption that hunting was the most important productive technique, and that it was performed exclusively by males. Indeed, some investigators view the cooperative activities of the hunt as essential to the social and intellectual development of the species:

> Hunting is the *master behavior pattern of the human species.* It is the organizing activity which integrated the morphological, physiological, genetic, and intellectual aspects of the individual human organisms and of the population who compose our single species. *Hunting is a way of life, not simply a "subsistence technique,"* which importantly involves commitments, correlates, and consequences spanning the entire biobehavioral continuum of the individual and of the entire species of which he is a member (Laughlin 1968:304, emphasis ours).

> . . . in the primitive human group of the early Paleolithic, hunting alone was able to give an impetus to the development of tools. It alone was able to support the collective group. Certainly, gathering had always existed, but it did not, and could not, play a predominant role in the first stage of social evolution—that of the primitive group (Debetz 1961:145–46).

The first quotation comes from a paper presented at an international symposium on Man the Hunter in 1966, and the second from a 1959 international conference on the Social Life of Early Man. As noted above, however, the importance of hunting by males was argued nearly a century before by Lubbock.

The image of females as dependents or nonproducers is nowhere better illustrated than in discussions of infanticide. Here too the conclusions of modern scholars parallel closely those of nineteenth-century theorists such as Lubbock and McLennan:

> If the local group is looked upon as a source of male-female pairs (an experienced hunter-provider and a female who gathers and who cares for the young), then it is apparent that a small group cannot produce pairs regularly, since chance determines whether a particular child is a male or female. If the number maturing in a given year or two is small, then there may be too many males or females (either *males with no mates* or *females with no providers*). The *problem of excess females* may not seem serious today or in agricultural societies, but among hunters it was recognized and was regarded as so severe that female infanticide was often practiced (Washburn and Lancaster 1968:302, emphasis ours).

In the latter statement, sexual stereotypes for the ancient and modern foraging situations are clear—females provide males with sexual and reproductive functions in exchange for economic support.

All modern evolutionary progressions stress hunting as the earliest stage of cultural development. Similarly, all emphasize the importance of keeping related *males* together in the same locality. Men sharing common kinship, it is argued, form the most cohesive, cooperative hunting groups. It is therefore not surprising that *patrilineal* (Steward 1955) and *patrilocal* (Service 1962) organizations remain undisputed as models of the typical Paleolithic community.

Before evaluating these theories and contrasting modern resurrections of sexual stereotypes with alternative hypotheses, it is necessary to consider briefly a recent elaboration and extension of the male dominance and man-the-hunter positions.

The Male-Bonding Hypothesis. As we have seen, the emphasis upon males as hunter-providers in ancient society is typically

attributed to their greater physical strength and lesser involvement in reproduction. This biological suitability is seen as
being tempered and molded by culture to form the basic division of labor within the conjugal family, and to create cooperative production groups outside that unit.

Recently the thesis has been advanced that these cooperative
patterns among males are primarily *biological* rather than cultural in origin. Tiger in *Men in Groups,* and along with Fox in
The Imperial Animal, argues that genetic factors based in the
human male's primate nature predispose him toward bonding
relationships with members of the same sex. Females, on the
other hand, have no such built-in codes, and are therefore less-
well-suited genetically for cooperative economic and political
activities.

Tiger bases his argument on the genetic residue allegedly
inherited by males from the original requirements of terrestrial
living. The transition from arboreal to terrestrial conditions was
accompanied by an increase in the general vulnerability of the
group. Tiger argues that this situation placed greatest selective
pressure on males. The requirement for group protection was
met by an increase in male size and strength, and by coordinated defensive behavior. Tiger proposes that not only sexually
dimorphic physical characteristics, but also the so-called bonding behavior itself become genetically imprinted.

The first truly human primates, the argument continues, were
already programmed for male-bonding. These bonding patterns
were simply extended from defense to activities of predation.
Males, at this point, became the *natural* hunter-providers, genetically endowed as they were with propensities toward interpersonal cooperation. Females, Tiger asserts, could not have
taken part in any aspect of hunting. In his own words, they
"would normally be pregnant or nursing their infants virtually
all the time" (Tiger 1970a:58). Decreased mobility, increased
frequency of miscarriages, and accident-proneness are cited as
inhibiting factors. The unfitness of females for the coooperative
activities of the hunt is elaborated in the following passage:

> . . . just as females who hunted with males
> would be at a long-run genetic disadvantage,

> so would those males who permitted females
> to join the hunting party. Even unencum-
> bered by pregnancy or infants, a female
> hunter would be less fleet, generally less
> strong, possibly more prone to changes in
> emotional *tonus* as a consequence of the es-
> trous cycle, and less able to adapt to
> changes in temperature than males. Also,
> they could interfere with the cooperative na-
> ture of the group by stimulating competition
> for sexual access (Tiger 1970a:59).

To the list of qualities connoting female ineptitude in the
hunt are added inferior locomotive ability, inability to throw
projectiles, inferiority in spatial and geographical perception,
and less aggressiveness. Tiger concludes that processes of natural selection favor those communities whose women acquiesce
to their basic biological roles:

> The contributions of non-maternal female
> behavior to the genetic pool would be less
> than the contribution to the pool of those
> females who *accepted* a clear-cut sexual dif-
> ference and enhanced the group's survival
> chances chiefly by full-time maternal and
> gathering behavior (Tiger 1970a:59, empha-
> sis ours).

It is in the hunting-defense bonding pattern of males—and
males alone—that are to be found the prerequisites of increased
brain size in evolving hominids. Only those males who learned
to cooperate and to successfully play the complementary roles
of dominance and submission to dominance made a significant
genetic impression on successive generations. Tiger concurs
with studies by Fox (1967) and Chance (1961), which contend
that the reduction of competitive sexual tensions within the
male-bonding unit and the development of emotional control
was directly responsible for cortical expansion. The resultant
increase in group cohesion is seen as fostering the positive
emotions of loyalty and the sense of guilt among male bonds-
men.

The end result of millennia of male-bonding in human evolu-

tion, according to Tiger, has been a structural or chemical difference in male and female brains, and a genetic program for
behavior which is *expressed in* but not *channeled by* culture:

> Of course, we do not know now the actual
> cortical-amygdaloid processes involved in
> bonding among men, or even the neurologi-
> cal differences among males and females in
> this respect. However, *for my purposes it is
> suggestive* that brain-process differences
> exist between males and females and that
> these certainly reflect themselves in sexual
> and reproductive activity and possibly in pol-
> itics and economics. . . . Given the over-
> whelming portion of human history in which
> females' chief functions have been maternal,
> it was presumably advantageous for females
> to be closely and uninhibitedly attuned to
> their young. For males this responsiveness
> could be a disadvantage beyond the point at
> which it does not interfere with political and
> economic activities (Tiger 1970a:66–67).

In sum, the male-bonding hypothesis of Tiger and Fox differs
little from the man-the-hunter position in terms of sex role stereotypes. Their significant departure from more traditional
theories lies in a stress on the priority of genetic over cultural
factors as the determinants of male and female behaviors.

Woman the Gatherer. Hypotheses on the origin of culture considered so far see males as the architects of all evolutionary advance, either by circumstance or natural endowment. This *androcentric* view of the universe is perhaps attributable more to
the influence of Euroamerican cultural bias on the conclusions
of its own sciences than to any sexist conspiracy. The question
of sex roles in ancient society, however, strikes at the heart of a
complex of issues over the nature of early human communities—issues long clouded by models based largely upon convenience or apparent logic. Woman the Gatherer is by contrast a
discussion of alternative theories on the evolutionary role of

both sexes. Many of these ideas are new, and presently stand only as isolated challenges to more traditional approaches, rather than as an integrated body of theory. They are presented here, therefore, in the context in which they arose: that of a critical examination of androcentric hypotheses. Three dimensions central to the male role in these theories—the sexual, social, and economic—will provide a forum for discussion.

Man the Id We have noted that most sexual stereotypes relate to unequal sexual aptitudes. Males are characterized as the sexually active half of the species. Indeed, Tiger argues that male sexual activity involves "more extensive higher cortical control" (1970a:48) than that of females! Sexual needs and sexual energy have also been closely linked with male aggressiveness and competition. Primate studies are offered in evidence to substantiate the thesis that males are innately hierarchical or *political*, with the more dominant males gaining sexual access to estrous females. This tendency for the structuring of aggressive relationships, we are told, provides the basis for cooperative activities and community organization, and becomes *genetically imprinted.* The political dominance of males, the argument continues, is easily transferred to economic control through the redirection of aggression from a defensive to offensive posture—from protection to predation. In short, this "authoritarian personality" theory of ancient society has no heroines.

One of the most cogent criticisms of this model is that it is based almost entirely upon observations of male-female behavior patterns in low-level primate communities. All androcentric theories, including those in the popular works of Ardrey (1961, 1966, 1970) and Morris (1967), take their major source of inspiration for the reconstruction of early hominid society from baboon troops. Baboon social life is relevant, they argue, because it represents a fully terrestrial primate adaptation. Many observers, however, have recently questioned this choice as both curious and convenient (see Weisstein 1971, Morgan 1972). Baboons are, after all, merely small-brained monkeys. Are not apes phylogenetically closer to man, and hence the more suitable subjects of study? Is the fact that baboon males exhibit behavioral characteristics in conformity with existing stereotypes a happy coincidence?

It is certainly difficult to support the elimination of anthropoid apes from major considerations of the possible nature of early hominoid and hominid social life. Although chimpanzees and gorillas are only semi-terrestrial, phylogenetic affinity and all the associated morphological and behavioral correlates may far outweigh the difference in ecological niche. It is indeed significant that the androcentric model is inapplicable to man's closest living relatives. As Morgan, in her tongue-in-cheek account of human evolution, remarks of androcentrists:

> It seems to me that they have taken a look at our kith and kin and rapidly concluded that the way chimps and gorillas behave doesn't *explain* anything. It all depends, you see, on what you are setting out to explain. If you are starting out with the premise that man is the most aggressive and bloodthirsty creature on the face of the earth, then these cousins of ours will be nothing but an embarrassment to you (Morgan 1972:179).

Unlike baboons, chimpanzees and gorillas rarely engage in either overt physical aggression or sexual competition over estrous females. According to Van Lawick-Goodall (1971), male chimpanzees in the wild express an extremely casual attitude toward coitus, and a complete disregard for competition or jealousy over sexual access. Similarly Schaller (1963) reports that male gorillas do not compete over females, and in fact show little interest in coitus.

Chimpanzees and gorillas *do* exhibit what some have called dominance patterns. Dominance among apes, however, is established by acts of *display,* that is, "showing-off," rather than by acts of in-group aggression. Display behavior appears to be performed by males for the benefit of males, and often takes on an almost theatrical character. Such performances involve charging, throwing objects, and pounding the ground (or, among gorillas, the chest). These energies seem to be directed toward generating as much commotion (and attention) as possible. Van Lawick-Goodall (1971) supplies a vivid account of the rise to dominance of a young male chimpanzee through noisy displays with a metal container he had liberated from the encampment. Any injuries arising from such behavior are typically the result of accidental proximity to the highly excited animal rather than of acts of premeditated assault.

Although dominance so attained may sometimes come into play in the presence of food, it is *not* exerted in the context of sexuality. Significantly, the dominance hierarchy among apes is generally *peripheral* to male-female relationships. What, then, is its function? Its origin? Perhaps an important question to consider in hominoid communities lacking a sexual division of labor is what males do with their time when not breeding. For females reproduction and rearing occupy, in addition to food-getting and food-providing, a large proportion of their life. In contrast, the most pressing responsibility experienced by male apes in a normal day is eating. The sexes differ, it seems, in two immediate respects: freedom for independent action and hormonal behavioral sets. It is in this context that Tiger's (1970a) argument is of interest.

First, it is true that adult males have more free time than adult females. Since higher primates are gregarious, social activities with other available community members often form an important part of daily life. Second, we know that the higher androgen levels of males are responsible for a greater potential for vigorous, aggressive activity. The gregarious nature of primates is often expressed in mutual grooming and play, and by males in *rough* play. The drama of displaying among apes may be interpreted as a highly structured play situation, wherein the actor and audience follow definite rules of behavior. In this case, aggression and energy are exerted more against the environment than against individuals.

Is display behavior among chimpanzees and gorillas *political?* Is the tenuous social ordering that results an example of Tiger's bonding? With the information now available, answers must be reserved on both questions. Display, like food-getting, is an *individual* act—in this case a social act of self-assertion and intimidation. It appears to confer no consistent advantage to the most impressive performer beyond the release itself. The status position thereby achieved is subject to frequent reallocation. The bonding of which Tiger speaks connotes *group* activity rather than the alienation of members through individual competition or acts of overt aggression (as among baboons). A highly adaptive communal activity for which males are genetically favored is *defensive* action. It is in out-group aggression, rather than in sexual competition or individual displays, that the basis for cooperative social relations lies. Such corporate action may have been well developed among fully terrestrial prehistoric apes, comparable in intelligence to modern anthropoids, who, unlike baboons, had already learned to control in-group aggression.

Does this mean, then, that collective action among males is innately determined? Not necessarily. Two inherited features predispose males toward defensive roles in the primate community—their independence from the responsibilities of childbearing and child-rearing, and their hormonal propensities for aggression. Both of these morphological and chemical traits make males more available and more suitable for the assumption of such tasks. Tiger's (1970a) male-bonding hypothesis is objectionable in that this *potential* for social action is equated with the inevitability of its occurrence.

The potential for the development of complex patterns of social interaction existed in ancient male *and* female hominoids. Just as hormonal levels predisposed males toward corporate aggressive activities, so females were structurally and chemically favored for the nurturing and socialization of young through the refinement of cross-generational systems of communication. The transmission of information essential for survival—the essence of culture—involved complex patterns of social interaction, *bonding* if you will, between mother and offspring on a level comparable to that of male special-purpose groups. The direct influence of male-female hormonal differences on social roles probably diminished in relation to the increasing brain size of evolving *Homo sapiens*. The development of intelligence and the elaboration of culture have allowed both males and females to step outside the limits of their own physiology, and to call upon a wide range of learned as well as hormonal motivations for behavior.

This use of a baboon analogy for the reconstruction of early hominid society may be dangerous and misleading. It has led to the equation of male aggressiveness with sexual competition, and to the assumption that patterns of *cooperation* arise from relationships based upon *coercion*. The alternative position, suggested by anthropoid ape behavior, is that sexuality, in-group competition, and out-group aggression are independent variables. The greatest potential for development of male-bonding relationships seems to lie in defense. Female bonding relationships, ignored in androcentric theories, are complementary to those of males. Whereas males tend to participate in activities directed toward the preservation of the community from external threat, females focus upon the continuity of the community through the nurturing and socialization of the next generation. The foci of male and female patterns of social interaction, especially among *Homo sapiens,* is influenced by, but not *determined* by, genetic inheritance.

Man the Family-Maker. The elimination of sexual competition as the focus of male relationships has important implications for hypotheses on early family structure. Andocentric theories cast males as regulators of sexual relations through coercion—as creators of exclusive mating relationships *for females* through the driving-off of competing subordinates. These so-called *one-male* groups or harems are argued as the first departure from random mating. They not only provide for recognized paternity of offspring, but also outline the domestic units for which males are thought to eventually play the role of hunter-provider.

These notions on the origin of the family are also based upon observations of baboon social life. If we turn again to our closest living relatives, the one-male group is entirely absent. Among apes the most enduring family relationship is that of a mother and her offspring. Close ties and cooperative behavior are based

upon common descent rather than the momentary or untrace-
able bonds of sexuality. This *matricentric* family, universal in
primate communities, is proposed by Linton (1970) as the most
likely unit of socioeconomic life in proto-human society. The
idea of males selecting and exclusively possessing females, she
argues, is a positively charged Euroamerican notion, and has
little or no resemblance to hominoid mating patterns (or indeed,
perhaps, to Euroamerican ones). In these communities, sexual
relationships are informal and temporary. Either the female or
the male may inaugurate the coital act, and there is no development of pairing relationships on the initiative of either sex.

Given the evolutionary tendencies for neoteny and increasingly long periods of infant dependency and socialization,
bonding between females and offspring and among siblings,
Linton argues, would be greatly strengthened. It is within this
unit that the fundamentals of interpersonal cooperation are learned. The concept of coercive or enforced paternity is unnecessary, therefore, to account for the origin of familial relationships.

Man the Hunter-Provider. The elimination of the one-male
group as a necessary precondition of family life in proto-human
society leaves many scholars uneasy. Is not the conjugal or nuclear family universal? On the contrary, some anthropologists
feel that the matricentric family has more cross-cultural validity
for human society, since it may be alternatively linked to one
male, several males, or no male at all (see Bohannan
1963:73–74). The insistence on pairing relationships among the
sexes for early society, however, is based upon two premises
(see Sahlins 1960): only in the creation of conjugal pairs can
males suppress their disruptive sexual competitiveness, and the
resulting nuclear family provides the sexual division of labor
necessary for survival. We have already cast doubt on the first,
or Freudian, rationalization. It is to the implications of the second that we now turn.

Androcentric theories of human cultural evolution, without
exception, cast males in the role of head of household and eco-

nomic provider. This, they propose, was accomplished through the development of hunting. According to Tiger (1970a), it was natural for males to engage in this cooperative activity, given their innate ability for bonding. It is out of the activities of the hunt that all good things come to pass for the genus *Homo*, such as intellectual development, food-sharing, tool-making, and even art (see Washburn and Lancaster 1968).

Recently the early development of hunting in human evolution has been brought into question. Jolly (1970), for instance, has indicated that traditional explanations (such as hunting, meat-eating, tool-using, bipedalism, or hormonal factors) are inadequate to explain the trend to the reduction of tooth size in fossil man-apes. He proposes, instead, two phases of hominid evolution: 1) seed-eating by "basal" hominids, and 2) meat-eating and vegetable-eating by "human" hominids. The first phase represented the characteristic foraging pattern throughout much of the Lower Pleistocene:

> The ability to exploit grass-seeds as a staple is not seen in other mammals of comparable size . . . presumably because the agile hand and hand-eye coordination of a higher primate is a necessary pre-adaptation to picking up such small objects fast enough to support a large animal. With these pre-adaptations, and the adaptive characters of jaws, teeth and limbs, the basal hominids would have faced little competition in the exploitation of a concentrated, high-energy food (a situation which would hardly have existed had they, as the "hunting" model demands, started to eat the meat of ungulates in direct competition with the Felidae, Canidae, Viverridae, and Hyaenidae). They would thus have attained a stable, adaptive plateau upon which they could have persisted for millions of years, peacefully accumulating the physiological adaptations of a terrestrial, "open-country" species. There is no reason to suppose that they would show radical advances in intellect, social organisation, material and non-material culture, or communication,

beyond that seen in one or other of the extant higher primates (Jolly 1970:21).

An initial vegetarian phase is certainly supported by archaeological evidence. One of the most consistent problems man-the-
hunter theories must deal with is the absence of projectiles in
the Lower Pleistocene. Dominant tool types in this long period
are hand axes and simple flakes. Their use for securing, pul-
verizing, and scraping vegetable matter arises as a real possibility in light of Jolly's theory (for a modern example of the use of
hand axes for this purpose, see chapter 7). The second phase, in
which hunting is added in increasing proportions, marks the
evolving hominids' rapid advance toward "human" status. By
the Middle Pleistocene projectiles and fire made their appearance, and there is evidence for the slaying of several game animals at kill-sites.

The significance of Jolly's findings for male and female roles
in hominid evolution is substantial. The vegetarian phase may
have characterized proto-human communities for hundreds of
thousands of years before the advent and perfection of hunting
techniques. What would be the social ramifications of such an
economic base? Unfortunately, when it comes to the social correlates of human evolution, Jolly succumbs to the androcentric
model by now familiar to us—that the community organization
of terrestrial *monkeys,* namely baboons, provides a valid picture
of ancient *hominid* social structure. We have rejected this
model because of its very limited occurrence among primates in
general, and among man's closest living relatives in particular.
If, instead, we replace the one-male group with Linton's (1970)
matricentric unit, a model of primate social structure emerges
which is equally applicable to ancient and contemporary vegetarian hominoids, and entirely in keeping with Jolly's two-
phased evolutionary scheme.

In agreement with Linton, the "seed-eating" phase of hominid evolution may have involved communities of terrestrial
man-apes in a social arrangement not unlike that of modern
pongids. Adult females, as heads of their own matricentric
units, would be primarily involved with reproduction, infant

care and socialization, and the gathering of sufficient seeds or vegetable products for themselves and their dependent young. Adult males would maintain no permanent attachment to these mother-child units—except to the unit of their birth. A significant deviation from the situation of modern chimpanzees would lie in the tighter bonding of males for defense. In keeping with what we know of modern gorilla and chimpanzee social life, it seems unnecessary to propose sexual jealousy, sexual competition, male-female pairing, and in-group aggression as necessary correlates of the terrestrial adaptation.

This type of community structure, wherein all adults foraged for themselves, may have continued for millennia with little change. As noted earlier, however, the increasing tendency toward neoteny and prolonged infant and subadult dependency would logically strengthen both social and economic bonds among matricentric family members. But what are the social implications of the advent of hunting? Is this the point at which males assumed the role of providers? Says Jolly:

> The latter [an ecological shift] may have involved the increasing assumption by the adult males of the role of providers of mammal meat, with the equally important (but often neglected) corollary that the females and juveniles thereby become responsible for collecting enough vegetable food for themselves and the hunters. The adult males would perhaps be behaviourally predisposed to hunting by an existing role as "scouts" (Jolly 1970:21).

For Jolly, labor specialization accompanying the development of hunting favored the initiation of food-sharing, tool specialization, and eventually new patterns of economic cooperation, which may have required the organization of what we now call kinship systems. Linton (1970) feels, however, that these patterns were foreshadowed in the matricentric family. Dramatic change in social structure with the gradual introduction of meat-eating may not have taken place:

> Food sharing and the family developed from the mother/infant bond. The techniques

of hunting large animals were probably much later developments, after the mother/children family pattern was established. When hunting did begin, and the adult males brought back food to share, the most likely recipients would be first their mothers, and second their siblings. In other words a hunter would share food *not* with a wife or sexual partner, but with those who had shared food with him: his mother and siblings (Linton 1970:12).

In short, the evolution of a male-female pairing arrangement, wherein food was accumulated and shared by sexual partners, seems to have developed in response to the adaptive advantage of *sexual division of labor* rather than the control or suppression of the primate libido. The division of tasks by sex may have occurred first within the extended matricentric family, with the cooperative efforts of males in hunting serving as a link between these units. Such links may have eventually become strengthened through the systematic exchange of formalized mating partners—the foundation of kinship and marriage systems.

It is perhaps also an oversimplification to polarize male-female economic roles along a gradient with hunting at one end and gathering at the other. Paleolithic big-game hunting often involved the technique of stampede and surround, which required active participation of a major portion of the community. In this case the division of labor occurred between those who drove the game into ambush, and those who did the killing. It is also an androcentric bias to divide the sexes into providers and dependents, or producers and nonproducers. It is fairly safe to assume that in ancient foraging communities, as in modern ones, the only nonproducers were dependent young, adults near death, and invalids. As we shall see in chapter 7, the greater portion of the diet in the majority of preagricultural societies is contributed by the gathering activities of women.

In a similar manner, we must reject the model that reserves cooperative social activities for the male. The formation of the nuclear family, argued by some androcentrists to be the cornerstone of human society, seems to be central to this argument.

That is, the ancient invention of marriage is seen as reducing sexual competition among males, and as opening the door for cooperative activities. Males, thus assured of the exclusive possession of their respective mates, are then free to engage in nonthreatening relationships with one another. By contrast, females are conceived of as exhibiting *increased* competition with one another for the achievement of these dependent, submissive relationships with males. Women become identified with the initiators of these unilateral pairing arrangements, and exist primarily as breeders, isolated beneath the veneer of male cultural accomplishment. The nuclear family model, therefore, compartmentalizes women and isolates them from one another through their articulation to men. Androcentrists argue that the primary allegiance of women is to their biological partners (those of both sexuality and descent), rather than to one another, or to society at large. Any communication among women that transcends these cellular units is therefore often interpreted as nonproductive, superfluous, or even frivolous (i.e., gossipy) in nature, and without significance for the maintenance or advancement of culture. However, when one objectively considers women's activities outside the domestic sphere, this model becomes invalid. While it is true that females bond to their offspring, and that they traditionally maintain some formal relationship with at least one male, their function as economic producers requires that they establish structured activities outside the domestic unit. Since the economic roles of human groups are often dichotomized by sex, the likelihood of female-female bonding in production is increased. As we shall see in chapter 7, gathering activities by women are not only central to the subsistence base of foragers, but are often undertaken both jointly and cooperatively.

DISCUSSION

We have seen how anthropology views culture and the roles played by females and males in its development. Our bias has been that present notions of the nature of the sexes may be fully understood only with a knowledge of their historical roots. In the nineteenth century, theorists seemed to be overwhelmed at the possibilities arising from an absence of sexual restraints in proto-human society. Stereotypes of males and females often paralleled their real or imagined roles in sexuality and repro- duction, and seldom deviated from the idealized Victorian model. Although a universal stage of descent through women was hypothesized, males were consistently painted as socially, politically, economically, and intellectually superior. The re- emergence of general evolutionary models in the twentieth cen- tury occurred only after an interval of intense criticism of pre- vious efforts and of concerted data-gathering. New models of human biocultural evolution were tremendously more sophis- ticated. Fossil and archaeological evidence was available as an aid in the reconstruction of early society. As we have seen, how- ever, modern theories are still largely androcentric.

In the final section of the chapter we outlined recent chal- lenges to traditional formulas for sexual division of labor, the or- igin of the family, and the biosocial aptitudes of males and fe- males. We have not offered a definitive solution to the problem of societal origins, but have attempted to clarify the nature of male-female behavioral stereotypes in modern anthropological theory. We are now better equipped to objectively examine the complementary and fluctuating roles of women and men in modern societies of varying complexity.

CHAPTER SEVEN

Woman the Gatherer

Our species has roamed the earth for at least 50,000 years, and our hominid forebears for several million more. Humans, however, have subsisted on the products of domesticated plants and animals for only a small portion of their existence—perhaps the past 10,000–15,000 years. In the phylogenetic and cultural development of *Homo sapiens*, therefore, hunting, fishing, and gathering have been by far the most important food-getting techniques. Because humans and prior human*oids* are genetically related, and because they may have employed essentially similar technologies, considerable interest has been generated in questions of the qualitative differences between them. What biological, social, and economic advances, for example, marked off human communities from nonhuman ones? What models do we have for the reconstruction of male and female roles during the long period called the Paleolithic or Old Stone Age?

As we have seen in chapter 6, anthropologists have relied on both intuition and the observation of contemporary primates for insights into the nature of this critical transition. Alternatively, however, they have pointed to a small number of modern societies, whose populations subsist solely by foraging, as structural relics of ancient times. These contemporary hunter-gatherers, although now intimidated to the point of extinction by more complex societies, have served as a model for the genesis of most current evolutionary stages. It is often argued that the nature of dominance and the division of labor by sex among modern foragers is a logical refinement or humanization of the genetically based sex behaviors observed in lower-primate communities. We have already examined alternative viewpoints on the relevance of primate models for the reconstruction of human social life. We must now consider the other end of the spectrum—the extent to which modern foragers may be taken as mirrors of ancient ones, and the nature of observable male and female roles in a large number and variety of preagricultural adaptations.

We shall approach our investigation of sex roles in foraging societies first from an economic perspective. That is, we shall want to identify the primary food-getting activities, and the way in which these tasks are allocated to women and men. This initial discussion will allow us to test models that limit the producer role to one sex. Second, the social implications of these relationships will be considered. Here we shall be primarily interested in the effect of subsistence technologies on the structure of local communities, and the possible influence of unilateral and bilateral kin arrangements on the family, marriage, and overall status differences among the sexes. After existing socioeconomic patterns in a large cross-cultural sample of modern foragers are profiled, we shall take a closer look at an individual society. As an example of sex roles among hunter-gatherers, we shall present a case study of the Tiwi of Melville Island, North Australia.

ECONOMIC BASIS OF FORAGING

Most hunters and gatherers of the historical period are now culturally or biologically extinct. These technologically simple societies have been at a disadvantage since the agricultural revolution. Throughout the past 10,000 years, they have become more and more encapsulated by cultures of greater complexity. The tremendous thrust of Euroamerican colonial expansion during the past four centuries, however, has greatly accelerated this process, and has now eliminated the foraging adaptation

from all but the most remote areas of the world. Because of the
accompanying loss of native territories, extermination of game
and other resources, and depopulation, remaining hunting and
gathering representatives have been greatly altered and simpli-
fied. Still, they provide us with a glimpse of what foraging societies may have been like throughout mankind's long preagricultural past.

   In the previous chapter we reviewed alternative models on
the economic importance of the sexes in early society. These
notions have had a tremendous influence on the interpretation
of male and female cultural roles. This is especially true for
societies at the foraging level, since both ancient and modern
representatives employed a similar tool inventory and sexual
division of labor. It is from observation of contemporary
foragers that the man-the-hunter hypothesis arose. We are
therefore interested in clarifying the actual subsistence activities of males and females in hunting and gathering societies,
and in noting the relative contribution of their respective productive efforts to the diet.

The Importance of Gathering. We selected 90 foraging societies
from Africa, Asia, Australia, and the Americas from the *Ethnographic Atlas* (Murdock 1967) to serve as our cross-cultural
laboratory for the correlation of economic and social variables.
Information coded in the *Atlas* on all of these societies was
collected by ethnographers well after they had been influenced
by technologically more complex peoples. It is important to
remember, therefore, that all modern foragers are acculturated
to a greater or lesser degree. In addition, all have experienced
an enforced alteration of their natural and social environments.
Thus, it is only with considerable caution that they may be
viewed as indicative of ancient adaptations. Although we include in our sample only noncoastal, pedestrian, hunter-
gatherers, these modern representatives occupy generally undesirable and nonproductive habitats, and are subsequently less
populous and less complex than even their most immediate ancestors. Our interest in contemporary foragers remains, how-

ever, because they have been so systematically utilized in evo-
lutionist and androcentric theory, and more simply because
they provide the only examples of preagricultural adaptations
available for direct observation.

Our first task is to obtain a clear idea of the relative importance of hunting and gathering in the subsistence of these societies, since the allocation of productive tasks is so often drawn
strictly along sexual lines—hunting is typically male, gathering
female. To obtain our answer, we shall first calculate the
average percentage of the diet contributed by gathering and
hunting in each of the 90 sample societies, after which we shall
tabulate the primary or most important subsistence activity.

Hunting fails to materialize as the dominant food-getting
technique among modern foragers in terms of raw frequencies.
The great majority of sample cases, over two-thirds, depends on
products of the hunt for only 30 to 40 percent of their diet.
Gathering by women, in contrast, is extremely important. The
same proportion of the sample depends on the products of gathering for 40 to 60 percent of the diet.

If we consider the primary or dominant subsistence activity
in each of the 90 societies, the central position of gathering by
women is further underscored. This tabulation appears in Table 7-1.

In Table 7-1, gathering is seen to compose the primary food-
getting activity of 52 of the sample societies (58 percent). In
contrast, only 25 percent of the foragers in question depend

Table 7-1. Primary subsistence activities in 90 foraging societies

PRIMARY SUBSISTENCE ACTIVITY	FREQUENCY	PERCENTAGE
Gathering	52	58
Hunting	22	25
Fishing	7	8
Gathering and Hunting equally	3	3
Gathering and Fishing equally	3	3
Hunting and Fishing equally	3	3
	90	100

primarily upon hunting for their subsistence. Similar findings
have been recorded by other investigators (see Lee 1968). The
model that stresses the provision of animal flesh as the focal
productive orientation of preagricultural societies, therefore, is
not supported by cross-cultural data.

It could be argued that the economic dominance of women
among modern hunter-gatherers is due largely to game deple-
tion and a subsequent reversal of subsistence priorities. Certainly most foragers have been driven into marginal areas where
resources are much less readily available than in their original
homelands. There seems to be little evidence, however, that
the gathering-to-hunting ratio has been significantly altered.
The availability of wild food plants tends to decrease proportionally in poor habitats. Moreover, societies fortunate enough
to occupy environments in which wild game is plentiful, such
as the Hadza (Kindiga) foragers of Tanzania, still depend heavily on the gathering activities of women—in this particular case
for some 50 percent of the diet (Murdock 1967:62). So reliable,
in fact, is the collection of wild plant foods that Hadza males
hunt only occasionally, and *individually* rather than collectively. In light of the evolutionary significance attached to hunting for the development of male-bonding, this observation is of
potential interest. Cooperative hunting perhaps occurs only
where the pursuit and slaying of animals requires the concerted
efforts of several individuals—for example, in the case of scarcity or where game animals congregate into large herds. If this
is true, then the use of modern foragers as models for Paleolithic life may distort our perceptions of the actual frequency or
universality of cooperative hunting by males, and of the
frequency with which women and children were also utilized
for large-scale drives.

Sexual Division of Labor. The allocation of productive tasks to
the sexes in foraging society generally follows a simple rule—
males provide the bulk of the animal protein, and women the
vegetable and fruit complements. There are, however, several
points of convergence in daily food-getting activities. As noted

above, women, along with other community members, participate in communal drives of herds in some ecological niches.
Females may also be responsible for the hunting of small game
or the collection of insects or reptiles encountered while gathering. In other cases they participate equally with males in fishing. The killing of large game, however, is universally assigned
to men. Although males assume some gathering duties in a
small number of foraging societies (7 of the 90 in the sample),
their primary economic roles are those of hunter and fisher.

A high value is attached to the acquisition of meat in all foraging societies. The hunt is a much more precarious endeavor,
however, than is the collection of nutritious stationary resources. It is because of this reason that the products of gathering
traditionally compose the dietary staples. Since women are almost
wholly responsible for the provision of these foodstuffs, their
productive contribution in foraging societies is substantial indeed.

In sum, the model of hunter-gatherers that characterizes
males as *providers* and females as *nonproducing dependents* is
totally unsupported. Indeed, women often assume the primary
responsibility for both productive and reproductive activities,
providing sufficient staples for their respective children and
marital partners while simultaneously making a considerable
temporal and social commitment to the next generation.

SOCIAL JUXTAPOSITION OF THE SEXES

The androcentric argument for male economic and political
dominance in ancient foraging society has also had an important
influence on models of kinship and social organization. As we
have seen, popular man-the-hunter constructs generally ignore
the social implications of the female role except with respect to
child-rearing. Rather, the cooperative activities of males in
food-getting, offense, and defense are often equated with evolutionary biocultural advance in the species as a whole. Given the
sheer inequity of contributions by the sexes portrayed in this
model, a male emphasis in the areas of kinship and social orga-

nization appears as a logical correlate. All modern characterizations of foraging societies that embrace the man-the-hunter
hypothesis (see Steward 1955; Service 1962) argue that a male-
centered social structure—a patrilineal or patrilocal organization—predominated throughout the Paleolithic era. It is to this
hypothesis we must now turn.

Kinship and Social Structure. Social profiles for hunting and
gathering societies are drawn largely on the basis of prevailing
patterns of descent and postmarital residence. As in the majority
of preindustrial societies, the criterion of sex is often utilized by
foragers in the formation and spatial distribution of social
groups. Since only one sex may be consistently distinguished as
the primary linkage in social networks, it is expected that relative status among women and men reflects this inequity.

The residence and descent patterns for our 90 sample societies, we would do well to recall
some basic terminology. The residence modes undertaken by
newly married couples may be most easily distinguished by
identifying the sponsor(s) of the new household. The sponsor
may be, for example, the wife's parents (*matri*local), the husband's parents (*patri*local), the husband's mother's brother
(*avuncu*local), or either or both sets of parents (*ambi*local). Such
residential patterns, when standardized over a number of generations, lead to characteristic patterns of descent. Matrilineal descent is most frequently associated with matrilocal (wife's
uterine kin) or avunculocal (husband's uterine kin) residence,
while patrilineal descent correlates highly with patrilocal (husband's agnatic kin) residence. Some societies claim affiliation
through both matrilineal and patrilineal lines. This type of descent is called *double* (bilineal). Finally, there are those societies, including our own, in which descent is reckoned through
both parents equally, but where lineages are absent. This variety is known as *bilateral*.

The residence and descent modes of our 90 sample societies
are correlated with one another and tabulated in Table 7-2.

From Table 7-2 it can be seen that foraging societies are over-

Table 7-2. Primary patterns of descent and residence in 90 foraging societies

RESIDENCE	MATRI-LINEAL	DOUBLE	PATRI-LINEAL	BILATERAL	TOTALS
			DESCENT		
Matrilocal	4			13	17
Avunculocal	1				1
Ambilocal			2	17	19
Patrilocal	2	4	21	25	52
No Data	—	—	—	1	1
Totals	7	4	23	56	90

whelmingly bilateral in descent. Male emphasis in both residence and descent, however, is strongly represented. Approximately 26 percent of the sample is patrilineal, and an additional 58 percent is patrilocal. Matrilocal residence, postulated by some investigators (e.g. Service 1962:60) to be nonexistent among foragers, is the dominant type in approximately 19 percent of the sample, while the ambilocal (alternatively matrilocal and patrilocal) variety accounts for an additional 21 percent of the total. According to the data in Table 7-2, then, the type of foraging society most strongly represented in the present sample is *patrilocal* in residence and *bilateral* in descent.

While these figures are instructive, caution must be exercised in their interpretation. The great majority of these data were compiled from ethnographic accounts written well after the conquest and subjugation of indigenous peoples. The economic and social fabric of these societies has changed considerably since their first contact with European intruders, and in the great majority of cases this change has proceeded in the direction of the ruling culture. In Table 7-2, for example, it is notable that although bilateral descent is by far the most common variety among foragers, nearly 80 percent of the sample societies have residential patterns (matrilocal, avunculocal, patrilocal) that encourage the reckoning of descent through *one* line only. The high incidence of bilateral descent is undoubtedly a recent development. It is perhaps more than coincidental that the bilateral system of kinship is also the characteristic pattern of

Euroamerican culture, and that bilaterality is itself encouraged by the economic individualism so often imposed upon indigenous peoples.

Much the same caution must be observed when interpreting the high incidence of male-orientation among foragers with respect to residential modes and local kin affiliation. It is argued in androcentric theories, for example, that the localization of related *males* is the only logical pattern for hunters and gatherers. As we have seen, however, the argument that male social dominance results from their role as economic providers is unsupported. The data in Table 7-2, when taken at face value, do indeed lend themselves to this type of conclusion. On closer examination, however, we find that 21 of the 52 societies designated as patrilocal have themselves a patterned alternative for permanent *matrilocal* residence. In other words, options for the localization of individuals related through maternal or bilateral kinship in foraging societies are not only available, but are chosen with great frequency. In our present sample, 58 of the 90 societies, or nearly 65 percent, have this option for permanent matrilocality.

The frequency with which matrilocality may be chosen by hunters and gatherers is all the more striking when the influence of Western culture is considered. An understanding of male emphasis in some foraging societies must take into account the diffusion of ideal sex roles from the dominant culture. In nearly every documented case of alterations in the reckoning of unilineal descent during the postcontact period, the direction of this change has been from matrilineal to patrilineal. Missionaries and early statesmen sometimes abhorred the matrilineal custom whereby a man devoted his primary responsibility to his *sister's* rather than to his own children, and in many instances literally imposed upon males a role more in keeping with Western European values.

What we conclude from these facts, figures, and anthropological jargon is that there is no consistent or universal pattern of male orientation in the kinship structure of foraging societies. Further, there appears to be no significant correlation between the economic importance of the sexes and the type of kinship

structure manifested by a given society. The productive contribution of women among foragers is substantial in all examples, and highly dominant in many. And yet, the frequency
of matrilineal descent and matrilocal residence, at least among
contemporary foragers, remains low. Likewise, patrilocality,
well represented in the present sample, occurs with high
frequency in societies where hunting by males meets with only
sporadic success. Indeed, the average contribution of hunting to
the subsistence base of matrilocal foragers (42.5 percent) is
greater than that found among the patrilocal representatives
(35.5 percent)!

The possibility of change in the kinship structure of these
societies in recent times, of course, may account for the obliter-
ation of former parallels, if any, among economic and social
variables. This eventuality, along with the a priori reluctance of
some anthropologists to accept the legitimacy of matrilineal and
matrilocal organization for the foraging level, indicates a need
for further research before the construction of stereotypes for
Paleolithic social life resumes.

Patterns of Equality. It is often reasoned that there is a necessary symmetry between innate behavior, productive potential,
the locus of kinship, and the locus of power. Males, for example,
have been portrayed as innately dominant, and therefore the
natural providers to and masters of their respective patricentric
families. Just as there exists in our large sample of foragers no
one-to-one correlation between the nature of descent and the
relative economic importance of the sexes, however, so there
appears to be no simple parallel between descent and the relative
social status of women and men. Patrilineal descent among
foragers, for example, does not indicate the subjugation of women.
Neither, of course, does descent through women indicate *rule* by
women. Males in matrilineal societies often reside with the
relatives of their spouses, but assume social and political status
positions not unlike those in patrilineal ones.

It is perhaps a peculiar and latent Western bias that the recognition and emphasis of paternity associated with patrilineal de-

scent is somehow linked with virility and male dominance, whereas the denial or deemphasis of paternity in matrilinal societies is identified with the social emasculation of males. Indications are that the nature of residence and descent in any society is a reflection of adaptive sociospatial arrangements for both the production and the maintenance of political stability, rather than a playing-out of the innate or acquired dominance of one sex over the other (see Martin 1974).

There are, however, some apparent differences in the way that men and women are regarded in matrilineal and patrilineal systems. The degree of sexual freedom granted to women, for example, often varies greatly between them. Since the local communities of most foragers in our sample have lost their unilineal character, such contrastive patterns are more easily seen in stable farming societies. If we categorize our sample according to the prevailing emphasis in descent or residence, however, even these fragmented peoples show some of the characteristic features to be discussed in more detail in chapters 8 and 9.

Data on types of premarital sexual activity are available for 51 of the 90 sample societies, and are presented in Table 7-3.

In Table 7-3, we see that approximately one-quarter of the foraging societies require women to be virgins at marriage, whereas a similar number prefer this situation but do not take breaches of sexual etiquette too seriously. Approximately 30 percent of our foragers fully license sexual experimentation by unmarried women, while half as many avoid the entire problem by marrying off their females before puberty. The interesting feature of these data lies not in their general profile, but in the contrastive patterning of female sexuality by matrilateral and patrilateral communities. Patrilineal or patrilocal foragers exert a significantly greater degree of control over the sexual lives of young women, strictly forbidding experimentation before marriage in nearly half of the cases. In contrast, less than 10 percent of matrilineal or matrilocal foragers promote mandatory virginity.

As we shall see in later chapters, such patterns are not unique to foragers, but relate to the varying importance attached to pa-

Table 7-3. Types of female pre-marital sexual activity in 51 foraging societies according to emphasis in descent and/or residence groups

PREMARITAL SEX	EMPHASIS			
	MATRI-LATERAL	PATRI-LATERAL	BILATERAL	TOTALS
Precluded by early age at marriage	3	2	3	8
Allowed; no sanctions unless pregnancy results	2	3	2	7
Freely permitted; no sanctions	2	2	5	9
Prohibited, but weakly sanctioned; not rare	4	6	4	14
Virginity required; premarital sex rare	1	12	0	13
Totals	12	25	14	51

ternity determination in all societies. Unfortunately, comparable data on the sexual behavior of women after marriage, their freedom to choose their own mates, or to terminate unwanted unions are not available. What evidence we have from individual case studies, however, indicates that the degree of freedom enjoyed by women after marriage may vary greatly with that granted before. In addition, foraging societies appear to be particularly oriented toward egalitarianism, not only in relationships among peers, but among the sexes as well. Although patriliny in more complex societies, for example, is sometimes associated with the exclusion of females from both wealth and power, portable or real property in societies at the foraging level is generally of such insignificance as to be irrelevant to social status. In addition, the economic base of hunters and gatherers is typically inadequate to support the accumulation of multiple wives by males, common in the patrilineal situation, as symbols of wealth and prestige. Rather, the dominant form of marriage is monogamy, and the sex roles therein appear to be both complementary and socially equitable.

Our most accurate generalization about the relative statuses of men and women in foraging societies as a whole is that the worlds of the sexes are separate but equal. In other words, because of the nature of subsistence among hunters and gatherers, the sexual division of labor is sharply drawn. The segregation of experience among men and women is related to these distinct but complementary economic and social responsibilities. Males typically hunt, fish, and share the social duties of maintaining the internal and external harmony of the community. Females gather, and assume the major role in the socialization and care of the next generation. In the majority of foraging societies, it is not the *tasks* assigned to the sexes that are ranked, but rather the relative proficiency with which they are performed. High status may attach itself to the successful hunter, the skilled gatherer, the bearer of many children, the healer of the sick, or the spiritual medium. As such, both women and men have the potential for greatness, for special talent, for charisma, for respect in the daily life of the community, and for wisdom in old age.

CASE STUDY: TIWI WOMEN

Now that we have drawn generalizations from a large sample of foragers, a closer examination of the participation of the sexes in the economic and social life of a specific society must be undertaken. We shall use this case-study approach in each of the following chapters as well. In every case, we have chosen a major ethnographic study that specifically highlights the life experience and lifestyle of women. The authors of these works will serve as our primary informants.

Until just recently, ethnographic descriptions of foraging societies written from an *estrocentric* (if we may coin a new word) perspective were practically nonexistent—perhaps in part because the majority of trained fieldworkers are men. The most important ethnographic data-gathering technique, participant-observation, is often practical or permissible only with informants of the same sex as the investigator. The cultural world of half the target population is thus left unrecorded. In addition, the theoretical bias of many anthropologists in the past has assigned only secondary importance to the socioeconomic role of women in so-called hunting societies. A welcome exception is the 1971 monograph by Jane Goodale entitled *Tiwi Wives*. This study provides an interesting glimpse of the lifestyle of women in a viable preagricultural society.

The Setting. The Tiwi are located on Melville Island, just off the coast of northern Australia. Goodale's study focuses on the members of a small community of approximately 200 individuals at a settlement known as Snake Bay. The land surface is forested, and well watered by rivers that traverse the island northward to the sea from a central ridge. These waterways are typically paralleled by thick tropical vegetation along their entire lengths, and often flow into mangrove swamps or open marshlands at their mouths. Marine resources—shellfish, crocodiles, fowl, and many varieties of fish—are abundant. The shore is also well endowed with fauna, primarily marsupials, reptiles, and birds.

The Tiwi have had considerable contact with the outside world. Melville and its sister island, Bathurst, were first cited in European logs by the Dutch in the seventeenth century. Although part of the coastline was then surveyed, and in the following century sporadic Portuguese slaving took place, the indigenous inhabitants of the islands were apparently little affected by these initial intrusions. The nineteenth century, however, ushered in a series of events that were to establish foreign populations gradually, but permanently, in the physical and cultural worlds of the Tiwi. It began with a French land exploration in 1802, and by a complete British coastal survey in

1818. By 1824 the British had established a small settlement, Fort Dundas, as a depot for mercantile activities, but this experiment was abandoned in 1829 after hostile activities by the indigenes and repeated failures in food production. Water buffalo abandoned by these would-be settlers were left to run wild and multiply on Melville Island until the turn of the present century.

At this point a notorious Australian adventurer and entrepreneur, Joe Cooper, established himself and a private army of mainland natives as resident buffalo-hide traders on the southeastern coast of Melville Island. It was Cooper, according to Goodale, who first gained a foothold among the once-hostile island inhabitants, and who established the flow of trade items on which they were to become dependent. His status as supplier of desired foreign goods was challenged only by Japanese pearlshell fishermen, who had limited trade relations with the Tiwi until the eve of World War II. Cooper's successful residency and stable relations with the indigenes, however, served as a magnet for Europeans of various persuasions and motivations. By 1906 the Australian Protector of Aborigines had visited Cooper's encampment, and by 1911 a Roman Catholic priest-missionary had not just set foot, but had set up shop, on neighboring Bathurst Island. The private reign of Joe Cooper came to a rather abrupt end shortly thereafter. So successful had this buffalo-hide business become, that the water buffalo itself was completely exterminated by 1915. With all the energies of a Hollywood antihero, Cooper then launched a campaign of timber exploitation for foreign markets. This new enterprise, however, depended upon the exploitation of the indigenes as well, and resulted in armed confrontations of such frequency and intensity that Cooper and his cohorts were officially banished from the island.

Through all of these decades of contact, therefore, the Tiwi had been exposed to the ways and the artifacts of foreign cultures. Still, in the absence of actual inland penetration by external populations, the Tiwi were able to continue their lifestyle in a manner congruent with past generations. However, seemingly inexhaustible foreign trade items such as cloth, metal tools,

flour, and condiments, drew Tiwi men and women into social
and economic relations with a continuing procession of
strangers. Until recently, the indigenes appeared to have struck
the happy balance in this interaction of minimal participation
and maximal rewards. In 1937, for instance, a government settlement was established near the old site of Fort Dundas. Its
express purpose was to saturate the Tiwi with desirable food
and material items to discourage the attraction for trading with
the Japanese.

During the Second World War, Tiwi cooperated with resident
allied military personnel for island-based operations. In the
postwar period, the Snake Bay Tiwi fell under the jurisdiction
of the government once again, while a nearby settlement was
placed in charge of a Catholic mission. In 1954, at the time of
Goodale's major fieldwork, the Tiwi still lived primarily in the
bush, although some children had been parcelled out to the
mission school. The description the author gives us is therefore
of a culture still able to practice its aboriginal ways at least to a
slight extent, and to engage in subsistence activities and the
sexual division of labor independently of the government settlement or its resources. The continuing encroachment of cyprus
pine lumbering operations had all but terminated native hunting activities by 1962. This new economic dependence, when
linked with the greatly intensified governmental acculturation
programs, make this final description of a viable, living, Tiwi
culture all the more valuable.

Men, Women, and Food-Getting. According to the data coded in
the *Ethnographic Atlas* (Murdock 1967), approximately 50 percent of the Tiwi subsistence base is contributed by gathering,
30 percent by hunting, and 20 percent by fishing. These figures
are entirely in keeping with the generalizations made earlier in
the chapter for a large cross-cultural sample. On closer examination, however, there are features of the Tiwi adaptation that are
atypical of contemporary foragers.

Perhaps the most striking and important of these is the sheer
abundance of natural resources. Available land protein sources

Plate 1. Cycad palm nuts are an important resource for the Tiwi.

Plate 2. A Tiwi woman and her dog make an efficient hunting team.

are the wallaby, bandicoot, a variety of lizards and rats, iguana, opposum, snakes, crabs, and oysters. Wild vegetables also abound, the most important of which are yams, a variety of sweet root, palms, and nuts. To this list may be added a category of "water and air" resources, such as fish, crocodiles, dugongs, turtles, ducks, geese, and other birds, which the Tiwi classify separately. Although food-getting is a daily activity for both women and men, no threat of starvation looms over the local community. Unlike the great majority of surviving preagricultural peoples, the Tiwi did not suffer territorial displacement by technologically more sophisticated populations, nor was their ecosystem significantly altered until well into the twentieth century. Although exceptional, therefore, in terms of modern representatives, the Tiwi adaptation may be more in keeping with foraging communities of the Paleolithic era.

A second way in which the Tiwi differ from other hunters, fishers, and gatherers is in the categorization and division of labor. The data presented by Goodale (1971) suggest that gathering and hunting are not strictly dichotomized by the Tiwi, nor is the assignment of these tasks made exclusively along sexual lines. Food resources in the environment, rather than subsistence techniques per se, are categorized as being primarily male or female. Ideally, animal life associated with the sea and air is assigned to men, while all land resources, both plant and animal, are classified as women's foods. Males, therefore, are typically occupied with fishing, and the hunting of birds and of aquatic reptiles and mammals. In contrast, women are responsible not only for the collecting of wild food plants and shellfish, but for the *hunting of land animals* as well.

Cutting across the sexual categorization of food resources and subsequent food-getting activities are the factors of age and marital status. Says Goodale:

> If a man had a lot of wives there was no need for him to help his wives in the bush collecting. His many wives could provide him and his nonproducing dependents with a balanced diet of meat and vegetables without his lifting a finger. But in the past young sin-

> gle men and those with only one or two
> wives almost certainly either accompanied
> their wives into the bush or went alone to
> hunt for opossums, bandicoots, and the like,
> as they do today (1971:154).

Among the Tiwi, then, there is no simple dichotomization of
subsistence activities by sex. Hunting and gathering are practiced by both men and women. An important factor in the division of labor appears to relate to the size and strength of the
prey animal, or the relative difficulty involved in its pursuit. For
example, although land animals fall within the female category,
hunting of the wallaby is reserved for men. Unlike the bandicoot or opposum, which may be successfully stalked and club-
bed, the wallaby must be chased down on foot and speared at
close range. Tiwi labor division, then, seems to relate to several
factors, among which are geographical location of resources,
presence or absence of economic complementarity among the
sexes, and the variable requirements of physical strength and
dexterity in the hunt.

Since hunting by women has received so little consideration
in the contemporary literature, we must examine this activity in
more detail. According to Goodale (1971), Tiwi women (sometimes joined by young men) formerly gathered shortly after
dawn each morning to plan the day's hunting and collecting
strategies. Each had four essential pieces of hunting equipment: a dog, an ax, a bark container, and a portable source of
fire. Dogs were well-trained, and exhibited great skill in locat-
ing such land game as bandicoots, which often sleep inside
hollow logs or trees:

> As the hunter walks through the bush, her
> dog darts from one fallen log to another, in-
> vestigating all in a broad line of march. A
> good dog is a beautiful thing to watch as he
> approaches a log, going first to one end and
> then to the other, giving each a careful sniff.
> Then he quietly works his way down the
> length of the log until he has located the
> exact position of the animal. Only then will
> he raise his voice to summon his owner, and

he sits down close to where the animal is
sleeping. The hunter may or may not test the
log further by inserting a long trimmed
branch down the inside of the log and twist-
ing it to obtain the evidence of hair. Whether
she does this depends on how much she
trusts her dog's judgment. Once the bandicoot is located, the hunter cuts a hole in
the log just large enough for her to insert her
hand and pull the animal out (Goodale
1971:167).

So highly did their Tiwi owners regard the dogs that a woman
addressed them in the same terms as she would her children. In
addition, these canines were adopted into the unilineal sib itself, which, as we shall see, stresses maternal or uterine links.

To the Tiwi female we may not only apply the label woman-
the-hunter, but woman-the-toolmaker as well. It is indeed significant that stone axes in this foraging society were made and
used primarily by women. They served as aids in gathering, for
stripping bark with which to make containers, and for striking
death blows to prey animals. In contrast, the predominant hunting implements of males were the mangrove spear with a fire-
hardened tip, and special-purpose throwing-sticks used in the
pursuit of low-flying birds.

Goodale notes that bush hunting and collecting by women
among the Tiwi were by far the most important productive activities:

. . . the women not only could but did provide the major daily supply of a variety of
foods to members of their camp. . . . Men's
hunting required considerable skill and
strength, but the birds, bats, fish, crocodiles,
dugongs, and turtles they contributed to the
household were luxury items rather than staples (Goodale 1971:169).

The economic aspects of Tiwi culture, therefore, seem to run
counter to those predicted by androcentric models of foraging
society. Although males make definite contributions to the daily
diet, women stand out as the primary producers, and occupy

roles of hunter and tool-maker often reserved for the opposite
sex in contemporary archaeological and ethnological theories.

Tiwi Geographical and Social Space. Although peoples of a
common Tiwi culture inhabited contiguous areas of Melville
and adjacent Bathurst Islands, they did not conceive of themselves as one homogeneous community or nation. In the past,
both islands were divided into independent political units,
seven on Melville and three on Bathurst. These autonomous
"countries" were named for and associated with various physical features in the environment. According to Tiwi informants,
membership in a country was life-long.

As in most primitive societies, these political units and the
resources they contained were broken down into smaller geographical divisions or subcountries, to which rather specific
claims were held by groups based on common kinship. In the
case of the Tiwi, however, the relationship of unilineal descent
groups to specific localities is clouded by at least two factors: at
the time of description the population no longer occupied the
various countries and subcountries of their island but had clustered around government settlements; *both* patrilineal and matrilineal affiliation are recognized, and neither variety of resultant kin groups appears to have been localized with any degree
of consistency.

Tiwi kinship and social relations are very complex, a characteristic shared with Australian societies in general. Our primary
reason for outlining the nature of geographical and social space
categories is to provide a basis for identifying the residential
group for which a woman provides economically, and for defining her social and political status within this group. As we shall
see, every individual in Tiwi society inherits membership in
two distinct sets of kinship networks, and these memberships
have varying significance for the daily lives of women and men.

Patrilineal Landholding Groups One's membership in a
country is said to be inherited from one's father. Thus, all persons occupying the same political unit are seen as descendants
of a common male ancestor. Country membership is compara-

ble, therefore, to our concept of nationality, with the addition of
a kinship link with the nation's founding father. This is the geographical unit within which people marry and spend their lives,
and the unit they defend against encroachment. Men sharing
membership in the same country compose what is known as a
landholding group. This means simply that all males in the
same political unit have inherited a common right to exploit its
resources.

Rights to a country's resources are more clearly demarcated
by the division of each into smaller subcountries, the boundaries of which are usually well-known. Closely related Tiwi
males organize themselves into groups approximating patrilineages. Each of these has jurisdiction and exploitation rights
over a given subcountry. In this way, the resources of each Tiwi
political unit are divided equitably, and their allocation is controlled by the administrative machinery of kinship groups. Patrilineages also typically maintain some kind of spiritual relationship with their respective subcountries, and often erect
shrines within their boundaries.

The association of patrilineages with specific subcountry territories would lead one to assume that they are closely identified in a residential sense as well. Actually, these descent
groups seldom manifest themselves as *local* groups. Thus, although related males share rights in a common territory, they
often do not *reside* there together. Goodale (1971:97) feels that
Tiwi patrilineal groups have never been localized. In other
words, the relationship between groups of related males and
land is primarily a conceptual one. As we shall see, the nature
of Tiwi marriage customs often dictates that men leave the residential group of their birth. What results is a pattern of residence that anthropologists call *ambi*local, wherein the newly
married couple may reside with or near *either* set of parents.
The Tiwi, therefore, use patrilineal affiliation to conceptually
define landholding groups, but not to create residential groups.

Local communities among the Tiwi are called *camps*. These
are the smallest units of geographical space, and there are typically several of them in each subcountry. Camps are generally
heterogeneous with respect to kin membership. A major reason

why a lack of symmetry exists between those who hold rights to resources and those who actually reside together may be that the Tiwi trace their primary kinship affiliations in the opposite direction: the most highly structured and important descent groups among them are matrilineal.

Matrilineal Social Groups Maternal linkage in Tiwi society is traced through a series of gradations beginning with one's immediate relatives and extending into increasingly larger groups. Whereas paternal affiliations define rights in land, maternal ones structure society through the control of marriage. There are five distinct levels of social space in the matrilineal descent system: the sibling set, sib, supersib, phratry, and moiety. Unlike patrilineal divisions, each of these levels represents an *exogamous* group (one that forbids marriage between its members). Matrilineal affiliations are thus of critical importance to *both* sexes, whereas patrilineal ones have their greatest relevance for males and the distribution of natural resources among them.

The smallest or lowest level of the matrilineal group hierarchy is the *sibling set*. This kinship unit, often called the "one granny" group, is composed of all siblings who share descent from a common mother's mother. These closely related individuals would include, therefore, one's own brothers and sisters, the brothers and sisters of one's mother, and the children of one's mother's sisters. This group of people, of both sexes, is joined by links traced exclusively through women to a common maternal grandmother. As we shall see, women in the same matrilineal sibling set often reside together for a significant portion of their lives by sharing the same or closely related husbands.

Sibling sets felt to be closely related to one another are grouped into common *sibs*. During Goodale's (1971) research, there were a total of 24 sibs in Tiwi society, created from a very sizeable but uncalculated number of sibling sets. The formation of sibs is identical to the collection of related matrilineages into clans in other parts of the world. The clan differs from the sib only in that the latter has no specific or designated ancestress (hence the exact relationship between component lineages is not always traceable). Their functions, however, are the same. Sib members may not intermarry and are bound together by obligations of mutual aid and loyalty.

The supersib, phratry, and moiety divisions are larger and more amorphous collections of sibs and groups of sibs. Goodale counted seven supersibs, four phratries, and two moieties in Tiwi society. While they are not nearly so important to the daily lives of women and men as are the sibling set and sib, such groups complete the categorization of the Tiwi population and make explicit the rights and obligations of each individual to every other member of society.

The supersib is simply a collection of closely related sibs that act cooperatively as a unit, primarily for the fulfillment of obligations involved in the exchange of marital partners with other sibs. Phratries are also composed of a collection of sibs, but the number is much larger and the integration and cohesiveness considerably weaker. According to Goodale (1971:79–80), the phratry is a group based more upon fictional than actual matrilineal kinship. In other words, phratries bind a large number of sibs together into a single out-marrying unit, but these sibs may not necessarily share a common ancestress. The largest level of matrilineal organization is the moiety, which splits the entire population into two great halves. This dual organization was reported by earlier investigators (Berndt & Berndt 1964; Pilling 1957), and though not specifically identified by Tiwi informants, was noted to be operative in Goodale's tabulations of marital unions.

In sum, every Tiwi man and woman, by virtue of matrilineal kinship, belongs to one of two great moieties. When choosing a marital partner, one must look to eligibles in the opposite half of society. Matrilineal divisions thus provide a conceptual order to society, defining every person's proper place and their rights and obligations toward others. Whereas matrilineal kinship groups structure social space, patrilineal ones define the relationship of individuals to their environment. Paternal relationships are not so formalized, however, as maternal ones, and serve largely as a mechanism for mapping out economic spheres of influence in each Tiwi country. Their members are not bound by rules of exogamy, and do not form homogeneous residential groups. In contrast, closely related women (belonging to the same sibling set) often *do* congeal into local clusters by virtue of the peculiarities of Tiwi marriage.

Two Perspectives on Marriage. Tiwi females are never really divorced from matrimony. In this society, they are betrothed even before their conception, and are the wife of one or another man from girlhood to old age. Our discussion of the role of women must, therefore, take into account that femininity and marriage are of one fabric.

But from what perspective are we to understand the dynamics of marriage and sex roles? One may examine the phenomenon through the eyes of either sex. However, since most ethnographers have been male, this seemingly obvious bias in perceptual focus has often gone unnoticed. We want first of all, then, to summarize briefly the nature of Tiwi marriage—the mechanics of betrothal, matrimony, and the inheritance of spouses. We shall then contrast the way in which Tiwi men (and male ethnographers) view the acquisition of wives with the way Tiwi women see themselves and their serial progression of husbands.

The Tiwi system of marriage diverges rather sharply from the Euroamerican ideal. For one thing, marriage partners are often widely separated in age, at times by two generations. Moreover, every man and woman generally has several spouses in one lifetime. Polygyny is the ideal, and men strive to accumulate as many wives as possible. Women, on the other hand, are typically much younger than their original spouses and are therefore passed on to surviving, and increasingly younger, male kinsmen several times during their lives.

From the male point of view, marriage is the primary road to wealth and prestige in Tiwi society (see Hart & Pilling 1960). Women are tremendous economic assets, and the accumulation of several wives can free a man completely from subsistence pursuits and allow him to engage in ceremonial and public activities. Those with large, surplus-producing polygynous households are able to command considerable power and influence, and are designated as "big men."

As in many cultural situations where maximal rewards are available only to a selected few, many obstacles stand in the way of individuals and coveted high-prestige positions. Foremost for men is the availability of or access to marriageable women. Females, as a form of "capital" in this society, are typically monopolized by the older men. Young men begin their respective careers by inheriting a widow, typically an old woman, from a deceased elder kinsman. Several wives may be accumulated in this way throughout a man's lifetime. The acquisition of a young virgin wife, however, is a complex procedure, and one that involves years of negotations and obligations.

In order to acquire a virgin wife, a man must enter into a contract before the future spouse is *conceived*. Arrangements are therefore made years in advance between the hopeful groom and the father of a married, pubescent woman. At the ceremony celebrating the young woman's first menstruation, an agreement is made whereby any daughters she subsequently bears will be automatically betrothed to the man in question, and will be delivered to him as wives when they reach their late girlhood. Once this contract of future marriage (between a man and the unborn daughter of a young woman) is finalized, the parties involved begin relating to one another as *in-laws*. The mother of the unborn bride (often herself a generation younger than the prospective groom) becomes a "mother-in-law" and the man her "son-in-law." Their relationship, known as *ambrinua*, immediately assumes an economic dimension. The son-in-law typically takes up residence in the camp of his young mother-in-law, contributing food and labor to her throughout her lifetime. Since he is often an age-mate of her own father, however, the economic commitment continues generally for the remainder of *his* life, some time after his eventual marriage to one or more of her daughters. It is for this reason that female members of a sibling set often remain spatially intact, while males with the same patrilineal affiliation to a given subcountry may become widely scattered.

For males, then, the road to fortune is paved with skillfully contracted marriages and the eventual establishment of a large and prosperous household. Women from this perspective appear as little more than pawns in the marriage game, being dis-

tributed and redistributed like chattels in a system over which
they have little or no control. Actually, however, all but the
most immature Tiwi women play an active role in the intrigue
of political manipulations executed by their sons and brothers:

> . . . as mothers and as sisters the women
> were not coerced by their sons or their
> brothers. On the contrary, sons or brothers
> wishing to use their mothers or their sisters
> in their political schemes (typically when
> those mothers or sisters became or were
> about to become widows) could only do so
> with the active collaboration of the women
> concerned. Tough-minded young widows
> could drive a hard bargain with their
> brothers as to where they remarried, since
> each needed the other to make the remar-
> riage acceptable to the tribe at large and to
> beat down other competitors (the dead hus-
> bands' brothers, for example) who wished to
> control the remarriage of the widows. Young
> girls thus had no bargaining power but
> young widows had a good deal. Old mothers
> with influential senior sons were extremely
> powerful. Any affront to an old woman was
> an affront to her sons, and some of the
> strongest influence networks were alliances
> of several senior brothers, in which their old
> mother seemed to be the mastermind and
> the senior sons largely the enforcers of what
> the old mother and her middle-aged daugh-
> ters (their sisters) had decided among them-
> selves (Hart & Pilling 1960:53).

Women, then, like men, were able to use their seniority and
cunning to secure favorable positions for themselves, as well as
beneficial alliances for their kinsmen. But are women merely
secondary participants in a men's world? How do they see their
own lifestyles as distinct from those of males?

The Dynamics of Female Gender. Goodale's description of Tiwi
culture gives us a perspective omitted in previous works. That
is, rather than portraying females as merely wives, it reverses

the field and sees them as women with a fluctuating inventory of husbands. The importance of this approach lies in the fact that the life of women may be seen temporally in a single thread, rather than as a disjointed series of intersections with the dynamic careers of various males.

Every culture is equipped with a set of categories called *age grades* with which to escort its members through the life cycle. Such arbitrary stages recognized by the Tiwi provide us with a convenient framework in which to examine female careers. Tiwi culture distinguishes among ten female status categories, relating to significant stages in the life cycle. In translation they are small girl, young girl, puberty, young woman, pregnant, mother of girl, mother of boy, barren women, menopause, and old woman.

The *small girl* status applies to the period between birth and marriage. A female infant is welcomed among the Tiwi both for her future continuation of the matriline and for her fulfillment of infant betrothal obligations undertaken earlier by her mother. Tiwi girls are indulged by members of the camp during early childhood, and establish close familial relationships with their classificatory mothers and fathers (full-siblings of their parents). As soon as they are able to walk, small girls begin to accompany their mothers into the bush on hunting and gathering expeditions. While economic skills are first learned within the context of play, the female child is soon instructed in the arts of swimming, tree-climbing, tracking, botany, tool-making, and tool-using. Goodale (1972:38–39) notes a case of two girls, aged seven or eight, who constructed a serviceable bark raft six feet long, four feet wide, and two feet thick with which to gather wild food plants in a local billabong (swamp). By the time a young female reaches the latter stages of small-girlhood, she has the basic economic skills to be a productive member of the residential unit of which she is a member.

Entrance to the *young girl* stage occurs at marriage. Unlike the situation in most societies, Tiwi girls are officially married *before* the onset of puberty. Early unions are supported by the belief that secondary sex characteristics, such as the development of breasts and mature genitalia, can occur only with the aid of sexual intercourse. At some point before puberty, then, the young bride is simply taken by her father to the campfire of the man to whom she had been promised before birth. In most cases he has previously joined her natal residential group. The first spouse of a young girl is considerably older than she. The ideal husband is, in fact, a real or classificatory "mother's father," and may actually be a member of the grandparental generation. It is the initial duty of the elderly spouse to gradually instruct his young wife in sexual intercourse, and to oversee her sexual maturity.

At her first menstruation, the young Tiwi wife begins the important and brief encounter with the *puberty* age grade. She is immediately isolated from the residential group in a specially constructed bush camp. There she is attended by her mother, co-wives if any, and other senior women of the community; she observes a number of taboos for the duration of her period. After menstruation has subsided, she is taken to a second bush camp where she undergoes one of the most important rituals in her adult life. The puberty age grade not only establishes a young wife as a woman, but as a mother-in-law as well. During this second isolation a woman is ceremonially introduced to the man who will become the husband of any daughters she may bear in the years to come. This relationship between a mother-in-law and her prospective son-in-law, called *ambrinua,* is particularly intense, and critical to Tiwi social structure. The son-in-law must immediately begin to provide food and favors to his young mother-in-law, and often joins her camp at this time. If she subsequently bears a daughter, the son-in-law must wait until the latter reaches the young girl status before receiving her as a virgin wife. It is for this reason that the age discrepancy between a woman and her first spouse exists.

After establishment of the *ambrinua* relationship, the young wife returns to the residential group and is automatically graduated to the next age grade, that of *young woman.* Between her first menstruation and her first pregnancy, a wife enjoys her greatest social and sexual freedom. Her status in the residential group reflects this period of limited responsibility, since she is not considered an adult until the achievement of motherhood.

During this interval, Tiwi young women traditionally engage in a series of extramarital sexual unions with lovers of their own age. Although this behavior is not officially condoned by Tiwi moral codes, it is both expected and tolerated if discretion is exercised. Such leniency is additionally encouraged by the fact that their young male agemates as yet have no women of their own.

Pregnancy usually brings an end to this extramarital activity. It is notable that abortions are practiced with some frequency by young women in order to delay the acceptance of child-bearing and child-rearing responsibilities. This appears to be a more recent phenomenon, however, since pregnancy was traditionally welcomed as the avenue to adult status.

Barren women are those who have failed to achieve pregnancy. These unenviable females are considered immature regardless of their chronological age, and never gain a position of importance in the community.

If the wife becomes *mother of boy,* fulfillment of *ambrinua* obligations are delayed. The new son is, of course, a member of his mother's sibling set, but leaves this residential unit when he reaches maturity and acquires a mother-in-law of his own. If the wife becomes *mother of girl,* another critical link in the matrilineal network is thereby added. Further, the mother's *ambrinua* is provided with a future wife, to be claimed a few years hence. Once the daughter is delivered as a wife, the son-in-law is bound to remain in the residential group of his mother-in-law and to serve her until her death. In return, he receives any of her subsequent daughters and adds them to his polygynous family.

Given the ramifications of the *ambrinua* relationship, then, the ideal residential pattern is matrilocal before the birth and marriage of the future wife, and until the death of the mother-in-law. The pattern of *sororal polygyny* (marriage of a number of sisters to one man) plus the *levirate* (inheritance of wives by a brother of the deceased husband) tends to encourage the localization of females belonging to the same matrilineal sibling set. The *ambrinua* relationship also guarantees that a woman will have several husbands in one lifetime.

The final age grades, those of *menopause* and *old woman*, connote both respect and power. As she progresses through a series of marriages, the Tiwi woman assumes with age the important position of eldest or senior wife. Her sexual activity is also gradually curtailed as her increasingly younger husbands become occupied with younger co-wives. Just as secondary sex characteristics and menstruation are thought to be initiated by sexual intercourse, so menopause is conceptually related to the slackening and ultimate cessation of sexual activity. A woman entering the post-menopausal age grade, old woman, gains considerable prestige in society and, if she is a senior wife or has a number of mature sons, power as well. As the eldest of the co-wives, a Tiwi old woman assumes the position of authority in the domestic group. In the daily activities of this unit, she sends younger co-wives on bush hunting expeditions while she relaxes at camp. Senior old women may also exercise the right to direct the nature of child-rearing within the polygynous family. The power of the old woman, however, extends beyond the limits of domesticity to an actual personal influence over kinsmen. Some or all of her co-wives may be real or classificatory sisters, toward whom she assumes a maternal role. Her co-wives and their respective daughters form a cohesive economic and social unit, often a matrilineal sibling set, which ideally remains articulated until her death. Sons of the old woman and of her younger co-wives, in contrast, eventually leave their natal domestic unit to assume residence with their own *ambrinua*. Mothers of these young men, however, still exert considerable influence over their sons, and are consulted whenever a crisis arises.

In summary, the lifestyle of a Tiwi woman in no way conforms to stereotypes of social inferiority, economic dependency, or political subjugation often assigned to the female in gathering and hunting societies. In this essentially matrilineal society, her biological sex is heralded at birth for the potential continuation and expansion of the uterine line in the generations to come. Rather than being socially repressed by a male authority figure, the life of a Tiwi woman is a long journey of changing sexual partners and social roles. It is only within this dynamic framework, independent of individual members of the opposite sex, that the entire spectrum of Tiwi womanhood may be appreciated and understood.

DISCUSSION

We have seen that one of the basic tenets of the androcentric model is male economic dominance. From the male assumption of the role of hunter and provider follows, we are told, the necessary correlates of male-centered residential and descent groups. We concluded from cross-cultural data that gathering, rather than hunting, is the primary subsistence activity of foragers. The economic dominance of women is illustrated rather dramatically by the Tiwi, whose diet not only depends upon gathering for the provision of half its staples, but whose women regularly hunt land animals as well. The concept of woman-the-hunter has never received attention in extant foraging models, nor has, certainly the notion of woman-the-toolmaker. The production and use of stone axes by Tiwi women as aids in gathering may have important implications for the archaeological interpretation of similar handaxes found throughout the Lower Paleolithic period.

On the question of social organization among preagricultural societies, our cross-cultural sample failed to reveal any necessary or universal pattern of male dominance. While the majority of modern foragers was found to be bilateral in descent and patrilocal in residence, some cases of matriliny and matrilocality are still present. Complicating the picture of aboriginal social organization among hunters and gatherers is the disruptive influence of contact with more sophisticated societies, a process that seems to initiate both the breakdown of unilineal groups (encouraging bilaterality) and an emphasis upon males (encouraging patrilateral organization). Still, we were able to find no one-to-one correlation between economic and social dominance among the sexes. In the few matrilateral examples in the sample available for investigation, hunting was of greater importance in the diet than was true for patrilateral societies.

The explanation of uterine organization among foragers as an aberrant pattern based upon the unusual importance of gathering is therefore unsupported.

In our closer examination of the Tiwi, we were able to see more clearly the shortcomings of the androcentric stereotype. Although the mapping of resources in this society was based upon agnatic links, the residential and descent system was not. Women in this society serve not only as the most important links in the structuring of social relations, but enjoy considerable sexual variety and social equality with males throughout their lives as well. That the matrilineal system has survived at all is perhaps attributable to the relative recency of foreign occupation on Melville and Bathurst Islands. Goodale (1971:229) notes, however, that an erosion of power among the old women had already begun as a direct result of colonial-national influence. This has been accomplished by : the discouragement of polygyny, thus eliminating the position of senior wife, and the refusal of government officials to recognize females as heads of the domestic group.

From our investigation of foraging societies, therefore, we must conclude that the status of economic dominance is traditionally occupied by women. This status is of importance only because it has been continually identified as the factor critical to the determination of social structure. As we have seen, there seems to be no reason to assume that residence and descent determination among foragers is significantly different from that which occurs at other levels of technoeconomic complexity. Whatever the causal factors of social organization in primitive society, there seems to be an equal potential for either matrilineal or patrilineal organization among foragers as an adaptive response to an as yet undefined set of antecedent conditions. Likewise, economic dominance in gathering and hunting societies seems to bear little relationship to the status juxtaposition of the sexes, which appears in most cases to be based upon both equality and complementarity.

Women in
CHAPTER EIGHT Horticultural
Society

Cultivation is a relatively recent development in the evolution of human society. It is likely that in the late Stone Age hunters and gatherers repeatedly experimented with controlled growing and harvesting of wild food plants, as a natural extension of gathering activities. Although we now traditionally associate cultivation with increased economic security, early attempts at plant domestication were probably for the most part more time-consuming and less productive than was foraging. Likewise, population density or organizational complexity among early cultivators may not have exceeded, or perhaps even equalled, that achieved by hunters, fishers, and gatherers in favorable environmental settings.

However tenuous its beginnings, cultivation eventually had a revolutionary effect on the course of human biocultural evolution (see Smith 1972). For the first time, human communities began to significantly alter their physical environments, and to exert control over the survival or extinction of plants and animals. The higher level of productivity that cultivation eventually guaranteed allowed greater numbers of people to congregate in increasingly smaller amounts of geographical space. Sedentary villages and greater population density themselves led to new challenges for effective human social organization. These were met with the development of enlarged and more complex kinship groups, voluntary associations, ranking systems, and, in some cases, new forms of political integration.

Preindustrial societies today have inherited both the technology and adaptive community organizations of ancient cultivators. They vary tremendously, however, in the extent to which they depend upon crops for subsistence, the relative sophistication of techniques, and the amount and quality of yield achieved.

Anthropologists therefore often find it convenient to divide cultivation into two categories, horticultural and agricultural. Horticulture—that is, farming with the benefit of hand tools only—is our focus in the present chapter. Agriculture, or intensive cultivation, which involves the use of the plow or irrigation, is the subject of chapter 9.

Prior to the colonial era most non-Western societies practiced horticulture. Taken as a group, they display a greater amount of internal variability in social, political, and economic institutions than any other adaptational type. We shall therefore have to consider the roles of women and men against a wide spectrum of dynamic institutional relationships. Our initial approach to this problem will be economic. Here we shall find that, as in many foraging societies, women continue their important role in production, but that this pivotal economic role tends to decrease as the overall productivity level of horticulturalists increases. Our second approach to the problem of sex role definitions will be a consideration of some of the more salient organizing principles of horticultural communities and their social groups. Since the population density afforded by cultivation is so often associated with unilineal descent groups, we shall examine in some detail the effects of matrilineal and patrilineal systems on the status of women and men. Finally, the interrelationship of economic and social variables will be illustrated with a case study of the lifestyle of women in Mount Hagen, New Guinea.

ECONOMIC BASIS OF HORTICULTURE

In order to summarize the general characteristics of horticultural societies, we have, as in the case of foraging, selected a sample from the cross-cultural inventory found in the *Eth-nographic Atlas* (Murdock 1967). These 515 societies represent each major geographical area of the world, and display a wide range of dependence upon cultivation for their subsistence. Pastoralists, defined in chapter 10 as groups who depend upon herding activities for at least half of their diet, are *not* included in the present horticultural sample.

Economic variation among horticulturalists will be examined according to the extent of their dependence upon cultigen production, and the way in which the sexes are involved in cultivation.

The only measure of the level of productivity coded for the sample societies is the percentage of the subsistence base filled by farming products. The 515 societies vary in their dependence upon cultigens in their diets from less than one-quarter to over three-quarters. This scale leaves much to be desired, since we cannot balance the stated yield of cultigens against the effort expended in their production. Still, correlations with other related variables suggest that cultivative dependence, as an index of relative productivity, is adequate for our purposes. Both community size and political complexity, for example, show an overall increase in proportion to the dietary importance of cultigens.

But how does the variable of sex relate to productivity in these societies? In the 515 sample societies, women dominate activities associated with cultivation in approximately 41 percent of the sample. The sexes are equal contributors in an additional 37 percent, while males are the exclusive cultivators in only 22 percent of the societies in question. It is desirable for our purposes, however, to note not just the relative economic importance of women and men in a large number of horticultural communities, but also to account for the above variability in sexual division of labor. When are farming activities more likely to be assigned to one sex than the other?

To answer this question, it is useful to observe the interaction of sexual division of labor and the degree of cultivation dependence, our index of productivity level. These relationships appear graphically in Figure 8-1, which shows some interesting contrasts between exclusively female, exclusively male, and equally male-female cultivative labor assignments. Women are most likely to be economically dominant in horticultural societies with low dependence on crops. While the frequency of exclusively male farmers remains minimal in the lower productive

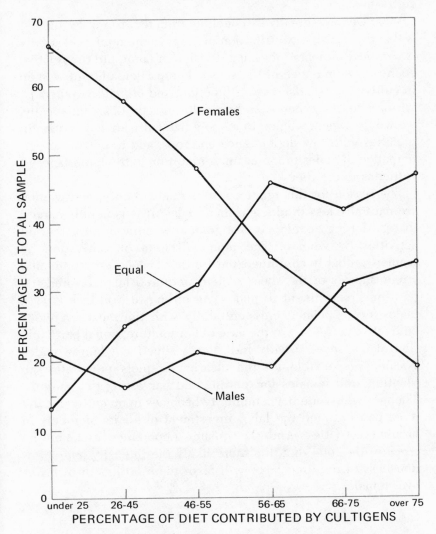

Figure 8–1. Sexual division of labor in cultivation for 515 horticultural societies in relation to the degree of cultivative dependence.

categories, it rises rather dramatically where cultigens compose over 65 percent of the diet. The assignment of equal and complementary cultivative tasks to women and men increases proportionally with productivity. The latter curve, it will be observed, is almost a mirror-image of that for exclusively female cultivators.

What we may tentatively conclude from the data in Figure 8-1 is that the variable contribution of crops to the total food supply is a critical indicator of sexual division of labor and the relative economic dominance of the sexes. The participation of women in cultivation is a *decreasing* function, and of males an *increasing* function, of reliance on horticultural activities. Statistically, we would expect women to monopolize cultivative activities in societies with low dependence on crops, and to enlist the participation of males in increasing proportion to the importance of cultigens in the diet.

The reason for this relationship is not, certainly, that women are naturally less productive than males. It is generally agreed that gardening developed as a gradual elaboration of gathering activities by women. The monopolization of cultivation by women probably continued until either special environmental circumstances or the sheer scale of required labor favored the part-time recruitment of males. According to Murdock (1937), males are associated cross-culturally with the most strenuous cultivative activities. In the case of horticulture, equal participation of the sexes usually indicates a situation wherein males become responsible for the clearing of plots preparatory to planting, and females for tending and harvesting the gardens. The more dependent a community becomes upon cultigens, the more concentrated the labor investment of *all* its members in farming activities. And the greater importance assumed by crops in the total diet, the more likely the intensity and strenuousness of required labor will favor the recruitment of males over females.

SOCIAL JUXTAPOSITION OF THE SEXES

The vigor and success with which cultivation is pursued in horticultural communities has immediate quantitative effects upon the nature of human social networks. The relative productivity of a society in the *leanest* season of the year is a primary determinant of maximal community size. Likewise, the variable density of human communities sets the challenge for effective structuring of social and power relationships. Horticultural societies throughout the world, and perhaps throughout time, have responded to these challenges with amazingly consistent types of organization. Social groups formed on the basis of unilineal descent surely compose one of the most universally adaptive institutions in cultural evolutionary history.

However, we shall next see that sociopolitical variation does occur, but within limits that are definable and at least partially predictable. We shall first summarize the range of this variability in demographic, social, and political dimensions for a reduced representative subsample of 104 horticultural societies; next, we shall investigate the relevance of this variation for male and female statuses, with special reference to the ramifications of the two basic types of unilineal organization—matrilineal and patrilineal. Unlike the situation of foraging societies, the nature of descent among horticulturalists appears to have a very important influence upon the flow of power, property, and social prominence. The sedentism that cultivation allows when accompanied by a high level of productivity is more conducive to the accumulation and storage of surpluses. Just as portable wealth may be amassed for its exchange value, so women are regarded and accumulated in many patrilineal societies for their child-bearing potential. As such, the nature of descent in horticultural societies may be a salient variable in the reckoning of women's overall status.

Sociopolitical Variation. Before we consider general female and male role configurations in matrilineal and patrilineal societies, we must examine the latitude of diversity with respect to a number of variables. More precisely, we are interested in the density, political level, and social organization of horticultural communities, and the way in which these factors relate to the patterns of economic production and sexual division of labor outlined above.

The average community size of horticulturalists varies between the almost unbelievable extremes of below 50 individuals to true urban clusters of over 50,000. The great majority of societies in the sample, however, some 79 percent, have average population units of under 400 individuals. An additional 12 percent range between 400 and 1000, whereas only 9 percent could be described as having protourban or urban aggregates (about 5000 people). Community size bears a direct relationship to the variable of cultivative dependence. All societies with communities of over 5000 individuals depend upon cultigen production for at least 60 percent of their diets. Conversely, although there is some minor overlap, some 80 percent of horticultural communities with less than 400 individuals depend upon cultigens for less than 60 percent of their subsistence. The economic predominance of either sex in production cannot be predicted with any degree of accuracy on the basis of community size alone. There is a related tendency in the data, however, for an increased participation of males in cultivative activities for communities over 400.

Just as population density relates to the variable production of cultigens, relative community size presents proportional challenges for the manipulation of power relationships. Horticultural societies are largely uncentralized politically. Only 5 percent of the societies in the sample could be classified as true *states*, and an additional 15 percent as *chiefdoms* (see Service 1962). All of these centralized political systems depend upon cultigens for over half of their subsistence. The remaining 80 percent of the societies sampled, however, are at the *tribal* level of integration, and represent the full spectrum of cultivative dependence. The categorization of these societies into state and nonstate political systems has no predictive value in the definition of female and male economic roles.

In our discussion of foraging societies, we noted the
frequently advanced hypothesis that the nature of social organization in a kin-based society is somehow reflective of the relative economic importance of the sexes. This notion appears to
be equally as sterile for horticulturalists as for hunters, fishers,
and gatherers. Although statistically women tend to monopolize
cultivation in horticultural societies, social groups based upon
patrilineal kinship predominate. Prevailing types of postmarital
residence in the sample societies are correlated with descent
patterns in Table 8-1.

Table 8-1. The relationship of residence and descent in 104 horticultural societies

RESIDENCE	DESCENT				
	MATRI-LINEAL	DOUBLE	PATRI-LINEAL	BILATERAL	TOTALS
Matrilocal	7			8	15
Avunculocal	10				10
Ambilocal	2		2	3	7
Patrilocal	4	4	55	4	67
Neolocal	2		1	2	5
Totals	25	4	58	17	104

Table 8-1 shows matrilineal descent predominates in approximately one-quarter of the sample. A similar percentage of societies possesses types of residence (matrilocal, avunculocal) associated with the localization of uterine kinsmen. In contrast,
the great majority of horticultural communities places primary
emphasis upon relationships among related males. Approximately 56 percent of the sample societies have patrilineal descent, and an additional 64 percent favor patrilocal residence.
As we shall see below, the prevailing rules of descent and residence bear little relationship to factors of productivity and the
division of labor by sex.

In summary, horticulture as a technoeconomic adaptation
allows for considerable variation in sociopolitical institutions.
Certainly, the extent of a society's commitment to and success
in cultivation serves as a limiting factor on both the size and the

relative complexity of its communities. As we have seen, however, the great majority of horticulturalists are uncentralized politically, and live in predominantly nonurban settlements. Unilineal kinship groups most frequently take on the major responsibilities of maintaining the social and political continuity of the community. Since these groups are formed by the systematic exclusion of *some* consanguineal relatives from membership at each generation, and of one sex from pivotal social and power positions in the local group or wider political community, it is desirable to investigate the more qualitative aspects of female and male roles as influenced by the prevailing mode of descent.

Matrilineal horticulturalists. Matrilineal societies compose only one-quarter of the present sample. They are, in fact, underrepresented in the primitive world as a whole. That there are many known cases of descent change during the historical period suggests that this comparatively low frequency may not have always been the case. Still, the precise adaptive advantage of *both* matrilineal and patrilineal types of organization among horiculturalists remains somewhat of a mystery to anthropologists. What are the precise antecedent conditions favoring descent through women rather than men among hand cultivators? Is there any causal relationship between sexual division of labor and determination of descent?

Matrilineal Antecedents A corollary to the androcentric argument of hunting priority and male dominance at the foraging level is that matrilineal descent is a maladaptive or aberrant form of social organization to be found only in situations of relatively unproductive gardening. In horticultural societies, we are told, matriliny's solitary and brief appearance is due to the unusually important productive role played by women. This argument has obvious weaknesses. As noted above, matrilineal societies do indeed occur with foraging adaptations, and are generally associated with subsistence activities in which gathering by women is *diminished* in importance. In horticultural adaptations there is some tendency for women to dominate production to a greater extent under matrilineal conditions than patrilineal ones. For example, 64 percent of the matrilineal societies in our sample assign cultivative tasks exclusively to women as compared to 50 percent of the patrilineal societies. This higher frequency, however, may be attributable to factors other than variability in descent. As noted earlier in the chapter, the level of productivity is highly correlated with sexual division of labor. Matrilineal horticulturalists in the sample depend upon cultigens for an *average* of 55 percent of their diets. In contrast, patrilineal examples have an average dependence of 68 percent. Therefore, the greater frequency with which matrilineal horticulturalists assign cultivative tasks to women may be merely reflective of overall lower productivity rather than descent per se.

These comparative figures leave many mysteries. Why are horticultural societies that trace descent through women associated with lower productivity? Is there, perhaps, something about matrilineal descent as an organizing principle that is especially adaptive for communities with low dependence on or low yield from cultivative activities? Considerable attention has been directed toward answering these and other related questions about matrilineal descent (see Schneider & Gough 1961), but conclusions remain tentative. According to the cross-cultural study of Aberle (1961), matrilineal cultivators are most likely to be found outside of or bordering on forested regions, and in situations where herds of large domesticated animals are absent. This set of conditions seriously limits the ecological range of matrilineal systems. Furthermore, matrilineal systems are in competition with more productive organizational alternatives, and tend to give way to patrilineal and bilateral ones.

Unfortunately, explanations such as these tell us more about the conditions under which matriliny may be expected to *disappear* among horticulturalists than those which give rise to the structure initially. In other words, matriliny is argued as strong possibility in the *absence* of factors encouraging descent through males, such as the accumulation and exchange of portable wealth or a high incidence of internal warfare (See Murdock 1949).

For our purposes, it may be more worthwhile to seek the adaptive advantages of matriliny in those features which underscore its uniqueness as an organizing principle. In societies stressing matrilineal kinship links, descent groups are composed of women and men who share a common ancestress. Since only women may pass this affiliation on to their children, men are peripheral to the formation and continuity of descent groups in the community. The female core of these kinship units is therefore often left spatially intact, and associated with specific cultivation rights in land.

The significance of matrilocal residence for the structure of matrilineal horticultural communities is considerable. Adult males must leave the locality of their natal matrilineal group at marriage and assume residence with their spouses. Related men, therefore, are distributed or dispersed throughout a number of uterine groups into which they enter as strangers. Because matrilocal societies engage in the *exchange of men,* local communities contain political leaders from several descent groups. Interestingly, kinship units within a given matrilineal political community tend to be more closely spaced than in the patrilineal situation (see Oberg 1955). The political consequences of related-male dispersal are especially important to questions of the adaptive advantage of matrilineal descent. Cross-cultural studies (see Otterbein and Otterbein 1965) have indicated that societies which prevent the localization of related males have a higher degree of internal political stability. Matrilineal descent groups establish a complex network of kinship ties and kinship loyalties which effectively cut across local corporations and potential special-interest groups.

Matrilineal horticultural societies, then, seem to be adaptive in habitats that allow considerable *stability* in human organization (the same is no doubt true for foraging adaptations as well). Matriliny is ideally an *open* system that disperses rather than consolidates its potential sources of power—its men. Such an adaptation seems to arise where resources are equal to or exceed those required to accommodate the needs of extant populations, and where competition between communities in the same niche is absent or infrequent.

The Disappearance of Matriliny The stability that strong matrilineal societies both require and promote seems to be at a premium in the ethnographic present. Some habitats, such as the tropical forest, may naturally select against matriliny because of the nature of and competition for resources, and the difficulties involved in the exploitation of this type of environment. Internal warfare is particularly intense in densely forested regions, and certainly favors a system that concentrates rather than disperses the basis of military organization, namely, related males. Other niches, while favoring the development of stable matrilineal organizations, may not be effectively exploited beyond a certain level of productivity without a fundamental reorientation in human organization. Any *in situ* development or external influence that places a premium on the production and accumulation of *surpluses* for the purpose of exchange militates against the integrative, static framework of matriliny, and fosters the crystallization of local groups which concentrate both wealth and defensive-offensive power in the hands of related males.

The great majority of surviving matrilineal horticulturalists have undergone standardized structural changes in an attempt to maintain existing descent groups in the face of rapid change (see Gough 1961). Avunculocal residence, a variety of postmarital residence, localizes *males* of the same matrilineage and is therefore often taken as an immediate and intercalary alternative to actual *descent* through males. A continuing male emphasis in matrilineal and avunculocal societies may eventually lead to patrilocal residence, first as an alternative and then as a dominant pattern. This typically signals the demise of matrilineal kinship groups, and their accompaniment or eventual replacement by paternal ones.

This sequence of residence and descent change is well documented in the ethnohistorical and ethnographic literature. Murdock (1959), for example, cites evidence for its occurrence over wide regions of Africa. The types of catalysts that may trigger such dynamic changes in social organization are illustrated by the case of the Tumbuka, a horticultural society of south central Africa:

The Tumbuka, prior to 1780, resembled most of the neighboring tribes in adhering to matrilineal descent, inheritance, and succession, in requiring matrilocal bride-service rather than a bride-price, and in permitting an ultimate shift to avunculocal residence.

Between 1780 and 1800 some ivory traders from the east conquered the Tumbuka and established the Kamanga kingdom. Under the influence of these patrilineal invaders, bride-service was reduced to a nominal period, the token bridal gift was increased to enable the husband to remove his wife almost immediately to his own village, and rights to inherit and succeed, after younger brothers had had their turn, were transferred from sisters' sons to own sons.

Around 1855 a new invasion, this time by the Ngoni, overthrew the Kamanga dynasty and subjugated the Tumbuka to new rulers with even stronger patrilineal institutions. In consequence of their influence the Tumbuka abandoned even nominal bride-service, adopted the full-fledged South African bride-price, or *lobola,* substituted the eldest son for the younger brother as the preferred heir and successor, and transformed what had originally been matrisibs into indubitable exogamous patrisibs (Murdock 1959:302).

Similar sequences of socioeconomic change, wherein matrilineal systems are replaced by more expansive, exploitative ones, have occurred widely in the primitive world. Matrilineal societies are most fruitfully viewed, therefore, as vanishing rather than aberrant phenomena. They are underrepresented in the ethnographic present not because they represent a curious mutation from an alleged universal standard of paternalism, but because the ecological adaptations and niches that this type of organization fosters and sustains have all but disappeared in the modern world.

Matriliny and the Status of Women The prevailing rule of descent among cultivators has rather immediate implications for the status of women. Whereas the position of females is quite variable in patrilineal societies, it is almost universally high in matrilineal ones. In the matrilineal situation, women are the focus of the entire social structure. Uterine links ideally provide for the allocation of resources associated with production, and also define the relationship of men and women, social groups, and political community segments to each other and to the larger universe. Although positions of public authority in matrilineal societies are consistently assigned to elder males in each descent group, actual power may often be concentrated in the hands of senior women. Females may therefore wield considerable influence in decision-making within the community when matriliny is dominant.

Since our horticultural case study below focuses on the position of women in a strongly patrilineal society, a brief look at female lifestyles in an equally strong matrilineal one will provide us with some interesting contrasts. The indigenous culture of the Iroquois Indians is a prime example of how women may command power and influence in a society stressing maternal affiliation (see Morgan 1851, 1881; Beauchamp 1900; Richards 1957; Brown 1970). The Iroquois, a confederacy of several related tribes, had a pervasive system of matrilineal clans and lineages. They lived in a highly favorable environment, and subsisted on a varied and nutritious diet of numerous cultivated crops, fish, and game. Although warfare with distant peoples was a common source of aggrandizement for males, the Iroquois home economy was generally stable and noncompetitive—a set of conditions apparently ideal for the evolution of a cultural system in which women played a central role.

Matrilineal kinship penetrated every corner of traditional Iroquois society. One's social identity, real and portable property, and succession to offices and titles flowed exclusively in the maternal line. Moreover, related women remained together throughout life, forming tightly knit residential as well as social units. Women of the same matrilineage or lineage segment, along with their children and imported husbands, typically occupied different compartments of the same large dwelling, known as a *longhouse*. Within this extended household their influence in domestic and economic affairs was paramount. They determined, along with other senior women, not only who would enter the longhouse as husbands, but often who would remain as well.

Brown (1970) argues convincingly that the key to elevated status for Iroquois women lay in their relationship to production and the distribution of wealth. As in a great number of horticultural societies, women were the exclusive cultivators. However a frequent accompaniment of matriliny—the manipulation of access rights to seeds and to arable land by matrilineal descent groups themselves—gave Iroquois women exclusive control over the production and storage of food. They were not only the primary producers, but collectively owned the means of production as well.

The significance of this control for the manipulation of power in Iroquois society was tremendous. Since food was wealth, and since the matrons of matrilineal descent groups supervised its distribution, women had available to them a mechanism for giving or withholding rewards. Women of the longhouse held in common a store of food, which they systematically allocated to their men and children. Since they had labored collectively to cultivate these food crops—and on land belonging to them by virtue of their common kinship—women were not obliged to feed men on demand, but more often did so as an act of good faith. The elder women would simply ask any male member of the longhouse whose behavior they viewed as objectionable to leave. Such eviction notices were apparently taken quite seriously, and provided an efficient instrument for terminating unsuccessful marriages and for eliminating persons incompatible with the larger longhouse membership.

But the power of women among the Iroquois extended far beyond the domestic unit. As in most matrilineal societies, the senior women or matrons of lineages and clans played an important role in political and social policy decisions. The Iroquois confederacy or League was headed by a council of chiefs. These representatives to the governing body were male, but gained and held office only with female approval. Eligibility for these positions was, first of all, determined matrilineally. Selection of chiefs from among eligible candidates, however, was also controlled largely by matriclan matrons. Their choice was relayed to council members for approval or veto. If the candidate was rejected by council members, another was nominated in his place until the selection was ratified. Moreover, matrons regularly monitored the performance of chiefs, and sent warnings to any whose actions were viewed with disfavor. If such undesirable behavior persisted, impeachment proceedings could be initiated against him.

Women also had an influential voice in the actual deliberations of the council. Matrons had a special representative of their own to present their position on all important issues. In addition, they had the power to veto war declarations and to introduce peace-making efforts. In this respect,the ownership of food by women had some interesting ramifications. Hunting was not undertaken on raiding missions, and warriors therefore depended entirely on women for portable supplies. War parties could therefore not begin an expedition without specially dried provisions sufficient for the entire journey. Women also allegedly controlled the collective assets or national treasury of the Iroquois, which consisted not only of stored food, but forms of portable wealth such as *wampum*.

Finally, women played a central role in the religious life of Iroquois society. Matrons had a voice in the selection of sacred leaders or practitioners, half of which were women. The sexes in this sphere of Iroquois culture had both an equal voice and equal representation.

The extent to which the Iroquois allocated power to women is sometimes considered unusual. It may be misleading, however, to attribute this phenomenon simply to the idiosyncrasies of an individual culture. We would argue, rather, that the *niche* of the Iroquois and the subsequent type of adaptive institutions for which it selected are unusual in the ethnographic present, although not perhaps in the ethnographic past. Several conditions combined in Iroquois society to favor the monopolization of productive *and* distributive roles by women. Their very successful ecological adaptation, combining horticultural skill with abundant natural resources, eliminated the necessity for economic competition among local communities. Matriliny and the symmetrical rule of matrilocality provided an effective organizing structure for the maintenance of political stability through male dispersal. The localization of related individuals seems itself to be a critical factor in the assignment of food production and distribution rights to kin groups, whether matrilineal or patrilineal. In this case, the segregation of kinswomen in one locality added the necessary geographical dimension to a group of cultivators already united by bonds of common descent. Related women, so congregated, formed both collective work groups and collective distribution groups. It is in the latter feature—the right of women to determine how the products of their labor will be allocated to others—that their access to power lies.

Common residence, then, appears to be critical for the control of resources and wealth by kinswomen. The maternal core of each descent group is reinforced by the spatial continuity of mother's mothers, mothers, mother's sisters, female siblings, their respective children, and imported spouses. Large matrilineally extended families are characteristic, as is monogamous marriage. Polygyny, where it occurs, is typically of the sororal variety. That is, a male residing matrilocally will marry a number of sisters, often serially as they reach puberty.

Any mode of postmarital residence that disperses related women jeopardizes their collective relationship to land and production. Such is the case with avunculocal residence, in which a woman joins her husband in or near the household of *his* mother's brother (a member of the husband's rather than the wife's matrilineage). Although the localization of men (as opposed to women) of the same matrilineage does not immediately threaten the survival of matrilineal descent groups themselves, it almost inevitably results in the transfer of some or all production and distribution rights to males who reside together. It also eliminates the pattern of collective farming by related women and encourages, in its place, the cultivation of individual plots allocated by the husband's matrilineal kin to each incoming wife. Avunculocal societies thus share many features with patrilineal and patrilocal ones. Kinship groups composed of matrilineally related males (often called *avuncu*lineages) persist, but the nature of family units within these groups tends to take on a collateral rather than lineal character. That is, extended families of several generations often disappear in the avunculocal situation, and are replaced by smaller, polygynous families geared toward the production of surpluses. In the matrilineal but avunculocal or patrilocal situation, then, females not only assume the role of stranger in the localized kin group of husbands, but also typically become co-wives to and economic competitors with other women.

To summarize, matrilineal descent appears to provide a very adaptive superstructure for horticultural communities in stable environments. It loses its adaptive value in the face of expansive, competitive, or more intensely exploitative technoeconomic systems. Because matriliny has been replaced by patrilineal structures so repeatedly in the primitive world, there is some question as to whether matrilineal descent may represent a universal stage in the evolution of culture as a whole. This may indeed be the case for compatible ecological niches throughout the world, but there are certainly environments that may have *always* selected against matriliny. It is perhaps more correct to assume that matrilineal adaptations may arise in any situation where highly integrated, stable kinship communities can effectively exploit a given environment, whether through foraging or cultivation. While matrilineal societies typically hold women in high regard because of their central role in descent group formation, the prevailing principle of *local* group formation has a strong influence on their degree of economic influence, and hence on their ultimate status in the community.

Patrilineal Horticulturalists. Societies tracing descent through males dominate the horticultural adaptation in the ethnographic present. Whatever the frequency of patriliny in the past, this type of organization has certainly been on the rise among kin-based societies in recent centuries. Because the antecedents of matrilineal descent systems are only imperfectly understood, the adaptive advantages of patriliny also remain somewhat of a mystery.

Patrilineal Antecedents In many androcentric schema, one

senses no immediacy on the part of theorists to *explain* the development of patrilineal horticulturalism. Since such models make the assumption of male dominance and agnatic local organization at the foraging level, cultivation represents merely a technological advance with quantitative elaboration rather than qualitative change in social organization. Matriliny thus becomes the albatross that must be accounted for. In the following statement, the theorist ponders over the development of matrilineal descent and uxorilocality (residence near the bride's parents) from his ideal foraging model based upon virilocal (near the husband's parents) residence:

> That patrilineal descent should occur in tribal society is not surprising, considering that virilocality was characteristic of band society and that the collaborative activities of males in fighting, hunting, and ceremonial activities remain prominent in tribal society. What is more difficult to explain is the widespread occurrence of matriliny. Inasmuch as matrilineal descent presupposes uxorilocal residence and the resultant matrilocal kin groups, the essential question concerns the rise of uxorilocal marital residence rules (Service 1962:120).

As we have already noted, matriliny is usually attributed to female productive acumen. The weakness of this argument is compounded by the fact that women are the major providers in patrilineal horticultural societies as well. Females dominate farming activities in 50 percent of our patrilineal societies, and participate equally with males in an additional 36 percent of the sample. Interestingly, there is no rise in the frequency of exclusively male cultivation with patriliny, which averages a meager 16 percent of the matrilineal horticulturists and 14 percent of the patrilineal sample. While descent and social labor division are intimately related, therefore, it appears that this relationship is not a genetic one. Rather, both are dependent variables, and represent adaptive responses to specific environmental circumstances relating to production.

In seeking the adaptive features of patrilineal social organization, we are aided by the large number of well-documented cases of actual descent change in process. By observing the conditions encouraging the transformation of matrilineal kinship groups, those favoring patrilineal organization are thereby highlighted. Some of the primary catalysts for the localization of related males have been identified by Murdock (1949). Two of these, the introduction of the plow and the dominance of herding in subsistence, will be considered in more detail in chapters 9 and 10. Central to all of these causative features, however, is a fundamental change in the nature of property, as Murdock notes:

> Especially important is the development of any form of movable property or wealth which can be accumulated in quantity by men. With such property, whether it be herds, slaves, money, or other valuables, prosperous men can offer a bride-price to the parents of girls which will induce them to part with their daughters. The concentration of property in the hands of men specifically facilitates a transition to patrilineal inheritance among peoples who have previously followed the rule of matrilineal inheritance, for men now have the power and the means to make effective their natural preference for transmitting their property to their own sons rather than to their sororal nephews. Warfare, slavery, and political integration all encourage patrilocal residence. War enhances men's influence and brings them captive (and hence patrilocal) wives and plunder wherewith to buy other women. Slavery provides a mechanism for purchasing women and enforcing patrilocal residence. Political expansion increases the power and prestige of the men and normally establishes a rule of patrilineal succession, both of which favor patrilocal residence (1949:206–7).

Murdock's statement deserves our careful scrutiny. The factors identified as encouraging patriliny, such as portable wealth accumulation, warfare, slavery, polygyny, and increased sociopolitical integration, all relate to fundamental changes in the nature of production. We have, then, the problem of the chicken and the egg. Does a particular marriage custom, an institution of servitude, or the birth of statehood arise in a cultural vacuum and *then* initiate patriliny? Are males merely being held in abeyance until their seizure of some form of portable wealth allows them to claim their own sons as their "natural" heirs? We would agree that the factors isolated by Murdock are highly correlated with patriliny, and that portable wealth is important in its maintenance. But we would argue further that these factors are *symptomatic* rather than causative, *dependent* rather than independent variables. In other words, features such as slavery, intrasocietal competition, and the systematic production of surpluses are based in economic adaptations fundamentally different from those of matrilineal societies. We feel that patriliny, as an *in situ* development, arises primarily because it is the most efficient way of organizing societies in specific kinds of ecological niches.

Under what conditions, then, is patriliny adaptive for horticultural societies? A number of insights are provided in a recent work by Ester Boserup:

> In female farming communities, a man with more than one wife can cultivate more land than a man with only one wife. Hence, the institution of polygamy is a significant element in the process of economic development in regions where additional land is available for cultivation under the long fallow system (1970:38).

Boserup notes that polygyny is a mechanism for increased productivity in the absence of the plow or of hired labor. But under what circumstances is greater productivity necessary or desirable? Certainly population density is important in several ways. As mentioned earlier, matrilineal societies do not appear to compete much over arable land or its products. Indeed, they both thrive under and promote stability. If the population increases beyond the point it may comfortably subsist on existing resources, productivity may decline—either because the number of available fields is reduced by the need for fallowing, or because inadequately fallowed land is cultivated despite its decreased fertility. In this situation, environmental resources may remain adequate only through competition with surrounding groups. In a similar manner, the availability of arable land may be a factor promoting the localization of males in densely forested regions, where both warfare and patriliny are of high frequency.

Cross-cultural studies have shown that in-group and out-group competition characterizes the entire social fabric of patrilineal societies. Whereas matrilineal horticulturalists spatially disperse their power groups, patrilineal ones concentrate related males into potentially explosive clusters. This phenomenon results from the overlapping of kin-based military and local groups. In the absence of a state political machinery, or at times in spite of it, officials are relatively powerless to prevent hostile confrontations along kinship lines. It is perhaps in this violent, competitive nature of patrilineal systems that their adaptive advantage lies. While matrilineal structures are accommodating and integrative, patrilineal ones are acquisitive and internally divisive.

Subsistence Farmers and Surplus Farmers The desire for greater productivity, the concentration of specific land parcels and portable wealth among males, and the trend toward smaller and more individualized kinship groups (polygynous and small extended families, as opposed to large collectives) must therefore be viewed in terms of the quality of interaction among societies in the same habitat. The localization of males would seem to be adaptive whenever critical resources are scarce.

Scarcity itself is a complex concept. It may be applied to cultivators who have barely enough to eat, or alternatively to those peoples who are well-fed but who experience ever-increasing requirements for the accumulation of wealth. Both types of ecological adaptations place a premium on maximal production, and both encourage intense competition over the resources of a given environment. We feel it is useful to make the distinction between *subsistence* farmers on the one hand, and *surplus* farmers on the other, and to note the common thread that, in some habitats, moves them both toward patriliny.

There are many types of subsistence farmers. We have already argued that most matrilineal horticulturalists fall into this category of cultivators, whose primary economic concern is the production of foodstuffs for direct consumption. These societies, it will be recalled, tend to be identified with habitats in which resources are plentiful. Horticultural lands are exploited extensively over a wide area and are then left to lie fallow for long periods. Since arable real property is both abundant and available, noncompetitive descent groups have evolved. Typically, matrilineal kin groups are concerned with the production of adequate food for their respective lineage and clan members, rather than with the maximization of resources through coercion or increased exploitation.

Patrilineal subsistence farmers, in contrast, are found in much less favorable habitats, where considerably more effort must be expended to attain similar rewards. Although an economic surplus may be desired, the productive yield of such societies seldom exceeds the basic requirements for survival. Patrilineal subsistence horticulturalism is prominent in areas of the world with dense tropical forests which, as Aberle (1961:668) has noted, appear to be prohibitive to matrilineal systems. Two ingredients seem to be essential. First, environmental resources are limited, and the acquisition and exploitation of farming plots requires considerable time and energy. Second, competition with communities in the same niche is high. Patrilineal principles of group formation provide a mechanism for the internal accretion of periodically overcrowded local groups through the creation of new ones. That is, sons or groups of brothers may split off from the original community and set themselves up in a new area, taking their wives with them. As we shall see in chapter 10, this feature of patriliny is also highly adaptive for pastoralists in marginal habitats. Perhaps even more essential to this adaptation, however, is the symmetrical rule of patrilocal residence. Consistent patrilocality generates in each community an effective military reserve of male kinsmen, whose charge it is to protect members and garden plots from outside encroachment.

Surplus farmers, in contrast, are found in habitats with abundant resources. They differ from the typical matrilineal adaptation by their possession of what may be called a *dual economy:* they are concerned not only with the production of adquate or even plentiful food, but are also deliberately geared toward maximal yields, the excesses of which are accumulated and exchanged. There are in these societies, then, two economic spheres. One is concerned with the production of food, including the network of rights and obligations associated with land, labor, and the distribution of crops. The second is concerned with the conversion of surpluses into portable wealth and their strategic exchange for prestige, status, and power. As we shall see, men and women generally have very different involvements with these two phases of production and distribution. Surplus societies are characterized by considerable economic competition and are typically nonegalitarian, regardless of scale.

The reason why surplus farmers are seldom matrilineal is not altogether clear. We would reason, however, that the diffusion of power and subsequent egalitarianism among males this type of social structure encourages would be maladaptive under the conditions just described. If we have to suggest possible reasons for the conversion of stable matrilineal societies into less stable, more flexible, or more dynamic patrilineal ones, population pressure and competition with outsiders may figure as prime contributing factors.

In patrilineal societies, whether subsistence- or surplus-oriented, women continue their role as primary cultivators, but the nature of both productive and distributive groups is fundamentally changed. The relationship of women to land and resources is now a consequence of marriage rather than descent. That is, as soon as local aggregates of related women are dispersed with the institution of avunculocal or patrilocal residence, the focus of their collective labor is destroyed. Instead, they become economic producers for and domestic appendages of their individual male spouses. Control of land and resource allocation is thus transferred from the hands of female producers to the manipulators and political caretakers of the new economy.

For economic support, men look not so much to their women as to their male kinsmen who now provide the factors of production (land, capital, and labor in the form of wives) for the establishment and expansion of their respective family enterprises.

Although a number of unrelated females may cultivate plots on land held in common by male members of the same kinship group, only rarely do they do so jointly or communally. There is a definite tendency for women in patrilineal societies to cultivate and provide foods individually, and for a relatively small unit headed by their respective spouses. Polygyny is typically utilized as a mechanism for increasing the yield of one-male households. Among our sample societies, 55 percent are reported to have independent polygynous households, either exclusively or in combination with patrilineally extended families. Co-wives typically occupy separate dwellings, cultivate separate plots, and contribute their yields partially to a large common store, and partially to their own private bins from which they feed themselves, their children, and, in rotation, their common husband. The wealth of individual polygynous males increases proportionally with the number of spouse-providers. The accumulation of additional wives entitles men to increased allocations of arable land from their lineage, and concomitantly greater surpluses of cultigens, which may be accumulated and exchanged. Women in patrilineal societies assume a dual role as producers of food and producers of children, and thus even themselves become valuable as moveable property.

Patrilineal organization, therefore, not only provides a *labor* structure for increased productivity, but also the *military* structure with which to defend the resources so accumulated. The relative success achieved by any society organized around clusters of related males depends greatly on the nature of resources available for maximum exploitation.

Patriliny and the Status of Women The dispersal of related women among the local kin groups of their spouses has similar, although more far-reaching, effects in patrilineal societies than in matrilineal ones. In the case of matriliny and avunculocality, women are removed from their natal household at marriage and become new residential members at the home of their husband's mother's brother. As we have seen, polygyny may even occur under these circumstances. Despite the spatial discontinuity of related women with the avunculate, however, they still form the loci of matrilineal descent groups and can depend on this membership for protection and security. With patrilocality, however, removal from the parental household is typically compounded by the usurpation of matrilineal kin groups by patrilineal ones.

In patrilineal societies, the husband acquires rights *in genetricem,* or rights in a woman as a child-bearer, before the marriage is consummated. Any offspring resulting from that union will subsequently belong to the father. This agreement, negotiated with the members of her father's kin group, is typically sealed with a payment in material goods of often substantial proportions, known as *brideprice* or *bridewealth.* A woman represents, in effect, an investment for the patrilineage of her father and that of her husband. For her own patrilineage, she has brought in portable wealth, which perhaps may be used to acquire a wife for her real or classificatory brother. In turn, the patrilineage of her husband anticipates her horticultural labor and her offspring, both of which help to guarantee the expansion and continuation of their ranks.

In patrilineal societies, the experience of patrilocality may be traumatic and oppressive for women in the early years of marriage. Often, a junior wife is granted adult status only after bearing a child, especially a male child. Until such time she may be treated as a minor, and frequently falls under the supervision of either a senior wife or mother-in-law. This relationship may be sterile and authoritarian—so much so that the daughter-in-law indicates her respect and submission with an elaborate etiquette of physical and social avoidance behavior (the mirror image of this phenomenon often occurs on the part of males with *their* mother-in-law). The inferior status of the new wife may also be indicated by her comparative lack of material items, especially in the domestic sphere.

Thus patriliny and patrilocality require that a woman leave the security of her natal household and assume the role of stranger in her husband's. There, the road to improved status is paved with obedience, diligence, productivity, and reproductivity. Although a woman may eventually achieve a position of respect and influence in a patrilineal community, she typically does so only in advanced age, and then by association with her sons or other prominent, close male relatives. Should a woman be mistreated at the household of her husband, she may usually exercise the option of returning to her parents. There she may air her grievances and encourage negotiations on her behalf among the lineages involved. Since, however, a permanent desertion from her husband would require her father to return the brideprice consideration, she is usually cajoled by her own parents into reassuming the role of dutiful wife.

Although the pressures for female conformity to the domestic-reproductive role and for their subordination to males are certainly great under the yoke of patriliny, the range of variation is substantial from one society to the next. Insofar as the control of economic production and distribution is reserved exclusively for males, the power of women in patrilineal communities is effectively limited. Conversely, however, insofar as women are able to circumvent traditional property relations, or to establish their economic independence outside the household, access to positions of influence is possible. Indeed, societies could be classified as "weakly patrilineal" or "strongly patrilineal" with regard to the economic rights they grant or do not grant to women.

In many parts of West Africa, for example, males in patrilineal, polygynous societies controlled the allocation of land and the distribution of wealth. Women were obliged to cultivate subsistence crops for themselves and their families, but significantly were entitled to accumulate any surpluses from their own labor that remained after obligations to their children and to the household common store had been met. These private residuals women took to marketplaces, indigenous to this part of the continent, for exchange. During the period of colonization, however, the degree of independence they enjoyed as occasional traders was in many cases greatly accentuated. Among the Afikpo Ibo of southern Nigeria, for example, women adopted cassava plants from Europeans, and inadvertently became the custodians of a valuable crop with which they eventually gained their economic independence from males (Ottenberg 1959). Women traders among the Nupe to the north enjoyed a similar florescence in wealth and power as a result of accentuated activity during the British occupation (Nadel 1942, 1952). In both cases, women were able to circumvent their secondary status in traditional society by successfully exploiting new avenues of economic activity.

In other patrilineal societies, however, few such opportunities exist. Cattle-herders of eastern and southern Africa, for example, had a similar pattern of patriliny and polygyny, but systematically excluded women from rights in portable as well as real property. In these societies, a classic dual economy was present (see Herskovits 1926). These distinct spheres of activity are sometimes referred to as the *subsistence* system and the *prestige* system. The subsistence economy was based on horticulture, in which women were assigned the bulk of cultivative labor. Since regular marketplaces in this region were unknown before colonization, females had none of the opportunities for individual entrepreneurship open to their West African sisters. They were also excluded from participation in the prestige economy, which was based on the ownership and exchange of cattle. Cattle were felt to have a very intimate relationship with human beings, and more especially with men and patrilineal descent groups. They were used as the principal form of exchange, especially for brideprice considerations, and the size and quality of a man's herd provided an index of his wealth and status. In these societies, then, women were obliged to cultivate for their husbands or their husband's patrilineage, but had no rights in land and little control over the distribution of their produce. Wealth and power were intimately related to cattle, and this source of accumulative portable property was forbidden to them. In our case study of the New Guinean Hagen below, we shall examine the position of women in a very similar type of dual economy, in which pigs rather than cattle provide the focus of the prestige system.

In such strongly patrilineal societies, we begin to see the outlines of sex role justapositions characteristic of more complex, intensive cultivators. Although we shall not discuss these patterns until chapter 9, it is essential here to bear in mind the variable extent to which domestic and extradomestic economic activities are included in the female repertoire. In foraging societies, there is little to distinguish these two spheres of activity. Much the same is true for the economic roles of women in matrilineal and matrilocal horticultural societies, where the production and distribution of food are symmetrical activities controlled by the cultivators themselves. Farming communities that localize related males, however, are often engaged in the production of surpluses, and hence have developed a dual economy—one set of activities associated with food production and subsistence, and another set of activities associated with the accumulation and exchange of capital.

In these traditionally patrilineal systems, women inevitably continue to perform the bulk of cultivative labor, but are often excluded from important extradomestic activities involving the exchange of portables. As we have seen, some societies permit extradomestic or "outside" involvement for women on a limited scale by granting them exclusive rights to excess produce. Although in the traditional context few women were able to accumulate sufficient capital to achieve positions of influence, colonialism often skewed the economic balance in their favor. As often as not, however, husbands monopolized the growing of profitable cash crops or performed wage labor, and left their women to the drudgery of subsistence farming. In those situations where women are confined to strictly domestic economic activities, we begin to see development of the basic male-female role dichotomy characteristic of more complex societies. Namely, the exclusion of women from major economic-event systems outside the household signals their increasing isolation from central roles in other societal institutions as well.

To summarize, we have contrasted patrilineal horticulturalists with matrilineal ones on both economic and sociopolitical bases. Patriliny is perhaps best adapted to situations where resources or access to them (i.e. control of arable land) are in great demand, whether through scarcity or abundance. Its adaptability lies in its unique organization of communities into internally divisive or accretive aggregates of related males. Patriliny and patrilocality provide the structure for both acquiring and protecting accumulative property. In this type of societal arrangement, women figure prominently as both food producers and child-bearers—not in their own lineages, but in those of their husbands. As such, they fall into the category of *human* resources, and may be so valued and accumulated by males. It is probably fair to say that status inequities among men and women are more pronounced in the patrilineal situation than under matriliny, and that far fewer feminine opportunities exist for the achievement of high status or the exercise of coercive power in the context of the local community.

Polygyny—Enslavement or Emancipation? We have so far been concerned with polygyny as an adaptive marriage and family type for horticultural communities in which a high level of productivity is pursued. It occurs in some 56 percent of the matrilineal societies in our sample, and in 55 percent of the patrilineal ones. The prominence of polygyny in horticultural adaptations merits a closer examination of its influence upon the social juxtaposition of the sexes. We are especially interested in the qualitative aspects of social roles for men and women, and the ways in which these may vary. The relative advantages and disadvantages of the polygynous situation in daily life (to the extent that they may be objectively measured) will be considered separately for each sex.

Those of us whose culture dictates monogamy as the correct and natural union, and places a premium upon sexual fidelity, may view polygyny as an institution that bestows great rewards upon men. Indeed, it is not uncommon for Westerners to attribute this form of marriage to the lechery of males. As we have seen, however, polygyny is primarily an adaptive economic arrangement rather than one conceived to offer sexual variety. The Tiwi are a good example of the way in which polygyny and sexual freedom for women may coexist and vary independently. In societies where polygyny is the general or preferred pattern, males may leave the monogamous state with considerable apprehension. The taking on of a second wife is often the subject of much joking among males. The disadvantages of multiple marriage are underscored in humor in much the same vein as the ribbing of a prospective bridegroom by his agemates in American culture.

The disadvantages of polygyny for males most commonly involve their complex and often problem-ridden interactions with co-wives. In the great majority of societies, a polygynous husband must distribute his favors equally among his spouses. The more wives a man acquires, the more nearly impossible it is for him to fulfill his responsibilities. Jealousies may erupt into open hostility if the husband favors a certain—often younger—co-wife. Such antagonisms are not only unpleasant, but disrupt the economic routine of the household. It therefore behooves the polygynous husband to maintain the delicate balance of equal treatment and to mediate, by act or deed, disputes that threaten the cohesiveness of the domestic unit.

If dissension among co-wives is a potential source of headaches for polygynous males, so is a high degree of esprit de corps. Co-wives who regularly cooperate may often utilize their close bondage as an instrument of coercion. If, for example, one wife develops a grievance with the husband, she may enlist the support of the others to strengthen her own position. In some cases, they may actually go on strike, refusing to farm, cook, or participate in sex until the dispute is settled and proper restitution made.

What motivates males to create such domestic hornet's nests? Two primary advantages accrue to polygynous husbands, both of which are related to resource accumulation. In those societies in which it is preferred, polygyny is seen as the primary avenue to wealth, prestige, and status. The economic advantage has already been noted: the more wives a man acquires, the more land will be allocated to, exploited, and controlled by him. Expansion of his household with additional women increases both the labor supply and productive yield. A second advantage of polygyny for males lies in the reproductive capacity of women. Wealth may also be measured in the number of progeny, i.e., in the growth of a man's own lineage or lineage segment. Since children are supported largely by the economic efforts of their own mothers, and since they too become productive members of the household, multiple progeny are an asset rather than a liability to polygynous husbands. The more children produced by co-wives, the more successful the family enterprise, and the more secure the husband in old age.

From a Western woman's point of view, it may appear that polygyny places males in a decidedly advantageous position. It is true that this type of marriage appears most frequently in situations where descent and property flow through men, or where the society is moving in that direction. All but one of the cases of polygyny in matrilineal societies, for example, occur with avunculocal residence: where localized uterine groups are composed of related *males* who inherit from their head of household, the mother's brother. Similarly, with the exception of one neolocal case, polygyny in patrilineal societies is universally associated with patrilocality. Wherever this pattern occurs, then, we can expect women to be residing in a strange group and producing and reproducing primarily for their husbands, rather than for themselves and their natal kin units.

There are many variables to consider in the reckoning of female status in polygynous societies (see Clignet 1970). Certainly in terms of descent we would expect the position of women to be higher in matrilineal societies, even with the spatial separation of kinswomen in groups with avunculocal residence patterns. This is because women maintain considerable influence within uterine kinship groups. Polygynous families in the patrilineal situation tend to become patriarchal with respect to the exercise of both domestic and extradomestic power. Within the patrilocal household, however, the status of women may be determined by factors quite extraneous to the individual personalities of husbands and wives. Among these are her relationships with co-wives, fertility, productive importance, degree of economic independence, freedom of movement, and the facility of divorce.

The relationship among co-wives is itself a complex issue. Every culture with well-developed polygyny institutionalizes this role behavior, whether along the lines of cooperation or extreme jealousy. Whatever the ideal qualities of co-wife interaction, these patterns are systematically learned as a prelude to womanhood. If polygyny is *sororal*, congenial relations among women seem to be greatly facilitated by personal association and common socialization experiences. Sisters are more likely to transfer preestablished bonding patterns to the new social milieu of the polygynous household. The *nonsororal* variety, however, is by far the most frequently chosen. Most polygynous societies have to rely upon incentives for cooperative behavior other than those grounded in common kinship.

The addition of a second or subsequent woman to a preexisting marital arrangement is often greeted enthusiastically by the original wife. Indeed, in some societies the husband adds another woman only at his wife's urging. She may play a major role in the perusal of eligible women, and her choice is considered seriously by the husband, since the wife is likely to select a woman with whom she feels good rapport. Women are motivated to seek additional co-wives both for companionship and to help relieve the burden of domestic chores. Mutual aid is especially valued during the latter stages of pregnancy and the immediate postnatal period. As mentioned earlier, cooperative co-wives working in unison may exercise a degree of coercive power vis-à-vis their husband through work stoppages or the withdrawal of favors.

There are several sources of disharmony, however, that can and do erupt in polygynous households. Disputes often arise simply out of the pressures of daily living, or may relate to the women's respective interactions with their common husband. Often the line between these two categories of potential discontent is difficult to draw, since most arguments seem to relate to one or another type of inequity. Should a co-wife make an accusation of laziness, for example, concealed resentments over unequal work distribution or participation may suddenly come to the surface. Similarly, disputes that periodically arise among half-siblings in the household may in turn involve their mothers, and provide a platform for the airing of an inventory of unrelated interpersonal grievances. Perhaps even more disruptive, however, are cleavages that develop in response to real or imagined favoritism on the part of the husband. A common source of jealousy is the sexual preoccupation of a husband with a favored spouse to the comparative neglect of the others.

Children in a polygynous household also provide the raw material for emotionally charged interactions among co-wives. Especially in the patrilineal situation, a woman may be measured by the number and qualities of her progeny. Sterility, comparative infertility, frequent miscarriage, or a high incidence of postnatal infant mortality can significantly lower the status of an individual co-wife and contribute to feelings of jealousy and envy. Similarly, a woman who has borne only daughters may grow to resent attention bestowed by the husband upon the sons, or approval heaped upon the mother of those who will continue his patriline in the next generation. Questions of inheritance are also a problem in polygynous households, since a number of half-siblings of the same father are often, in varying degrees, eligible to inherit his property or rights to property use. Some societies solve the problem by making the eldest son of the first wife the sole heir of the household. Remaining sons are allocated specific land-use rights to allow them to relocate. Unless the precise allotment of the father's wealth is defined, by custom or oral proclamation, before his death, the estate may become carrion over which both sons and mothers do battle.

For Westerners, the disadvantages of polygyny for women may seem to outweigh any obvious benefits. In many cases, however, co-wives may enjoy greater individual freedom than traditionally tolerated in monogamous female role definitions. Where independent polygynous families are the rule, co-wives and their respective children frequently occupy separate dwellings, which are in turn visited by the husband for both food and sexual activities. These matricentric units are typically self-supporting because of the cultivative efforts of each co-wife on her individually assigned plots or fields. Although a wife is bound to feed her own family, and to contribute a share of produce to a common store for the entire polygynous household, she may be entitled to accumulate any remaining surpluses for her own private use. This pattern is especially prominent in societies with well-developed marketplaces. Here women gather to exchange their surplus cultigens for other horticultural products, or material items for themselves and their children. Matricentric units are certainly independent in this situation—so much so that relationships of co-wives with their husband and with each other may assume a secondary position to relationships outside the household. A co-wife is, in essence, her own producer of raw materials and her own entrepreneur. The institution of polygyny may, therefore, provide an opportunity for women to include themselves in the primary economic (masculine) focus of patrilineal societies—the acquisition, accumulation, and control of moveable property.

Sexuality, Marriage, and Divorce. As we have seen, the status of women in polygynous societies is reflective of the nature of social organization, patterned relationships among co-wives, husbands, and half-siblings, and the degree of economic independence attained. In the latter case, freedom for independent action seems to be a critical ingredient in the escape of women from rigid patriarchal controls. This freedom may also be measured along other dimensions, such as the number and kind of approved sexual outlets, and the control of a woman over her own marital status.

Available information on female sexual freedom for the societies in our sample is scant, and limited to the regulation of premarital intercourse. Data are available for only 40 of the 104 cases, only 15 of which are polygynous. Still, apparent differences between matrilineal and patrilineal horticultural societies are worth noting. Five types of premarital sexuality for women are tabulated according to descent in Table 8-2.

Since our sample is quite small, we must be cautious in drawing any firm conclusions. As seen in Table 8-2, however, matri-

Table 8-2. Types of female premarital sexual activity in 40 horticultural societies according to descent

| | DESCENT | | |
PREMARITAL SEX	MATRILINEAL	PATRILINEAL	TOTALS
Precluded by early age at marriage	1	2	3
Allowed; no sanctions unless pregnancy results	0	4	4
Freely permitted; no sanctions	8	10	18
Prohibited, but weakly sanctioned; not rare	1	6	7
Virginity required; premarital sex rare	0	8	8
Totals:	10	30	40

lineal societies are overwhelmingly permissive in their attitude
toward premarital sex for women. The two exceptions are both
avunculocal, polygynous societies. Patrilineal examples, in contrast, are much more disparate in their patterning of female sexuality. Although freedom is not entirely foreign to patrilineal
societies, a full two-thirds of those for which there are data exert
some type of controls over the sexual life of women. The reason
for this difference no doubt lies in the importance attached to
the establishment of paternity in patrilineal communities. In
general, then, we may expect restrictions on female sexual expression before marriage to occur more frequently with patriliny than in societies where the mother-child link is primary.

The choice of a marital partner in horticultural societies with
unilineal descent groups is seldom entirely determined by either the bride or bridegroom. More typically, marriage represents a union of kinship groups rather than individuals. For this
reason, men and women are joined more on the basis of their
kin affiliation than on any Western notion of romantic love. Virtually every woman in a horticultural society, therefore, is married at least once, largely by parental urging and arrangement.
Her sexual expression in marriage may be strictly limited to her

spouse, or may be extended outside this relationship with varying degrees of approval by society at large. Among the Ba-Ila of
southeastern Africa, for example, a woman may take on publicly
recognized lovers who formalize the sexual arrangement with
payments to her typically polygynous husband (Murdock
1959:367).

An extreme of sexual and marital freedom is found among
several cultures in Northern Nigeria (see Meek 1931). Here the
great majority of societies are patrilineal, patrilocal, and polygynous. In this situation one may ordinarily expect a high
degree of male dominance in social and sexual relationships. In
many cases, however, women have actually turned the marriage
system to their own advantage. Two ingredients seem to be essential. The first is easy divorce. Women in these societies often
formalize their relationship with a lover by deserting their husbands. The second element is a mechanism for compensating
the original husband for his loss. It is possible in these societies
to substitute the return of the brideprice with a child. Thus, if a
woman becomes dissatisfied with her marriage and enamored
by a lover, she may leave a child permanently with her husband's descent group and run off. In this way no financial hardship is caused her father. Indeed, after a series of such marriages, fathers may become considerably more secure through
the accumulation of their daughters' brideprices. As for the
woman, she needs only to bear one child to each husband, or
beg her father's indulgence, and she is free to move on to a new
spouse.

We have, then, a full spectrum of sexual expression and freedom for women in horticultural societies. It appears that fewer
restrictions, at least in the premarital period, exist under matriliny than patriliny, and that these differences may relate to the
relative importance of paternity determination. Considerable
latitude, however, seems to exist in patrilineal societies in the
postmarital period. Although data are not available, we may
hypothesize that extramarital liaisons may be more frequent in
the polygynous situation. Since the legal husband is the pater
of any children a wife bears during their marriage, regardless of

the biological father, the paramour relationship does not present an immediate threat to the solidarity of the family.

CASE STUDY: HAGEN WOMEN

It is now time to illustrate these generalizations with a more intensive examination of the role of women in a specific society. Ethnographic data on women in horticultural societies is comparatively abundant (see Albert 1963, Earthy 1933, Gessain 1963, Laurentin 1963, Leith-Ross 1939, Smith 1954). The great majority of these field studies have been undertaken by European women anthropologists in Africa. Cultures on this continent have an extremely high incidence of female cultivation, polygynous marriage, and—at least in the recent past— partrilineal descent. In general, African women enjoy a high status in non-Muslim indigenous cultures, and a generous measure of freedom in both economic and personal pursuits. Moreover, traditional African state political bureaucracies inevitably included females alongside males in monarchical positions, and at times in governmental ministries as well. Because the data are best for Africa, there is a tendency to equate the role of women in these societies with the horticultural adaptation as a whole. As noted above, however, there is considerable variation in the overall status of women among hand cultivators.

We have chosen to examine the female role in a non-African horticultural society, the Hagen of the western New Guinea highlands. Data for our case study is provided in a 1972 work by Marilyn Strathern, *Women in Between*. The Hagen exemplify patrilineal horticulturalism in the extreme. Here the patterns of male dominance and male superiority over females are similar to those of agricultural communities. Hagen society provides a glimpse at the lifestyle of women beneath the veneer of institutionalized inferiority. Our initial task will be to define the material basis of Hageners and the economic dimension of sex-linked behaviors. We shall then take a closer look at the critical integrative roles played by women as links in the social and trading networks. The Hagen give us an appreciation of the *intercalary* status of women in patrilineal societies, namely as bridges between the male-centered kin groups of fathers and husbands. Finally, we shall contrast these subordinate roles of women with their unique position and powers in the supernatural area.

The Setting. The Hagen live in the Western Highlands District of New Guinea in the vicinity of Mount Hagen, a peak rising to 13,000 feet above sea level. The people studied by Strathern (1972) occupy the lower hillsides, at 5000 to 7000 feet. There the terrain varies from flat, rolling grasslands to steep-sided and heavily forested valleys. Despite the elevation, tropical conditions prevail.

Terrain angularity poses no deterrent to cultivation. The Hagen farm extensively on the slopes of this region. Individual garden plots are often constructed on steep ground and demarcated by ditches or wooden fences. Crops include sugarcane, bananas, taro, yams, sweet potatoes, coffee, and a variety of vegetable plants acquired through Europeans. The Mount Hagen region has no clearly marked monsoons, although rainfall is somewhat more prominent from October to March. Because of the virtual absence of seasons, crops are planted and harvested throughout the year.

As was true of many other areas of New Guinea, Mount Hagen remained isolated from the outside world until quite recently. The first European expedition into the area did not occur until 1933. An airstrip constructed shortly thereafter provided a foothold for European exploration and eventual settlement. Despite successful pacification of the immediate area, however, intertribal warfare among Hagen communities was not effectively curbed by the Australian administration until well after World War II. The 1950s marked an invasion of missionaries, the ubiquitous vanguard of Westernization. By the mid-1960s the Mount Hagen settlement had achieved the status of a prosperous town.

Population density throughout this region is high. The

Hageners themselves, some 75,000, are organized into independent tribes of 500 to 6000 people, with an average of 1000 individuals per political unit. Within these tribal groupings are patrilineal clan, subclan, and lineage divisions. Typically the clans composing a single tribe represented the largest conglomerate to unite against a common enemy. In the past, however, clans within the same political community occasionally took up arms against one another. Similarly, political alliances among clans in different political units were sometimes maintained through intermarriage and trade alliances. Traditional Hagen tribes, therefore, were largely collections of geographically contiguous patriclans which, under certain circumstances, rallied to defend a common territory. More typically, however, component clans within these tribal units acted as independent agents in the initiation or severing of alliances with others. Each clan categorized alien kinship groupings as allies, minor enemies, or major, perpetual enemies. The distinction between the latter two categories, based largely upon the seriousness, duration, and degree of violence in armed confrontations, was an important one in traditional Hagen society, since minor enemy clans were often the source of incoming spouses.

Each clan is divided into a number of subclans, the male members of which often reside or meet together in a single men's house. Subclan leaders, or "big-men," gain their positions of prominence largely through their special abilities in trade and the accumulation of portable wealth. Although these positions are not formalized, big-men were formerly influential in the settlement of disputes and in the negotiation of peace between warring kinship groups.

As might be expected, European intrusion in recent decades has precipitated certain changes in Hagen society. At the time of investigation the patrilineal clan, subclan, and lineage systems were still intact, although the lure of town life had already given rise to a permanent expatriate population. The prohibition of warfare by Australian authorities, however, has considerably altered the traditional legal and power structures of Hagen communities. Since the early 1960s, all serious disputes (those which in the past might have precipitated a military confronta-

tion) must be heard before a governmental court. Lesser disputes, however, are now heard by informal bodies of councillors
appointed from each clan by the administration.

The abandonment of warfare has been greatly facilitated by
the introduction of foreign currency. Hageners may now engage
in economic rather than military competition. (Indeed the accumulation and exchange of valuables has much in common
with physical combat.) Currency finds its way into village communities through wage labor on local plantations, the sale of
horticultural produce, and the raising of cash crops. This gen-
eral-purpose money has infiltrated traditional systems of exchange as well.

Although missionizing efforts have been rather vigorous since
the early 1950s, Hageners have generally been reluctant to part
with their adaptive institutions. Strathern (1972) notes, for example, that polygyny persists as the preferred type of marriage
among all but baptized converts. The picture which emerges,
then, from a cursory view of Hagen society is one of a viable
culture lured by Westernization, yet with a strong foothold in
traditional institutions.

Women, Pigs and Produce. One of the more significant facts of
life for Hagen women is their spatial segregation from their
natal kinship group. Residence after marriage is generally patrilocal; the new wife takes up residence in the vicinity of her
husband's patrilineage. There she will cultivate, tend her livestock, raise her children, and perhaps die. It is also there that
she will remain essentially an alien for the duration of her stay,
never to be completely trusted, always a potential source of
misfortune through individual malice or supernatural sanctions.
In order to understand the ramifications of this intercalary status, we shall first define the nature of economic dichotomization
among women and men. In the following section, we shall consider the mechanics of female linkage between patrilineal descent groups of fathers and husbands. Finally, we shall examine
the less mundane, symbolic connotations of gender status and
sex behavior, with an emphasis upon Hagen notions of female
pollution.

Plate 3. Hagen woman gardening at her brother's settlement.

In the traditional economy of Hagen society women are the primary producers. When a new wife enters the settlement of her husband's kin, she is allocated specific garden plots at the first new clearing of land. From these resources she is expected to plant and cultivate a variety of crops with which to support her husband and offspring. Males have a limited twofold involvement with cultivation. They perform the heavy labor required to prepare garden plots for planting, and they are involved in the cultivation of crops such as bananas and sugarcane, which are considered essentially "male" because of the strenuous labor involved in their harvesting. Such crops may therefore be planted, tended, and gathered by men, or in some cases planted by women but harvested by males. In contrast, women regularly cultivate sweet potato, maize, green vegetables, yams, and a variety of taro. Garden plots lack the linear symmetry and order characteristic of open fields in other horticultural societies. Rather, disparate crops are planted sporadically throughout the plot, with no spatial segregation either by species or "gender."

In addition to garden plots allocated to a woman by her husband, she may also look to other males for land-use rights. Not uncommonly, plots will be donated by the father and brothers of a woman both before and after marriage. These she may continue to plant. Even though these gardens may be some distance from her husband's settlement, and therefore left untended for considerable periods, individual harvesting rights remain intact.

Women acquire their rights to cultivate, then, through males. They can neither own nor transfer landed property. Rights to the productive yield of such allocated garden plots, however, are both exclusively and individually held by women. Says Strathern:

> Irrespective of whether help was given in the initial preparation of a garden, assertions of crop ownership rest on who planted them. . . . Cowives do not plant for each other. A woman has near absolute rights of control over her crops, which she may regard as holding even against her husband and children. They may go into her garden, but strictly should not harvest any of the produce without permission (1972:23).

Indeed, many domestic disputes originate in accusations of trespass and the theft of produce. These disagreements are common among spouses, co-wives, wives and children of co-wives, and even among parents and children. Female members of the same settlement may also argue over the specifics of land allocation after the clearing of a new area has been undertaken by males. These altercations typically involve women, such as co-wives or mother- and daughters-in-law, who are competing for individual shares of the limited resources of one male (the husband-son). In addition, the continued allocation of gardens by a husband to sisters residing in different patrilocalities is a potential source of interpersonal conflict.

Interestingly, some Hagen women pursue rather elaborate measures designed to exert limited control over land allocation itself. By improving the land in their individual gardens, the women may strengthen their claims to continued use-rights of that particular plot. A favored technique is the planting of certain species of trees (an activity otherwise performed by men). Although such improvements are no guarantee of land control, tree planting on plots in either the husband's settlement or that of the father or brother seems to be accompanied by a degree of informal but recognized privileges for women vis-à-vis land.

Hagen women are therefore obliged by their culture to assume the role of producers of primary foodstuffs. Although they neither own nor distribute landed property, they are entitled to use-rights from both spouses and kinsmen, and may, through individual effort, exert some influence over the allocation of these resources. In the latter case, trees planted by some women as a form of insurance against relocation to another garden plot may subsequently be exploited by their spouses for wood. As Strathern notes, women have specific but variable claims to garden yields:

> A woman may or may not expect to be notified of the use to which her menfolk put the trees she has planted. At the other end of the scale are her sweet potatoes and vegetables which should never be taken without her knowing, and which she prefers to gather herself anyway. Between these fall the male crops (bananas, sugarcane); a woman likes to be told, but also recognizes the right of certain men to help themselves (1972:26).

These limited or exclusive rights of women to produce, however, are not inalienable. If, for example, plots cultivated at the settlement of a brother are not harvested when ready, he himself may lay claim to the produce. Conversely, in the event of desertion or divorce, women lose not only their interests in garden plots allocated by their husbands, but also the right to harvest any personal crops already under cultivation. During these and other situations of crisis, women commonly take up residence in the vicinity of their brothers or parents. Separation and divorce thus underscore the importance of maintaining garden plots outside the husband's settlement, and illustrate the intercalary position of women between parental and spousal lineage territories.

The linkage of Hagen kinship groups through women is nowhere better illustrated than in the raising and distribution of pigs. When a woman marries, she typically brings as a dowry to her new residence a number of breeding pigs. These animals form the core of the young couple's future herd. The relationship of women to pigs is both utilitarian and emotional. Hageners charge women with the tending and raising of these valuable animals; the size and quality of individual herds is the object of much effort and personal pride. Females maintain a close physical relationship with pigs, allowing them to forage in the bush during the day, but stalling them in their own homes at night. As other dependents in the household, they are fed produce from the individual garden plots of their female herders. Strong emotional attachments are not uncommon. For Hagen women, the breeding sow takes on an air of elegance generally unappreciated in our own culture. Sickness among pigs is met with elaborate nurturance and care, and women express grief openly at the theft or death of a favored beast.

The relationship of men to pigs is contrastive, and underscores the primary distinction between the sexes in the Hagen economy. Whereas women assume the role of *producers*, males see themselves first and foremost as *transactors*. That is, men not only control the distribution of wealth within their own kinship groups, but regularly engage in a myriad of economic partnerships with other individuals or groups. This ceremonial exchange, called *moka*, involves pigs and shells, and is the central focus of male activities:

> *Moka* transactions with pig and shell valuables follow standardized forms and may accompany performance of religious cults, payment of war indemnities, and funeral and childbirth gifts; bridewealth is a precursor of *moka* exchanges between affinal kin. *Moka* can be conducted quite privately between individual partners; or a clan, divisions or combinations of clans, may come together in public display, each man giving to his own partner, but jointly celebrating the whole wealth of the group. Public transactions take place at ceremonial grounds and are often

> accompanied by dancing. They are a vehicle
> for the expression of competition between
> groups, assertions of strength and prosper-
> ity, and claims to prestige (1972:10).

Women play no active or direct part in *moka* exchanges, and therefore have no formal claim to the pig herds under their care. Ideally, their role is to take charge of the breeding and natural growth of the herd, and to increase productivity of the gardens on which the nutrition of pigs depends. A wife is expected to provide, in essence, the material and personal support for her husband's social advancement—his elevation to, perhaps, the status of big-man through skillful transactions and oratorical prowess. Because of the efforts expended in the care of pig herds, however, and the emotional attachments that sometimes develop toward certain animals, women often endeavor to play less passive roles in the economic transactions of their husbands. Indeed, they often see themselves as essential (if behind-the-scenes) participants in *moka* exchanges. Women may be entitled to a voice in decisions concerning the distribution of pigs raised under their care, and may actually, in exchanges with their own kinsmen, act as official go-betweens. In both cases, however, the participation of women is attributable more to their intercalary position in Hagen socioeconomic structure than to any political influence per se. The status ambiguity of women must now be examined in more detail.

The Intercalary Gender. Women form the binding pins that link Hagen patrilineages and clans in an elaborate system of economic exchange and power relationships. Their position is somewhat like that of a character in two distinct and articulated dramas. They are essential to the plots of each, but are always in a supporting role. Hagen culture stresses the relationship between males or groups of males *through* women. For this reason, the social identity of females is inextricably blended with becoming a wife and an affine. Marriage is symbolized as the road linking one kinship group with another, and along which both women and *moka* flow.

The almost anonymous role of females in the articulation of male-centered kinship groups first comes into focus at adolescence. This is a time of great activity for young women. After puberty they are often excused from the gardening and domestic labor in which they have participated since they were small girls and begin to attach increasing significance to peer-group activities. At this time in the life cycle of women—and continuing for perhaps two to three years—courting parties are held in their honor on any ceremonial occasion that brings two or more clans together. Commonly, these parties are held in the evening after a *moka* festival, and attract large numbers of young men. They provide a public occasion for ritual displays of mutual attraction between the sexes, referred to as "turning heads." The latter consists of the couple kneeling on the ground face to face, pressing their foreheads together, and rocking back and forth to the love songs chanted by observing guests.

This behavior may be engaged in with several partners over the course of a courting season. A man toward whom a young

Plate 4. Young married Hagen women visiting their home clan for a *moka* festival.

Plate 5. Unmarried Hagen girl dancing at a *moka* festival with her brothers.

woman has indicated a preference by "turning head" at more than one party, however, typically invites her back to his settlement to spend the day and subsequent night. At her parting, often at the beckoning of an elder kinswoman, she is oiled and painted by the male relatives of her suitor and receives gifts on behalf of her own father and brothers. Although such excursions may eventually lead to serious matrimonial negotiations, they formally involve no further obligation for either set of kinsmen. Sexual intercourse is prohibited throughout the entire courting period—a rule enforced by a liberal use of chaperones.

Serious intentions on the part of a couple may be indicated by the mutual exchange of small gifts, or more directly by the bestowal of presents upon the young woman's father by the suitor. Some initiative in the choice of spouses is taken, therefore, by the couple involved. Final approval of the union, however, rests with the parents concerned, who maintain the right to dissolve any relationship that appears undesirable to them. The characteristics sought in a potential wife are indicative of her larger status and role positions in Hagen society. A primary consideration in this regard is industriousness. Says Strathern:

> Hard work is the mark of a good wife, and young girls are encouraged to show their capacity for work. The mother is supposed to tell her daughter: "You are a girl, and you can never forget your netbag and digging stick. Your father and brother have made gardens and you mustn't neglect weeding them. In the morning you must harvest food for breakfast, then when the sun is warm you can weed the gardens. At night you should bring sweet potatoes back to cook—but you mustn't eat all the tubers yourself: leave some for your father and brothers who will be hungry when they come home. When you have a spare moment, use it to make a headcovering for your father or a netbag for yourself. When the pigs come in, herd them into the house and see they have food. You cannot get up and leave your netbag and digging stick, and go to sit down in the men's

house. The men are there talking, and you
have no business there. Or if you wander
around the paths and roads and neglect your
gardens everyone will see, and they'll say,
"Oh, this woman is no worker—never mind,
we shall not marry her!" (1972:133–34).

A young woman who appears energetic, therefore, is highly
valued for her future productive capacity, both as a cultivator
and pig-breeder. The size of a bride's dowry is often interpreted
by women as an indication of her family's gratitude for her labor
before marriage. The production of food is one of the very few
areas in Hagen culture where males acknowledge their dependency on women. Female ambitiousness underlies the entire
basis of household maintenance and growth and the provision
of *moka* goods.

A second quality valued in a potential bride is virginity.
Women bear the final responsibility for observation of premarital sexual taboos, and their overall character during courting activities may fall under the scrutiny of potential in-laws. Promiscuous behavior on the part of women before marriage is thought
to be indicative of postmarital sexual infidelity. As we shall see,
this belief relates to Hagen equations of genitals and intercourse with uncleanliness, and of frequent sexual activity with
both danger and abnormality. On a more mundane level, the
fear of future spousal infidelity and desertion of the husband are
bound up with his economic dependency and questions concerning the political loyalty of the wife (whose own kinsmen
may be actual enemies of the husband's people).

A third and critical factor in marriage arrangements concerns
the kin affiliation of the prospective bride rather than qualities
of the woman per se. Marriages are roads for interclan economic
and political alliance, and are therefore negotiated both to sus-
tain existing relationships and to create new ones. Hageners, for
example, prohibit unions with close kin or among lineages with
whom an alliance has already been sealed by an existing marriage. Preferred in-laws are individuals who belong to a more
distant kinship group, and whose relatives will create new avenues for *moka* transactions. For this reason, women from clans

classified as "minor enemies" may actually be preferred as incoming spouses. In the past, when warfare was endemic, women were sometimes exchanged to cement political as well as economic alliances.

As soon as both sets of parents give their approval to the union, negotiations over the amount of bridewealth to be transferred to the woman's kinsmen begin. In the drama of marriage rituals and exchanges the intercalary status of the new wife is symbolically reenacted. The bride begins the proceedings as a representative of her own people. Ritually oiled and decorated, she visits the household of her prospective spouse bearing solicitory gifts of shells and cooked pork. With these she hopes to impress her future affines, and to encourage generous brideprice contributions on her behalf. The next few days are taken up with direct negotiations between the respective kinsmen of the couple over the amount of valuables to be transferred. The climax of these proceedings occurs at the groom's settlement with the actual display of the bridewealth, comprised of shells and live pigs, and their presentation to the kinsmen of the bride. This is a time of elaborate bickering among the two sets of kin over the size and quality of goods. Through it all the bride remains little more than a helpless observer:

> The bride is in an ambiguous position. Success or failure in the exchanges involve her own reputation. But the gap between this and her actual control of events (largely in the hands of men) can lead to strain. She is an actor in the proceedings, at some junctures a central one, but has little control over the actual bargaining for wealth. While her approval for the transactions is sought, a negative answer is often regarded by her menfolk as subversive as flight. A girl may become unhappy or angry if the proper gifts are not made to her relatives; default on her kinsmen's part may put her into a similar position of frustration (Strathern 1972:115).

Since the first bestowal of solicitory gifts by the bride, she has remained in the company of strangers at the settlement of her

husband. Her intercalary status, underscored by the juxtaposition of her father's and spouse's kin groups during brideprice
negotiations, is somewhat modified by the new friendships she
begins to establish with the women of her new locality. Following the transfer of marriage valuables on her behalf, the social
identity of the new wife is symbolically transferred to the residential group of her husband. This is dramatically illustrated in
a final gift of pork from the groom's kin, in which she plays a
central role:

> The pork, still on the bone, is packed into a
> netbag. The groom's kin lift this on to the
> bride's forehead; an unmarried sister of the
> groom may help her carry some if the pre-
> sentation is large. Staggering under the
> weight, she bears this ahead of her affines,
> who make their entrance behind her. Helped
> off by her own father and brothers, she lays
> the pork before them and then retires to sit
> with her husband's female relatives. Her role
> as bearer of valuables between the two sets
> of kin is clearly symbolised. It is also taken
> as a sign of her own acquiescence in the
> marriage. The bride who willingly carries the
> burden of pork will not later run away, but
> will, one is told, stay with her husband and
> bear him many children (Strathern 1972:119).

At the completion of this complex series of exchanges, a new
wife formally changes her residential membership. This incor-
poration, however, is never complete, and for the remainder of
her life she must regularly balance these relationships, placing
one foot, one set of loyalties, one emotional weld in the community of her father and brother, and the other in that of her
spouse. Hageners recognize the cultural duality built into the
female gender as almost a necessary evil—women serve as
bridges for male trading partnerships, but at the same time
wield the awesome and unmanipulable powers of production
and fluctuating, subsurface emotional commitments.

Hageners share with many Melanesian cultures the practice
of physical segregation on the basis of sex. Closely related men

typically sleep and center their social activities in a large men's house, while women and their respective pig herds occupy separate and individual dwellings. Because of this practice, a new wife does not actually live with her spouse, but rather joins the household of her mother-in-law. The emphasis upon virginity, modesty, and shyness between the sexes contributes to the fact that marriges may not be sexually consummated for an additional six months. It is in the mother-in-law's household that a woman undergoes the most difficult period of adjustment of her early married life. As among the Wodaabe Fulani (see chapter 10), a young, childless wife is at first completely dependent upon her husband's mother for subsistence, and must reciprocate with displays of respect and cooperative labor. At the next clearing of land, she may eventually acquire her own strip of arable land with which to support herself, her husband, and pigs. In marrying, however, she inherits her spouse's obligation to aid and support his mother in old age. For this reason, the two women typically continue their coresidence until the old woman dies, or the size of a wife's family requires a separate domicile. Although the relationship of a woman and her husband's mother may be reserved, latently hostile, or openly competitive, the mother-in-law is her most important link to successful community integration.

The interaction of the new wife with other members of her husband's settlement is characterized by varying degrees of restraint. Males of the parental generation must be granted particular respect. According to Hagen traditions, one should avoid addressing or even referring to affines by their personal names, and should not walk directly behind them lest the threads connecting that person to his clan ancestors be violated. A partial exception is the husband's father, whose back is not avoided, and who may assume a protective role over his daughter-in-law vis-à-vis other community members. If the new wife's husband is a polygynist, her adjustment may be further complicated by hostile relationships with his older spouses. Hageners institutionalize jealousy and competition as the normal state of cowife interaction, and much energy is spent in winning the husband's favor at the expense of others. Although the first wife is accorded some prestige by virtue of seniority, favorite wives are typically those who are superior producers—sex and economics are intimately related:

> A central component of the concept is sexual jealousy, and brides are traditionally given magic stones to make them attractive to their new husbands. These, or similar stones would also bring them success in pig breeding, for sexual attraction and economic success are seen to go together. A skilful manager is thought to endear herself to her spouse, and conversely the favourite wife is give preferential treatment in the allocation of valuables (Strathern 1972:52).

In contrast to the restrictive, competitive relationships at her husband's settlement, those with her natal kin are affectionate and informal. New brides make frequent trips home to enjoy the warmth and support of their lineage-mates. Of particular intensity is the bond between brothers and sisters. It is in the settlement of her brother that she will typically maintain separate gardens, and to which she will go in times of trouble.

The husband's attitude toward his wife's kin reflects the ambivalence of her own position. A man must exercise a high degree of restraint in his relationship with his wife's immediate relatives. He is eager to win their approval, and to pave the way for future *moka* exchanges through the maintenance of good relations. For this reason he acquiesces to his wife's desires to visit her home kin since, in essence, she acts as his emmissary for subsequent trading networks. On the other hand, the husband often fears that his wife's home kin may exert influences over her that would threaten his own position. Hagen men believe that a wife's mother can exert her will over a daughter by threatening to withdraw her emotional support. Similarly, men fear that a wife's brother or father may encourage her to stay permanently in their household in the hope of securing a larger brideprice for her elsewhere. Separation and divorce are most frequently initiated by young, childless women. It is for this reason that the early period of marriage is particularly delicate, and that serious economic transactions between male affines are not commenced until after a child has sealed the union.

The relationship of husbands and wives is almost secondary, an anticlimax, to linkages between their respective kinsmen. A primary bond is their economic complementarity, and the tenor of their interactions reflects the wife's productive capacity and the husband's skill in trade. We have yet to examine, however, the affective dimension of male-female relationships. For this we must consider those characteristics which, in the eyes of men, place all women in an inferior, but at times awesome, category.

The Dangerous Gender. All human societies rationalize their adaptive labor divisions and social groups as being somehow reflective of the natural order of the universe. Sex and gender are invariably associated with an elaborate set of stereotyped behaviors which stress the inevitability of extant conditions in a given society. For the Hagen, dichotomization of the sexes has supernatural as well as mundane dimensions.

Women in this culture are felt to be not only less well suited than men to engage in prestigeous trading negotiations, but less *genetically* fit for these activities as well. The natural inferiority of females is based upon the notion of their alleged inability to reason clearly. Women, Hagen men argue, have several "minds," rendering them fickle emotionally, and entirely incapable of the levelheadedness required in economic transactions. As a category of humanity, females are mere "rubbish," suited only to the more menial occupations of food production and pig-herding. They lack the oratorical skills that embellish ritual and informal gatherings, and play a generally silent, passive role in focal community activities. Those exceptional females whose behaviors are overtly aggressive are categorized negatively as either promiscuous or disobedient wives. These "strong" women, while embodying many positive male behavioral attributes, are both resented and feared by men. Indeed, they are viewed as a reflection of the ultimate depravity of womankind.

Despite the social inequities among women and men in day-to-day, mundane relationships, the world of the supernatural opens new vistas for the exercise of female power and influence. Although they are often degraded by men, women are also greatly feared for their unique powers to exercise malice through silent, unseen channels. We shall consider three different avenues of supernatural coercion open to Hagen women, both living and dead.

One supernatural dimension of the female concerns the special relationship of husbands and wives after death. Hageners believe that the marital bond is generally unaffected by the mortality of spouses. The ghostly spirits of husbands and wives are joined after death, and may exert their will upon the living. A dead woman is especially feared by Hagen men, precisely because of the intercalary position she occupied during her lifetime. This special status continues after death. A woman may not only join the ghosts of her own patrilineage in monitoring the social behavior of her living kinsmen, but she may also heap revenge upon her living spouses, children, and affines. Female ghosts are thought to be especially jealous of the living, and are able to inflict sickness and death upon the entire clan of the widower. This action is particularly feared if the woman has died young and childless, or if she is otherwise embittered, such as by the contemplated remarriage of her living spouse. For this reason an elaborate ceremony of ritual banishment must be performed by the widower and his fellow clansmen after the death of a wife to symbolically sever the marital bond, and hence her supernatural influence over them.

The relatively secure position of women *after* death is in sharp contrast to their vulnerability to ghostly malice while living. A woman's intermediate status between the kin groups of her father and husband, renders her subject to the controls of *both* sets of clan ghosts. As such, women are often used as scapegoats to punish the offenses of men:

> Whereas a married woman comes under the influence of two sets of ghosts, the husband is not controlled by his wife's clan ghosts. . . . It is the wife who becomes iden-

tified with the husband, and not the other way around. She may be identified to the point of victimization for her husband's crimes. . . . On the other hand, she may suffer directly because of her intermediate position. Ghosts ordinarily control only their own cognates. If brothers-in-law steal from each other, whether it is the sister's husband or the wife's brother in the wrong, the linking woman becomes vulnerable to attack from ghosts from either side who themselves cannot directly influence the affine. The loss of the wife (or the children) is a blow against her menfolk (Strathern 1972:126–27).

A second supernatural dimension of the female gender concerns the manipulation of substances called *mi*, which are associated with each Hagen political unit. *Mi* are totems characteristically representing species of leaves, or alternatively of stones and dogs. Material forms of these totems are publically ingested by Hageners to bring about a desired end. *Mi* substances are powerful in that they are backed by the authority of clan ghosts. A person professing innocence in a dispute, for example, may swear on the *mi* of his tribe, thereby requesting death at the hands of clan ghosts if guilty as accused. Women, so often powerless in the negotiations that directly affect their lives, may utilize *mi* as a coercive tool against their own kinsmen. If, for instance, a woman's parents have coerced her to enter or remain in an undesirable marriage, she may attempt to force their capitulation by threatening to eat *mi*. This act of desperation, the grim foreboding of suicide, was in the past a common occurrence in Hagen society. Strathern (1972:115) notes a case of suicide as recently as 1963, in which a young bride hanged herself in a dispute with her parents over dowry pigs.

A third supernatural dimension of the female gender, and that which has the most far-reaching implications for male-female interaction, concerns the awesome physical sexuality of women. If the power of Hagen men lies in their ownership and distribution of wealth, the power of Hagen women is based in the generalized fear of their genitalia and physiological periodicies. Although relegated to an inferior status by males in mundane affairs, the superior potency of women in the supernatural arena stems from their unique abilities to both pollute and poison those who would unduly exert their dominance over them.

To understand the polluting influence of women, we must note briefly Hagen biases on the nature and use of genitalia. Sex organs of both men and women and sexual intercourse itself are associated linguistically with the adjective "bad." As in traditional Western European culture, exposure of the genitals is an offensive and shameful act; private areas of the body are regarded as "dirty." The Hagen concept of uncleanliness for female genitalia is extended much further than that of male counterparts. The genitals of women are regarded as contaminating to anything they touch. Females must therefore take special care in the placement and disposal of skirts and other articles of personal clothing. In addition, women cannot step over another person, cooking fires, or especially over any food, cigarettes, or other items destined for human consumption. The reservation with which Hageners regard their genitals is reflected in a corresponding discouragement of frequent sexual intercourse. Coitus is thought to be enjoyable, but stringent rules regulate times and places in which it may be engaged. Interestingly, Hagen sexual partners conclude the intercourse ritual by spitting to symbolize their aversion to the release of genital fluids.

Hagen women may act as polluting agents in both passive and active ways. In the passive sense, males view mere contact with female genitals as physically and spiritually weakening. Frequent intercourse is thought to rob a man of his vitality, make him old before his time, and even to result in flabbiness in the skin. Women are in every physical respect, therefore, antithetical to male success. Because of their contaminating influence, females must retire to a segregated menstrual hut during their monthly periods, and during childbirth. In addition, women are eliminated from male rituals, and segregated from the infirm lest they prevent their recovery. Such powers of pollution, however, may be actively manipulated by women to achieve a desired effect. If driven to the point of frustration or outrage, a woman may express her contempt by exposing her genitals to the offending person, or by deliberately stepping over a cooking-fire. These antisocial acts constitute serious violations of social and ritual etiquette, and must usually be followed by some form of material restitution to the wronged party.

Strathern offers a vivid example of how the polluting powers of women may be used as an instrument of coercion. In this particular case, a Hagen woman was overcome with jealousy when her monogamous husband decided to take on a second, younger wife. The quarreling that ensued between them ended in his striking her with a stick. But her anger was not diminished. Indeed, it was further aggravated by the fact that some of the pigs under her care were to be used for the other woman's brideprice. When the men came to claim the pigs in question she protested vigorously, and again the husband resorted to physical violence to prevent her interference. She was struck with an axe and bound while the pigs were slaughtered and the meat carried off to the new bride's kinsmen. Still undaunted, she assaulted the new bride upon her return home in the company of the now-polygynous husband. With this, the man became enraged and broke the arm of his senior wife with a blow from a wooden stake. The superior physical power of the husband had apparently prevailed, and the objections of the senior wife, this "rubbish" person, were effectively disposed of. With relentless determination, however, unabashed or perhaps driven anew by her injuries, the angered woman decided to exercise her powers of pollution to achieve the elusive goal:

> The husband and his new bride, along with others including the story-teller, were still in the house when the first wife climbed on to the roof, tore a hole in the thatch and urinated on those below. She shouted out that the husband should either get rid of the second woman or she would set fire to the house and kill her. At this point he gave in (it was surmised he feared the wife would kill him as well with poison) and sadly told his young bride to return home. Shame at his

> wife's actions made him compensate with a
> pig those who had been insulted by her pub-
> lic exposure (Strathern 1972:255).

In commiting this public act, the senior wife symbolically transferred the dispute from the mundane to the supernatural arena. Whereas the husband had both the authority and power to subdue her within the domestic context, he was forced to withdraw when presented with the prospect of facing his senior wife on a battleground where superior physical strength offered no advantage. The exposure of her genitals served not only as an outrage of sufficient magnitude to discourage the new wife from continuing the union, but also bared the weapons of an even greater threat—homicide by poisoning.

Among Hageners, there is a specific association between poison and menstrual blood. Female genitals are not only polluting if exposed or contacted, but may actually contain an agent lethal to human beings. Death by poisoning through the ingestion of menstrual blood is a major fear of Hagen men. Women are thought to engage in such machinations by adding an imperceptibly small amount of blood to the food of an unsuspecting victim. It is for this reason that females must suspend their normal domestic routines during menstruation. Poisoning may also result from sexual intercouse, although death in this case is not instantaneous. Coitus is prohibited during menstruation because of the belief that blood may be absorbed through the penis. The poisonous effect of such activity is cumulative. The blood is thought to localize in the chest of the victim, and to eventually cause suffocation. A nosebleed at or near death is taken as an indication of such poisoning. Women are held ultimately responsible for these deaths since, Hagen men argue, they may deliberately lure an unsuspecting lover during menstruation without his knowledge or acquiescence.

Some of the latent hostility that Hagen men direct at women, therefore, may have considerable basis in a generalized fear of female supernatural reprisal. Women have easy access to the necessary ingredients for poisoning, and as food-preparers and lovers a man's own wives pose the greatest threat to his physical well-being. In addition to personal motivations, husbands fear that women may be led to homicide at the urging of their own kinsmen. Such killings, wherein the wife acts as a kind of proxy murderer, are especially feared when the woman comes from an enemy clan, or where in-law relations are otherwise strained on an interpersonal or intergroup level. These special powers of women, and the inability of males to control them, account for the lack of trust that tempers the quality of interaction among wives and their in-laws throughout life.

Although channels for the exercise of power are available, Hagen women who deviate from their ideally subordinate, submissive roles are severely reprimanded by males. Indeed, the treatment of recalcitrants gives vent to male hostilities, replacing their feelings of powerlessness with overt displays of force. In the past, public beatings, rape, and torture of women suspected of misusing their genitals was apparently commonplace. Interestingly, runaway wives, promiscuous women, and alleged poisoners are symbolically equated by Hageners. Male reaction to and retaliation for these acts varies more in intensity than in kind. This stems largely from the fact that all such violations of moral or criminal codes by women have similar disruptive effects on intra- and interclan relations. Sexual infidelity, desertion, and the threat of domestic sabotage all negate the productive responsibilities of women on which a man's daily food and the raw materials for trading depend. These acts also serve to destroy the economic networks among intermarrying groups so important in *moka* exchange.

Strathern suggests that male anger may also be fanned by the fact that these acts are clandestine. It is perhaps this power of silence that best characterizes the affective side of womanhood in Hagen society. Notions of female fickleness, political treason, and sexual disloyalty (*all* women are viewed as promiscuous at heart), appear to be generated by the system that suspends women between the localities and special interests of their consanguineal and affinal kinsmen. They remain the silent pawns who on one plane are submissively shuffled in the service of men along roads for *moka*, but on another plane are surreptitiously destructive, severing these networks or transforming them into avenues for poison. Any denial of their traditional role by women is by definition either criminal or treasonous. It therefore behooves men to exert their dominance over women in the name of social control, and to rationalize this precarious tenure with an elaborate lore of female inferiority. By treating poisoners and other "strong" women severely, their supernatural power may be temporarily subordinated to the mundane authority of males. And while the guilty are publicly humiliated and punished, other Hagen women watch, and then return to their homes to grow vegetables, to herd pigs, and some perhaps—as men fear—to meet a lover, to leave the menstrual hut prematurely, or to foul the food of an invidious husband.

DISCUSSION

It is a difficult task to generalize about horticultural societies as a whole. As noted at the beginning of the chapter, hand cultivation is an ancient technoeconomic adaptation, which triumphed over foraging in limited areas of the world about 10,000 years ago. It eventually provided the basis for sedentary communities, increased population density, and complex sociopolitical superstructures. Our cross-cultural sample revealed a tremendous amount of variation in the relative level of productivity achieved, as measured by dependence upon cultigens in the diet. Most horticulturalists, however, support population aggregates of nonurban proportions, and few achieve true statehood.

Matrilineal and patrilineal horticulturalists seem to differ fundamentally in their dependence upon cultigens and their overall economic strategies. Communities that localize related women and disperse men appear to be particularly adaptive in environments with plentiful and relatively uncontested resources. The localization of males and eventual patrilineal descent seem, in contrast, to result from a reorientation of production toward greater exploitation of resources in competition with others.

The position of women in horticultural society fluctuates with socioeconomic variables in fairly standardized ways, although their precise relationships remain only imperfectly defined. We have noted, however, that women play the major economic role as producers. They are likely to be the exclusive cultivators in situations of low productivity, and to enlist the labor of males in increasing proportion to the importance of cultigens in the diet. Whereas in matrilineal societies women cultivate for the benefit of their own lineage, in patrilineal ones farming activities are undertaken primarily for the husband or his immediate kin group. As we have seen, over half of the patrilineal societies in our sample utilize the institution of polygyny to increase the yield of both cultigens and children for the individual patriarch.

The Hageners provide a good example of the adaptive features of patrilineal horticulturalism in an area of contested resources. The slopes of Mount Hagen are densely populated, and warfare, at least until recently, was endemic. Polygyny has been utilized extensively to increase the wealth of individual households. Of particular importance to males in this society is the collection of pigs for *moka* purposes. Hagen women are valued not only for the production of basic foodstuffs, but for the provision and care of the raw materials with which males may accumulate shell money and increased social status in the community.

The social status of women appears to be uniformly highest in matrilineal societies where the local community is organized around related women. Any form of residence, such as patrilocal or avunculocal, which removes women permanently from their natal household both threatens their security and encourages descent through males. The status of women is more highly variable and uncertain in the case of patrilineal descent. As we have noted, women are more likely under these circumstances to be subject to rigid sexual controls. Even where polygyny is the norm, however, considerable freedom may be expressed in illicit or formalized paramour relationships. Polygyny itself holds advantages and disadvantages for both sexes. The important question for women seems to be how much latitude for independent action is granted in domestic, sexual, and especially in economic relations.

Returning once again to the Hagen, women are political

minors in every important sense. Unlike many African horticulturalists, polygyny seems to offer no escape from the throes of
female inferiority. This is perhaps importantly related to the
overlapping of trade networks with political alliances, hence
their monopolization by males. Even though Hagen women
maintain exclusive rights to certain crops under their care, there
are no markets at which they may exchange their surpluses and
extend their social horizons. As we have seen, stringent controls
on the sex life of women both before and after marriage also
relate to the high value Hageners place upon the extension and
maintenance of *moka* networks through stable marital unions.
What appears as a system of general tyranny on the part of
males, however, is nicely counterbalanced in the Hagen supernatural belief system. It is in this arena that women recoup
some of the power they are denied in daily affairs. Even though
the act of poisoning is a reprehensible crime, the threat of its
use is considered as little more than a social blunder and is generally effective in checking male dominance. The Hagen culture thus provides for the maintenance of an adaptive system of
patriclan alliance while simultaneously placing a mechanism of
checks and balances in the hands of female subordinates.

Women in Agricultural Society

CHAPTER NINE

The development of hand cultivation led to a proliferation of societal types. Some were certainly more successful than others in terms of productive yield. Since horticultural techniques are fairly uniform, the influence of environment seems to have been of great importance. We can speculate that those societies which found themselves in regions with abundant arable land often organized their communities around the localization of related women. These matrilineal societies utilized female kinsmen for the joint exploitation of communally owned fields, and related males as carefully placed binding pins between lineages and local groups. In environments where there was considerable competition for resources, or where, for any reason, greater productivity was valued, the localization of related males was perhaps favored. As we have seen, polygyny is an adaptive institution under these circumstances, since a male may engage several women simultaneously in the business of crop-growing and reproduction.

In such places as Northeast Africa, Southwest and Southeast Asia, Central America, and the Andean highlands, the continuing demand for greater productivity led to the independent development of advanced cultivative techniques. The simplest of these involved the revitalization of soils through organic fertilization, and the harnessing of animal power to prepare the land before planting. A second critical innovation was the artificial diversion of water to fields under cultivation. Manuring, use of the plow, and irrigation—individually or in combination—provided the economic base for some rather spectacular sociocultural developments, including the earliest civilization.

The demand for increased productivity may well have precipitated the demise of matrilineal horticulturalism through new patterns of male localization and polygynous marriage. Similarly, the exploitative patterns favoring patrilineal horticulturalism as an adaptive system were themselves eventually to contribute to its obsolescence. As we shall see, the advanced techniques developed to increase productivity almost invariably demanded the active participation of *males* in cultivation. This represented a significant break with the past, and was to have effects upon the status of women so dramatic that they linger to the present day.

In this chapter, we shall first investigate the significance of economic changes accompanying the agricultural transition. We shall compare a sample of societies utilizing advanced cultivative techniques with horticultural ones with respect to their level of productivity, population density, political complexity, and the sexual division of labor. We shall be interested not only in how, but in why agriculture developed, and why the productive role of women was usurped by males. Our second task will be to investigate the social consequences of the nonproducer role for women. Here we shall find that the pattern of male social dominance becomes greatly exaggerated. Families decrease in size and are more clearly patriarchal, and an elaborate mythology concerning the natural inferiority of women takes shape. Finally, we shall briefly glimpse the lifestyle of women in an agricultural society with the help of a case study of sex roles in an Iraqi village.

ECONOMIC BASIS OF AGRICULTURE

In trying to account for the origin and development of agriculture, it is easy to fall victim to a generalized notion of progress. We could say, for example, that mankind *naturally* evolved from simple to complex, and that the agricultural and urban revolutions were an inevitability of human evolution. Obviously, the cultural accomplishments of our species have not moved along any predetermined course, but have arisen as adaptive responses to a constantly changing set of external conditions.

One persistent feature of human communities consistently linked with economic strategies is population density. As population size increases in relation to available resources, rights to arable land tend to become more strictly drawn. This situation favors the development of techniques both to increase the immediate yield of cultivated fields and to maintain their fertility season upon season:

> Female farming systems seem most often to disappear when farming systems with ploughing of permanent fields are introduced in lieu of shifting cultivation. In a typical case, this change is the result of increasing population density which makes it impossible to continue with a system necessitating long fallow periods when the land must be left uncultivated. When a population increase induces the transition to a system where the same fields are used with no or only short fallow periods, this change often goes hand in hand with the transition from hoeing to ploughing; when the land has to be used continuously, it becomes worthwhile, and indeed necessary, to undertake a large initial investment—the removal of tree stumps and bushes and land levelling— which must precede plough cultivation (Boserup 1970:32–33).

Intensive cultivation appears to have developed in a limited number of centers in the Old and New Worlds (see Childe 1942, 1951; Braidwood and Willey 1962). Wherever these innovations first took place, increased productivity and population growth seemed to have been engaged in a constant footrace. Urban centers arose, and with them socioeconomic classes and divisions of labor based upon criteria other than sex. The production of surpluses for the purpose of exchange became an end in itself, and complex military-governmental structures arose to pursue, control, and defend the increasing flow of wealth. Sub-cultural differences distinguished urban communities from their breadbaskets, the peasant outliers, much as they do today in industrial societies.

The diffusion of advanced agricultural techniques beyond the political domains of innovative centers has been determined largely by the productive requirements of target populations. Northern European societies, for example, with their relatively dense settlement and limited growing season, accepted intensive techniques very early. In contrast, the great majority of sub-Saharan societies of Africa (save those along the desert fringe and eastern highlands) still maintain a successful horticultural adaptation despite their proximity to the Egyptian florescence for nearly 6000 years. Says Boserup:

> Understandably, villagers usually show little enthusiasm for plough cultivation as long as they have land enough to apply shifting cultivation and can cover their protein supply from hunting and fishing or from cattle kept in grazings far from the villages and the crops. And the more the work of hoeing is done by women, the less likely will men be willing to change from hoeing to ploughing (1970:34).

To this statement we might add that all cultures display a degree of resistance to change, and more especially when extant conditions are adequate for the continuity of the community. The agricultural transition, although promising a much greater yield, involves a considerable expenditure of labor. Domestic animals must usually be stalled and tended, and their manure methodically collected and distributed over the fields. Irrigation requires not only the digging of ditches, but their maintenance and some reliable system of water control.

Those societies adopting intensive cultivation were no doubt unaware of its full implications. The existing sexual division of labor was almost immediately contradicted, precipitating corresponding changes in the structure of sociopolitical groups. In

order to examine the characteristics of these agricultural societies cross-culturally, we have again chosen a sample from the
Ethnographic Atlas (Murdock 1967). Three possible sources of
agricultural development are represented in these 93 societies.
The ancient Egyptians and their modern descendants, for example, lie in one of the original centers of innovation, and are
the benefactors of an *in situ* development. Other societies, such
as the Ethiopian Amhara, received advanced cultivative techniques in ancient times through diffusion from adjacent areas.
Finally, there are those agriculturalists—once peripheral to ancient civilizations—who, through colonial expansion, have pro-
ceded to aid the diffusion of these techniques millennia later.
The Spaniards are one such example. Despite tremendous differences in the relative longevity of agriculturalism among sample societies, their overall structures are amazingly consistent.

The Plow, Irrigation, and Productivity. All societies in the sample utilize the plow or irrigation in cultivation, and approximately one-third employ manuring as well. Subsistence techniques are distributed as follows:

Plowing only	5
Irrigation only	29
Plowing and Irrigation	30
Plowing and Manuring	29
Total	93

Variation in the choice of intensive techniques largely reflects the availability of water and of suitable domesticated draft
animals. Taken as a whole, there is no significant difference in
productivity among sample societies choosing one or the other
type of agriculturalism.

Perhaps one of the most effective ways of illustrating the increased productivity and complexity of agricultural communities is to contrast them with the horticulturalists considered in
the previous chapter. Since the two samples are of equivalent
size (104 horticulturalists vs. 93 agriculturalists), we may compare their frequencies with respect to a number of variables.

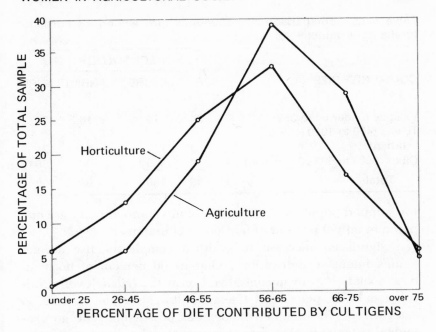

Figure 9–1. A comparison of the contribution of cultigens to the diet in 104 horticultural and 93 agricultural societies.

The effects of plowing and irrigation are illustrated in the degree of dependence upon cultigens. Agricultural productivity statistics are contrasted graphically with horticultural ones in Figure 9–1. From this figure we note that agricultural societies show an average dependence upon cultigens approximately 10 percent greater than do horticultural ones. Corresponding changes in population density and political complexity, however, are certainly disproportionate to such a small increase, and point up some of the inadequacies of cultivative dependence as an index of overall productivity. Population density, however, is perhaps both a cause and an effect of intensive cultivation and productive success. Consider the dramatic increases in community size in the agricultural societies for which there are data in Table 9-1. Village communities account for some 79 percent of the horticultural societies for which there are data, in comparison to only 24 percent for sample agricultural societies. In contrast, 55 percent of the intensive cultiva-

Table 9-1. A comparison of community size among 43 horticultural and 66 agricultural societies

	TECHNOLOGY			
COMMUNITY SIZE	HORTICULTURE		AGRICULTURE	
	F	%	F	%
Villages (under 50 to 399)	34	79	16	24
Towns (400 to 1000+, non-urban)	5	12	14	21
Cities (5000 to 50,000+, urban)	4	9	36	55
Totals	43	100	66	100

tors support population aggregates of urban proportions, as compared to only 9 percent of horticultural examples.

A significant increase in political complexity also accompanies intensive cultivation. Whereas 80 percent of horticultural societies were uncentralized or at the *tribal* level politically, only 46 percent of the agricultural sample may be so
categorized. The number of societies possessing state governmental machinery rises from 5 percent among hand cultivators
to 35 percent among intensive cultivators.

Agricultural societies, threfore, are not merely exaggerations
of horticultural ones. Rather, the greater density factor, which
may have precipitated both intensive techniques and its own
continuing growth, represents a qualitative change—a genuine
evolutionary advance. As populations grew, so did the challenge for effective socioeconomic controls. In the majority of agricultural societies, political centralization and statehood accompanied the transition to intensive farming. The urban
revolution, at least so far, has been a point of no return. For
each civilization that falls, another rises in its place, at times
from its own womb.

Sexual Division of Labor. What happens to the juxtaposition of
the sexes in the economic sphere with the agricultural transition? Once again the contrast with horticultural communities is
well marked. We shall first consider the actual dimensions of
these differences, and then notions that have been advanced to
explain them.

Table 9-2. A comparison of sexual labor division in cultivation between sample horticultural and agricultural societies

| CULTIVATION TYPE | TECHNOLOGY | | | |
| | HORTICULTURE | | AGRICULTURE | |
	F	%	F	%
Female	52	50	15	16
Male	17	17	75	81
Both sexes equally	35	33	3	3
Totals	104	100	93	100

As seen in Table 9-2, agricultural societies are tremendously
consistent in their assignment of cultivative tasks. Some 81 percent delegate males for farming as compared to only 17 percent
of our horticultural sample. Female cultivation, so central to
societies employing hand tools, shrivels in importance to a
mere 16 percent in agricultural cases.

Why do societies widely separated in both time and space so
consistently place the bulk of responsibility for intensive cultivation on male shoulders? Boserup (1970) argues that women
often abandon cultivation by default. With few exceptions,
wielding of the plow in field preparation is a masculine task.
The time-consuming labor of weeding the growing crops is significantly reduced or even eliminated by initial plowing of the
soil. Since weeding is traditionally assigned to women, they
may literally (and perhaps happily) find themselves out of a job.
Retirement to the domestic scene, however, is not always
guaranteed:

> . . . this advantage for the women does not
> last if the pressure of population increases to
> the point where it is necessary to use very
> labour-intensive techniques and to plant very
> labour-intensive crops in order to maintain
> the customary income from a smaller area of
> land. With irrigation, weeding may become a
> heavy burden for the women, and so may the
> transplanting of paddy. But men also get
> more work to do under irrigated farming
> than under plough cultivation of dry crops,
> for digging of irrigation ditches in the fields,

the lifting of water from wells and canals, and the repair of terraces and bunds are usually men's work (Boserup 1970:34–35).

According to the data in Table 9-2, Boserup's suggestion of continuing recruitment of women for cultivative tasks in agricultural societies is definitely a minority pattern. A closer examination of these exceptional cases in the sample yields no easy correlation with density. In some societies where women predominate in cultivation, it appears to be merely a continuation of the horticultural pattern wherein the plow has been introduced by culture contact. Among the Swazi of southern Africa, for example, the use of the plow has been merely superadded to male activities focusing around cattle, while female cultivation continues as before. In addition, special historical circumstances involving the mandatory contracting of males into private industry has also affected labor division at the village level throughout this region. Or, to take another example, the equal participation of men and women in agricultural societies employing irrigation may be encouraged by a *supra*subsistence economy. The Chagga of the Mount Kilimanjaro region of Tanzania produce coffee as a cash crop in addition to daily foodstuffs. Here the active participation of *all* adult members of the community may not be precipitated so much by density as by the desire for profit-making. The situation to which Boserup alludes, in which population density takes precedence over the intervening variables of culture or foreign money economies, may be especially relevant for areas of eastern Asia where human reproductive capacity has seen its finest hour.

An alternative explanation for male usurpation of cultivative tasks in the agricultural adaptation is associated with the dialectical materialism of Karl Marx (1965, orig. 1857–58) and Frederick Engels (1972, orig. 1884). An essential tenet of their philosophy is that control of sociopolitical institutions falls to those who control the means of production. At a certain point in cultural evolution, they argue, the production of surpluses led to an emphasis upon portable property as an avenue to both status and power. The communal kinship group, which they envisioned as being organized on the matrilineal plan, gradually disintegrated as shared rights to cultivate landed property became increasingly less important. The eventual destruction of matrilineal organization and its replacement with the smaller patriarchal family was identified with the marriage of males and portable wealth:

> All the surplus which the acquisition of the necessities of life now yielded fell to the man; the woman shared in its enjoyment, but had no part in its ownership. The "savage" warrior and hunter had been content to take second place and the woman down into the second. And she could not complain. The division of labor within the family had regulated the division of property between the man and the woman. That division of labor had remained the same; and yet it now turned the previous domestic relation upside down simply because the division of labor outside the family had changed. The same cause which had ensured to the woman her previous supremacy in the house—that her activity was confined to domestic labor—this same cause now ensured the man's supremacy in the house. The domestic labor of the woman no longer counted beside the acquisition of the necessities of life by the man; the latter was everything, the former an unimportant extra (Engels 1972:221).

It is doubtful that either Engels or Marx, with their limited ethnographic knowledge, were aware of the productive importance of women in foraging and horticultural societies without surplus accumulations. They viewed sexual division of labor as remaining essentially unchanged through time. The domestic role of women, it seemed to them, became degraded only when it assumed a secondary place to the accumulation of portable wealth as "socially productive work." The male, with his quest for supremacy in the household, and his eventual overthrow of the system in which descent and property rights flow through females, arises clearly as the villain in their scheme. Women thus become just another exploited group in the emergent class society.

The notion that women's participation in production is intimately related to their relative status in society indeed has merit, and will be discussed at greater length below. It is unnecessary to propose a theory of sexist or class conspiracy, however, to account for the position of prominence assumed by males in both the family and production. We must look, rather, for the adaptive advantage of this type of labor assignment. Again, we are reminded of the basic biological differences among the sexes. Males are on the average physically stronger than women; and because of their small temporal commitment to reproduction and child-rearing, they are more mobile. It is precisely because of these natural propensities that males are selected for the herding of large domestic animals in pastoral societies (see chapter 10). The utilization of animal power is merely an extension of herding activities into an area of heavy work also typically reserved for males: the preparation of arable land for planting. Similarly, the digging and maintenance of irrigation ditches requires a considerable degree of strength and investment of time, often at substantial distances from the household.

The male-provider–female-domestic division of labor arose with intensive cultivation, therefore, simply because it worked. As long as cultivation was of the extensive or shifting variety and not of overwhelming importance in the diet, women could handle the primary reproductive and productive responsibilities of society. As soon as crops became of utmost importance, but significantly when they began to be cultivated with intensive techniques requiring considerable strength, time expenditure, and a lack of spatial contiguity to the domicile, men arose as the most fit farm laborers.

It is now time to consider the social consequences of this reversal.

SOCIAL JUXTAPOSITION OF THE SEXES

The adoption of intensive farming by formerly horticultural societies thrusts new economic roles upon both men and women. Changes may begin subtly, almost imperceptibly, until—

perhaps over a single growing season—the community is se-
duced into a complete contradiction of its former pattern. This
not only disrupts domestic and extradomestic routines in the
household, but requires a critical realignment of social institutions, norms, and values.

We shall first examine the structural changes in kinship
groups and family organization that accompany the agricultural
transition. Next, we shall look at the effect of these adjustments
upon the role and status of women, especially with regard to the
social significance of domestic labor and the quality of male-
female interaction.

Social Networks and Domestic Units. In chapter 8, we noted
that the great majority of horticulturalists in our sample, some
60 percent, were patrilineal. To reiterate, this type of social organization, especially when accompanied by polygyny, is particularly well adapted to expansive, exploitative horticultural
productive systems designed to increase the yield of individual
households. It is therefore not surprising that patriliny continues to be strongly represented in agricultural communities as
well. Undoubtedly the great majority of these societies were
patrilineal before their adoption of the plow or irrigation—techniques that allowed them to *continue* their quest for
higher productivity.

Agricultural societies in the sample, however, show a coun-
tertrend in the nature of descent and the localization of kinsmen. Patrilocality drops from 75 percent among horticultural
samples to 66 percent in agricultural ones. Similarly, the incidence of patriliny decreases from 60 to 50 percent. These
changes are related to a trend toward the dissolution of kinship
groups based upon unilineal principles and their replacement
with compact bilateral units. Losses in horticultural and agricultural societies respectively are in the patrilocal-patrilineal categories attributable to an increase in neolocal residence from 5 to
14 percent and in bilateral descent from 15 to 37 percent.

The tendency for kinship and domestic groups to decrease in
size is illustrated more dramatically with the variable of family

Table 9-3. A comparison of family types among 104 horticultural and 93 agricultural societies

| | TECHNOLOGY | | | |
| | HORTICULTURE | | AGRICULTURE | |
FAMILY TYPE	F	%	F	%
Extended	—	—	1	1
Extended with polygynous	27	26	12	13
Extended with nuclear	18	17	42	46
Polygynous	27	26	5	5
Nuclear with polygynous	26	25	12	13
Nuclear monogamous	6	6	20	22
Totals	104	100	92	100

organization. Primary types of families are tabulated for both horticultural and agricultural societies in Table 9-3.

If we take our samples as representative of horticulturalists and agricultural societies as a whole, two trends seem to accompany the adoption of intensive techniques in cultivation. One is a sharp decrease in the incidence of polygyny. This type of family is no longer the adaptive structure it was under horticultural conditions. Since males are the primary cultivators in agricultural societies, the accumulation of multiple wives becomes an economic liability rather than an asset. Therefore, the tendency is for domestic units to become reduced to a single conjugal pair. This second trend, namely nuclear monogamy, seems to be encouraged both by the new division of labor and by the increasingly urban character of agricultural communities.

A decrease in the size of kinship and family groups seems to accompany increases in productivity with both horticultural and agricultural adaptations. Our present samples are too small and the data inadequate to raise this point beyond the level of speculation. Still, if we view the various aspects of social organization as economic strategies, a number of regularities may be observed. Matriliny and patriliny, for example, appear to represent quite distinct patterns of horticultural exploitation. Their adaptational value seems to relate both to specific environmental conditions and intersocietal relations. The matrilineal strategy, at least in its pure matrilocal form, lends itself more to the maintenance of larger extended families and communal systems of land tenure. The patrilocal-polygyny economic strategy, with its patrilineal correlate, seems to initiate a very gradual but perceptible trend of individuation in land tenure and among related households. This is not to say that patrilineal kinship groups are not based upon the same principles of communality as their matrilineal counterparts. The very fact that they localize related males, however, encourages internal divisiveness within these units.

Polygyny, strongly associated with patrilineal organization, represents the first departure from the larger extended family. As noted earlier, it is associated as an economic strategy with optimal cultivative production under horticultural conditions. In terms of kinship group atomization, it lies midway between the extended and nuclear families. Instead of sharing both land-use rights and cultivated produce jointly with other members of the lineage or clan, polygynous households are traditionally economically independent and in competition with one another for any resources held in common by virtue of descent. In the matrilineal-matrilocal situation, males may technically be heads of household, but have no rights to land in the domestic unit in which they reside. With patriliny and polygyny, however, the household head becomes an individual entrepreneur of sorts, accumulating wives, children, increased land allotments, and increased cultigen yields as a family business. If increased population density renders uncultivated land increasingly scarce, this type of family structure is more conducive to the conversion of individual use-rights in land to individual *tenure.*

With the adoption of intensive cultivative techniques, the polygynous family becomes obsolete. The process of individuation in family structure intensifies as women assume an increasingly nonproductive economic role. Rights to land held in common by a number of related household heads may persist for some time, especially where their joint labor continues to be adaptive—such as in the preparation and maintenance of irrigation ditches and water-control systems. Nuclear, bilateral, and neolocal families as an economic strategy arise largely under urban conditions. These highly mobile, independent units are perfectly adapted to a market economy, wherein labor itself is an exchangeable commodity that may be used to acquire all the other necessities of life. The high level of productivity achieved with intensive cultivation thus allows the aggregation of communities specializing in the manipulation rather than the actual production of foodstuffs. Nuclear monogamy may diffuse from urban to rural areas as the latter become increasingly dependent upon the expanding market economy, or it may arise independently where population pressure on land results in the creation of fixed boundaries and private ownership.

The Inside-Outside Dichotomy. As the level of productivity in society increased, kin-based production and consumption units decreased in size and complexity. They did so in response to new economic strategies. Women's status and role in society was also subject to constant revision. Economically, females have occupied the role of producers first for large extended households, and then for smaller one-male polygynous groups. As we have seen, there is a general lowering of female status from the matrilineal to the patrilineal situation, but polygyny itself often allows a high degree of independence and self-expression for women. With the innovation and spread of intensive cultivative techniques, however, women dropped out of the mainstream of production for the first time in the history of cultural evolution. The consequences of this reversal in economic roles permeated every corner of their social experience.

What did the assumption of an exclusively domestic role mean for women? A ubiquitous accompaniment of the agricultural transition was the erection of rather rigid categories, corresponding to the new pattern of sexual division of labor, which distinguished the production of goods for consumption from work connected with the domicile. This conceptual distinction of domestic and extradomestic labor, or what we call the inside-outside dichotomy, had the effect of isolating the sexes from one another, and women from public life. Decreased spatial

mobility for females is one of the outstanding characteristics of
the agricultural adaptation:

> Because village women work less in agricul-
> ture, a considerable proportion of them are
> completely freed from farm work. Sometimes
> such women perform only purely domestic
> duties, living in seclusion within their own
> homes, and appearing in the village street
> only under the protection of the veil, a phe-
> nomenon associated with plough culture,
> and seemingly unknown in regions of shift-
> ing cultivation where women do most of the
> agricultural toil (Boserup 1970:25–26).

Indeed, many agricultural societies place a high value upon
the lifelong restriction of women to the physical confines of the
domicile. Such is the ideal pattern in those embracing the Islamic region. The segregation of women, known as *purdah*, is
often a sign of wealth, since secondary personnel must be available to handle those domestic tasks which would remove wives,
however briefly, from the household grounds. The quality of
male-female relationships in a patriarchal, agricultural society is
illustrated in the following description of sex roles among the
Kanuri of northern Nigeria:

> In upper class families, women are in *pur-
> dah* (restricted to the household) and live at
> the back of the compound furthest away
> from the entrance. They leave the compound
> only on rare occasions and even then they
> must seek the permission of their husbands
> well in advance. They are usually accom-
> panied on such excursions by servants who
> may escort the upper class lady half way
> across the emirate to visit her own family for
> a ceremony at which her presence is
> required. On the other hand, peasant women
> must go to the well at least twice a day for
> water, and in some villages this means a
> walk of several miles. These women work on
> the farm plots of the various members of the
> household during the short growing season

and sell cooked foods. Ordinary women use the occasions away from their husband's households to meet and talk freely with other women, and sometimes, of course, with other men.

For the most part relations between husbands and wives are highly formalized. They avoid using one another's names in conversation. In public only the most necessary interaction takes place between them when other people are around. Women walk generally behind their husband when the two are going somewhere together, and even in the household the woman remains or should remain inside the compound. When he is not working, the husband sits most often in the hut or in front of his household. A visit to a Kanuri household brings the husband to the entrance hut if he is inside, and at the same time the wife retreats out of sight. For the most part women remain in the company of women, and men with men. Only in a few rare cases have I ever observed public expressions of friendliness between a husband and a wife.

Cultural tradition has ordained that men are the dominant members of society, and women, more specifically wives, are to be submissive. This is both Islamic and Kanuri. It is good and seemly for a women to obey her husband and to appear humble in his presence (Cohen 1967:42–43).

Such norms of sexual behavior are not, of course, limited to Islamic regions. Much the same quality of interaction among men and women is characteristic of peasant village life in southern Europe.

As may be expected, the tendency for agricultural societies to isolate their women is dramatically reflected in the area of sexual freedom. Types of premarital sexual activities and their sanctions are tabulated for 53 agricultural societies for which there are data in Table 9-4.

When compared with horticultural data in Table 8-2, the data

Table 9-4. Types of female premarital sexual activity in 53 agricultural societies according to descent

PREMARITAL SEX	DESCENT			
	MATRILINEAL	PATRILINEAL	BILATERAL	TOTALS
Precluded by early age at marriage	0	3	0	3
Allowed; no sanctions unless pregnancy results	1	1	1	3
Freely permitted; no sanctions	3	3	5	11
Trial marriage; sanctions if pregnancy results	0	0	1	1
Prohibited, but weakly sanctioned; not rare	1	5	7	13
Virginity required; premarital sex rare	0	12	10	22
Totals	5	24	24	53

for Table 9-4 present some interesting contrasts. While the few matrilineal representatives remain predictably permissive, patrilineal and bilateral agriculturalists exercise much more stringent controls over the sexual life of young women than do patrilineal horticulturalists. Since, in both situations, the societies in question are male-centered and place a high value upon determination of paternity, observable differences may relate to variation in spatial mobility for women. In horticultural societies their role as producers—that is, field workers and active local traders—demands both freedom of movement and social interaction. The narrowing of economic activities to the household with developed agriculturalism, however, tends to limit the social horizons of women to similar boundaries. The life cycle of females in this situation seems to radiate around their development of skills in one domestic unit and their ultimate transfer, with commensurate compensation, to another at marriage.

Although no data on postmarital sexual activities of women are available for our sample, we know from individual ethnographic studies that extramarital liaisons are generally prohibited and severely sanctioned (see Mohsen 1970). Some societies (indeed some states in America) permit the murder of a woman by her husband or her own kinsmen if she is discovered in an illicit sexual act, but this courtesy is seldom if ever extended to women. In contrast, extramarital liaisons are often acquiesced in, permitted, or even formalized for males. Asymmetrical privileges may also be extended in the area of divorce. The ease with which marriage may be terminated by Muslim males is famous, while a similar action may be discretely requested by women only in cases of sexual impotency. Successive divorces typically have no effect upon male eligibility, but may seriously hinder a woman's chance of remarriage.

Agricultural societies, then, generally prefer to keep a woman as isolated from public interaction as possible. Indeed, her value as a potential spouse may depend upon the degree of innocence and mystery she is able to maintain. The social segregation of the sexes accompanying intensive cultivation thus surrounds the woman with a highly charged set of taboos. Perhaps more than with any other economic adaptation, the behavioral sets of men and women in agricultural societies are diametrically opposed by culture. Sexuality is certainly one of the most dynamic examples of role complementarity. As the sexual life of women falls under the control of society, so sexual activity for women becomes a social obligation symbolically detached from individual gratification. For females, nonparticipation in extradomestic production, protective spatial isolation, premarital chastity, and institutionalized frigidity go hand in hand.

Because economic duties and primary social foci for women

are both limited to the immediate confines of the domicile, females become largely social appendages of their fathers and
husbands. With the disappearance of large communal kinship
groups, women are increasingly isolated from the security of
and identification with their own natal kinship aggregates. Polygyny, once offering considerable spatial mobility and a degree
of social and economic independence to women, disappears as
an adaptive pattern with developed agriculture. As family units
shrink in size and increase in self-sufficiency, women come to
rely upon their husbands for subsistence. In many cases, economic dependence is complete. Female labor, encapsulated as
it is, becomes focused upon repetitive, monotonous tasks inside
the domicile. Their isolation from "outside" activities eliminates access to avenues of political power and the control of
property, both real and portable. In sum, the overall status of
women in agricultural or peasant society is one of institutionalized dependency, subordination, and political immaturity.

Why did women assume this inequitable social position? Did
the usurpation of cultivative tasks by males make this juxtaposition of the sexes somehow inevitable, or did males deliberately
seize the opportunity to limit the social horizons of women?
Once again we must eliminate any conspiracy theory of cultural
evolution. It is probably safe to say that the agricultural transition in various parts of the world led to similar labor divisions
and hence to role stereotypes among the sexes. All cultures
wrap their adaptive institutions in an elaborate mythology. In
the case of sex behaviors, the new producer role for males was
accompanied by a wealth of favorable, positive stereotypes em-
phasizing their physical, intellectual, and emotional fitness for
"outside" activities. Women, who may have only recently left
the bulk of cultivative labor to males, are rather abruptly redefined as the sex best suited for menial, repetitive, and non-
creative tasks associated with domestic routines. Their physiological aptitudes for child-bearing and child-rearing are
traditionally emphasized, and henceforth provide the major avenue for socially recognized self-accomplishment. The physical
and socioeconomic isolation of women from the fundamental institutional event systems of these cultures is traditionally ac-

companied by biases stressing their *inability* to cope physically
or intellectually with such activities, and their ubiquitous need
for both the supervision and protection of males. This dependency theme for women is underscored in religion, morality,
and law among agricultural socieites, and shows great persistence, even in those subsequently swept by the industrial revolution.

Caste, Class, and Colonialism. Now that we have presented the
general profiles of women's role in the two major types of farming communities, we must comment briefly on intervening variables that may impinge upon traditional patterns of male-female
interaction. The sexual divisions of labor in horticultural and
agricultural societies, so important to the definition of male and
female ideal behaviors, may be significantly altered by outside
cultural influences. Furthermore, the quality of male-female interaction within these societies may not be fixed, but may instead be in a state of modification according to distinct and fluctuating social contexts. Two primary sources of variation will
concern us: sexual interaction across caste or class lines in
highly stratified societies, and the effects of European colonialism upon indigenous economies, divisions of labor, and sex behaviors.

The tendency for agricultural societies to be associated with
greater density, productivity, and protourban or urban communities introduces complex social stratification as a complicating
factor in norms of sexual interaction. Centralized political systems are typically characterized by economic specialization and
the subsequent development of social classes. Similarly, the expansive economies of agricultural societies make more likely
actual territorial expansion of political units into areas occupied
by distinct cultural groups. The amalgamation of these subordinate populations to the intruding state, if they are not assimi-
lated, results in the generation of racial or ethnic subcultures
and their possible fossilization into caste divisions.

Since both castes and classes are *ranked* in the societies that
embrace them, an entirely new dimension is added to domi-

nance and subordination patterns among the sexes. For example, in caste societies, wherein an individual's lifelong status is determined by birthright, men may be regarded as superior to women in their own caste but inferior to women of castes higher than their own. Social classes that place great importance upon ancestry may assume a similar significance for male-female interactions across these socioeconomic and subcultural divisions. In agricultural societies with open class systems, where overall status is *achieved* rather than ascribed by birth, the prestige of upwardly mobile males may be extended to their wives and daughters as well. Such upper-class women may be submissive in the domestic context, but command deference from any male whose status is lower than that of their social reference point—their husband or father. Where women in agricultural societies profit socially from their class or caste membership, this coveted position may usually be traced to a consanguineal or affinal relationship with dominant males.

Of all the intervening variables in traditional male-female juxtapositions, however, European colonialism ranks high in disruptive potential for both horticultural and agricultural communities. The assault on indigenous sex roles occurred along many fronts. Colonial administrators and missionaries took the initiative in inculcating European institutions and value systems. Since the culture they brought with them had a strong patriarchal base, the social and economic horizons of colonized males were characteristically broadened at the expense of women. Christian theology was, in many ways, as restrictive upon female roles as was Islam. The purported virtues of chastity and sexual fidelity were among the first foreign biases to be impressed upon subordinate populations. But the system of morality the colonists sought to impose had much deeper economic prerequisites. Polygyny, much to the chagrin of men of the cloth, remained in force as long as it provided the most adaptive social structure for maximal production.

The most effective type of warfare waged against indigenous institutions and sex role behaviors was economic rather than ideological. As we have seen, any change in sexual division of labor has important ramifications in the social arena as well. Co-

lonial administrators, because of their own cultural bias, defined the basic household unit as the nuclear family with the
husband-father at its head. In cases of matrilineal descent, the
entire authority structure and principles of kinship group formation were thereby undermined. Further, the household head
was placed in the position of primary economic responsibility
by colonial governments. As in European culture, the husband
was expected to provide food and material items for members of
his domestic unit—a role quite foreign to males in most horticultural societies. In some cases, men merely increased their
participation in cultivative tasks within the bounds of the existing technology. In most, however, the economy of colonized
societies was significantly altered, and the reins of these new
forms of production were placed squarely in the hands of the
chosen heirs of European technology—male household heads:

> . . . Europeans showed little sympathy for
> the female farming systems which they
> found in many of their colonies and in those
> independent countries where they settled.
> Their European acceptance that cultivation
> is naturally a job for men persuaded them to
> believe that men could become far better
> farmers than women, if only they would
> abandon their customary "laziness" (Bos-
> erup 1970:54).

One of the enticements for men to become involved in farming was the simultaneous introduction of intensive techniques
and cash crops (not to mention frequent taxation payable only in
foreign currency). In many cases, males were instructed in
types of cultivation that guaranteed higher yields, and at the
same time provided sources of portable wealth and status. Old
horticultural techniques were often continued by women, along
with their responsibility for providing dietary staples. Although
in some cases females may persist in the cultivation of food
crops, this activity is no longer accorded the same social significance:

> Such a development has the unavoidable
> effect of enhancing the prestige of men and

of lowering the status of women. It is the men who do the modern things. They handle industrial inputs while women perform the degrading manual jobs; men often have the task of spreading fertilizer in the fields, while women spread the manure; men ride the bicycle and drive the lorry, while women carry headloads, as did their grandmothers. In short, men represent modern farming in the village, women represent the old drudgery (Boserup 1970:56).

Enculturation of males to the dominant society thus typically begins with their recruitment into the mainstream of the colonial economy. This may take the form of intensive cultivation of cash crops or actual wage labor. As subjects of the earliest educational efforts, and the primary links to desired foreign material items, men soon assume a social position superior to that of women. This asymmetry may also be extended to rights in land, and eventually to actual land ownership. Because males have been chosen as intermediaries between the old and new traditions, it is they who deal with "outside" activities—those involving the intrusive culture. "Inside" activities, identified with women, become conceptually limited to the domicile, and at times to cultivative tasks associated with daily staples.

Where the colonial regime is particularly exploitative of indigenous wage labor—where, for example, males are recruited into industry for extended periods and return to segregated regions with little or no accumulated capital—women may remain the primary producers for village households out of necessity. In these situations a sharp dichotomy in technological sophistication and productivity develops between urban industrial centers and rural agrarian ones where villagers may live at *sub*-subsistence levels. In general, however, the more dependent that males become in their involvement with the economy of colonial or developing nations, the more, in turn, women become dependent upon men. Thus, as males begin to consistently exchange goods and services for part or all of the domestic necessities, the cultivative labor of women diminishes in scope and importance.

What we have called the inside-outside dichotomy, therefore, may be imposed upon horticultural peoples through the introduction of intensive techniques and cash crops, or through industrial wage labor. Both encourage portable wealth orientation for and accumulation by males, a decrease in the productive importance of women, and the development of the independent nuclear family. The increasingly domestic, subordinate role for women, underwritten in Christian and Islamic morality, thus becomes a self-fulfilling prophecy generated in economic conditions and rationalized in religion.

The case study that follows offers us a unique opportunity to view the effects of the agricultural adaptation upon male-female roles in a society where the veiling and seclusion of women is a requirement of daily life.

CASE STUDY: EL SHABANA WOMEN

The informants for our agricultural case study are spouses, Elizabeth Warnock Fernea (1965) and Robert Fernea (1970), who spent the first 18 months of their marriage (1956–1958) in the tribal sector of a small Iraqi town, Daghara (El Nahra). Robert Fernea, then a predoctoral anthropologist pursuing his dissertation research, lived in the economic, social, and political world of men—a world largely foreign and taboo to the settlement's women. Elizabeth Fernea, a journalist, agreed to conform to the local custom of female seclusion, and thereby to experience firsthand the life of El Shabana (El Eshadda) women behind the protection of veils and mud wall enclosures. Her fascinating narrative, *Guests of the Sheik,* when combined with the more formal anthropological data of Robert Fernea's *Shaykh and Effendi,* provide us with a rare opportunity to view simultaneously the full spectrum of male and female roles in a highly dichotomized agricultural society.

The Setting. The village of Daghara lies within the Mesopotamian zone encompassed by the great Tigris and Euphrates Rivers. It was in this vast, arid, alluvial plain that one of the earliest irrigation civilizations was born approximately 7000 years ago. Nourished by the controlled diversion of waters from the seasonally flooding twin rivers, complex states and empires dominated the area which is now southern Iraq for millennia. A significant break with the past, however, occured in 1258 A.D. when the ancient capital of Baghdad was overrun by the forces of Hulagu Khan. For the next seven centuries, until the British assumed control following World War I, centralized political systems linking the countryside to urban centers virtually disappeared. In the rural areas, smaller autonomous tribal groups continued much as had their ancestors, although with renewed challenges from their at times hostile physical and political environments.

One of the primary challenges for tribal peoples of the countryside was the effective control of water. Southern Iraq is a land of seasonal extremes. Rain is rare from May through October, and temperatures sometimes soar to 125 degrees in the summer months. Winter, in contrast, may bring freezing temperatures and torrential rains, which cause the great river basins to flood unpredictably and uncontrollably. After the fall of centralized political systems in southern Iraq, the coordinated control of dikes and reservoirs throughout rural zones was discontinued. Although tribal groups, at the local level, continued to divert water to their fields and exhibited considerable expertise in adapting to or altering surrounding conditions, their control over water left much to be desired. Planted fields were continually threatened by persistent summer droughts, which dried up irrigation canals, or by winter rains, which washed away both crops and fertile topsoils. In addition, the competition of neighboring political units for the control and use of available water often led to open hostilities.

During the late 1950s, the people of Daghara settlement were the benefactors of a centralized water control system begun by the British and continued and expanded by the Iraqi government. The disastrous annual flooding of the Tigris River, which regularly invaded even the city of Baghdad, was effectively controlled by 1958. The Euphrates Valley south of the capital, however, is relatively flat and still subject to the unpredictable meandering of waterways. Areas converted into marshes one year may the next be abandoned by rivers charting a new course southward. Villages such as Daghara are thus subject to some of the same uncertainties of flooding and drought as in the days of political decentralization.

In Daghara itself, seasonal climatic extremes are commonplace. Winter rains, which persist for several days at a time, turn the town and surrounding countryside into a mass of mud that is often impassable to wheeled vehicles and even a discouragement to animal and pedestrian traffic. Disease and death are common during this cold, wet season because of the lack of adequate nutrition, heating, and medical aid. Spring brings dust- and sandstorms. With summer, skies are cloudless and temperatures extremely high. Water shortages are most critical during this extended arid season, when crops, domesticated animals, and humans struggle against hunger, heat exhaustion, and dehydration. Between the extremes of summer and winter, spring and fall offer moderate temperatures and adequate moisture for both pasturage and the cultivation of crops.

The tribal people of Daghara, the El Shabana, cultivate barley, wheat, and to a much lesser extent wet-rice. Fields are prepared for planting in the fall. Low, rectangular plots are plowed with the aid of horses. They are then sown by the scattering of large amounts of seeds on the freshly turned earth. A portion of the low mud walls that surround each field is then removed to allow periodic flooding from a nearby irrigation ditch. The cultivation of rice requires a constant water supply (an increasingly rare phenomenon in Daghara). In this case fields are seldom plowed, but rather are flooded and trampled to remove surface irregularities. Rice seed, which has been germinated in seed beds, is then broadcast in the padis, which are kept inundated until harvesting time nears. Vegetable gardens are also sometimes cultivated by women in the immediate vicinity of their domiciles. Date tree groves in this permanent settlement are owned by individual families, and provide abundant fruit from which can be derived an amazing variety of food products.

In the cultivation of cereal crops, no weeding is done and no fertilizers are applied. Fields are ideally left fallow for one year. In the past, tribal groups simply moved to new areas as the surrounding countryside's fertility became diminished. Rural populations were thus able to maintain essentially horticultural settlement patterns to which had been added the plow and irrigation. In recent times, however, physical and social factors have both posed additional problems for the El Shabana farmer. Daghara's region suffers from a progressive salination of the soil—a condition that, encouraged by poor drainage, results in the accumulation of mineral salts and renders the soil infertile. The traditional solution, in which farming families migrate, has recently been discouraged by land registration programs. As a result, soil deterioration is progressing even more rapidly than before, encouraging indigenous peoples to abandon agriculture more and more for herding or for urban wage labor.

The settlement of Daghara in many ways represents a cross-section of southern Iraqi social and occupational groups. It

Plate 6. Iraqi woman and child from a village near Daghara.

houses peoples of similar cultural heritage, but of highly variant lifestyles and social outlooks. The El Shabana compose only one segment of this busy administrative center. We shall first be interested, therefore, in the relationship of the tribal barrio or sector to other ethnic divisions in Daghara, and in the hierarchical internal structure of the El Shabana themselves. We shall then examine the lifestyle of El Shabana women and men in more detail.

The Town and Its People. Daghara is a settlement of approximately 3000 people, and the administrative center of a district of some 26,000. The populated area of the town is bifurcated by the Daghara canal, a tributary of the Euphrates River and the source for local irrigation networks. This waterway is in a sense a social boundary as well. The town has three main groups of citizens: government officials and their families, people of the market or *suq,* and tribespeople. Each group views its membership as exclusive, socially distinct, and morally superior with respect to outsiders; each segregates itself spatially within the settlement.

In 1958 Daghara contained somewhat fewer than 100 administrators, including police, clerical workers, engineers, teachers, and medical personnel. The majority lived on the north side of the canal, east of the main road, although some of Daghara's educated, Western-oriented citizenry, or *effendi,* occupied the opposite southern bank as well. This latter area was the site of the civil servant's clubhouse, a modest structure that served as the hub of *effendi* social life. Among the civil servants themselves, cliques were formed primarily on the basis of age and educational experience. Older administrators generally lacked Western training, and were the most politically conservative segment. Among all personnel, they were the least likely to be transferred or promoted. The middle-aged *effendis,* who were educated during the British occupation, tended to hold the highest administrative positions and had the greatest stake in maintaining the status quo. These officials, such as the mayor and doctor of Daghara, often traveled some distance to other

villages, towns, and cities to socialize with individuals of similar status. The youngest and most liberal *effendi* subgroup was
composed largely of teachers, who were employed at the segregated girls' and boys' schools in Daghara. Although educa-
tors were often very dedicated to the overwhelming needs of
the community, the majority of civil servants avoided any deep
involvement with market or tribal peoples. All but the older *effendis* could look forward to promotions and subsequent
transfers to other towns.

The people of the market also congregate on the north side of
Daghara Canal, but to the west of the main road. Merchants
wear traditional attire called *dishdashes* (long robelike garments), and place primary emphasis upon extended patrilineal
kinship. Many own their own dwellings in Daghara, as well as
individual stalls in the *suq*. Shopkeepers and tradesmen make
their living by retailing items such as cloth and other manufactured goods purchased wholesale in the cities, or by providing
needed services such as smithing in exchange for currency or
produce. The ethic of individual competition among market
people is unpopular and rare; economic ambitiousness is instead expressed by the extension of the family enterprise to
other *suqs* in neighboring towns. Merchants tend to form a
closed, endogamous cluster of families, and like the *effendis*, to
congregate separately for social purposes in the community's
several coffee shops. The nature of their economic activities,
however, casts them into secondary relationships with both
civil servants and tribespeople. Administrators depend for basic
foodstuffs upon *suq* shopkeepers, or poorer merchants who
spread their goods informally along the canal edge. Since the
great majority of tribespeople produce no extensive surpluses,
they are dependent upon the merchant community not only for
manufactured items, but at times for the bare necessities of life,
especially in lean seasons and before harvesting. Debtor and
creditor relationships therefore tend to dominate interactions
between merchants and tribesmen.

The focal group of our case study, the El Shabana, form a
tribal cluster on the southern bank of Daghara Canal, which in
1958 contained from 450 to 600 adult males. (Because of the

traditional patrilineal emphasis, women and children are seldom included in census statistics.) The El Shabana are one of
12 tribes in the region, some 5000 strong in adult male membership, forming a loose confederacy known as the El Aqra. Politically, each component tribal unit has a leader, one of whom
assumes the position of *ra'is* or "paramount sheik" of the entire
El Aqra confederacy. During the time of the field study, the El
Shabana head, Sheik Haji Mujid Atiyah El Sha'lan, occupied
this important position. The tribal sector of Daghara was thus a
political and religious center for traditional activities over a
wide region. There, men of the El Shabana and other El Aqra
tribes gathered in the huge *mudhif* or guesthouse of the sheik
for all important cultural and ritual occasions. Such regular
visits were taken as a sign of respect and allegiance to the
sheik's authority, and contributed to the cohesiveness of both
the tribe and the confederacy.

Within the El Shabana and other tribal units, patrilineal descent and what anthropologists call the principle of segmental
opposition form the ideal organizing structure. Put simply, descent is traced through males only, with the correlate that at
each new generation sons begin their own respective sublin-
eages (rather than continue the single patriline of their father).
Small patrilateral families are thus typical, along with households in which brothers jointly share certain economic rights or
resources. The precise relationships of lineages and sublin-
eages, spanning generations, are set to memory and form the
basis of alliance and cooperation within the tribe. In the past,
closeness of kinship appears to have had a spatial dimension as
well. That is, the closer two males were related, the closer spatially would be the arable land to which they held cultivation
rights. In recent times, however, the relationship of tribal peoples to land has been disrupted by drought and land registration
laws. Near the turn of the century, the temporary drying up of
Daghara Canal encouraged many farmers to abandon their
fields, or to sell them cheaply. As a result, the largest and most
fertile parcels are now owned by the sheik and his brothers.
These men have become, in essence, estate-holders, and the
majority of El Shabana tribesmen tenant farmers or *fellahin*.

The El Shabana thus share a cultural world quite independent of and distinct from the marketpeople or of the *effendi* representatives of the modern Iraqi state. The merchant's profit motive runs counter to the tribal conception of honor based upon generosity and valor. Although shopkeepers provide needed products and services to the Daghara population, they also hold the impoverished El Shabana tribesmen in a state of constant economic dependency. Similarly, the *effendi*, with their modern concerns for national policies and for individual mobility, as well as their shedding of traditional garb and custom, represent to the El Shabana a degeneration of ancient moral tenets. Relations have at times been further strained by the exercise of excess authority by resident administrators in the legal affairs of tribesmen.

In general, however, the three segments of the Daghara community strike a balance between mutual exclusiveness, interdependency, and respect. The El Shabana sheik and the *mukhtar*, the elected official of the marketplace, are both legally recognized by the Iraqi government, and must be consulted by the *effendi* mayor in all important administrative matters. High-ranking members of the merchant community may visit the tribal *mudhif*, or, along with El Shabana notables, be welcomed at the civil-servant clubhouse. Furthermore, and perhaps most significantly, all three community segments are joined by the Islamic faith, and by the performance of its rituals.

Men, Women, and Purdah. It is difficult to discuss the economic, political, or social networks of the El Shabana—or perhaps even to ponder the physical setting of the tribal community—without reference to the variable of sex. As in most cultures, El Shabana men and women are thought to be quite distinct creatures with disparate temperaments and potentials. But in Daghara, as in much of the Islamic world, such differences are a self-fulfilling prophecy encouraged not only by a conceptual dichotomization of behaviors, but also by an actual physical segregation of the sexes in daily life. El Shabana women observe the religious prescription of *purdah*, which requires their abstention from public view and free social intercourse.

The architecture of Daghara's tribal sector in many ways reflects this duality of experience. Housing consists largely of modest rectangular dwellings constructed with mud walls and strung closely along narrow streets. Surrounding each house is a high, solid, mud wall topped with a generous covering of thorny brush. These enclosures, with their bolted gates, stand as miniature fortresses against the entry or penetrating eyes of strangers. The treasures they protect are not primarily material, for the El Shabana are a poor people with little portable wealth. Rather, they stand in purported defense of female virtue—an overt marker of the boundaries of social and sexual experience. It is in the world of interior courtyards and, when male visitors are present, more distant rooms of the domicile that women ideally spend their lives. Males, in contrast, focus their activities outside the household in the streets, the marketplace, the sheik's *mudhif*, and in the fields of the Daghara countryside.

Such high priority is placed on the seclusion of women from males that couriers are extensively used to run the essential errands that would normally take females outside the household. Only the poorest, most pitiable woman, for example, would herself venture to the *suq*. But there are times, of course, when domestic activities, attendance at religious rituals, or the mere visiting of neighbors draws women into the adventure of the street. On these and all other occasions where males are present, women are shrouded from head to foot in concealing garments, which expose only their eyes to those of strangers. These long, black cloaks, or *abayahs*, though quickly discarded in the privacy of their homes and at informal gatherings of women, are an essential ingredient of respectability in mixed company.

Despite its concealing qualities, the *abayah* serves not so much as a form of portable seclusion as a mechanism of flight from one controlled social situation to another. Any female excursion from the household must be approved in advance by the male, and women must proceed directly to the destination in question. Casual walking for pleasure by female companions in the streets or the surrounding countryside of Daghara is practically unknown. Although women may occasionally venture from the settlement to cultivated fields, they are always escorted by their husbands or other male kinsmen on whom their safety and good reputation depend.

Such precautions—the confinement of women behind locked gates and *abayahs*—relate, of course, to the regulation of female sexual expression. The *abayah* covers a woman's body, and, symbolically, the pride of the lineage. As many other patriarchal societies, the El Shabana feel that only by maintaining the social and sexual purity of the women of a household may a lineage arrange suitable marriages and thereby ensure its continuation. In this society, the familiar requirement of virginity is extended to concealment of the entire body as well. Courtship is eliminated altogether, and it is not until the new husband lifts the veil of his bride on their wedding night that he is either pleasantly or unpleasantly surprised. Males, in contrast, have no sexual restrictions either before or after marriage and may, in accordance with Islamic custom, take as many as four wives simultaneously.

The wide gulf between the introverted behavior of females and the relatively uninhibited, extroverted behavior of males characterizes other social contexts as well. In public, spontaneous, open conversations between the sexes are taboo, as are expressions of familiarity or affection among spouses. Within the household, relationships are essentially paternalistic, and reflective of the extension of asymmetrical privileges to men in the culture as a whole. Women are expected to display modesty and deference toward their husbands. Meals, for example, are served first to the males of a household; the leftovers are later consumed by women and children. Females have no public voice and no legal status apart from their subordinate relationship to a male parent or spouse, and are in effect insulated from the major political activities of the community. They therefore remain jural minors throughout life, and are prohibited from the exercise of independent action by those who claim responsibility for their deeds. Such actions as daily purchasing, freedom of movement, educational instruction, and certainly marriage are subject to prior approval by the male household head. Failure to secure such approval or deliberate defiance of a rule of behavior results in severe physical punishment at the hands of a father or husband which, in the past, included execution.

Growing up female among the El Shabana is thus a long lesson in acquiescence. Both sexes are convinced at an early age, by instruction and the observation of culturally determined behavior, that male and female natures are unavoidably contrastive and opposed. Males, they observe, are the *born* politicians, warriors, heavy laborers, and economic transactors. Women, in contrast, are *naturally* more retiring, and less capable of the decision-making and independence of action required for such activities. Given her innate vulnerability and sense of personal modesty, what normal woman would dare enter this dangerous world of strangers! The segregation of the sexes is therefore perceived as a common-sense accommodation to a law of nature, rather than a system that maintains an efficient sexual division of labor or balance of inequality. Such folk theories, reiterated even today by social scientists (see Tiger 1970a), are part of our agricultural heritage and are interesting examples of how cultures rationalize their adaptive institutions.

By Western standards, at least, it would seem that the extension of asymmetrical privileges to males makes their task of conformity to ideal cultural roles a rewarding experience. That is, social, political, and economic dominance are traits more easily accepted by the chosen sex than by the subordinate one. It would be a mistake, however, to portray El Shabana males as tyrants, or their wives, sisters, and daughters as downtrodden underlings. Women do not appear to feel particularly oppressed by men or by the requirements of *purdah*, but rather seem to enjoy the good company of females within the security and comfort of locked gates and concealing garments. For with the asymmetrical privileges of males come asymmetrical responsibilities—responsibilities for digging irrigation ditches, plowing fields, tending and selling livestock, paying household debts, defending the honor of the lineage, and going to war. Responsibilities so heavy that dominance becomes an honorific status rather than a social concession; responsibilities so awesome that the high mud walls add an air of pleasant encapsulation to the domestic, nurturant, and socializing activities of women.

Producers and Processors. As we have seen, the El Shabana view male and female as highly dichotomous categories of humanity bridged by an elaborate etiquette of behavior. This pattern of interaction is designed by their culture to underscore and preserve the monopolization of primary economic, social, and political roles by males and male-centered kinship groups. A significant observation here is that inequality in some productive situations, whether among the sexes or among social or ethnic groups, may have adaptive value for the survival and perpetuation of a given society at a given point in time.

But do men monopolize *all* important cultural roles in agricultural communities? Do women occupy themselves solely with cooking, cleaning, baby-making, and child care? While these domestic tasks are certainly important, the economic responsibilities and contributions of El Shabana women are considerable, and extend far beyond the context of household maintenance. In the cultivation of staple cereals, men control the distribution of land rights and water, and assume full responsibility for the digging and maintenance of irrigation ditches and for overall field supervision. Women and children, however, are not prohibited from field labor, and may indeed be recruited for planting and harvesting activities. In addition, the growing of vegetables is left almost exclusively to women, who cultivate small gardens within their walled courtyards.

Females, therefore, do play a role in primary food production. Their involvement with staple crops, however, is greatest *after* harvesting. By and large, the processing requirements of raw produce in agricultural societies are significantly more time-consuming than among foragers or horticulturalists. Agricultural production inevitably involves the cultivation of grains, which must be hulled, washed, winnowed, or pounded into flour before use. Although these tasks also beset horticultural cereal-growers, societies employing intensive farming techniques tend to far surpass the former in yield and attendant volume of processing requirements. The reduced mobility and limited growing season of agriculturalists place a high priority on the storage of food for future use. Thus, women in agricultural societies, while relieved of many of their former productive responsibilities, inherit labor involving the conversion of raw materials into usable goods. Agricultural production is a two-stage process, involving not only the amassing of harvested crops, but their subsequent transformation into a variety of storable products prior to actual food preparation and consumption.

If males are the primary producers among intensive cultivators, women are the systematic manufacturers. Among the El Shabana, Fernea (1965:216) refers to the cleaning of rice and flour by women as an "everlasting task." Vegetables such as okra must also be specially processed for future use, while perishable dates are dried or converted to syrup and vinegar. Women are responsible for the manufacture of nonfood items as well. Following the shearing of sheep, for example, females of the household wash the wool in the Daghara Canal and bring home the fleece to dry. Wool is then spun into thread and subsequently woven into cloth. When these seemingly endless processing tasks are combined with the cyclical event systems of reproduction, child care, laundering, cleaning, and food preparation, it would seem that El Shabana women have little time to venture from the domicile, to explore avenues of self-expression, or to build social networks. But the very complementarity of male and female economic roles dictates a certain parallelism in work and leisure cycles. Both farming labor and processing labor, for instance, are unevenly distributed over the annual growing season. In addition, the overwhelming majority of men and women work *individually* rather than in communal groups at their respective tasks. *Both* sexes, therefore, tend to experience daily, weekly, and monthly fluctuations in activity and in socializing opportunities.

In addition to the economic tasks performed in the households of their husbands, some females engage in small-scale independent pursuits. One woman of Daghara, for example, specialized in churning butter, while others raised lambs and chickens. Still others combined economic gain with social activity and individual talent. Women skilled at sewing, embroidery, and crocheting were contracted by others for the making of *abayahs* or decorative clothing and bedding. Daghara also boasted a tatooist who for a fee adorned the bodies of young

women with provocative designs. Religious specialists or *mul-
lahs* led women's prayer meetings during Islamic holy day celebrations, and were compensated for their services and marked
off from others by their eccentric personalities. Despite their
legal dependency upon males, then, El Shabana women experience a degree of economic independence in extradomestic pursuits. These activities are limited in scope and necessarily secondary in terms of expenditure of time when compared to
domestic obligations. Still, the performance of services forms an
important rallying point for female social interactions.

A second deviation from the general economic impotence of
women lies in their accumulation of jewelry. Gifts of ankle and
arm bracelets, necklaces, and earrings of gold may be bestowed
upon a woman by her father, fiancé, or husband. Elizabeth Fernea learned of the importance of jewelry in her early encounters with the sheik's harem:

> I asked Selma how much her ankle brace-
> lets cost.
> "Forty pounds," she said proudly, "for
> one," and pulled out the pin so that it could
> be taken off and examined. It must have
> weighed at least half a pound. "All gold,"
> she added.
> The women began pointing out her indi-
> vidual necklaces and bracelets, telling me
> the cost and the Arabic name of each. Later I
> estimated that Selma wore on her person at
> least $1000 worth of gold. She said that the
> pieces of jewelry had been presents from her
> father and from the sheik, and repeated, "It's
> mine, my own."
> This was literally true, I found. A woman's
> jewelry is her own insurance against disas-
> ter, and the community may take action
> against men who attempt to seize their wo-
> men's gold (Fernea 1965:33).

The amount of gold accumulated varies considerably with socioeconomic standing. Selma, the favored wife of the sheik, was
especially well-endowed, but the majority of women in the El
Shabana settlement were less fortunate. Amina, a slave girl at-

tached to the sheik's household, for example, came from an extremely large and poor family. At a mere 15 she had been married to an elderly man who left her nothing at his death but the gloomy prospect of returning to the squalor of her father's household. Since the sheik had purchased her and installed her in his domestic service, Amina's life had been happy. On one occasion, however, she lamented to our informant: "If your husband is really kind to you . . . get a lot of gold jewelry from him while you are still young. You never know what will happen" (Fernea 1965:74). With respect to gold, Elizabeth Fernea was somewhat of a curiosity to village women. If her husband could afford to decorate his house with such prestige items as a radio or refrigerator, why had he not decorated his wife with fine jewelry? Such was the query of the settlement tatooist and beautician:

> I replied that I did have some gold in America which I had left behind for fear of losing it on the long trip to Iraq.
> "Wear it, wear it, you silly girl," Qanda burst out. "What good does it do lying in a box far away?" Then she launched into a short, earnest sermon about the value of gold as ornament, but secondly and most important, the necessity of gold in every woman's life as insurance in case her husband should die or leave her or divorce her. I had not heard such an eloquent statement of the "diamonds are a girl's best friend" theory in a long time (Fernea 1965:134).

The prospect of poverty for women deserted by their husbands is a very real fear in the tribal settlement. Chances of remarriage (and hence the reestablishment of economic complementarity) are limited, and widows, divorcees, or wives without husbands must be enterprising in order to survive. Personal gold may also be sold by women to provide educations for their children, especially in instances where sons have fallen into disfavor with their father.

If we were to sum up the economic role of women in El Shabana society, the complementarity of their tasks with those of males and the mutual dependency of the sexes should be emphasized. In terms of real estate or use-rights, women are propertyless and hence dependent on males for access to raw produce. Women without men must part with their savings or throw themselves enthusiastically into extradomestic pursuits in order to purchase basic food items from others. But males are equally dependent upon women for the processing of produce and the manufacture of essential nonfood items, in addition to the performance of domestic routines. Although our informants cite no statistics, one would assume from their accounts that bachelors or widowers living alone are rare or entirely absent in the tribal settlement, their marriage or remarriage being greatly facilitated by the custom of male initiative in pairing arrangements. As we have seen, women may further their economic value by engaging in extradomestic services or enterprises. Although household revenue is still largely under the supervision of male heads, women can and do accumulate portable wealth in the form of gold, the possession and transfer rights of which are inalienably theirs.

Behind the Abayah. The inequality of men and women seems to permeate all interactions across sexual lines. This situation greatly encourages bonding patterns *within* rather than between these groups. Herein, perhaps, lies the key to our understanding of the adaptive nature of such alienating cross-sex relationships. The El Shabana cultural system both requires and perpetuates male bonding in a setting where intensive cultivative techniques are applied and where, until recently, competition for resources is high. It is a system that effectively maintains the inside-outside dichotomy of sex roles so central to the agricultural adaptation. Males, linked by kinship networks both socially and politically, assume the primary responsibilities of basic food production, the distribution of wealth, and the maintenance of favorable power relationships.

It is perhaps small wonder, then, that in such societies anthropologists have tended to overlook the activities of women as merely secondary and supportive, or to assume that husband-fathers form the central focus of female identity and social relationships. The agricultural adaptation, however, has often had the effect of polarizing *both* men and women into cohesive, homogenous social units. Commonality of experience among male-female dyads is often limited to their special-purpose functions within the household. These interactions, although essential to economic complementarity and reproduction, may be peripheral to the primary reference groups of *both* sexes. In other words, the conjugal family may provide a point of articulation between male and female worlds, but the focal social group of neither.

Cultural systems like that of the El Shabana thus encourage the formation of social networks along sexual lines, which may exceed in everyday importance simultaneous relationships across sexual boundaries. Such bonding patterns seem equally likely to occur among women as men.

To Westerners, mandatory seclusion of females may bring visions of gloomy solitary confinement in an unending abyss of domestic drudgery. In the absence of plumbing, modern appliances, and in many cases electricity, much hard work is performed by the El Shabana woman. In addition, within the household they are not only manual laborers, but social inferiors as well. The world of women, however, extends far beyond the limits of the domicile to a rich network of peer relationships. It is in this latter context that women learn how to view themselves as well as their more limited relationships with males.

One of the basic elements of esprit de corps among those living behind the *abayah* is the requirement of seclusion itself. From an early age, girls are encouraged to develop warm, open relationships with females only. Physical and social settings must be dichotomized into masculine and feminine, structured and unstructured, proper and improper. The world inside high mud walls and concealing garments provides the stage for industriousness, comradery, and self-expression. Outside these boundaries lies a vast inventory of experience which is both fascinating and potentially dangerous. Just as girls and women flock to strategically placed peepholes along courtyard walls to view an object of interest, so they scurry excitedly when the sound of a gate threatens to penetrate their camouflage.

The sense of personal modesty and shame that both encourages and maintains sexual segregation, however, is not an exclusively feminine trait. If a male intruded so unexpectedly as to confront a woman without her face veil, the embarrassment would be his as well. Men reportedly do not even discuss women publicly; such comments are considered highly improper. The discomfort El Shabana men display in situations where female contours are exposed or where men and women interact freely is illustrated by an incident related by the sheik. The latter, undoubtedly the most well-traveled and sophisticated man of the tribal settlement, was once forced to flee a burning hotel during a vacation in Cyprus. Fernea relates:

> Hustled downstairs and out onto the lawn, the four Arabs were greeted by a sight which Haji told Bob he never forgot. All the hotel guests were assembled on the lawn, attired in odds and ends of clothes which they had been able to don quickly in their flight from the burning building. Some wore almost nothing. These half-clad men and women were talking and joking together, and Haji, coming from a society where strange men and women *never* talk together, and the women are always covered up to their eyes, found the scene very upsetting. Eventually the fire was put out, and little damage had been done. The guests returned to their rooms, but Haji had had enough. Next morning he packed his bags and returned to Lebanon (1965:174).

But for women, the consequences of social or sexual impropriety go beyond personal uneasiness or temporary embarrassment. The maintenance of sexual purity, personal modesty, and good character is a serious matter, for women bear the final responsibility for undue familiarities. The *abayah* thus conceals potentially provocative body parts, while the social prohibition of free conversation among opposite-sexed strangers discourages the initiation of casual relationships. The mobility of women, restricted during the day, is entirely prohibited after dusk except for special ritual observances. Many of the temptations and opportunities for pre- or extramarital liaisons are thereby culturally eliminated. But such rules, of course, are sometimes broken. Young girls, while remaining sexually chaste, may in the spirit of adventure scurry together through the darkened streets to spy on a special event at which their presence is prohibited. On occasions such as marriage ceremonials, women of all ages may risk disciplinary action to catch a glimpse of the elaborate spectacle:

> In the alley we almost collided with a black-veiled figure who turned out to be the sheik's daughter Samira. She and Laila dissolved in helpless laughter at the comic coincidence of their meeting.
>
> "Watch the slops," giggled Laila, pulling Samira out of the center of the road.
>
> Samira let out a mock scream and clung foolishly to the side of the house nearest us. This brought on more laughter, until we were silenced by Laila.
>
> "Shhh," she said sternly. "We must be quiet. The sheik doesn't know Samira is out, but she says the guards are looking the other way tonight so all the women can see the dancing. Alwiyah is out too. They are the two bravest."
>
> We took hands and moved along in the general direction of the Sayid's *mudhif,* heading toward a yellow glow of light which was reflected in the sky above the flat roofs of the houses. Somewhere a donkey raised his head and brayed fiercely; Samira clung to me and screamed; we all laughed again. There was much laughter in the crowds that moved along with us—high-pitched giggles of children, deep laughter from old women experiencing again, without tension or pain, the excitement of their own wedding nights, long since past (Fernea 1965:143–44).

Such breaches of seclusion regulations are expected, and
punishment of recalcitrants is often only a formality. But violations that reflect negatively upon a woman's character are
serious indeed. Fernea (1965:256–66) relates one such incident
in which she was accompanied by Laila, a niece of the sheik, on
an afternoon ride in the country with the girl's school teacher,
the latter's cousin, and his driver. In conformity with social custom, the women sat together in the back seat of the automobile
and did not engage in coversation with the men. The three
female companions were subsequently dropped off for a pleasant stroll in the countryside, and later met the cousin and driver
for their return home. What had seemed like an innocent adventure assumed nightmare proportions shortly after their arrival in
the settlement. Mohammed, the Ferneas' otherwise demure
houseboy, excitedly admonished our informant for her conduct,
and proceeded to tell her of the possible repercussions of the afternoon excursion:

> . . . "Sitt, you are a foreigner and although
> you wouldn't, I should think, want to ruin
> your good name, you don't have to live here.
> The schoolteacher's cousin is a very bad
> man; he drinks and gambles and stays with
> bad women in Diwaniya."
> . . . "Laila is in great danger," he said. "If
> anyone"—he paused and repeated "—any-
> one were to know that she went riding with a
> strange unmarried man without men from
> her family present, she could be killed. Her
> father would have to do it to save the honor
> of the other women of the family. Do you un-
> derstand?"
> . . . "What shall I do, Mohammed?"
> "You must deny that Laila was with you. Say
> it was a cousin of the schoolteacher. I know
> Laila went and so do some of the children
> who saw you go, but I will deny it and so will
> the children because they like Laila" (Fernea
> 1965:261–62).

And so the lie became the official version of the day's events,
saving Laila from, at the very least, a severe beating from her fa-

ther. Laila's father admonished Robert Fernea sharply, however, for permitting his wife to be in the company of such a
rogue. Elizabeth Fernea, who had thus placed both her husband and Laila in awkward positions, had to react submissively
to the polite reprimands of Laila's sisters. Although the people
of the settlement were secondarily aware of Laila's excursion,
Mohammed's silence and the unanimous acquiescence of concerned women in essence negated the serious breach of conduct. Laila had learned her lesson, and after our informant's
tongue-in-cheek reassertion of Laila's innocence to harem
women some two months later, the matter was officially
dropped.

The necessity of maintaining the purity of unmarried girls
relates to the strict requirement of virginity at marriage. As
noted earlier, the maintenance of a bride's mystery must extend
even to the appearance of her facial contours. Girls, however,
are often aware of their future husband's identity and physical
attributes even as children. Ideally, El Shabana marriages are
arranged between the children of brothers. Often such unions
involve brother-sister exchange, wherein male cousins marry
one another's sisters. This type of reciprocal transposition of
women eliminates the need for brideprice, which in this society is so substantial that its accumulation often poses a serious
obstacle to matrimony. A prospective bride in any case has little
control over the choice of her marital partner, which is approved by her mother and negotiated by her father. A young
bride's sadness may be great if she has been promised to an old
man or to someone from a strange settlement who will take her
from the security of her natal family and childhood friendships.
Cousin unions, however, seem to be the object of great anticipation. The following conversation on the subject took place between Elizabeth Fernea and Laila.

"Would you want to marry your cousin?" I
asked. "Would your older sister Sanaa want to
marry her cousin?"
Laila looked shocked. "Of course," she
said. "Sanaa is to marry Sheik Hamid's son
Ahmar. She has always known she would

marry him and she has been in love with him for years."

"But how can she be in love with him if she never sees him?" I asked. "Doesn't your father arrange the marriage, and doesn't she wait until the wedding night to be with him for the first time?"

"Yes, yes," said Laila impatiently, "but Sanaa has known Ahmar since she was a baby. They played together all the time till Sanaa put on the abayah and went to sit in the house. She watches for him when he goes by our house; we tease her about him." She looked at me oddly. "Naturally she wants to marry him; who else would she want to marry?" (Fernea 1965:158).

Once the engagement is negotiated by prospective in-laws, the bride-to-be may receive gifts of gold from her fiancé and purchase jewelry from the dowry contributed by her female friends and relatives. This will be worn on her wedding day. The bride is literally displayed before women friends and relatives at her father's house before the actual ceremony takes place. Typically she is seated on a special white cloth and dressed in the finest garments her family can afford. Her makeup is the province of the local tatooist, who also may add permanent designs to her calves, buttocks, breasts, or other body areas. Unless the new wife is to live in a distant settlement, the bridal bed on which the marriage will be consummated, with its finely embroidered and crocheted sheets and pillowcases, is also displayed to guests. The women known to the bride thus gather to sip water and smoke cigarettes, to cheer and praise the young woman and her finery, and to ponder the husband's reaction when he first removes her veil.

Simultaneous with the bridal viewing, food and entertainment are provided by the groom's parents for his friends and relatives. After men of the prospective husband's family have finished feasting, musicians and dancers perform. The climax of the entertainment focuses on a male dancer who dons female clothing and engages in a frenzied display of pelvic movements, symbolic of the sexual activity that awaits the newlyweds. The entertainment is ended by the arrival of the *mullah*, the holy man who performs the ceremony. He leads attending males down to the canal for ritual washing, and then to the home of the bride. The groom and *mullah* enter the dwelling, which is now occupied only by the bride and the respective mothers of the couple. Interestingly, after the vows have been spoken and papers signed, the mothers-in-law remain in the bridal chamber to witness the sexual consummation of marriage. This, according to El Shabana custom, must be done to verify the virginity of the bride.

On one occasion, Elizabeth Fernea and a number of female friends secreted themselves in the darkness outside a bride's household just as the consummation of marriage was to take place. She offers the following description of the ensuing events:

> The mullah came out.
> "He has gone to his bride, I think" said Laila.
> The drum roll continued and the crowd shifted uneasily, whispering and chattering to each other.
> "It's taking him a long time," cackled one old lady. "What's the matter with him, is he sick?"
> "Shh," said Sherifa sternly, "mind what you say," but the lady continued to cackle.
> Minutes went by and the crowd grew quieter. The drum roll continued.
> There was a loud cry within, and in a few minutes the bridegroom emerged smiling. After a triumphant volley of rifle shots, the groom's friends and relatives pressed forward to shake his hand. The women surged into the compound to congratulate the bride, who would remain in her room, and to see the bloody sheet displayed by the bride's mother and the groom's mother, incontrovertible evidence that the girl was a virgin and a worthy bride (Fernea 1965:147–48).

Following the wedding, the bride takes up residence near her husband's kinsmen which, in the case of cousin marriage, involves a move only to a different household in the settlement. Bonds with women of her own lineage and with female friends are therefore maintained. But now that the long years of strict segregation from a male partner have officially ended, does not the conjugal relationship become the focus of female social activity and identity? Although there may be considerable affection among spouses, their personal interactions are limited, and revolve largely around food and sex. Despite the stringent cultural requirements for chastity and sexual abstinence before marriage, frigidity is not viewed as an inevitable feminine condition. On the contrary, women are socialized to cherish future opportunities for sexual intercourse:

> The passion was important; the married women would giggle and tell the unmarried ones that they had yet to learn how much fun it could be to sleep with one's husband.
> "Always?" I asked.
> "Of course," they would reply. "If we did not enjoy sleeping with them, how could we love them?"
> I thought to myself, truly how else, for they seldom saw their husbands except to serve them at meals, and at bedtime (Fernea 1965:186).

Thus, for a woman, the conjugal relationship provides a stage for both pleasure-seeking and social approval. Her position vis-à-vis her husband, however, remains subordinate and unequal, and places her in his service in exchange for emotional and material rewards. In this domestic context, a wife receives approval for exceptional skills in crafts, housekeeping, and especially in food preparation, since in accordance with Arab custom, she must play hostess to any and all male guests.

But an adequate wife must also bear children. Responsibility for barrenness among the El Shabana falls always to the woman, and is a legal ground for divorce. As in most patrilineal societies, a woman feels especially pressed to produce a son who will carry on his father's line. Men whose wives have given birth only to daughters are the object of joking among their peers, a situation bound to influence the esteem in which a wife is held. In the world of men, daughters are at best a mixed blessing. Although they are revered for their domestic labor and for their exchange value at marriage, they will eventually leave their natal household and make no further substantive contribution to their fathers. To our informant's surprise, this preference for male children was reiterated rather strongly by her friend Laila, one of nine sisters: "Boys are really the best, Beeja; they can take care of their mother when she's old. What good are girls?" (Fernea 1965:294). Nevertheless, a strong bond is felt to exist between mothers and daughters—a bond, as among fathers and sons, based perhaps in the timeless narcissism of self-duplication.

A new wife's motivations for immediate pregnancy are therefore rather complex. Children, on the one hand, will help to cement the marriage and provide a degree of social insurance against divorce. The production of male heirs will also win her the favor of her husband. It would be a mistake, then, to view the childbearing efforts of women as merely unselfish boosts to the husband's social prestige. The wife and mother roles provide for women the most reliable sources of economic and social security. Keeping a husband is an essential ingredient of economic complementarity, whereas pleasing one brings the promise of gold or other accumulable wealth. Daughters provide a social reincarnation in the next generation, while sons may be relied upon for support and a position of honor in old age.

Since the interaction of men with their wives and children is limited, the matricentric family is an important unit of socialization and a basic cell in the more extended social networks of women. As we have seen, the requirements of seclusion have the effect of segregating women from men, but not from one another. Indeed, the fact that relationships across sexual lines are so limited in scope seems to throw women into more intense association with one another. Fernea observes:

> . . . friendships among women were much more important and much more intense in this segregated society than in our own. Where the men spend the major part of their

> time away from women, the women have to
> depend on each other for company, for sup-
> port, and for advice. A man might be a de-
> voted father or brother or a loving husband,
> but in El Nahra [Daghara] he was seldom, if
> ever, a companion. I never heard a woman
> discuss her emotional attitude toward her
> husband or her father or brother, but long
> hours were spent in debates about the fidel-
> ity or indifference of women friends. Natu-
> rally these friendships became most serious
> for women who were single or childless or
> widowed, but even married women with
> large families had close women friends for
> whom they composed poems or cooked spe-
> cial sweets (1965:255).

During her early stay in Daghara, our informant was viewed
as an object of curiosity, joking, and pity by women of the settlement. Her longing for companionship was exacerbated by the
teasing and rejecting behavior of those women who paid rare
visits, and for a time it seemed that she would remain a social
outcast. Like strangers in all cultures, Elizabeth Fernea was vic-
timized by the ethnocentric viewpoints of those upon whom
she had intruded:

> "Poor girl," Kulthum had said, summing it
> all up. No mother, no children, no long hair,
> thin as a rail, can't cook rice, and not even
> any gold! What a sad specimen I must have
> seemed to them. I smiled again at my image.
> What kind of charity combined with compas-
> sion had persuaded them to take me in?
> (Fernea 1965:316).

Only later did she learn that her initial feeble command of Ar-
abic had caused many to question her intelligence, and hence
the desirability of her company. For among women, sharpness
of wit is greatly appreciated, and joking behavior is a cherished
element of informal conversation. Once her friendship had
been sought and received by a niece of the sheik, however,
Elizabeth Fernea earned a sponsorship into the ranks of
women. From that point forward, her daily activities and per-

sonal experience were merged with those of other settlement females, so much so that escape from group membership was sometimes as difficult as previous attempts to obtain it. On one occasion, for example, the Ferneas were overjoyed by the visit of two American male engineers to their home. The prospect of conversing in English, playing cards, and consuming a case of beer was especially inviting for Elizabeth Fernea, whose interaction not only with Americans, but also with men, had been so long denied. No sooner had the guests arrived, however, than several village women appeared at the gate. In an act of seeming consideration, they had come to "keep her company," assuming that, by custom, she would be left alone huddled in her *abayah* while her husband entertained his guests. She was thus forced to spend the entire evening with her female companions within agonizing earshot of the festive drinking and card-playing of the men of her own culture. It was only after the evening and the last drop of beer had been spent that the women sleepily bid her goodnight, convinced of their heroic gesture of loyalty.

But despite the solidarity of female social groups, Westerners (themselves just emerging from agricultural sex molds) may question the legitimacy of a system based upon inequality. How, they ask, can women be truly happy if they are disenfranchised and have no voice in community affairs? The assumption that contentment naturally follows the option for or exercise of coercive power is, of course, an ethnocentric one. So too is the elevation of male, community-management activities to the highest level of significance. The majority of event systems in El Shabana society that could be termed "political" are outside the daily experience of women and may affect their lives only indirectly. Their most significant social arenas, at least in the ethnographic present, encompass the household, the family, and female corporations. In these contexts women do exercise a degree of control over their own destinies. As in all other aspects of El Shabana culture, however, the power of women is differently conceived and derived. Whereas male authority is based on the control of material resources and physical coercion, female influence is solicited from the supernatural.

In this respect, we see some similarity with the exercise of power by females in Hagen society (see chapter 8). El Shabana women, however, command no such potential for wielding their bodies in a poisonous fashion. Rather, they tend to rely upon a limited number of female specialists from whom may be purchased amulets or charms to achieve a desired effect. Such icons may be used as contraceptives to protect an individual from illness or the Evil Eye, or to win the favor of a loved one. Control over reproductive functions is also sought in this way, primarily for the inducement of pregnancy or for the determination of a child's sex before birth.

But such magical power may be drawn upon for malicious purposes as well. One of the most common breeding grounds for such action is the prospect of polygyny. In Daghara, fear of the dissolution of marriage is perhaps exceeded only by the fear of supplantation by a new wife. Women speak of the threat constantly, dreading a losing battle for dominance in the household, an unequal distribution of favors by the common husband, or his sexual preoccupation with a younger, more attractive wife. These fears, however, seem to be entirely out of proportion to the actual incidence of polygyny. In the tribal settlement of 108 households, Fernea (1965:163) was able to find only 9 with any past or present incidence of multiple marriage. In this and perhaps other societies where jealousy among co-wives is culturally patterned, the institution of polygyny poses more of an economic hardship than an advantage. In other words, multiple marriage is of low frequency because it is maladaptive in situations of agricultural production. Social attitudes toward polygyny therefore move in line with economic realities. Its decreasing frequency is rationalized by attribution to often-unrelated phenomena.

Some women in the tribal settlement, for example, credit the low incidence of polygyny to their own initiative. Fernea (1965) relates the case of a woman, notorious for her disgruntled character and domestic ineptitude, whose husband had decided to wed a respected widow with two young children. The proposed arrangement met the approval of concerned villagers, since it was felt that the husband would not only make a substantial domestic improvement, but also provide needed support for the fatherless family. The present wife, however, was enraged, and borrowed taxi fare from her mother to enlist the aid of a wise woman some fifty miles away:

> By late afternoon everyone in El Nahra [Daghara] knew where Hussna had gone, and her husband, sitting nonchalantly with friends in the coffee shop, was eyed curiously by acquaintances and passers-by. What would happen? Even I stared at the ordinary-looking man as Laila and I walked by on our way to visit the school. Abad's hand trembled a little, perhaps, as he raised his glass of tea to his lips, but that was all. The widow kept to her house. We were told that Hussna had returned late the same night, and that in the morning the widow's oldest boy was sick with fever and dysentery. The child recovered, but Abad abandoned his plan of taking another wife. Hussna reigned alone and triumphant in her slovenly house and Abad was seen more and more often in coffee shops. Within a few months the widow and her children were forced by economic circumstances to leave the village and move in with relatives in Diwaniya (Fernea 1965:161–62).

In another case, the youngest and most favored of the sheik's three wives was thought to have achieved her position of prominence by consulting with the so-called Book of Stars. There is some disagreement across age and sex lines, however, over both the respectability and the potency of such magical formulas. It is generally recognized that belief in these supernatural manipulations runs counter to the teachings of Islam. Still, the attraction of magical aids is great, and even the younger women of the settlement or those familiar with the Koran condone their use for other than malicious or sinful purposes. Males are publicly sarcastic and sceptical about the powers of wise women, but show by their actions much less conviction in their own personal invulnerability to such forces.

The locus of female power thus rests in this uncertainty, in psychosomatic phenomena, and in the social pressure that results from bringing disputes to public forum through supernatural means. It also most certainly rests in their value as childbearers, socializing agents, housekeepers, and processors—roles in every respect complementary to those of males and vital to the continuity of the community.

The Expanding Frontier of Baghdad. Rooted as they are in the agricultural past, traditional sex roles throughout rural Iraq are gradually experiencing the assault of modernization. In the cities, industrial technology is making many of the same demands for a mobile, open labor force that occurred in nineteenth-century Europe (see chapter 11). Although moral sentiment for the seclusion of women is still strong, females are attending secondary schools and universities in increasing numbers. This portal to the outside world has greatly encouraged extradomestic employment. Moreover, Western women living in urban areas, with their revealing garments, freedom of movement, and comparative equality with men provide glaring examples of viable, alternative sex behaviors.

In Daghara itself, changing economic factors have already impinged upon traditional El Shabana sex roles. The increasingly poor yields achieved by independent farmers and sharecroppers have encouraged a seasonal or permanent migration of males to the cities for wage labor or higher education. This growing absenteeism, particularly by young men, has had a tremendous impact on the social horizons of women. Because of the shortage of marriage partners standing in the proper kin relationship, matrimony is no longer so automatic as it was:

> I had wondered why Moussa's beautiful daughters were unmarried, and also why three of the sheik's marriageable daughters were still sitting in the harem. There was no one for them to marry. Prohibited by the code of their tribe from marrying men other than first cousins or similar close relations,

they were trapped by circumstance, by social
forces within Iraq which they were powerless
to change. One was an unusual case, an
elopement. But the sheik's sons and his
brother's sons were something else, something new. These young men had been sent
to Baghdad to study in the new co-educational colleges there and they had emerged
with Westernized ideas. They wanted to
marry educated girls who could be companions as well as wives and mothers. The
boys could find such girls, for Bob had told
me that Jalil was hoping to marry a pretty
schoolteacher in Diwaniya and the sheik's
brother had reportedly quarreled with his
two sons over the issue. The girls were the
ones who suffered, destined to stay year
after year, unmarried, in their fathers'
houses, passed on finally in their old age to
their married brothers to support. An empty
and meaningless life, the reasons for which
they would never be able to understand (Fernea 1965:159–60).

But traditional barriers against education for village women
were being lifted even by the late 1950s, and attendance at
school and subsequent outside employment are beginning to
replace the extended confinement of domestic spinsterhood. An
increasing number of young women are thereby achieving *effendi* status on their own initiative, and beginning, however
gradually, to deviate from old moral prescriptions for both dress
and social interaction. Even during the Ferneas' stay, younger
women, although still veiled in public, had begun to abandon
their traditional black robes for printed housedresses (Fernea
1965:128). Moreover, the progressive and outspoken fiancée of
Daghara's *effendi* engineer, boldly announced her intention to
abandon the *abayah* entirely following their marriage (Fernea
1965:308).

External forces that have encouraged the horizontal mobility
of El Shabana men have thus had a similar although somewhat
delayed effect upon women. The advancing poverty of Daghara's countryside has removed men from the soil, and in doing

so has upset the delicate balance of economic complementarity among the sexes. Divorced, deserted, and widowed women are more likely to remain without partners than in the past, and to call upon their own talents for survival. Married women in larger towns are already seeking full-time employment such as nursing outside the home to supplement their family incomes (Fernea 1965:238). Wage labor appears not to reflect negatively on the character of women if domestic obligations are met, and for many has taken the place of more traditional craft specializations and related enterprises. Thus, the system that insulates women from the outside world, from men and, ironically, from the comparative isolation of housewifery in modern nuclear families, seems to be a vanishing phenomenon in the face of sweeping technological advance.

DISCUSSION

The transition from horticulture to agriculture involved an overall increase in productivity, population density, and political centralization. The tendency toward urban aggregation was paralleled by a general decrease in family size and the generation of bilateral kinship units. For our purposes, however, the most significant alteration accompanying the adoption of intensive cultivative techniques involved the sexual division of labor. As we have seen, males usurp the position of women as primary producers in the great majority of agricultural societies. The economic horizons of women are thereby gradually limited to the physical and social space of the domicile. Entirely new mythologies appear to redefine the innate aptitudes of the sexes with respect to domestic and extradomestic horizons. For women, this involves an elaborate syndrome of subordinate, submissive, and dependent behavior—a permanent adolescence—in their relationships with males. On a scale of social and political maturity, a woman's role is strangely intercalary. Although she exerts dominance over her children, she is cast in a childlike role in the presence of adult males, including, ironically, her own mature son. If the patriarchal family structure

does indeed generate strong cross-sex and cross-generational af-
fections among parents and children—Freud's famous Oedipal
and Electra complexes—it is perhaps less of a mystery if this
uniquely ambiguous position of women is taken into consideration. Within the context of the domicile there is little to distinguish the behaviors of mothers and female child-peers in their
relationships with males. Their conceptual merging is therefore
easily accomplished. Perhaps only in a patriarchal culture could
we expect the melodious longing: "I want a *girl* just like the
girl that married dear old Dad." Similarly, for women, behavioral patterns standardized in relationships with their own fathers, save actual sexual contact, are indistinguishable from
those ideally assumed toward a prospective spouse.

Complex social stratification and the intrusion of foreign cultures may add new dimensions to the juxtaposition of the sexes.
Since no major colonizing power has been organized on the
matrilineal plan, the effect of such political expansions has been
an elevation of the status of males at the expense of females.
The most dynamic revision of agricultural sex roles, however, is
initiated by fundamental changes in the nature of production.
Economic systems that are best fostered by the efforts of both
sexes in basic extradomestic tasks tend to reverse the trend of
sexual dichotomization. Two deviations from farming adaptations, pastoralism and industrialism, must now be examined.

Women in Pastoral Society

CHAPTER TEN

Foraging, horticulture, and agriculture have been considered as the three primary economic adaptations in cultural development prior to the mercantile and industrial age. A fourth option, herding or pastoralism, has an antiquity comparable to that of horticulture, although its origins and evolutionary status have been the subject of scholarly debate for some time. Interest in pastoralists as predators on settled communities goes back to the fourteenth-century scholar Ibn Khaldun (1958). During the Enlightenment, scholars such as Turgot (1844, orig. 1750) proposed herding as a general stage in cultural evolution following foraging and preceding the development of cultivation. In the nineteenth century, emphasis was placed upon changes in social organization rather than on technoeconomic factors as the marker for evolutionary stages. Morgan (1877), for example, saw pastoralism as a secondary development of horticultural communities, important primarily because it involved a form of portable, accumulable wealth, which precipitated a change in the reckoning of descent. This position was amplified by Engels (1972, orig. 1884) who, like Morgan, interpreted the herding adaptation as the first deviation from settled matrilineal horticulturalism, and the first step toward the enslavement of women.

Modern works on the evolution of culture, such as those of Steward (1955) and Service (1962), are based upon progressions of increasing sociopolitical complexity. Since their concern is not primarily economic, the specific problem of pastoralism is ignored. It is now generally agreed, however, that independent herding communities did *not* antedate the domestication and systematic cultivation of plants. As we shall see, the majority of pastoralists depend upon gardening for at least part of their diets. The hypothesis that herders represent spinoffs from sedentary farming communities is supported by known historical origins of modern pastoralists, and by the gradual fluctuation of many of these groups between nomadic and settled life (see Barth 1961).

Pastoralism appears to represent one extreme on a continuum of dependence upon herd animals and cultivation for subsistence, in which segments of sedentary tilling communities may, during periods of scarce resources (i.e., droughts, overpopulation), come to depend increasingly upon the products of their herd animals for subsistence. Food on the hoof allows greater geographical mobility, and the invasion of ecological niches unsuitable for, and hence uncontested by, cultivators. During periods of plenty, when the size of one's herds becomes cumbersome or provides the wherewithal for purchase of arable land, pastoral segments may be repatriated to villages. It is not at all unlikely that pastoralism has followed this cyclical pattern since its earliest development. The question of whether independent herding represents an intial departure from horticulture or from agriculture is still unanswered. It appears, however, that pastoralism is an option open to both variants of cultivators.

Our first task will be to outline the general characteristics of the pastoral adaptation, and to distinguish its major variants. As we shall see, the economic and social juxtaposition of the sexes reflects specific variation in food-getting activities. The lifestyle of women among the Wodaabe Fulani of northern Nigeria will then be examined as our case study.

ECONOMIC BASIS OF PASTORALISM

Since many settled farming communities possess large domesticated animals, and since many nomadic herding communities depend upon cultigens for subsistence, it is often difficult to arbitrarily draw a line between horticulturalists and agriculturalists on the one hand, and pastoralists on the other. Those societies in the *Ethnographic Atlas* (Murdock 1967) which emphasize herding vary in their dietary dependency on these activities from nearly 100 percent to only 50 percent. Since the latter figure appears to represent the baseline of herding dependency in the absence of sedentism, and since this level is represented by such typical herders as the Nuer of the Sudan, we decided to define as pastoral those societies in which the meat and dairy products from herd animals constitute *at least half* of the diet.

Our present sample consists of 44 societies that meet this criterion. These representatives will allow us to explore the range of variability in subsistence, community, and political structure, and the sexual division of labor among pastoralists. Our goal will be to derive a model that will allow us to predict the economic juxtaposition of women and men on the basis of subsistence emphasis.

Herding as a Way of Life. Old-world herding societies are limited to Central and Southwest Asia, and the northern, Saharan, Sudanic, and eastern areas of adjacent Africa. In the New World, pastoralism, such as that of the Plains Indians, was purely a post-contact development. Similarly, animals such as the llama and alpaca of the South American Andes, although herded by agricultural communities, never provided the basis for an independent, nomadic way of life. In our present sample, 12 societies are found in sub-Saharan Africa, 22 in the circum-Mediterranean region, and the remaining 10 in Eastern Eurasia.

Quite a wide variety of animals have provided the basis for pastoral economies, depending upon their adaptability to specific environments. All of these, including the cow, camel, sheep, goat, horse, and reindeer, were domesticated in Asia. Their dispersion from these centers of origin has been accompanied by the spread of culture traits, and often actual population migrations, into adjacent areas. Because of the rather recent radiation of animals and traditions from a limited number of innovative centers, a large proportion of modern pastoralists embrace the Islamic religious tradition. Of our sample societies, 29 herd cattle, 11 camels, 2 reindeer, 1 sheep and goats, and 1 horses.

Despite the diversity in the type of animal employed, all pastoralists face a common problem—the constant demand for fresh pasturage. Depending upon the natural endowments of the environment in question, and upon seasonal variations, herd animals must be moved continually as the grass cover of immediate acreage is denuded. For this reason, some or all members of pastoral communities must be nomadic, seminomadic, or semisedentary. *Nomadism* usually refers to the adaptation requiring constant movement of the entire local community from place to place according to the demands of the herd. In these situations, wandering is never aimless or haphazard. Typically, nomadic pastoralists follow a set route between known grazing lands and waterholes. Points along these highways are often followed in a set progression, with a single cycle taking several months or even years to complete. An alternative variety of spatial mobility among pastoralists is called *transhumance*. This type consists of seasonal movements, usually triggered by the annual onset and cessation of rains. Such herding communities often vacillate between dry-season and wet-season settlements, whose size and composition may be affected by the availability of pasturage and foodstuffs.

Pastoral societies generally lack the surpluses of settled horticulturalists and agriculturalists. Extended droughts or epidemic diseases can wipe out large segments of the herds on which they depend. It is perhaps for this reason, as well as for the accumulation of individual wealth, that the *size* rather than the quality of herds is given greatest emphasis in most pastoral societies. Even under optimal conditions, however, herders are characterized by a relatively low level of food production. Ubiquitous personal devotion to their animals as well as motivations for herd expansion typically eliminate their butchering for meat. Animals are slaughtered only if they are dying or infirm, or if their use for ritual sacrifice is required. Dairy products, and in some cases blood, are the major contributions of animals that require a considerable, indeed sometimes disproportionate, expenditure of physical and emotional energy.

The low productivity level of pastoralists, when coupled with the requirements of periodic or constant movement, militates against the formation of complex sociopolitical units. The great majority of herding societies are politically uncentralized, and typically articulate small unilineal local groups into loose confederacies recognizing common headmen. Exceptions sometimes occur among those societies, on the periphery of prosperous agricultural communities, which have exerted their military prowess and political influence through the exaction of tribute. Among the horse and sheep herders of Central Asia, for example, aristocratic, commoner and slave classes are recognized (see Forde 1949:328–51). Similarly, camel herders of the eastern Sahara distinguish hereditary serfs and nobles (Murdock 1959:316–17), while former cattle pastoralists in the Great Lakes region of eastern Africa invaded settled horticulturalists and placed themselves on the top of elaborate caste-class and political hierarchies (see D'Hertefelt 1965; Albert 1963). Although some form of ranking generally accompanies the integration of population segments into political confederacies, complex sociopolitical institutions of the types mentioned are exceptional among herders.

Facultative and Obligative Pastoralism. It is important to remember that pastoralism is an economic *specialization*—a mechanism whereby population segments of mixed farming communities (those utilizing both cultivation and domesticated animals for food) may expand into relatively unoccupied and uncontested areas by reversing the priorities of their subsistence activities. Although an emphasis upon herding at the expense of cultivation is an essential of this transition, the pastoral community is never entirely independent of crops. All but 10 of our sample societies, for example, undertake some form of supplementary gardening activity themselves. This variety of pastoralism is called *facultative*. Crops may also be acquired through trade with or the plunder of settled communities.

Herders without cultivation are called *obligative*. They display a renewed supplementary dependence upon hunting, fishing, and the gathering of wild food plants.

The ramifications of obligative and facultative pastoral adaptations are evident in such variables as settlement pattern, community size, and political complexity. Obligative pastoralists typically occupy habitats, such as tundra or desert steppe, that cannot support settled life based upon cultivation. These communities are highly mobile. Eight of the 10 obligative pastoralists in the sample are fully nomadic; the remainder wander seasonally. All but one of these societies, a petty chiefdom, falls within the *tribal* level of Service's (1962) sociopolitical classification. Data on community size are available for only 7 of the 10 obligative herders, but all fall below 200 individuals, with the majority below 50.

Facultative pastoralists in the sample include societies with a dependence upon cultigens for 25 to 50 percent of their diets. With such a range of variation, we would expect corresponding disparities in the degree of nomadism and population density. Predictably, those who derive only one-quarter of their food from gardening are highly mobile. Of the 13 societies in this category, 5 remain fully nomadic and 8 are transhumant. The degree of wandering among facultative pastoralists decreases proportionally with the importance attached to stationary cultivated plots or fields. In the 12 sample societies with a cultigen dependence of 30 and 40 percent, for example, only 2 are fully nomadic, 6 are transhumant, and an additional 4 have assumed fully sedentary communities. In contrast, the remaining 9 sample societies, which attach an equal importance to herding and cultivation, vary exclusively between sedentism and transhumancy, nomadism having become inappropriate and maladaptive.

The greater degree of permanency characteristic of facultative pastoralism is reflected in community structure. Unfortunately, data on community size are available for only 12 of the 34 sample societies, so no useful comparisons may be made with obligative cases. There appears to be a tendency, however, toward greater density, since cases of villages of up to 1000 individuals

are reported. Again, if we convert the *Ethnographic Atlas* categories to those of Service (1962), the majority of facultative so-
cietes are on the *tribal* level politically. It is significant, however, that centralized political communities (10 chiefdoms and 7
small states) together compose over half of the 32 cases for
which data are available. There is a definite tendency for highly
stratified pastoral societies to be primarily dependent upon
their herds rather than upon cultivation for subsistence. This
correlation is probably attributable to the fact that such societies
have exerted their political influence over adjacent agricultural
communities, from whom they obtain cultigens and other goods
either through trade or tribute.

Sexual Division of Labor. Because the distinction between facultative and obligative pastoralism relates directly to subsistence
emphasis, the economic roles of men and women may be expected to vary accordingly. Nevertheless, it is generally noted
that females make only a small contribution to the diet of herders. When viewed as a whole, the participation of women in
production does indeed appear low among pastoralists. In our
present sample, approximately two-thirds assign herding activities exclusively to males, while the remainder recruit women
for dairying. Similarly, in the area of cultivation men are dominant in half of the sample. Of the remaining societies, approximately half assign cultivation to women exclusively, and half
distribute farming tasks equally among the sexes.

We have seen that women are barred from both the tending
and dairying of herd animals in two-thirds of the sample, but assume milking duties in a significant proportion. Their participation in cultivation, however, is more reminiscent of agriculture
than of horticulture. They are the primary farmers in only one-
quarter of the sample. Although these statistics give us a general or composite profile of sexual division of labor, they have
no predictive value. Why do women dairy in some pastoral societies and not in others? Does the assignment of cultivative
tasks follow a pattern similar to that outlined for sedentary tillers?

In order to answer these questions, we must look closer at the *interaction* of herding and cultivation as subsistence activities. If our 44 sample societies are categorized on the basis of the relative importance of farming, we are provided with a consistent framework with which to correlate both settlement pattern and the division of labor by sex. For the sake of convenience, four types of cultivative dependence are distinguished here: 1) *high,* where cultigens compose half of the diet, 2) *moderate,* where cultigens average 30 or 40 percent of the diet, 3) *low,* where cultigens make a dietary contribution of under 25 percent, and 4) *none,* where obligative pastoralism is present. When these types are compared with characteristic labor divisions and settlement patterns in Table 10-1, recognizable patterns begin to emerge:

Table 10-1. Sexual division of labor and settlement pattern in 44 pastoral societies according to their dependence upon cultivation

	SEXUAL DIVISION OF LABOR		
AGRICULTURAL DEPENDENCE	HERDING	CULTIVATION	PRIMARY SETTLEMENT PATTERN
None	Equal	—	Nomadic
Low	Men	Men	Semi-nomadic; nomadic
Moderate	Men	Equal	Semi-nomadic; Semi-sedentary (transhumant)
High	Men/Equal	Men/Women/Equal	Sedentary

Those societies with a high dependence upon cultivation display the greatest degree of diversity in sexual division of labor and settlement pattern. This tends to support the hypothesis of the generation of pastoralists from settled communities of tillers. Males predominate in both herding and cultivation, but women dairy and cultivate in one-quarter of the cases, and farm equally with men in an additional 12 percent. Variation in cultivative labor assignment may itself be related to the nature of the parent farming community—whether it is horticultural or agricultural. Societies with a high dependence upon cultigens are in an intercalary position with respect to their commitment to herding. While some occupy a number of villages serially according to the seasons, all are characterized by permanent communities, some of which boast considerable populations.

Pastoralists with moderate cultivative dependence are highly consistent in their labor assignments by sex. As herding increases in importance, both tending and dairying of animals become more exclusively male occupations. Cultivation decreases proportionately, but there is a dramatic increase in the participation of women. The commitment of these communities to herding is reflected in their greater tendency toward mobility. The majority are transhumant, moving themselves among established villages, or their entire settlements, according to the seasons.

Herding societies with a very low dependence on cultigens in the diet are highly male-dominant economically. Animal products increase in importance, as does the spatial mobility associated with their demands for pasturage. Although the majority of these societies maintain the pattern of seasonal movements, a significant proportion have become nomadic throughout the entire year. The only form of cultivation is sporadic gardening, the produce of which is used as a dietary supplement; it is taken over almost wholly by males. Herding continues to be primarily off-limits for women, although a number of societies with extremely low cultivative dependency (6–15 percent) assign dairying to women.

The final variety, obligative or noncultivative pastoralism, is characterized by sexual complementarity in productive tasks. That is, males generally tend the herds and females reassume dairying operations. Gathering by women replaces sporadic gardening as a vegetable source, and assumes similar proportions in the diet. As expected, the dominant settlement pattern for these communities is one of constant movement.

In sum, as the importance of herding increases in pastoral societies, so gradually does the participation of women in herding activities. Although some dairying is undertaken by females in each of the types distinguished, it becomes a dominant pattern in the absence of cultivation. Conversely, as the importance of cultivation decreases in pastoral societies, so does the participation of women as cultivators. Although females dominate farming in some settled pastoral communities, their participation is shared with males in societies with moderate dependence upon cultigens, and is usurped completely by males when there is only sporadic gardening.

In attempting to account for these patterns of sexual division of labor, many anthropologists have sought and been content with essentially folk explanations of economic behavior. Murdock (1959:360–61), for example, accounts for the presence or absence of dairying by women with the presence or absence of religious or ritual taboos. While these ideological traditions are interesting, they function primarily as cultural rationalizations for, rather than explanations of, human behavior.

To explain economic phenomena, we shall have to look to economic causal factors. Interesting in this respect are the observations of Dupire concerning the variable assignment of dairying tasks among pastoralists of northern Nigeria:

> Apart from the period of married life preceding the birth of the first child and the month or two following upon each time she gives birth, there is no period in a woman's life when she may not do the milking. However, although the reason why Bororo men do not undertake this task is because they have never learnt to do so, should the necessity arise, they would not hesitate to assume this feminine role. Thus it is the very conditions of existence that have determined cultural choice. This is proved by the fact that among the semi-nomad Fulani of the Niger it is the men who practice the technique of milking, while the women are unversed in it. The reason why, in this society, it is the herdsmen who have learnt how to milk, is because they spend half the year, parted from the women, looking after the cattle in the bush at some distance from the village. The few milch cows left behind in the village are milked by the older men, while the butter is churned by

women. It is obvious therefore how much
these habits, which sometimes persist long
after there has been a change in the mode of
life, are functional in origin, and not based
on any magico-philosophical concepts of ir-
reducible differences between the sexes
(1963:75–76).

This explanation is of interest because it relates to the seasonal migration patterns of many other pastoralists. The variable
of transhumance does indeed allow a measure of prediction in
the fluctuating patterns of sexual division of labor. In those pastoral societies where transhumance is characteristic, males dominate both tending and dairying. This may be attributable to the
fact that both men and herd animals wander together for a good
portion of the year around seasonal "home bases." Economic
roles in this situation may be greatly influenced by who goes
with the herd and who stays behind. This physical segregation
of women and animals may be given a sacred rationalization totally unrelated to actual economic preconditions. Cultivation,
often in the form of sporadic seasonal gardening, may also be undertaken largely by males simply because crops are planted on
the move and left unattended until their maturation.

In pastoral societies where the entire community remains
together throughout the year, women tend to participate in
herding on a status equal to that of males. The greatest
frequency of dairying by women is found in both fully nomadic
and fully sedentary communities. Similarly, it is in the latter
category that women tend to be importantly involved in cultivation.

Concerning the division of labor between the sexes in pastoral society, therefore, we conclude that whenever the members
of a community remain together, whether in the fully nomadic
or fully sedentary state, the economic participation of men and
women will move toward equality and complementarity. Conversely, whenever the members of a community must segment
or disperse along sexual lines, male-female roles with respect to
herding and cultivation will be differentiated.

SOCIAL JUXTAPOSITION OF THE SEXES

The relatively small productive role of women in pastoral societies is duplicated in the daily affairs and social structure of their
communities. In our sample, 36 of the 44 herders have patrilineal descent groups, while patrilocal residence characterizes an
additional 33 societies. We shall initially be interested, therefore, in why such a skewing toward male dominance in the
social organization of pastoralists is present. Of similar concern
is the way in which marriage and family structures compare
with the general profiles already drawn for patrilineal horticulturalists and agriculturalists. The discussion of the overall status
of women among herders will be undertaken in the spirit of balancing patriarchal influences of Islam with the range of variability in non-Islamic and exceptional cases.

The Male Locus of Kinship. The near-universality of patriliny
among pastoralists has caused much speculation over the decades. One popular explanation points to the association of
males with herd animals as sources of wealth. As we have already noted, nineteenth-century scholars such as Engels (1972)
emphasized the implications of male monopolization of both
property and the means of production for the institution of male
sociopolitical dominance. A similar catalyst is noted by Murdock (1949), who emphasizes herd animals as a source of portable wealth which falls into the hands of males because of their
natural association in subsistence activities. The significance of
this development lies in the potential for payments to be offered by the groom to his father-in-law at marriage in exchange
for the permanent removal of the bride and her subsequent
children from her natal kinship group. In other words, herd
animals provide the wherewithal for bride-price considerations
and the generation of localized agnatic descent groups.

While portable wealth and its exchange by males at marriage
is a common feature of both patrilineal societies and matrilineal
ones in transition, this pattern appears to be a symptom rather
than a catalyst of change. Why should males *want* to acquire

rights in women and children in the first place? If we assume this to be a "natural" consequence once the opportunity arises, then we are once again trapped in the cultural idealism and teleology of the past century. As with the case of patriliny in other types of technoeconomic adaptations, we shall have to look for those features which promote group survival in order to account for its near unanimity of occurrence.

As we have seen, pastoralism requires the type of social groups that can survive conditions of low productivity, considerable movement, and community segmentation. It is perhaps in the inherently *divisive* nature of patriliny that its adaptive advantage for herders lies (see Sahlins 1961). We noted that among settled peoples the segmentation and competition of lineage groups are the source of much internal discord (as well as increased productivity). The same mechanism among herders assures the spatial redistribution of the population at each generation and lessens the threat that resources will be overexploited. The dispersion of lineage segments, however, does not eliminate the complexity of power relationships. Indeed, pastoralists are notorious for their militarism, both internally and against foreign cultures. But in the case of herding societies, both the economic and political consequences of patriliny are adaptive. That is, the multiplication of localized subsistence and power units at each generation promotes survival by inhibiting the geometric population growth of stable, settled communities. At the same time, these new lineages maintain precise blueprints of their relationship with one another and with parental lineages. Although this overall organizing structure sometimes offers few safeguards against internal feuding, it does provide a ready mechanism by which the groups may unite against a common external enemy.

Patrilineal descent groups, therefore, seem particularly suited structurally to the pastoral adaptation. There are at least two other contributory factors, however, to the high incidence of descent through males—the nature of pre-pastoral parent communities, and ideological and material influences from the outside. An intensive variety of horticulturalism or agriculturalism may itself have given rise to patriliny before herding became the dominant theme in subsistence. Furthermore, the vast majority of pastoralists in the Old World lie geographically in the path of Islam. The spread of this religious system to both sedentary and herding communities has typically left patriarchy in its wake. We must take care, however, to differentiate the ideological system itself from other cultural innovations that may have accompanied its spread. Islam has traditionally diffused by way of actual population migrations or religious wars. Technoeconomic changes, such as the introduction of new domesticated animals and intensive agricultural techniques, have sometimes come in the wake of these intrusions. It is likely that these changes in productive and political relations have a greater determining influence upon the maintenance or creation of patrilineal descent groups than does the mere acceptance of foreign religious dogma.

An interesting case in point are the Tuareg camel herders of the Sahara. Two of the cultural groups within this larger ethnic community, the Ahaggaren and Asben, appear in our sample and are the sole matrilineal pastoralists. Although these and other Tuareg groups adopted Islam, at least nominally, from invading Arabs after the eleventh century, the patriarchal family did not accompany this transition from Christianity. Neither, significantly, did agriculturalism or the pattern of alternating nucleation and dispersal associated with transhumancy. Tuareg groups are fully nomadic and maintain close sociopolitical ties among the local groups that form the building blocks of centralized chiefdoms. Although they maintain a moderate dependence upon cultigens, they have relieved themselves of the responsibility of agriculturalism—and hence the requirement of transhumancy—through the subjugation of settled Sudanic populations.

Of the 34 pastoralists in the sample engaging in some kind of cultivative activities, 16 employ the plow or irrigation, and an additional 5 societies apply manuring or crop rotation. A substantial number of even casual gardeners have a knowledge of intensive techniques. This would tend to support the hypothesis of former agriculturalism in prepastoral times for many herders, and of an earlier development of patriliny. Whatever the ultimate derivation of agnatic organization, however, its near universality among pastoralists probably relates more to its specific adaptive nature than to survivals of past adaptations or conformity to new ideological systems.

Marriage, Sexuality, and the Domestic Unit. As mentioned in previous chapters, the nature of domestic units varies with the nature of technoeconomic adaptation. Polygyny, for example, was found to be highly correlated with horticulture, but to be of comparatively low frequency in agricultural societies. We accounted for this fact by noting the increasing liability of multiple wives in proportion to their divorce from production. The problem among herders, perhaps because of their diverse origins, is somewhat more complex.

The ideal domestic unit among pastoralists has been stereotyped in the literature as the nuclear monogamous family (see Forde 1949:408; Honigmann 1959:325). When the family types of the sample societies for which there are data were tabulated, however, the following distribution was found:

Extended with polygynous	13
Extended with nuclear	6
Polygynous	12
Polyandrous	2
Nuclear with polygynous	7
Nuclear monogamous	3

The high incidence of polygyny among herders is somewhat perplexing in light of existing models. When family types are correlated with levels of dependence on cultivation, no causal relationship is apparent. Similarly, data from our sample societies yield no positive relationship between the nature of domestic units and the relative participation of the sexes in herding and cultivation.

If we look more closely at the *type* of cultivation undertaken by pastoralists, however, or at its absence, distinct patterning in the nature of domestic units is evident. In those societies where cultivation is undertaken with horticultural techniques, regardless of the importance of the cultigens in the diet, polygyny characterizes 72 percent of the total as compared with only 22 percent for nuclear families of any frequency. An identical profile is found with obligative pastoralists, whose statistics are a comparable 60 percent and 30 percent, respectively. In contrast, herders employing agricultural techniques have only a 33 percent incidence of polygyny and a 60 percent frequency of nuclear families.

There is, then, a correlation between pastoralists and their probable parent communities with respect to the nature of domestic units. It is tempting to attribute the high incidence of polygyny to a continuation of sedentary patterns after their productive usefulness has disappeared. That is, although women no longer represent wealth in productive potential, their reproductive and exchange value continues as a source of prestige for males. The persistence of polygyny may also be encouraged by the teachings of Islam, so widely accepted among pastoralists of both Asia and Africa.

What does the near universality of patriliny and male-centered domestic units mean for the status of women in pastoral societies? Once again there is considerable variation. Those herders embracing Islam or those with agricultural parent communities have tended to inherit many notions of female inferiority which had their origin in the inside-outside dichotomy of sedentary intensive cultivation. The patriarchal authority structure, whether in polygynous or nuclear families, represents perhaps the most common social juxtaposition of the sexes among pastoralists. That is, there is typically a strict dichotomization of the sexes conceptually, and the assignment of opposite and complementary behaviors. With few exceptions, males control both social and political affairs, and manage the flow of property by birthright. Women assume a position of submission or often actual avoidance in face-to-face public encounters with real or potential husbands.

This surface dominance of males may be counterbalanced by a substantial degree of social and economic independence for women in the broader nonconjugal context. Forde (1949) notes that considerable variation in female status exists among central

Asian pastoralists in terms of the degree of domestic isolation, social freedom, and required labor. He concludes that the stereotype of female subjugation often assigned to pastoralism is most frequently rooted in former agricultural adaptations or in adherence to agricultural religions, and may comprise only the veneer of social relationships:

> The explanation of the low formal status of women among the Asiatic pastoral peoples generally takes an economic form. The herding of beasts is essentially a man's work, and women, providing so little and being economically so dependent, are regulated to an inferior rank. This may to a certain extent be true, but it must be borne in mind that this formal status may have little relation to actual daily life, and that such behavior patterns as the relations between the sexes may survive over long periods of time. Their explanation often lies in the remote historical past and not in any present realization of the need for assigning a particular status. The economy may in the present merely play the passive role of permitting the accepted status to survive (Forde 1949:409).

The influence of specific culture histories upon female status is also suggested in the data on sexuality. Types of premarital sex for women are tabulated by descent for 23 herding societies for which there are data in Table 10-2.

We see in Table 10-2 none of the sharp skewing toward preferred virginity characteristic of settled agriculturalists, but rather a mixing of typical profiles for intensive and extensive cultivators. Closer examination of sample cases indicates a regional correlation, which may indicate past historical influences. Premarital sexual freedom, for example, is prominent among herders of Sudanic and sub-Saharan Africa and of eastern Asia, while greatest restrictions occur in southwestern Asia and the adjacent Sahara.

The persistence of sedentary cultural patterns, or the evolution of social arrangements seemingly incongruous with the

Table 10-2. Types of premarital sexual activity for women in 23 pastoral societies

| | DESCENT | | | | |
PREMARITAL SEX	MATRI-LINEAL	DOUBLE	PATRI-LINEAL	BILATERAL	TOTALS
Precluded by early age at marriage	0	0	1	0	1
Allowed; no sanctions unless pregnancy results	0	0	1	1	2
Freely permitted; no sanctions	0	1	7	1	9
Prohibited, but weakly sanctioned; not rare	1	0	3	0	4
Virginity required; pre-marital sex rare	0	0	7	0	7
Totals	1	1	19	2	23

pastoral way of life, testify to the importance of historical influences in sexual juxtapositions. Among the Toda herders of Asia, for example, both matrilineal and patrilineal descent groups are reported, as well as polyandrous marriage (the union of a woman to two or more men). The most interesting case of incongruity, however, occurs among the Tuareg camel herders of the Sahara, whose women not only provide the loci of matrilineal kinship groups, but are relieved of domestic duties by subordinate servile populations:

> The men spend most of their time in herding, in raiding, and protecting client caravans, whereas the women are relieved of all economic and most household responsibilities by Negro serfs and slaves. With their time thus freed, the women devote themselves to the fine arts. Music and poetry are exclusively feminine accomplishments. Whereas only a few men are literate—approximately one-third in the Azjer tribe—all women can read and write in the peculiar Tuareg script,

which is derived from a Libyan alphabet of
the fourth century B.C. Moreover, at least
among the northern Tuareg tribes, the bulk
of all livestock and other movable property is
owned by the women (Murdock 1059:407).

This pattern is all the more exceptional in the fact that Tuareg
herders are also at least nominal Muslims:

> The Tuareg woman enjoys privileges un-
> known to her sex in most Moslem societies.
> She is not kept in seclusion nor is she dif-
> fident about expressing her opinions pub-
> licly, though positions of formal leadership
> are in the hands of the men. Frequently
> beautiful and commonly mercurial in temper-
> ament, she places little value upon pre-
> marital chastity, stoutly defends the institu-
> tion of monogamy after marriage, maintains
> the right to continue to see her male friends,
> and secures a divorce merely by demanding
> it—and she is allowed to keep the children.
> The shock of early Arab travelers at this state
> of affairs is understandable and was ag-
> gravated by the fact that the men were
> veiled and the women were not (Murphy
> 1970:297–98).

In sum, it is difficult to point to any single pattern of economic adaptation or social juxtaposition of the sexes among pastoralists as a whole. As we have seen, the involvement of
herders with cultivation, and hence the size and permanence of
their communities, varies from an equal vying for importance
with herding to a complete lack of participation. Sexual division
of labor seems to be importantly related to the degree and nature of mobility required for the successful execution of subsistence activities. The pattern of transhumancy, when coupled
with a low dependency upon cultivation, results in the greatest
degree of isolation from production for women.

Since the great majority of pastoralists have both a dependence upon cultigens and an acquaintance with horticultural
and agricultural techniques, we have held that their origins lie
among sedentary tillers rather than among foragers to whom

herd animals have been added. Links with parent communities are indicated not only in economic institutions, but in sociopolitical ones as well. The overall status of women in pastoral societies, while sometimes modified by universal religions such as Islam, appears to be more reflective of cultural traditions born in the horticultural or agricultural communities from which they originally segmented.

CASE STUDY: WODAABE FULANI WOMEN

Studies of women in herding societies are indeed rare. This is perhaps because of the bias that the economic, political, and social dominance of males, which is common to pastoralists, leaves little in the female role that is of interest to anthropologists. A more practical problem lies in the frequent segregation of the sexes in these societies, an obstacle difficult to overcome for the typically male investigator. The hardships of pastoral life may also have to some extent discouraged women anthropologists from considering them as objects of ethnographic study. A welcome exception is found in the work of Marguerite Dupire (1963), whose fieldwork among a group of nomadic Fulani cattle-herders provides us with an interesting case study.

The Setting. The term Fulani refers to a large number of related societies whose distribution extends across the African Sudan from Senegal eastward to Cameroon, and beyond to parts of modern Chad (see Murdock 1959:413–21). Linguistic evidence suggests they originated in the extreme western region, where they arose as a cultural and genetic amalgamation of indigenous black Africans with infiltrating Berber herders from North Africa. These pastoral Fulani populations, although genetically mixed, remained phenotypically distinct from their sedentary neighbors. Some clustered as ethnic majorities in their area of origin, while others began the long journey eastward in search of fresh pasturage on the fringes of horticultural sedentary communities. This initial expansion, begun in the twelfth century,

followed closely on the heels of the introduction and acceptance of Islam in the western portion of the Sudan. The Fulani,
therefore, were among the primary proselytizing agents of the
new religion. During the twelfth and thirteenth centuries they
had expanded from their Senegalese homelands to portions of
modern Guinea and Mali. By the fourteenth century they had
reached the area of the Niger River bend, and by the fifteenth
century, northern Nigeria. Vanguards of the Fulani migration
had established themselves in southeastern Nigeria by the
eighteenth century, and in parts of Cameroon and eastern Chad
during the nineteenth.

These movements were, for the most part, achieved peace-
fully by nomadic Fulani. Those pastoralists who became sedentary in horticultural communities and commercial centers along
the way, however, were sometimes led to wars of conquest by
charismatic, pious ritual leaders for the stated purpose of Islam-
izing subordinate populations. Thus, within the Fulani group
itself, there grew a cultural and to some extent genetic split
between nomadic pastoralists and sedentary tillers or city
dwellers. It was from the latter group that famous conqueror
Usman dan Fodio arose to forcibly consolidate northern Nigeria
into a single Islamic empire between 1804 and 1809—a political
unit that was to remain intact until British contact in 1903.

The Wodaabe, like many other Fulani pastoralists of the
larger Bororo subgroup to which they belong, remained aloof
from such essentially urban developments. Their wandering
lifestyle, like that of the ancient Fulani, has often made them
the object of contempt and ridicule among sedentary populations, who point to their lack of commitment to cultivation and
orthodox Islamic customs as evidence of their inferiority. In
keeping with the traditions of all pastoralists, however, the Wodaabe highly value their mobile, independent lifestyle, and
view sedentary tillers as permanently bound, encapsulated, and
pitiable populations.

The Wodaabe Fulani occupy an area north of the union of the
Niger and Benue Rivers in the arid savanna belt sometimes referred to as the Sudanic fringe. They depend primarily upon the
dairy products of their cattle, and to a lesser extent on their

sheep and goats. Wodaabe pastoralism is of the facultative variety, since the sporadic gardening of cereals makes a small contribution to the diet. The physical environment of the Wodaabe
is incapable of supporting settled communities of cultivators,
but receives sufficient water during the rainy season to meet the
requirements of pasturage for their herd animals, and for the
planting and germination of carefully timed but untended garden plots.

We shall approach an understanding of the female role in
Wodaabe society by examining first the nature of domestic units
and the participation of women in the daily tempo of camp life.
We shall then explore the more qualitative aspects of growing
up female in this culture, as well as the dimensions of womanhood, by tracing the florescence of gender roles from birth to
maturity.

Men, Women, and Camp Life. The basic physical units among the
Wodaabe Fulani are temporary encampments made up of patrilineally related polygynous or extended families. The social juxtaposition of the sexes conforms generally to the patriarchal
model, by now familiar to us. There is a strict segregation of the
sexes both conceptually and spatially within the camp, and
males assume, at least ideally, the dominant role in all social interactions. These relationships are beautifully symbolized in
the physical layout of Wodaabe camps. Dupire vividly describes this balancing of sex, seniority, and space criteria.

> Within the camp, the arrangement of the
> women's huts, of the cattle enclosures, and
> of all material objects always follows the
> principle of sex differentiation. When the
> members of an extended family live together,
> the eldest of the heads of the component in-
> dividual families—the father or eldest
> brother—takes up the position furthest to the
> south, with his juniors following in order of
> seniority. But within each separate po-
> lygynous group, each man's wives will ar-
> range their huts in hierarchical order in the

opposite direction, that is, from north to south. The eastern part of the camp is the women's domain, and the western the men's. Behind each hut (to the east of it), the woman washes her cooking utensils, and also herself. Here she can be metaphorically protected from view, if not actually so, since the hut is no more than a simple screen of thorn, unroofed. This is also the place where she will be buried. The man, on the other hand, does his work on the other side of the hut, for the cattle corral is to the west, near the entrance to the hut, and it is in this corral, or a little beyond it, that his grave will be dug. Because they come under the sphere of masculine activities, the calves are tethered in a row running in the masculine direction, from south to north, arranged according to age, from the oldest to the youngest; while the calabashes belonging to the women are arranged on a raised table in order of decreasing size running in the feminine direction from north to south. In the foreground, then, are the men and the goods that belong specifically to them, while behind are the women with their property arranged in a hierarchy like the men's and according to the same principle, the essential difference between them being expressed by an inversion of orientation: to the women belong the east, and the direction north-south; to the men, the west, and the direction south-north (Dupire 1963:50–52).

The dichotomization of the sexes in the spatial arrangement of the camp is mirrored and perhaps encouraged by the division of labor in subsistence activities. Statistically, the Wodaabe depend upon herding for over 85 percent of their subsistence, with the remaining 15 percent or less being contributed by the cultivation of millet. Both of these activities are dominated primarily by males, although women figure importantly in herding and dairying tasks connected with food production for their own matricentric units.

This seeming contradiction may be clarified by distinguishing the types of herd animals critical to Wodaabe subsistence, and the varying rights in livestock granted to women and men. By far the most important animals, in terms of both food and prestige, are cattle. Their association with males, at least in terms of labor connected with tending, is largely attributable to the arduousness of these activities. Cattle must daily be driven back and forth to pasture, at times considerable distances from the encampment, and the seemingly simple task of watering reportedly takes half the night during the dry season. When added to the temporal and spatial requirements of motherhood, these tasks are incompatible with other demands placed upon the female.

Among the Wodaabe, however, the dairying of cattle is assigned to women. Each wife receives a specified number of cows from her husband; with them she supplies herself and her children with milk and milk products. Although these cattle are owned by her husband's patrilineage, she may hold exclusive use-rights. Women also have limited claims on two other categories of cattle. A new wife eventually brings to her husband's herd a small number of cattle she has received from her father, plus those cows that have been offered for her brideprice. Custody of these animals is in actuality transferred from the patrilineage of her father to that of her husband. Such cows are at least conceptually separated from the remainder of the herd for eventual inheritance by a woman's sons, and are not disposed of without the wife's consent. While cattle, therefore, are not specifically *owned* by women, females may act as important links in their distribution.

In addition to the dairying of cattle, women are responsible for both the tending and milking of smaller domesticated animals. Unlike cows, sheep and goats may be owned exclusively by women. The most frequent way to acquire them is through the enterprising activity of marketing butter. During the winter, large quantities of excess butter from the dairying of milch cows are stored in calabashes. These surpluses belong solely to the wife, and may be exchanged for small livestock, personal items, or cash during visits to town marketplaces. Cereals, salt, and condiments are also purchased in this manner.

In the Wodaabe division of labor we see many features in common with patrilineal horticulturalism. Women enjoy a tremendous degree of economic responsibility and freedom, and are in essence the heads of their own matricentric units during their husbands' frequent absences. Polygyny in this case mirrors the situation among cultivators, with the exception that women use the *cattle* rather than the land of their husbands to provide for their respective offspring. Their use-rights to productive resources acquired through males are exclusive and complete. Just as the polygynous wife is in horticultural societies the sole owner of any surplus produce from her fields, so Wodaabe women accumulate excess stores of milk by converting it into butter.

The degree of financial success achieved by individual wives is influenced by such seemingly unrelated factors as the size of her husband's herd, the number of co-wives, the amount of rainfall in a given year, and the number of children she bears. The common thread linking these variables is the simple matter of supply and demand. The number of milch cows a wife is assigned by her husband is determined by the number of animals at his disposal and the number of times they are reapportioned. Polygyny is generally a source of irritation for women, since the addition of each new co-wife means a reduction in the size of milch cow allotments for earlier spouses. This economic competition places a strain upon co-wife relationships among the Wodaabe, and institutionalized hostility is not uncommon. The amount of surpluses accumulated by women is also influenced by the number of offspring they are required to feed from rather fixed resources. The largest herds of sheep and goats are owned by childless women, whose lack of maternal prestige is compensated for by fewer material responsibilities and the subsequent opportunity for accumulation of wealth in livestock. A long dry season, however, may hinder the petty entrepreneurial activities of even the most prosperous women in camp. Even though males are technically responsible for cattle expenses and for supplying members of their households with clothing and millet, a poor harvest may necessitate bartering for cereals with sedentary tillers. In these instances women may be required to offer some of their small livestock as units of exchange.

The question of why men tend cattle and gardens, and why women dairy returns us to a hypothesis advanced earlier in the chapter. Since the Wodaabe are fully nomadic (the community members remain together throughout the year) the participation of the sexes in herding is convergent. Labor assignments assume a spatial bipolarization related to the proximity of tasks to the domicile. Complementarity is achieved in the categorization of dairying as an inside and tending as an outside activity (this is in contrast to other Bororo Fulani groups, whose transhumancy and male dispersal result in the merging of cattle-related tasks and their exclusive assignment to men). Similarly, the cultivation of millet falls to those who wander far from the camp in the course of other subsistence activities. In this case, rude garden plots are planted by men in areas that coincide with the projected location of community encampments during the harvesting season.

The Dynamics of Female Gender. The social, spatial, and economic dichotomization of the sexes evident in daily camp routines begins early in the lives of Wodaabe children. Male and female infants are handled differently and adorned with distinct sex-typed amulets. By the age of two or three female children have their ears pierced, and begin to wear the jewelry and hairstyles of older girls. Future adult tasks are imitated in play behavior with toy calabashes and dolls. The acquisition of these skills is therefore a long and gradual learning process of participant-observation.

Between the ages of four and five, girls in Wodaabe society are instructed in the basic code of morality that will guide their behavior thereafter. The significance of marriage is impressed upon the young girl, and she learns the identity of her future husband. Among the Wodaabe infant betrothal is the common

and preferred pattern. Because of this society's highly structured nature of male-female relationships among opposite-sexed
close kinsmen of either consanguineal or affinal types, it is essential that children learn both the system of kin categorization
and the associated appropriate behaviors while very young.
Girls are informed of those males with whom sexual contacts
and familiarity would be incestuous or inappropriate, and toward whom they must react with both submissiveness and timidity. Among the most tabooed figures is the girl's future husband. She must henceforth avoid all contact with him until their
marriage, and may never speak his name.

Between the ages of six and seven, girls begin to participate
seriously in the domestic routine of the household. Sewing,
weaving winnowing mats, and mending and decorating calabashes are now refined individually rather than acted out as a
group play activity. Similarly, mothers (or at times grandmothers) are greatly aided by the daughter's contributions in
the seemingly endless tasks of babysitting, and of pounding
grain and drawing water for daily household use.

At the first signs of maturity a young girl embarks upon what
many Wodaabe regard as her happiest years. From the age of
nine or ten years until her marriage, girls take part in evening
dances attended by bachelors and married men ranging widely
in age. It is here that the girls are introduced, at times forcibly,
to sexuality. Parents, who view this period of experimentation
and acquisition of sexual skills with both tolerance and amusement, are completely permissive. Young people are expected to
engage in a long series of brief love affairs, but to honor in their
choice of partners the taboos against incest as well as those
against the selection of future spouses and close affinal kinsmen. The equality and openness shared by lovers during this
period contrasts sharply with what will characterize the future
husband-wife relationship. Professions of devotion are often expressed publicly in poetry and in song, and young women
proudly relate their lists of sexual conquests. The increasing
sociosexual sophistication so acquired by a woman, however, is
not transferred to her upcoming and inevitable marriage to a
man who is both a stranger and the object of a decade of ritual

avoidance. The self-praise and extrovertive confidence of a young adolescent girl may be quickly converted to modesty and embarrassment at the mere mention of her fiancé's name.

Depending upon when the agreed bridewealth payments are completed, arranged marriages may take place any time after the young woman's first menstruation. As soon as the union is officially underway, the future bride is ritually isolated for a period of three to five months. During this interval she may neither see males nor engage in sexual intercourse. The seclusion is terminated with her removal by the groom's kinsmen to the household of her mother-in-law. This event is thought to be especially traumatic for the new bride, so much so that she is expected to flee home to her parent's compound the first night before the marriage is consummated. At the end of several days, however, she is once again claimed by her husband's kinsmen, and must then begin the difficult period of adjustment to early married life.

Marriage is regarded as a particularly painful experience for a young wife because it demands the immediate adoption of a new lifestyle. First, she must eventually, although not immediately, give up her open love affairs and sexual freedom. More importantly, however, she is rather abruptly cast into a strange and demanding household. The period of marriage before pregnancy is regarded as a mere apprenticeship during which the young woman of only 14 to 17 must depend upon the resources and stern guidance of her mother-in-law. She has no domicile of her own, and therefore must sleep outdoors with her husband on a mat donated by his mother. In addition, the wife must depend upon her in-laws' cows and domestic utensils throughout the probationary period, since she owns none.

Interpersonal relationships among the new bride and her in-laws are sterile in comparison to the frivolous exchanges enjoyed with her peers before marriage. The father-in-law and elder brothers of her spouse are surrounded by taboos laden with sexual overtones, and must therefore be avoided. Her mother-in-law is a figure of considerable authority now and in the years to come. The bride must regard her with both restraint and respect, and be submissive to her demands. Much the same set of behaviors characterizes the husband-wife relationship, which might best be described as puritanical, distant, and cold. It is considered out of place for a wife to appear at her husband's side in public, and any display of warmth or affection betweem them is highly inappropriate. This is in stark contrast to the interactions of lovers, and a primary reason why pre- and early post-adolescence is a time cherished by women.

The young bride escapes this circle of restrictive relationships by frequent visits to her own kinsmen. The Wodaabe feel that the separation of a girl from her parental camp is very stressful. Her kinsmen therefore insist that she be granted this mobility, and often arrange marriages between closely spaced families, perhaps those of full brothers, to guarantee such geographic proximity. New brides also ease the strain of adjustment by resuming their attendance at evening dances, and by renewing friendships with former lovers. This sexual freedom is permissible throughout the probationary period of marriage. Its purpose at this stage in a young woman's life, however, is not sexual experience but to gain additional assurance of early pregnancy.

Pregnancy provides the key both to temporary escape from the husband's camp and to adult status. After the fifth month, the prospective mother is allowed to return to her parents' camp, and to remain there until the child is weaned. During her long stay at home, the new mother and child are indulged by their relatives. This is considered a time of great happiness for the young wife, and she does not see her husband nor communicate with him directly for well over two years. During this interval the husband exercises restraint in making inquiries about his wife and child to avoid feelings of "shame," and sends gifts through established intermediaries.

When the child is finally weaned, the young wife returns with her child to her husband's parents. This second arrival, however, has none of the traumatic connotations of the first. She has now proudly achieved adult status, and brings with her a dowry in cattle and household goods. Her husband welcomes his family's arrival because of the independence he may now request from his father. The young family characteristically moves out of the father's camp to establish their own household and to begin tending, dairying, and expanding their own herd. No longer must the wife sleep outdoors on the mat of her mother-in-law and be forced to use the resources of others. She now has her own house, mat, utensils, cows, and her own child. This new economic and social autonomy symbolizes the final sealing of the long process of marriage.

Despite the newfound autonomy of the conjugal pair, and the increased status and respect that now attaches itself to the wife-mother, relationships among spouses remain essentially unchanged. Their interactions continue to be distant and cold for the duration of the union, and she may no longer legitimately or openly seek love affairs outside her marriage. Other immediate members of the household, such as co-wives, also typically fail to develop warm, spontaneous relationships. Since, as mentioned above, these women tend to be economically competitive, their social exchanges are often tainted with suspicion and hostility.

The further removed, it seems, a woman is from her immediate domestic unit, the less strained emotional and social attachments become. Among those in her husband's locality, a woman's sisters-in-law are often the most trusted friends. These women are free of the potentially disruptive competition over household resources, and share a comradery and patterns of mutual aid similar to cooperative co-wife interactions in many horticultural societies. Similarly, the relationship between a woman and her mother-in-law, although always characterized by restraint, usually warms over the years. For example, it is not at all uncommon for a woman to donate a daughter to the household of her mother-in-law to aid her in old age. Such a gesture symbolizes their growing affection and mutual respect.

Despite these secondary relationships, a woman remains a comparative stranger among her husband's kin. So important is the maintenance of close ties with her parental camp considered for a wife's emotional well-being that any prolonged separation constitutes adequate grounds for divorce. Indeed, the tensions created within Wodaabe domestic units among spouses and co-wives make the termination of marriage a frequent occurrence. For males, divorce may be obtained simply by renouncing a wife. Women who become discouraged with a marital relationship typically leave the camp of their husband without prior announcement, taking all household items with them. In accordance with the rules of patrilineal descent and inheritance, however, a wife must leave any weaned children plus the cattle transferred from her father's herd to her husband's (the original brideprice). Moreover, the deserted spouse will usually seek some type of additional material compensation. The wife who flees her husband's household usually does so to join a lover. This mechanism allows women an avenue of escape from arranged marriages and their patterned emotional sterility. In fact, Wodaabe Fulani women may contract a number of unions with spouses or lovers, using their own parental camps as islands of security between relationships.

Whether a woman remains with her initial husband throughout life, or whether she changes partners frequently, she remains one of the more mobile and independent units of Wodaabe society. Beneath the veneer of patriarchy and the patterns of dominance and submission, a woman may find considerable freedom of expression. The division of labor places her in the position of a small-scale entrepreneur, maximizing the yield of milk and converting available surpluses into material wealth over which the husband has no claim. Although such accumulations will be inherited by her sons and may not be transferred to another camp or locality (save domestic and personal items), the pattern of domestic isolation and economic dependence which so often characterizes the agricultural adaptations is nonexistent. Further, the very rule of patrilineal filiation aids in the mobility of women by freeing them from the responsibilities child custody entails. An unhappy wife can desert her husband with the full knowledge that any children she has borne will be adequately cared for by other members of his household. In advanced age, if she has outlived both her latest husband and the desire to remarry, a woman may then attach herself to the camp of one of her sons to spend the remainder of her days with him, his herd, his wife or wives, and her grandchildren.

DISCUSSION

Pastoralists embody many of the features of tilling communities set to motion. Because all either participate in some variety of cultivation or acquire these products from sedentary societies, it is likely that the herding adaptation has its origin in horticulturalism or agriculturalism rather than in foraging. Certainly in terms of political structure, kinship, marriage, and male-female role definitions, their affinity to cultivators is close indeed.

The generalization that pastoral societies are overwhelmingly male-dominant may be accurate and at the same time deceiving. In the economic sphere, for example, males typically control the ownership, distribution, and tending of herd animals, and may extend their activities into dairying and cultivation as well. As we have seen, however, variation in the assignment of subsistence tasks is both considerable and predictable. While the participation of males in tending may have certain biological prerequisites, the fluctuating allocation of dairying and gardening labor between the sexes seems largely to reflect the nature of community movement and settlement pattern. Among the fully nomadic Wodaabe Fulani, for example, the assignment of dairying to women contrasts with that of related neighboring groups whose transhumancy patterns separate females from both cattle and men during a significant portion of the year. Similarly, the isolation of women from cultivation is often correlated with their lack of spatial mobility necessary for planting gardens in areas which the entire encampment will occupy only weeks or months later. In societies such as the Wodaabe Fulani, where dairying is a female occupation, women and men are equally dependent upon the labor of one another for the care and exploitation of cattle. Even though herd animals are owned by males, women play a primary role in the conversion of this resource to food products and secondary accumulable wealth.

In this and related social respects, a number of pastoralists show affinities to patrilineal horticulturalism. Where women dairy, there is a tendency for the productive output of herd animals also to fall into female hands. When coupled with a persistent pattern of polygynous marriage, the social and economic juxtaposition of the sexes is very similar to that of patrilineal hoe cultivators. In both cases, resources are controlled by males, but their productive yields are extracted and to a greater or lesser extent distributed by women. This economic independence, even when accompanied by a patriarchal value system, appears to greatly enhance the status and mobility of women outside the immediate domestic unit.

There are some herders, however, for whom agriculture provides a more comparable model. As we have seen, a significant number of facultative pastoralists utilize such intensive techniques as plowing, manuring, and irrigation in their limited farming activities. These same societies favor nuclear over polygynous families, and more often exclude women from productive activities. The so-called inside-outside dichotomy, born in agricultural conditions, continues to foster the domestic encapsulation of women, and to isolate them from active participation in event systems outside the household.

In sum, variation among pastoralists may be influenced by at least three factors. The first, as we have seen, is their specific adaptation to a given environment. Variables such as settlement pattern and the interaction of herding and cultivation have an important influence on the final allocation of tasks according to sex. Second, the culture history of a given pastoral society may exert a definite sway on socioeconomic institutions and sex role definitions. Many characteristics, for example, seem to be attributable more to membership in common culture areas than to any obvious adaptive advantage in a given environment. Those herders developing from sedentary communities in sub-Saharan Africa, for example, are more likely to be characterized by hoe cultivation, polygyny, permarital sexual freedom, female economic independence, and easy divorce. Those pastoralists whose cultural roots are in the Near East or the adjacent Saharan region tend to yield an opposite pattern with respect to the same characteristics. The reason for these distinct profiles need not be lost in the vagaries of cultural relativity; more likely, it may be found in distinct geneses of pastoralism from horticulture on the one hand, and agriculture on the other.

A third and final factor that may influence the juxtaposition of the sexes in pastoral society is culture history of a different sort—recent diffusion of ideas rather than cultural origins. Here we are speaking primarily of the spread of Islam throughout areas of high herding dependency. As noted earlier, the Tuareg camel herders of the Sahara provide a good argument against the inevitability of male social dominance patterns among practicing Muslims. But this ethnic community is a mere island in a sea of patriarchy. Major religions of the Western world developed out of cultural traditions based in agriculturalism. All emphasize the patriarchal family, and rationalize status inequalities and dominance-subordination patterns among the sexes in an elaborate dogma. The impingement of such value systems upon foreign cultures is perhaps most apparent in pastoral societies with horticultural parent communities. Among the Wodaabe Fulani, for example, patriarchal dominance patterns among conjugal pairs and within domestic units are incongruous with relationships outside, and appear to be responsible for much disharmony in the household. This situation is very reminiscent of the sedentary Kanuri cultivators of neighboring Nigeria (see Cohen 1967), among whom the indigenous and Islamic recipes for sex role juxtapositions have virtually come to blows at the grassroots level. The high incidence of Kanuri divorce (some 80 percent) indicates the degree of stress generated by such an adjustment, and may provide a clue to the apparent contradictions among the Wodaabe Fulani and similar pastoralists of nonagricultural origins.

In short, the role of women in pastoral society is determined by a complex interaction of ecological and historical factors. Both point to the origins of herding in settled cultivative communities, and to the persistence of institutional configurations born in these traditions long after their adaptive advantage may have disappeared.

CHAPTER ELEVEN

Women in Industrial Society

The situation of modern industrial society shows clearly the legacy of the past. In this chapter, we shall be concerned with the persistence of agricultural sex role definitions, their gradual modification by industrial economies, and the way specific cultures have attempted to deal with conflicts arising from the clash of old domestic stereotypes and renewed productive demands for female labor.

WOMEN, MEN, AND MACHINES

The adaptive advantages of the male-provider and female-domestic roles were greatest at the agricultural stage of cultural evolution. As a pattern of sexual division of labor, it is associated with a rural, feudal, or peasant economy in which the small patriarchal family persists. Males, as we have seen, take over the responsibilities of farming when techniques requiring the use of large domestic animals, heavy labor, and absences from the vicinity of the domicile are adopted. Ironically, the surpluses and broadened exchange networks generated by intensive cultivation led to conditions that were to gradually undermine this new domestic and extradomestic relationship among the sexes.

Urbanism, one consequence of increased production, encouraged an early departure from agrarian labor divisions. Preindustrial city dwellers were not cultivators, but full-time artisans, craftsmen, traders, and wage laborers who exchanged their goods and services for the necessities of life. Divorced from a communal production system, households became greatly reduced in size to accommodate the new basic economic unit, the single conjugal pair and the offspring. Urban nuclear families were considerably less secure than their agrarian counterparts. Many of the mutual-aid functions of consanguine kinship groups were lost in the individualism and anonymity of the city. Male-female dyads became, therefore, increasingly codependent in their joint labor for household sustenance and survival. The domestic-provider dichotomy born in the agricultural adaptation was sufficiently elastic, at least in broad outline, to survive the onset of the urban revolution. Males continued to assume their responsibilities for economic support outside the household, whereas the absence of excess personnel that characterized extended families placed even heavier domestic demands upon women.

But for the vast majority of urban families—those of the lower classes—the agrarian labor division by sex was at least a partial failure. The productive efforts of males were often inadequate to ensure the survival of the family unit. Women, therefore, began to deviate from their homebased economic roles with some minor or full-time participation in the money economy. Economic partnerships among spouses often included extradomestic responsibilities for females, such as the vending of products acquired or produced by their husbands. In many cases, the traditional duties of women were simply compounded by the performance of domestic services in upper-class households. Tensions arising from the clash of socially idealized sex roles and the economic realities of domestic life may account for the frequent reemergence of the independent matricentric family under urban conditions through the phenomenon of male desertion.

Challenges to the agricultural role juxtaposition of men and women, then, in both economic and social dimensions, were already underway in the urban centers of feudal and mercantile societies. The invention and use of the steam engine for the manufacturing of marketable items further exaggerated these trends. Machines invalidated previous criteria for the division of labor by sex. Whereas males were recruited for producer-provider roles among intensive cultivators largely on the basis of strength, machinery theoretically reopened most professions to both sexes.

The effects of industrial technology upon male and female roles were significantly tempered by social class variables. During the late 1700s and early 1800s, broad gulfs in the wealth and status of European city-dwellers were characteristic. Those aristocratic families inheriting their wealth from old feudal estates, or bourgeois families rising to a position of power through the control of hand manufactures and trade in preindustrial times, constituted a small category of haves in a sea of have-nots. Sexual division of labor in aristocratic families often consisted merely of dichotomous spheres of management. Since financial security excluded men from subsistence activities and women from domestic ones, smooth functioning of the household became a matter of successful supervision of the estate on the one hand and of the servants on the other. Although notions of innate behavioral differences were elaborately underscored in both costume and leisure activities, upper-class men and women had greater equality than those of lower classes with respect to the distribution of wealth, power, and opportunities for the development of individual potential.

Bourgeois families strove toward and at times achieved the opulent lifestyle of the aristocracy, but tended to be the most conservative segment of early industrial society in the retention of traditional sex roles. The position of men in social-status hierarchies was intimately related to their success as providers and manipulators of wealth. Women were generally excluded from financial concerns and certainly from extradomestic labor; ideally they clung to their husbands' arms, provided an embellishment at social functions, and served as a silent partner in the upward thrust of the family enterprise. Unlike the aristocratic woman, the bourgeois wife typically had no prestigious heritage or independent resources to fall back on, and found

herself both dependent upon and confined by the social identity of her spouse.

The broad base of early industrial Europe was made up of
working-class families, and it is there that industrialism initiated the greatest changes in traditional, agrarian sex roles. Just
as the machine had replaced muscle, so social class replaced
sex as a primary criterion for industrial labor division. So great
was the demand for workers, and so precarious the existence of
lower-class families, that *all* of their members—men, women,
and children—sold their labor in the factories of Europe. In society at large, the profit motive took precedence over previous
biases favoring the domestic isolation of women in blue-collar
families. The economic exploitation of both sexes was rationalized with elaborate pseudoscientific arguments stressing the innate inferiority of proletarians. Just as, in the agricultural adaptation, women were classified as genetically unfit for
nondomestic tasks, so with industrialism an entire social class
was deemed suited only for those tasks which culturally fostered a rapid development of the new economy. Within the
working-class families themselves, traditional sex role definitions conflicted with the demands of urban poverty. Females returned to production out of necessity, and in doing so were
abruptly encumbered with unmanageable workloads. Industrial
labor for women was added to, rather than substituted for, domestic responsibilities. Men held on to their legacy of patriarchal authority all the more tenaciously in the face of shared provider roles. The rapidity with which these changes were
imposed upon recently arrived agrarian families, and the lack of
urban social services, led to considerable disruption and disharmony in spousal and parental relationships.

However initially traumatic for the family structure and domestic economy of the masses, the industrial revolution in
Europe initiated gradual but permanent trends toward sexual
equality and sex role convergence. Industrialism was simultaneously woman's great enslaver and great emancipator. Machine production and the development of sophisticated systems
of market exchange required the combined efforts of both sexes.
The number of women stepping beyond the economic and so-

cial horizons of the domestic unit was considerable, and continues to grow with each decade. As we shall see, however, agricultural sex role definitions have had great resiliency, and have tended to lag behind the economic realities of modern society.

In sum, the earliest development of urbanism in the evolution of human culture occurred with the agricultural adaptation. All industrial nations have developed from this base, and therefore share a similar legacy of adaptive social features. Developing industrial societies made two significant breaks with the past. First, the extended patriarchal family was destroyed and replaced with the more flexible and compact nuclear family. Second, the labor horizons of women were once more extended to production, while domestic obligations and associated sex mythologies were, to a greater or lesser extent, preserved.

During the twentieth century, industrialism provided the technology for two distinct systems of economic production and distribution, socialism and capitalism. We shall now briefly explore the ramifications of these variant systems for female and male roles, using for our industrial examples the Soviet Union and the United States.

THE SOCIALIST ALTERNATIVE

The industrial revolution posed one of the greatest social challenges in human history. Mass-production techniques required the recruitment of labor on a scale never approached before, and resulted in the accumulation of enormous surpluses. As in earlier urban developments, these resources and products were unevenly distributed in the population; control fell to a minority class who claimed rights either through heredity or entrenched political power. For the vast majority, early industrialism meant long hours at the factory, low wages, substandard housing, malnutrition, disease, and early death. The abominable conditions in nineteenth-century factories and urban slums led humanitarian philosophers such as Karl Marx and Frederick Engels to call for a political coalition of workers against their oppressors (see Marx 1888, orig. 1848). The revolution they both predicted and attempted to propagate called for a complete redistribution of wealth (with equal shares for equal work), the abolition of private property, and the control of production by the state.

Such an upheaval never materialized in Western Europe, but in Czarist Russia the cleavage between the old aristocracy and propertyless peasants and workers broadened to a violent confrontation in 1917. When the bloodshed had ceased, the victorious Bolsheviks began reorganizing society along lines that would eliminate inequalities based upon both class and sex. These legislated changes were to have far-reaching effects on the status of women in the Soviet Union.

Our first task will be to trace the fluctuating legal position of Russian women from prerevolutionary to modern times. We shall then examine more closely the model female role in Soviet culture, and compare the ideal of sexual equality with the realities of both homelife and the world of work.

Women and the Law. Before the Bolshevik revolution, the economy of Czarist Russia was predominantly agrarian. The Russian family conformed to the patriarchal model shared with the rest of rural Europe. Within the household, the male head had almost absolute authority over his sons, daughters, and spouse, all of whom were considered political minors. Although males could eventually escape the constant domination of family heads and set up their own miniature dictatorships, females were permanently bound to a subordinate role by fathers and husbands. Women had no voice in political affairs, and could not inherit their father's estate. In a society where the Church imposed heavy controls over marriage, sexuality, and reproduction, both divorce and birth control were outlawed. The life of a rural peasant woman in prerevolutionary times, then, was entirely focused upon child-bearing and the performance of domestic labor on behalf of a dominant male.

Following the revolution, Bolshevik political architects recognized the necessity of destroying the old patriarchal, feudal power structure (see Mace & Mace 1963, Marshall 1970). As long as sons were bound by tradition to an allegiance to their fathers and overlords, potential bases of resistance to the new regime remained. All aristocratic claims to landed property were therefore eliminated by government seizure, and laws were passed to enforce equality among parents and children, and among men and women.

With the elimination of patriarchal authority, the nuclear family began to rise almost by default. Industry attracted increasing numbers of young men and women to the cities. There they congregated into urban communes or peer collectives, and were encouraged to inform on recalcitrant or politically subversive parents. The goal of sexual equality was furthered by legislation known as the Family Codes, passed in 1918 and modified in 1926. In them, the institution of marriage was completely secularized. Mutual consent was required to counter the former practice of forced unions. The ceremony itself consisted of a simple registry of couples. Common-law or unregistered unions were also recognized as legitimate arrangements. Similarly, children arising from any union were pronounced legitimate, and were held to be the joint responsibility of both parents. For the first time, birth control was legalized and promoted, and divorce was made possible. The termination of marriage was first referred to the civil courts, but after 1926 either party could end the marriage by simply unregistering the union.

The break with old systems of morality and sex role definitions was thus immediate and sharp. Postrevolutionary legislation, designed primarily to destroy the old base of political opposition, simultaneously introduced social changes which in Western Europe would develop only gradually over several decades. Russian women were suddenly granted their freedom from the secondary status imposed on them by parental and Church restraints. They could now work in rural collective farms, migrate to the cities, explore sexuality, terminate unwanted pregnancies, exercise individual choice in cohabitation or marriage, and escape undesirable partnerships. But despite the seriousness of intent on the part of revolutionary legislators, the contrast with former patterns was so great that some cultural lag was inevitable. Although, for example, sexual equality and freedom was immediate, free and legal abortions were generally unavailable until 1920, and illegitimacy survived until 1926. There existed for a time a frantic reshuffling of moral codes, during which the inequality of women lived on in a generation of people socialized in the old tradition.

Although considerable progress toward sex role convergence was made during the second and third decades of the twentieth century, by the mid-1930s the pendulum had begun to swing toward a new conservatism in the drawing of sexual and marital guidelines. A substantial revision of the Family Codes designed to reinforce the conjugal unit coincided with Joseph Stalin's rise to power in 1936. In that same year abortions were outlawed, ostensibly to increase the Soviet birth rate. Simultaneously, a government program of monetary bonuses was instituted for families with over seven children.

The thrust of legislated change, however, came in 1944 with the passage of new marriage and divorce codes which, in effect, eliminated Bolshevik reforms. Common-law marriages were declared illegal, and the illegitimate status for children of such unions was reinstituted. The new legislation not only prohibited children born out of wedlock from taking their father's name, but the latter could not be held financially responsible. Instead, the government took over the initial burden of support; the mother received allowances until the child was 12. The institution of marriage was further bolstered by making its termination nearly impossible for the common man or woman. Divorce cases were returned to the discretion of the courts, and, as before the revolution, favorable decisions were prohibitively expensive and difficult to obtain.

All of the reforms passed during the Stalinist regime had an inhibiting effect upon the mobility and personal freedom of women. With the elimination of common-law unions and legalized abortion, marriage became the only approved heterosexual outlet. As sexual beings, women had once more become wards of the state. While the regulation of males with respect to reproduction remained unchanged, or was even somewhat relaxed, females were summarily herded into matrimony and professional motherhood with considerable fanfare. In 1944, for example, the system of monetary bonuses for achievement in baby-making was extended to mothers of over two children. These premiums were collected for the first four years of the child's life. The production, therefore, of at least one bonus child during that interval guaranteed an uninterrupted flow of governmental allotments. Encouragements toward the assumption of a purely domestic role also took on an air of patriotism. Distinguished service in baby-making was congratulated by receipt of the Maternity Medal (over five children), the Order of Maternal Glory (over seven), and the title of Mother Heroine (over ten).

These rather dramatic changes in the sociolegal position of Russian women paralleled developments in the family. The Bolshevik revolution coincided with early industrialization and increased demands for a large, mobile work force. The patriarchal family with its feudal structure, economic and political autonomy, absolute control over youth, and unequal sex roles was dysfunctional in terms of the requirements of an industrial division of labor. It was also antithetical to the new political order, and therefore was abruptly destroyed rather than allowed to dissipate gradually as in Western Europe. The sudden demise of the patriarchal family was perhaps only possible through the extreme relaxation of social and sexual controls that characterized the 1920s. During this interval, however, problems involving the domestic sexual division of labor remained unresolved. Hanging in the balance of universal employment for women and men were the tasks of child-rearing and household maintenance, as yet unclaimed by nonfamilial institutions.

By the mid-1930s, then, the conjugal unit, which had been rising to prominence in urban areas since the revolution, was simply given official legal priority in Soviet culture. Although an imperfect structure in terms of the conflicting demands it placed upon women, it provided a stable economic unit in a society striving desperately for industrial development and population growth. The cultural rationalization for the institution of marriage and family reforms was again political. Just as the Bolsheviks saw the peer collective as a base of resistance against feudal authority, so Stalinists envisioned the stable nuclear family as a socialization agency for the instillation of state values and state allegiance.

The Dialectic of Female Roles. Since the revolution, extradomestic labor has always played an important part in the Soviet definition of womanhood. Indeed, their active and enthusiastic participation in production has been stressed as a patriotic duty. Field and Flynn (1970) sum up the ideal Soviet female role as follows:

> Comrade Positive is the prototype of the femme engagée, the heroine of production who, in spite of tremendous obstacles, finds it possible to combine useful, productive work or study, with her family life and obligations. Like a tower of strength, she provides continuity and support to those around her and is able to transcend the narrow circle of her family. This positive, if somewhat manic and hyperactive, type of woman is endowed with endless energy and boundless devotion to the cause of building a communist society (1970:271).

Ideally, then, the Soviet woman should be self-sacrificing, but aggressive with respect to shared or common goals. She must regard her work outside the home as the source of ultimate pleasure and comradery, and be constantly vigilant for new opportunities to contribute to the welfare of the local community or larger society.

The antiheroine of Soviet womanhood is epitomized by one who centers her social and work experiences entirely around the domicile. Such women are viewed as lazy or even sycophantic, allegedly living off the efforts of others while contributing as little as possible. Joint pressure by former coworkers may be applied in these instances to coerce the recalcitrant out of the home and back into the factory or community service. Recurrent or persistent cases, however, are viewed as being particularly objectionable, their lack of initiative carrying with it a latent aura of political subversion.

The work obligations of Soviet men and women, then, are essentially identical; both are expected to play an active role in industrial production or community services. But how do Soviet women deal with the syndrome of domestic tasks inherited from the agricultural adaptation? Obligations such as child-rearing, household management, and household maintenance descend upon the majority of married women and compete with extradomestic labor for both their time and energies. The schizoid role obligations of women between the home and the factory have posed a persistent problem, the responsibility for which has fallen to the individual rather than the state. Domestic labor has been defined as irrevocably female in gender, menial, and generally devoid of any redeeming social value. As such, it constitutes just another obstacle women must overcome to reach their ultimate goal of full-time employment.

This dilemma in female role-playing has been further complicated by the postwar emphasis upon child-bearing. In the absence of adequate state nursery facilities, the Soviet woman is forced to rely upon the services of friends or relatives if she wishes to work. A reluctance to do so arouses the anxiety of being labeled a lazy or "bourgeois" wife. Social pressure is also experienced by the father of young children, in that he is keeping his spouse from meaningful, rewarding, productive labor by capitalizing on her domestic services.

The Soviet woman, then, is encouraged to develop individual skills apart from her obvious physiological aptitudes for reproduction and nurturance. Unlike her male counterpart, however, she must do so with the handicap of sizeable domestic obligations. Her patriotism is subject to intermittent review and renewal as long as the housewife and mother roles exclude outside employment. But in the world of work she is ideally a comrade—an equal partner—joining other women and men in the giant enterprise of state production and redistribution. To discover if this cultural ideal is ever attained, we must examine more closely the position of women in the Soviet economy.

Workers and Comrades. The Bolshevik Revolution freed over half of Russia's adult population from purely familial domestic labor and channeled it into state production. For about a decade after the political insurrection, the majority of women remained in rural areas, where they joined other workers in farm collectives. Their urban counterparts participated prominently in the textile industry, or filled some of the domestic roles (housemaids, wet nurses) vacated by others. After the first decade, industrialism became the dominant technology of the new state, and the government began to encourage an exodus of rural laborers to the cities. Women subsequently branched into the full spectrum of urban industries along with their male coworkers.

One of the significant encouragements for a governmental program stressing female extradomestic employment was the increasing shortage of male laborers. Russia suffered a tremendous loss of population during the Bolshevik Revolution and both world wars. Whereas the sex ratio was nearly equal before the revolution, there were 107 women for each 100 men in 1926. The ratio of women rose slightly to 108.7 in 1936, but then rose sharply to 150 immediately after World War II; by 1959 the ratio had dropped to 122.1:100, but among those over 32 years the ratio was an astounding 166:100 (Alexandrova 1967).

Certainly, without the concerted labor of women Soviet industrial development would have been severely retarded. Dodge (1966) estimates that nearly one-half of all Russian men alive in 1939 died during World War II. In 1933 some 35.5 percent of all mill workers were female. This figure rose to 40 percent by 1941, and to 52 percent in 1942. The tremendous loss of males during the last war accounts for the continued importance of women, who today constitute 45 percent of all factory workers (Alexandrova 1967).

Female industrial laborers frequently fill such positions as welders, tractor operators, or boiler stokers. They have traditionally monopolized the lower echelon and unmechanized positions requiring the greatest degree of physical labor. Significantly, women constitute the great majority of sanitation personnel. Although female engineers and crew foremen are not unknown, men often qualify for administrative positions largely on the basis of sex alone (see Alexandrova 1967).

Some of the revolutionary idealism and safeguards for female industrial workers have lingered, however. All pregnant employees, for example, receive a paid maternity leave encompassing two months before and two months after parturition, the option of a three-month unpaid extension, and a guarantee of the same position and wage scale upon their return to the job. Factories are also prohibited from requiring women to lift or move heavy loads. While maternity leaves tend to guarantee jobs on which female status in the community depends, the great majority of mothers have no day-care facilities at which to leave their newborns. The idealized worker role, therefore, either forces a mother to "pay to work" or to risk the loss of respect among her comrades by remaining at home with her infant. Similarly, load limits for women are systematically ignored, especially for those in stevedore and construction positions.

In the professions we see familiar patterns. (A professional is one who has qualified for and received a free high school or university education. Such persons thus inherit an obligation to repay the state through employment.) Even in careers with educational prerequisites, women are most likely to be found in those jobs associated with nurturance and socialization and to occupy lower-level positions. Women are concentrated in medical and educational professions, although all fields are theoretically open to them. In the former, women are clearly dominant. Female physicians and nurses constituted a mere 10 percent of the total before the revolution, but this figure rose to 75 percent after the last war. Interestingly, however, 92 percent are found in lower-echelon positions categorized as "average medical personnel," while males dominate administrative and top surgical, clinical, and research positions (Alexandrova 1967). Similarly, among teachers, the lower the grade the more likely it will be taught by a woman. In addition, the higher the administrative position in the educational system, the less likely it will be occupied by a woman.

During wartime, in rural farming collectives, women took

over the greater burden of cultivation in addition to their domestic responsibilities. Much of the hard labor, such as plowing, planting, and harvesting, was done without the aid of machinery. After the war, when machinery became more generally
available, it was operated by males rather than females.
Women, however, continued to perform similar tasks largely by
hand. Today, men still dominate the mechanized, less strenuous labor with which both higher status and income are associated. They also tend to be twice as likely as rural women to have
a higher education, and they virtually monopolize administrative positions on collective farms.

The Chimera of Equality. In urban or rural areas, skilled or unskilled professions, women experience little of the equality envisioned by Bolshevik reformers. In the performance of her patriotic duty, the Soviet woman is most likely to be found in the
lowest ranking jobs with the lowest pay and the greatest energy
investments. The world of work, propagandized as the only true
source of individual pride and accomplishment, means for the
majority of women factory workers and farmers hard, physical,
unmechanized labor with little chance for advancement. Even
though women constitute some 47 percent of the national work
force, administrative posts in the governmental bureaucracy, as
well as the Communist Party apparatus itself, are largely closed
to them.

On the domestic scene, a woman is still expected to bear and
raise children, keep house, and serve her husband. All these
obligations must be met in addition to outside employment—
and in the absence of automobiles, self-timing ovens, automatic
washers and dryers, and one-stop supermarkets. As a wife and
as a woman, she still struggles under the yoke of renewed Stalinist puritanism. Although abortion has been recently legalized
once again, pregnancy control (as opposed to *birth* control) is
still poor because of the unavailability of contraceptive devices.
Women, rather than men, are still held responsible for out-of-
wedlock pregnancies and births. Young Soviet women not uncommonly experience several abortions before marriage, and

have yet to achieve the degree of sexual equality enjoyed by
their grandmothers in the aftermath of the Bolshevik Revolution.

THE CAPITALIST ALTERNATIVE

We shall return to possible future trends in the Soviet female
role later in the chapter. First, however, we shall contrast the
productive and domestic contributions of Soviet women with
their American counterparts. We shall examine why a blue-
collar revolution failed to materialize within the developing
Victorian and American economies, and we shall see how the
course of industrial development affected both female recruitment into production and the accompanying cultural definitions
of womanhood.

Western and Eastern Europe shared a similar technoeconomic and cultural heritage. At the beginning of the nineteenth century, both were predominantly agrarian but with increasingly important urban centers of hand manufacturing and
domestic and foreign exchange. When the machine revolu-
tionized the production of consumer goods, England, for example, mirrored Russia in the passage of laws specifically designed to encourage the migration of farmers to urban
blue-collar positions. European nations shared the social ano-
mie of this population redistribution, and struggled to maintain
their political *status quo* in the face of gross inequities.

Western Europe's involvement in maritime trading networks
seems to be critical in its ultimate aversion to socialist upheaval
and its dedication to the maintenance of capitalism. Africa, Asia,
and the New World had become the economic lifelines of vast
foreign empires. Access to the high seas, colonialism, and the
eventual enlistment of proletarians abroad contributed to the
rapid industrial development of Western Europe. The resultant
prosperity of these nations eventually relieved the gross oppression of domestic working classes, and gave rise to extremely
elastic political systems specializing in the avoidance of revolution through minimal redistributions of internal wealth.

One of the primary enticements of capitalism for the average laborer was the irresistible but elusive pot of gold. Disparities in wealth and power generated by early industrialism were rationalized in capitalist cultures with an elaborate ideology of upward mobility through skill, effort, and cunning. Poverty was redefined as a condition of the unfortunate or unlucky from which the truly competent, ambitious man or woman could escape. Thus the bourgeoisie, rather than becoming an object of concerted revolutionary activity, provided the model for economic aggressiveness and social emulation.

The prosperity achieved by capitalist magnates in Western Europe and in America filtered down to working-class segments on a scale unimagined by Marx and Engels. Despite serious confrontations of private industry and labor, the resiliency of capitalist political institutions allowed economic growth to remain a full step ahead of social unrest. Especially in America, it was increasingly possible for blue-collar workers to attain the material accoutrements of the bourgeoisie.

Women's Role in American Prosperity. The economic development of the United States was in many ways quite unlike that of Western Europe. Beginning initially as a frontier of mercantilist England, America soon assumed a strategic importance in New World trading networks. The American Revolution was more an effort by the American bourgeoisie to control and expand their own economic horizons free from foreign skimming and restraint than any idealist proletarian revolt. With the establishment of the United States as a free agent in world trade, America became not only an equal competitor, but also the largest supplier of New World goods to Western Europe. In the place of colonies abroad (with the later exception of Liberia), American capitalism was nourished by the resources of a constantly expanding contiguous frontier. And in the place of a large indigenous and recruitable work force, economic development was almost wholly dependent on a continuing flow of immigrants. America thus held the advantage of selective recruitment and controlled distribution of its productive labor both before and after the industrial revolution.

The nature of participation of male and female immigrants in the developing American economy was influenced by socioeconomic class, cultural heritage, and historical circumstance. African "immigrants," because of their special pariah status, were channeled into distinct economic and social roles. Male and female slaves were exploited equally. Following the abolition of slavery, black women continued in the field work and domestic occupations, while the men began to clamor for the lowest-order jobs cast off by substantially more recent immigrants.

The numerically and culturally dominant segment of the new republic consisted of white, Anglo-Saxon, Protestants. This basal population and their descendants played a major role in the development of American core culture, and asserted social and political dominance over successive waves of immigrants with different religious beliefs and physical appearance. Thus, for example, newcomers from Ireland, Eastern Europe, and the Mediterranean region were likely to occupy lower-class socioeconomic positions for some time after their arrival. As in Europe, social class was always an important variable in defining the scope of women's economic role. An additional factor, the general availability of laborers, was especially relevant to the United States where the bulk of man- and woman-power was recruited from abroad.

In preindustrial times, labor in America had been in short supply. Women in the cities and settlements played active and vital nondomestic economic roles:

> In colonial America women became butchers, silversmiths, upholsterers, jail-keepers, printers, apothecaries, and doctors (or "doctoresses," as they were then called). Women helped their men, and when they became widows, which happened frequently, they had no choice but to go on running the farm, store, mill, newspaper, shipyard, and even the ship. Nantucket Quaker wives managed substantial enterprises for years while

their husbands went on whaling trips (Bird
1970:20).

The ever-increasing demands of city-dwellers for food and of
the economy for resources lured incoming settlers westward
along the growing frontier. Life was hard in these new rural ex-
panses, and women worked as equal partners with men in the
business of survival. Significantly, frontier areas throughout the
world have been the most liberal in granting legal equality to
women. It was in the western states, where women acted as the
custodians of farms, businesses, and even worked for wages as
domestics and teachers, that the right to vote was first extended.
In the rural South, racial and social class variables were more
important in the determination of female status. Poor women,
irrespective of racial classification, often spent the greater part
of their lives at hard labor in the fields. Wage labor, however,
traditionally divided along racial lines, channeling black
women into domestic service and white women into the horror
of early cotton mills. Women of Southern aristocratic families,
as those of wealthy urbanites in the North, were nonparticipants
in economic development; they and their husbands continued
the bourgeois tradition of Europe and provided the model of
conspicuous consumption and idleness toward which the majority of Americans would eventually aspire. Individual farms
were generally more successful in the Northeast and Midwest,
and often joined the members of minimally extended families
and hired hands in a single capitalist venture. Women in this
situation generally enjoyed a much more secure existence than
did their counterparts in the Western prairie or on the share-
cropper farms that dotted the South. Northern farms were capable of producing food beyond subsistence requirements, and
surpluses were bartered or sold for other consumer goods.
Northern women, therefore, also played a central role in the
economic success of the rural household, in this case through
the production of clothing, canned goods, prepared meats, and
other home-based industries.

Despite this regional variation in rural America, women consistently performed essential extradomestic labor throughout

most of their lives. Early industrialism and the increasing attraction of wage labor and the cities greatly exaggerated this trend. Approximately two-thirds of the American population was still rural in 1890, but urbanism had been spiraling since the end of the Civil War. The wholesale exploitation of young women from propertyless native-born and immigrant families in the "sweatshops" of large cities is a gruesome saga. The appalling poverty of early urban families required the continuation of some rural subsistence techniques. Early urban clusters were strung out like untidy patchworks of miniature farms, with livestock and gardens bound awkwardly within yard enclosures. Food, especially daily staples now easily available at supermarkets, was provided by the efforts of women. At a time when serial pregnancy and years of child-rearing responsibilities were avoidable only through sterility or menopause, and when the burden of domestic tasks was undertaken without the benefit of running water, electricity, or appliances, the life of married women was hard indeed.

Still, some women found it necessary to supplement the family income with independent wage labor as well. A 16- to 18-hour day was not uncommon for those who took in laundry, served as midwives, became seamstresses, took in boarders, or performed domestic labor in the homes of the more fortunate. Widows or women with unemployed or invalid husbands and dependent children—an apparently common situation—were especially imperiled. Worse still were situations where the spouse was an alcoholic or otherwise parasitic on the family resources, since women had no independent legal status apart from their husbands, and hence no right to their own earnings.

Although some of these unfortunates found their way to the factories as well, the majority of married women remained in their homes with dependent children, bringing if necessary the world of work to their own doors. Offspring in poor families, however, inevitably entered the labor market, in an effort to supplement the total income of the domestic unit. Significantly for women, both sexes were recruited equally by factory management. By the 1890s, there were already over a million women working in factories; they constituted about half of all textile and tobacco product workers. Most were young and unmarried, and of immigrant status or parentage.

Conditions in the early factories were dangerous and unhealthy for both sexes, and were compounded by work weeks that often extended over 80 hours. Women, however, inevitably inherited the most menial, repetitious, and unskilled of these industrial tasks, and thus received the lowest salaries and had the least opportunities for advancement. They also allegedly fell victim to unscrupulous employment agencies, many of which cheated them of their salaries or were involved in the recruitment of prostitutes. Working conditions in factories around the turn of the century are outlined in the detailed analysis of Smuts (1959), who states:

> Many factories, especially in the garment and food industries, were overrun with vermin. The New Jersey Bureau of Labor Statistics reported, in 1888, that the linen thread spinners of Patterson [sic] were "compelled to stand on a stone floor in water the year round, most of the time barefoot, with a spray of water from a revolving cylinder flying constantly against the breast; and, the coldest night in winter . . . those poor creatures must go to their homes with the water dripping from their under-clothing . . . because there could not be space or a few minutes allowed them wherein to change. . . ."
> The lint-filled, moisture-saturated atmosphere of the Southern cotton mills led to constant expectoration, and floors were slimy with a mixture of sputum and tobacco juice. In other industries, the atmosphere was even more dangerously contaminated by tobacco, glass, mica, or brass dust, or by the fumes of naptha, lacquer, paint, and other volatile materials. In all of these industries, tuberculosis, pneumonia, and less serious respiratory infections were common.
> In the shoe industry women scrubbed the excess glue and dye from the finished prod-

uct with bits of rag dipped in hot, soapy water. The water soon became a black, corrosive solution of glue, dye, and soap which stained the hands beyond cleansing, rotted the skin, and ate away the fingernails. Artificial flower makers developed horny, spade-fingered hands from constant use of hot irons to press their delicate creations to shape. Arsenic, lead, mercury, and phosphorus were used in a variety of industrial processes, usually with little or no effort to prevent poisoning (1959:76–77).

Although the bulk of the female work force was found in factory environments such as these, a number of "white-collar" positions also began to open to women. During the Civil War, women established themselves in clerical positions in formerly male-dominated business offices. Women, in addition, assisted and then largely replaced male sales clerks as store owners became convinced of the advantages of their diligence, courteousness, and low wage scales. Teaching and nursing stood for some time as the only female professions, but both at first required only limited and informal prerequisite training. Education for schoolteachers, for example, often went little beyond grammar school. The establishment of women's colleges and women's limited admission to coeducational medical and law schools occurred only decades after the Civil War. Still, the teaching profession was virtually monopolized by women following the war, and universal education for children was made possible largely through their general availability to school boards—at low salaries. As in the employment of women in industry, these clerical, sales, and professional positions were typically occupied by females who were unmarried and under the age of 25.

Women in the broad base of society, in the lower and lower-middle classes, played a continuingly significant role in both the preindustrial and industrial development of the American economy. After the turn of the century, and especially in the aftermath of World War I, however, there was a significant change in the image of women as workers, wives, and mothers. Despite their persistent and increasing participation in the nation's economic growth, a positive value began to attach itself to the *non-producer* role for women, and on behaviors that were both dichotomous with and complementary to those of males.

Ladies, Girls, and Women. The question of whether a mature female shall be categorized as a lady, a girl, or a woman may appear to represent a futile exercise in semantics. In modern society there are many occasions when these terms may be used interchangeably. And yet the subtle shades of meaning that contrast them seem to be critical markers of the ultimate definition of ideal female gender roles in American culture. Two indices, maturity and social standing, were initially important as status indicators. Womanhood in the nineteenth century was associated with marriage and motherhood. Females employed in industry, although physiologically mature, were typically single, and hence "working girls." Interestingly, the reference to employed females as "the girls in the office" regardless of age or marital status has had considerable longevity in our culture. Its use has been encouraged by the diminutive position it implies and also by the rather recent cultural glorification of youth by women themselves.

Ladies were initially females who did not work by virtue of their membership in financially secure families. Their refined behavior, domestic preoccupation, and dependent, noncompetitive behavior patterns came to be associated with upward social mobility, and hence formed the cornerstone of American femininity.

The question of why American women assumed a social identity incongruent with their overall economic contributions is certainly an interesting one. Even though, in the last century, women worked side by side with men in field and factory, there was never, as in the Soviet Union, a legislated or informal sense of equality among the sexes. Factory jobs themselves were "sexed" according to the degree of mechanization, skill, prestige, and commensurate salary. In American society, economic development proceeded rapidly enough to allow the preservation of old, preindustrial gender roles. The mass participation of women in blue-collar labor that characterized a significant part of the nineteenth century, for example, was eliminated before inroads toward comparable social equality could be well established. Male immigrants from Canada and Ireland began to pour into the United States by 1850, and to gradually replace women in unskilled factory positions. Improved machinery, such as the replacement of the steam engine with the electric motor and the development of assembly line techniques, also played a role in eliminating the manual and semi-mechanized tasks once assigned to women and children only.

A number of developmental trends thus combined to remove women from productive roles that placed them in the same social and work contexts as males. Perhaps the single most important of these was a significant increase in the financial security of families with each generation. America, by comparison with European nations, had become a rich land where even poverty-stricken urban households could raise themselves to a comfortable level through the combined work efforts of several of their members. Successive family units found it increasingly possible to keep their children in school and, significantly, to keep their women, married or unmarried, at home. Piecework performed by wives at home for large companies was gradually eliminated through the efficiency of mass production. Their domestic burdens were similarly lightened by the technological revolution that brought electricity, indoor plumbing, and increasingly sophisticated appliances to urban and suburban households. Female idleness, associated in the past with the gentlewoman and social standing, began to fall within the reach of an emergent middle class. There soon came a time when *any* woman could be a "lady"—when she did not *have* to work, but could assume a dependent status and focus her entire energies around the compulsive performance of household routines and the custody of domestic harmony.

The way the great majority of American women have regarded themselves and their ultimate role in society has been subject to historical influences. Says Bird:

> Generally speaking, frontier conditions—
> wars, revolutions, and feverish boom times
> which provide urgent work for all hands—

have motivated men and women to similar or
androgynous goals. By contrast, periods of
slow or orderly economic growth such as the
first and fifth decades of this century have
cultivated masculinity or femininity as goals
in themselves. In these periods, men are encouraged to submit to industrial discipline in
order to make money as the primary way to
prove their "manliness," while women are
encouraged to stay at home and be "feminine."

Androgynous periods are often marked by
feminist movements which assert the right of
women to independent action. Male-
dominated or masculinist periods, on the
other hand, encourage women to define
themselves in terms of their relationship to
men. The two philosophies have alternated
just frequently enough to keep every generation of American women from using their
mothers as models (1970:21–22).

Despite the cyclical fluctuations in the recruitment of women
into the labor force and associated advances toward legal equality, there has been a tremendous consistency in female role-
playing. In the nineteenth century, for example, the vast majority of women who worked outside the home were single, and
terminated their employment immediately upon engagement or
marriage. Motivations for employment, even in the professions,
seldom included the achievement of career-related goals.
Women worked out of a sense of responsibility to a struggling
household, but also to escape parental controls, to acquire the
material accoutrements of "ladyship," and to find a husband. Indeed, employment of women served (and continues to serve) as
rite de passage between girlhood and womanhood—between
the roles of dutiful daughter and dutiful wife. The mass of
American young women were always a part of the larger capitalist adventure, hoping to secure a hypergamous relationship and
to find their personal achievement through that of their spouses.
Despite the miserable, often inhuman, conditions of early factories, women rushed through their gates with great enthusiasm:

> Most working women did not act as though they were crushed by their lives as workers. North or South, they had spirit and energy to fight on occasion, to sing and tell ribald jokes over the noise of machines, to go home and stay up half the night converting their last week's pay into new dresses and hats for the following Sunday, to leave the factory on Saturday night with a week's wages, and shop until the last stores closed at midnight (Smuts 1959:98).

The author adds this insightful observation:

> The attitudes of people toward their own conditions are always circumscribed by what they are accustomed to and what they can reasonably hope for. From today's vantage point, or even from the viewpoint of the middle and upper classes in 1890, the working women of 1890 labored under intolerable conditions. The average working woman, however, had no burning sense of being wronged. She went to work, not because she had to in order to eat, but because she thought that, on balance, she would be better off if she worked. What she got from work was usually very much what she had expected. If she had come from Europe, or from a poor farm in America, what she found was sometimes considerably better than what she had expected. When she thought of something still better, she was more likely to hope for an early marriage to a good husband than for an easier job or higher pay (Smuts 1959:93).

And American prosperity brought, if not better husbands, earlier marriages and decreasing demands upon women for drudgery both outside and inside the home. The cries of early feminists and reformers, themselves members of largely upper-class families, fell on deaf ears so long as the doors of economic gain remained open to conjugal pairs. Dichotomous sex roles, rather than disappearing, became an index of social class. Supposedly inherent differences among men and women were exaggerated in dress, etiquette, and literature. As the need for female extradomestic labor subsided, there grew a body of cultural arguments stressing the unfitness of women for such tasks. Factory labor, for example, was gradually viewed as an endangerment to the physical and moral well-being of young women. Their celebrated purpose in life, namely child-bearing, was thought to be imperiled by labor that placed a stress on delicate female reproductive organs. Further, an unmarried "girl" could fall victim to unscrupulous males outside the protective dome of her natal household, and could acquire dangerously independent notions and spendthrift habits incongruent with future wifely duties. Prolonged education was also viewed as a threat to femininity. Respected voices were raised mourning the hazards of learning to female health and sanity. Those few women who were motivated to pursue professional careers were, in order to avoid job termination, legal encapsulation, and serial pregnancy, forced to remain single and thereby be held up as examples of the depravity of female aggressiveness and achievement orientation. Women were to live for reproduction, but not to speak of it; to defend the fortress of morality, but to shield their eyes from immoral things; and to cheer their husbands to victory in a world largely hidden from their view and daily experience:

> Purity, modesty, and lack of passion were among the most valued of the qualities generally attributed to women. Since men were viewed as naturally lustful and aggressive, women's reticence seemed to serve as the principal defense of moral standards. Like other essential feminine qualities, however, the virtuous instincts were viewed as extremely vulnerable. To prevent their defeat, it was necessary to minimize young women's opportunities for unsupervised association with men, and to isolate them from any source of knowledge about or interest in sex. Indeed, polite convention insisted that there be no reference in public to the physical basis of sex. Ladies were expected to refer, if

> absolutely necessary, to limbs rather than
> legs. There were even some—in the seven-
> ties and eighties if not later—who clothed
> the limbs of their pianos in modest ruffles.
> The girl who did not live up to such ideals of
> feminine propriety was likely to be viewed
> as a temptress and an outcast (Smuts
> 1959:117–18).

These notions of womanhood remain an important part of American core culture, although they have been somewhat eroded in recent decades. The domestic isolation of women was erected as an ideal, but in reality was seldom achieved. In the previous century, women of families financially secure enough to deliver them from extradomestic labor traditionally filled their spare time with some type of external voluntary, philanthropic, or recreational activities. Females of the leisure class were the first social workers, fund-raisers, and reformers. Unlike their brothers, they also often took advantage of their idle premarital years to complete their high school education. Near the turn of the century, the mushrooming demand for office workers, teachers, nurses, clerks, and telephone operators provided a respectable avenue of escape for "ladies" before marriage, and of upward mobility for women of lower-middle-class families.

The modern American woman owes her present position in society, happily or unhappily, to this unique cultural heritage. At the beginning of the twentieth century, she was essentially an economic and political minor, whose intellectual development and sexual expression were sharply curtailed by society. She was a preconceived notion, a cherished product of her own instincts. If he was the dynamic, she was the static; if he was the rollercoaster, she was along for the ride. This was her *natural* place, or so her culture told her. But history has a miraculous way of altering genetic codes, of muting the immutable. America in the twentieth century was forced to call upon the productive efforts of women as never before, and in doing so, to define them anew.

Thoroughly Modern Millie. The early twentieth century was a time of great reformist, unionist, and feminist activity. Female social workers, drawn largely from the upper classes, pushed for and achieved legislated improvements in the working conditions of women. Suffragettes complained bitterly about wage and legal inequities between the sexes, and began to exert pressure at state and federal levels. Women's causes, however, were substantially improved as a result of World War I. The response of women to the requests of political and military leaders to fill domestic and foreign labor shortages was enthusiastic. In both factories and businesses, they performed men's tasks, and performed them well. Following the war, a significant change in the image of womanhood swept American culture. By 1920, women had been granted the right to vote, the option of divorce with alimony, and access to birth-control information and devices. Although the "lady" image of modesty, virtue, purity, and domesticity persisted, both higher education and employment outside the home for unmarried women certainly threatened "femininity." The flapper symbolized the epitome of the new woman, liberated of her endless corsets and set to music. The fashion industry boomed, and the major thrust of the feminist movement was dampened by the contentment which concessions short of total equality, such as the franchise extension, provided.

The Great Depression brought renewed objections to female labor. If there were no jobs for men, how could women hope to remain in the ranks of wage-earners without further damaging male opportunities? But women continued to seek and find employment in unskilled and underpaid positions traditionally reserved for their sex alone. Indeed, the mass unemployment of males may have been responsible for the continuing increase of female workers as supplementary breadwinners during this decade.

With the outbreak of World War II, civilian and military labor shortages were again immediately filled by women. So wholehearted was the war effort, and so great was the demand for labor, that nearly all occupations and salary scales were opened to women. Such new culture heroines as Rosie the Riveter

arose to characterize the breaking down of previous barriers to
skilled and manual positions. Women as a social group blos-
somed with their new occupational freedom, and interestingly
began to wear pants publicly for the first time. A second significant development lay in the pervasiveness of recruitment itself.
Previous labor shortages in America had primarily been filled
by young, single women. The institution of marriage all but
closed the doors of employment to women. The social impropriety of wives working outside the home was in some states and
institutions even underscored by laws prohibiting its occurrence. This barrier, however, also fell during World War II, and
marked a significant break with the past. For the first time,
women of all ages and marital statuses entered extradomestic
employment, setting the trend that continues to the present day.

By the end of the 1940s, a significant portion of the life cycle
of women had been altered. The average age at marriage was
continually decreasing. Males no longer postponed wedlock for
an extended period dictated by the convention of financial security. Although the majority of women continued to place primary emphasis on child-bearing, many worked until their first
pregnancy to help establish the new household. The net result
of earlier marriages, along with improved birth control methods,
was a shortening of the child-bearing phase. By the time the
majority of married women had reached middle age, they were
no longer encumbered with time-consuming responsibilities for
preschoolers. An entirely new category of female labor was
thereby made available for exploitation.

Despite the culturally inevitable layoffs of women after the
war and their replacement by men, they continued to flock into
their more traditional clerical and sales positions and "nurturant" professions in order to meet the demands of an expanding population and economy. The re-romanticism of love and
motherhood and the subsequent trends toward marriage and
baby-making in the postwar period thus had little effect on female participation in the labor market. Mothers were younger
than ever, and ready to resume their productive roles outside
the home in the prime of their lives. Culturally, however, an effect of the new romantic and maternal emphasis in female role

definitions was a reticence in the arena of equal rights for women. Gross inequities in salary scales and blatant discrimination in job placement and advancement opportunities were commonplace in women's everyday work experience. And yet, as in the nineteenth century, the majority of female workers did not desert their typewriters, switchboards, or blackboards:

> Without quite realizing it, we have come to depend on a work force of married women who do not think of themselves as workers and are not treated seriously on the job. Only when we look back into history do we see how they have been pulled into wage work and pushed back home at the convenience of the changing economy. Women make no noisome ghettos, join few unions, rarely organize demonstrations, come when they are called, and go quietly when bidden (Bird 1970:45).

According to a 1969 government publication, *Handbook on Women Workers*, women compose approximately 37 percent of America's labor force. Some 42 percent of all women of working age are employed, and within this group three out of every five are married and 38 percent have dependent children. A full half of these workers are 40 years of age or older. Occupationally, clerical positions are held by over one-third, while professionals and technicians (including teachers) account for only 15 percent.

Despite the passage of various equal employment practice and wage scale laws over the past three decades, and of Title VII of the 1964 Civil Rights Act, sex discrimination is still a central theme of American life. This fact is illustrated in Table 11-1 with a comparison of the average salaries of men and women 14 years of age and older by occupational category.

If we control for educational preparation among women and men, these inequities persist. Table 11-2 compares the median income of persons 25 years and older by sex and educational level.

If women continue to make such a significant economic contribution to American society, why does social discrimination

Table 11-1. Median wage in 1972 of full-time, year-around workers, by occupational category and sex [a]

OCCUPATIONAL CATEGORY	WOMEN	MEN
Professional, technical workers	$8,946	$13,826
Managers and Administrators (except farm)	7,289	13,783
Clerical workers	6,196	9,978
Sales workers	4,649	11,904
Craftsmen	5,893	10,694
Operatives	5,145	8,880
Nonfarm laborers	4,807	7,723
Private household workers	2,609	—
Service workers (except private household)	4,701	8,109
Farmers, farm managers	—	5,808
Farm laborers, foremen	—	4,689

SOURCE: U.S. Bureau of the Census 1973:129.
[a] Dashes indicate an inadequate population base for comparison.

persist? Certainly, the cultural heritage of masculine superiority and domestic isolation is still an important factor. But, as we have noted, this bias has been compromised repeatedly in times of need, only to be reclaimed with the first boatload of home-coming soldiers. Unlike the Soviet Union, the United States has never suffered a severe or prolonged shortage of males in the

Table 11-2. Median income in 1972 of full-time, year-around workers, by educational attainment and sex

EDUCATIONAL ATTAINMENT	WOMEN	MEN
Elementary school		
Less than 8 years	$ 4,221	$ 7,042
8 years	4,784	8,636
High School		
1 to 3 years	5,253	9,462
4 years	6,166	11,073
College		
1 to 3 years	7,020	12,428
4 years	8,736	14,879
5 years or more	11,036	16,877

SOURCE: U.S. Bureau of the Census 1973:121, 125.

work force. There has, therefore, never been a persistent need for major sex role redefinition.

The strong family focus of women in American society persists largely because sufficient demands have not yet arisen to replace the family as a primary socialization agency. Thus, if and when labor requirements draw the majority of women into the work force, other cultural institutions will arise to fill the housewife-mother roles. Sex roles definitions will then be modified accordingly. At present, however, women are trapped in the vicious circle of *labor interruptus.* Employers and professional schools are reluctant to train or advance young women, anticipating their marriage and/or pregnancy. Females who do manage to complete their preparation for employment may often, by convention, leave the job market for five years or a decade, only to find on their return that they are shortchanged in terms of openings or qualifications. Since the woman over 40 is likely to be married, and to view her employment as a contribution to the family income rather than as an individually fulfilling career, she is less aware of and less sensitive to her subordination to males.

In recent years we have heard the loud protests of feminist reformers, raising many of the same issues that troubled their sisters over a century ago. Again, such women typically come from families of the upper-income brackets, and are well educated. Like earlier feminists, they compose only a small minority of the total population. But these facts should not dismiss the feminists' importance. Those who have spoken out against sexism tend to be women who are achievement-oriented, who take their careers seriously, and who have thereby become aware of obstacles to female advancement. Feminists, then—even without regiments of common women at their sides—have tended to vocalize the cultural disequilibria that foreshadow actual legislated change. The militants of any reformist movement function as weathervanes of the larger society. They not only encourage change, but are themselves products of changes already in process.

In the past decade the oppression of many minority groups in

American society has been effectively challenged. The Civil Rights Act of 1964, originally intended to guarantee equal opportunities to all regardless of color, religion, or national origin, was reluctantly extended to prohibit discrimination on the basis of sex as well. Women thus rode on the coattails of blacks and other minorities in the achievement of equal legal status. The whole concept of womanhood in the 1960s and 1970s has undergone very rapid modification. In the mass media, for example, there is a frankness that was unthinkable only a decade ago. Television commercials stress the social significance of brassieres that "lift and separate," the importance of vitamins with iron "because you're a woman," or the efficacy of special pain-relievers for "the trying times." There is a tremendous emphasis upon physical attractiveness specifically relating to bodies. Madison Avenue, for both fun and profit, instills the fear of rejection due to underarm odor, bad breath, foot odor, vaginal odor, or off-white teeth. Women are portrayed not only as sex objects, but as individuals pursuing their own sexual goals. The slogan "You've come a long way, baby" is certainly a truism, even for nonsmokers.

How can we explain these recent modifications in the feminine image? There are a number of factors related to the postwar American economy and its effect on social institutions that have contributed to the recognition of women as *individuals*, apart from their relationships to fathers and husbands. Although the wife-mother role is still central, the participation of women in extradomestic labor has increased steadily since World War II. Women have come to so monopolize positions in the vast communications networks of this nation that a joint strike for a single day would virtually paralyze the American economy. The indispensability of the mass of underpaid clerical workers and telephone operators has become more apparent with each decade. Even if women themselves do not view their labor as especially significant, the fact that nearly 42 percent collect regular paychecks is certainly modifying former stereotypes of economic dependency. Their breadwinner roles are also encouraged by recent economic recessions. During periods of

high unemployment, women are less likely to be affected than
are men, and hence often assume the major financial burden of
household expenses.

The increasing realization by women of their ability to "make
it on their own," along with the mounting pressures of a highly
technical society, have perhaps contributed to the booming divorce rate in America. The matricentric unit is beginning to
again claim a respectable position alongside the conjugal one.
Most of the areas of life formerly delegated to women, such as
household maintenance and the socialization of young, have
been taken over to some extent by public institutions and private agencies. The working mother may thus free herself of the
daily responsibilities of such domestic tasks by delegating them
to others.

Perhaps most striking, especially to those socialized in previous generations, are changes in the sexual orientation of
women. The true "lady" was ideally timid, ignorant of physical
sex, a virgin before marriage, and chaste thereafter, save for periodic submissions to her virile spouse. Since males are portrayed as sexually aggressive and irresponsible, women bear the
burden of preserving morality through nonparticipation or natural frigidity. The elimination of sexual desire in women
requires the expenditure of considerable energy by socializing
agents, and the isolation of females from situations where such
feelings may be aroused. The entrance of single women into the
money economy in the previous century removed many such
barriers to free social intercourse, and provided women with
some of the earliest opportunities to make decisions about their
own bodies. Many social commentators agree that the flapper of
the 1920s represented the first official departure from the Victorian image of womanhood. It was in the post-World War I years,
when the employment of single women was commonplace and
respectable that full female body contours were highlighted in
fashion, and that the daring suggestion that women had sexual
needs was advanced. American culture of successive decades
has not questioned the possibility of female sensuality so much
as the proper channels for its expression.

The sexual freedom of women and notions on the propriety of female employment have developed in a somewhat parallel fashion. At first prohibited from extradomestic labor, women were subsequently permitted to participate only before marriage. Presently, children rather than marriage take priority over working outside the home. More and more women, however, are maintaining their participation in the labor market through the use of domestic and child-care services. Sexual frontiers have expanded in a similar progression. At first denied their sexuality, women were gradually allowed to express passion— but to one male and within the institution of marriage. Acceptable channels of sexual expression, just as motivations for employment, were subject to class variation. Although premarital sex is still informally tabooed for women in the larger society, resistance is considerably diminished if the woman is engaged, or at the very least "in love." Virginity and chastity, however, are certainly doomed as majority phenomena for mature, unmarried women in American society. The facility with which effective birth control devices may be procured has gone far in segregating sexual activity from conflicting emotions of love, fear, and guilt.

But what if we are experiencing just another high point in an endless cycle of feminist and masculinist phases? Will the 1970s launch limited vanguards against sexism, only to be followed by a period of renewed romanticism of home, family, and chastity? The future, of course, is impossible to predict with any certainty. Still, a continuation of this cyclical trend is contradicted by present economic prospects. Unless the United States begins a systematic program of foreign military conquest, it is unlikely that the American economy can continue to expand at its present rate. The old "sky's the limit" notion for energetic newlyweds is no longer realistic for the vast majority. What this means for women is that they may be increasingly less able to measure their own and their family's achievement solely by their husbands. Rather, women can expect to work outside the home, either to pursue a career or to supplement the total income, for a considerable part of their lives. It is presently dif-

ficult to conceive of economic conditions that would permit the
size of the female work force to be significantly reduced in the
near future.

With respect to the sexuality of women, it seems just as unlikely that Puritanism will be resurrected. A major economic
and ecological issue that confronts the entire world, overpopulation, has been largely responsible for the recent availability of devices to prevent pregnancy. Barring another World
War, a baby boom and the attendant glorification of motherhood
such as that of the 1950s would certainly be maladaptive. The
need to control population growth has encouraged legitimate
public discussion of reproduction by women and men alike,
which has informed both sexes about the pleasures and responsibilities of sexual activity.

THE INDUSTRIAL PATTERN

In the twentieth century the involvement of American women
in wage labor has fluctuated significantly in phase with wartime
and peacetime economies. Yet, during this century there has
been an overall trend for women to become full-time wage
earners. Typically, these working women are either unmarried,
married and childless, or mothers with school-age children.
Most American women devote some years of their lives to raising young children, and during this interval do not often engage
in extradomestic employment. However, these women no
longer hesitate to work before and after this interval. Female
workers are no longer considered *déclassé*, nor is the fact of
their employment an undue embarrassment to either spouse.
The recent wave of feminist activity and legislation for economic and social equality among women and men parallels and
continues trends initiated during earlier phases of high female
employment.

Russian women have contributed to the market economy
throughout the twentieth century. The legislated sexual equality that came on the heels of the Bolshevik Revolution occurred
in response to Russian requirements for a large and mobile

work force. The female contribution to that work force was systematically maintained as a result of periodic depopulations of Russian men during every major episode of armed conflict in the twentieth century.

After World War II, the Soviet Union experienced a curious dilemma—one that was placed squarely on the shoulders of its female citizens. Although the labor of women in the factories, farms, and professions was critical to economic recuperation and development because nearly half of the USSR's mature males were eliminated during the war, Russia was at the brink of a serious population crisis. It soon became apparent, therefore, that women would have to make even greater contributions to the state. Material and honorific incentives were then instituted to encourage marriage and child-bearing as a patriotic but temporary departure from wage labor. Recently, the purely domestic, wife-mother role for Soviet women has begun to make subtle advances in popularity. The woman who forsakes all for her husband and children is winning a new place in Russian fiction. Increasing amounts of revenue are being channeled into cosmetics and women's clothing, and there seems to be a growing appreciation of material items and leisure activities.

Does this mean that entirely opposite trends in the patterning of sex roles are developing in the Soviet Union and America? We argue, on the contrary, that capitalist and socialist industrial experiments have been amazingly similar with respect to the role played by women. In each case, whether formally or informally, women have remained subordinate to males in work and social contexts. In the Soviet Union, it is largely the continuing shortage of male laborers that accounts for the active extradomestic life of women. Sex roles *per se*, however—with the possible exception of the immediate postrevolutionary period— were never equal or convergent. Women have assumed positions similar to those of their American counterparts during wartime. Interestingly, the apparent trend toward a re-romanticism of the Russian wife-mother model mirrors developments in the United States. That is, the demand for female blue-collar workers in the Soviet Union is beginning to drop off for the first time since the industrial transition. Automation is slowly replacing the largely manual positions reserved for women, and the sex ratio among citizens below 40 years of age is rapidly approaching normal proportions.

Economic prosperity and the replenishment of the Soviet work force with males, therefore, have recently created a situation similar to the peacetime United States. A parallel trend, the dichotomization of women into occasional, part-time, and career workers, is also emerging. The universal work ethic for Soviet women seems to be providing a mechanism for this division without serious compromises of existing role definitions. That is, women whose ambition it is to pursue a full-time career are taking advantage of the child-care and household services of those who prefer employment in the domestic milieu. Soviet professional women not only have smaller families, but provide legitimate part- or full-time occupations for the apparently swelling ranks of family-oriented comrades.

The female role in the United States and the Soviet Union is thus in many respects similar. The prolonged demand for female factory workers, farm laborers, construction workers, teachers, and medical personnel earned a fair degree of formal or legal equality for Russian women. But, as we have seen, social and political equality with men has lagged far behind governmental claims, and, as in the United States, has yet to be won. Surprisingly, sex role convergence in America appears to have made more substantial advances. Despite the cyclical masculinist and feminist periods in American history, legal and social equality have proceeded more uniformly. It is perhaps easier to rectify recognized, formal inequality than it is to relieve the internal injustices of a system claiming to be free of them. The future Soviet economy may indeed produce a more substantial number of professional or career women through the creation of adequate collective child-care centers, but it has yet to liberate its growing numbers of domestic comrades from the drudgery of household routines. A universal distribution of modern conveniences such as self-timing ovens, frost-free refrigerators, automatic washers and dryers, and the automobile will have to await further Soviet economic development. And when such prizes of industrial production have been won, Russia will share with the United States the inheritance of a new generation of affluent, well-educated, and energetic women who will again seek self-fulfillment outside the home, but on an equal footing with their male peers.

Industrial societies thus share the potential, the luxury, of invalidating most of the dichotomous behavioral sets assigned to women and men. Is, then, sex becoming obsolete? This is certainly an important question, and one that should be viewed within the comparative perspective we have now gained.

WOMEN IN THE FUTURE

Introduction. What is the future of the female of the species? As we have seen, her evolutionary past has involved multitudinous adaptations to different social environments. Yet throughout our examination of some of these adaptations certain patterns have emerged. In this final section we shall attempt to use our knowledge of these cultural regularities to predict the evolutionary future of womankind.

Anthropologists have no special prescience. We cannot, therefore, predict small details of culture change such as the future whims of Parisian designers. We could make some guesses on the matter in accordance with our appreciation of the fact that clothing styles tend to be cyclical (see Kroeber 1919) and to reflect social status. But, what women will be wearing in the future, whether hemlines will go up or down, or whether clothing styles of men and women will become even more alike than they are today, is not of great concern here. Perhaps such guesses are best left to our readers.

It would also be unwise to attempt to predict the rate of evolutionary change in social life. We really have no way of knowing what woman's place will be in a decade, or a century, from now. Cultural changes have a tendency to occur at different rates and anthropologists are not yet able to fully anticipate these shifts in the momentum of change.

General trends in social life, however, can be anticipated.

With the insight we have gained about the workings of cultural systems, it is possible to analyze the society of which we are a part.

The Demise of Gender. The major trend for men and women in the future, as we see it, is that gender roles will become increasingly unimportant. History teaches us that gender roles have been ubiquitous, occurring in every known society extant today, and in those of the reconstructed prehistoric past. But history does not teach us that these roles are fixed or inevitable.

What we have learned is that the complementary roles of women and men have had the function in human life of organizing societies in such a way that each group performs separate tasks, thus eliminating the need for everyone to do all tasks on an individual basis. Gender roles are a means of social specialization. In the past this usually dimorphic form of specialization has affected all aspects of social organization: the socially preferred places for women and men cut across the economic, religious, and political activities in societies.

Sexual anatomy is one of the simplest criteria for the social classification of people. A person's sex is normally determined easily at birth. Thus the allocation of a newborn child into the social group to which he or she will belong for the rest of his/her life is rapid, unambiguous, and permits early training that helps to insure the transmission of culture from generation to generation. The simplicity of using the principle of sex for the classification of activities that have nothing to do with reproduction explains the ubiquity and durability of this practice.

In addition to sex criteria, principles such as age, social class, caste, or occupation also can provide means of marking off specialized groups within societies. A major evolutionary trend recognized by anthropologists is the increase in modes of sociospecialization with an increase in organizational complexity. In small-scale societies with relatively simple technologies, the division of the population into specialized groups is based on only a limited number of criteria (i.e., age, sex, common kinship). Large-scale, industrialized societies, however, are segmented in a greater number of ways, and the social groups so formed are more numerous and more cross-cutting in their membershps than those in smaller, less complex societies.

Gender roles seem to be increasingly dysfunctional in complex societies. The division of persons into two groups is becoming increasingly opposed to the requirements of social segmentation required in industrialized, urban environments. The plethora of different occupational specializations required in these societies are most efficiently met by training people for their occupational roles on the basis of talent and aptitude rather than on the anatomy of their reproductive systems. Caroline Bird (1971) outlines the cost to society of keeping women in what economists call customary work. That is, work without pay. Although the presence of unpaid or underpaid workers can benefit some segments of a society, such a situation is usually detrimental to society as a whole.

People who have become interested in this aspect of the present status of women see a partial analogy with the history of American blacks. They argue that slavery was abolished because it became too costly to maintain. The more recent Civil Rights Movement can also be understood, in part, by analyzing the price society pays to keep a large class of underpaid workers with underutilized talents, when such talents and occupational skills are greatly in demand. In this general sense American women, unpaid as housewives or underpaid in most "feminine" occupations, cost society more than it can afford.

Predicting that women will become increasingly absorbed in the wage work force is not mere speculation about the distant future. This process is already well underway. Increasingly greater numbers of women each year are opting for full-time professional careers or to return to work after their small children start attending schools. Bird (1971) discusses several social processes that combine to permit this trend. First, women now have many non-child-bearing and non-child-rearing years because of fertility control, nutritional advances, and medical care. Second, compulsory education requires that children be away from home during many hours of the day; because education is usually co-educational, it ideally exposes boys and girls to the same instruction. Thus in America today a great deal of cultural information is passed on to young people regardless of their sex. Third, women have sampled wage employment and apparently like it. This process was accelerated by World War II, which removed a large number of male wage earners from their jobs. The vacated positions were filled by women, many of whom continued working in the economically booming postwar years.

Some observers of the present social scene have wondered whether the old dichotomous sex roles will be replaced by new ones (see Rosenberg and Sutton-Smith 1972). We believe that this is unlikely because the social categories of sex are not merely human devices contrived to guarantee the mutual physical attraction necessary for the continued survival of the species. Rather, societies have perpetuated sex categories to facilitate socioeconomic interdependence and cooperation among group members. In industrial societies this interdependence is now insured by other, more complex and more appropriate forms of integration. Gender categories thus have much less adaptive significance in modern societies than in ancient ones.

If women become integrated into the work force, who will raise the children, clean the house, do the shopping, and perform all the other necessary tasks of maintaining a household? Many of these responsibilities undoubtedly will be shared by men and women. However, it may be expected that much of this work will become professionalized. Professional cleaners with specialized equipment can clean a house much more efficiently than one woman working with less adequate equipment (Bird 1971). Many items can be ordered by phone and delivered, thus saving many hours of time formerly spent by women waiting in supermarket lines. It is likely that children will continue to be raised by their parents, but with fathers participating in the education of their children as fully as mothers. In addition, there will often be other adults who are close to and responsible for the youngsters. Day-care centers may be expected to become more prevalent, thus allowing preschoolers more opportunity to interact with agemates than is now usually possible.

There are people who fear such changes. Because most people have been raised to equate their personal worth with their closeness of fit to sex role stereotypes, the loss of the stereotypes will mean the loss of self-identity for some. The man who judges his own worth on the basis of his ability to support a woman will lose his sense of self-worth if his wife ably supports herself. Likewise, the woman who feels fulfilled by being a "good wife and mother" will be profoundly shaken by social expectations for her to be a well-informed and occupationally active member of society.

New models of behavior for men and women will undoubtedly permit greater personal self-development than traditional gender roles allow. Such changes are already well underway. As social scientists we consider them inevitable. As women we herald them.

References

Aberle, David.
  1961. Matrilineal descent in cross-cultural perspective. In *Matrilineal kinship*, eds. David M. Schneider and Kathleen Gough, pp. 655–727. Berkeley and Los Angeles: University of California Press.

Albert, A.
  1961. The mammalian testis. In *Sex and internal secretions, Vol. 1*, ed. William C. Young, pp. 305–365. Baltimore: Williams and Wilkins.

Albert, Ethel M.
  1963. Women of Burundi: a study of social values. In *Women of tropical Africa*, ed. Denise Paulme, pp. 179–216. Berkeley and Los Angeles: University of California Press.

Alexandrova, Vera.
  1967. The Soviet Union. In *Women in the modern world*, ed. Rafael Patai, pp. 387–489. New York: Free Press.

Anastasi, Anne.
  1958. *Differential psychology: individual and group differences in behavior*. New York: Macmillan Company.

Angelino, Henry, and Charles L. Shedd.
  1955. A note on berdache. *American Anthropologist* 57:121–126.

Ardrey, Robert.
  1961. *African genesis*. London: Collins.
  1966. *The territorial imperative*. New York: Atheneum.
  1970. *The social contract*. New York: Atheneum.

Bachofen, Johann.
  1861. *Das Mutterrecht*. Basel: Benno Schwabe.

Ball, Donald W.
  1967. Toward a sociology of toys: Inanimate objects, socialization, and the demography of the doll world. *The Sociological Quarterly* 8:447–58.

Bardwick, Judith.
1971. *Psychology of women: A study of bio-cultural conflicts.* New York: Harper and Row.

Barry, H. A., M. K. Bacon and I. L. Child.
1957. A cross-cultural survey of some sex differences in socialization. *Journal of Abnormal and Social Psychology* 55:327–32.

Barth, Fredrik.
1961. *Nomads of south Persia: the Basseri tribe of the Khamseh confederacy.* Oslo: Oslo University Press.

Bateson, Gregory.
1947. Sex and culture. *Annals of the New York Academy of Sciences* 47:647–60.

Beach, Frank A.
1965. Retrospect and prospect. In *Sex and behavior,* ed. Frank A. Beach, pp. 535–69. New York: John Wiley & Sons.

Beauchamp, William.
1900. Iroquois women. *Journal of American Folk-Lore* 13:81–91.

Berndt, Ronald M., and Catherine H. Berndt.
1964. *The world of the first Australians.* Chicago: University of Chicago Press.

Bird, Carolin.
1970. *Born female.* New York: David McKay Company, Inc.

Bogoras, Waldemar.
1904–9. The Chuchee. In the Jesup North Pacific Expedition, ed. Franz Boas. *Memoir of the American Museum of Natural History,* vol. 7.

Bohannan, Paul.
1963. *Social anthropology.* New York: Holt, Rinehart and Winston.

Boserup, Ester.
1970. *Women's role in economic development.* London: G. Allen and Unwin.

Bowers, Alfred W.
1950. *Mandan social and ceremonial organization.* Chicago: University of Chicago Press.

Braidwood, Robert J., and Gordon R. Willey, eds.
1962. Courses toward urban life. *Viking Fund Publications in Anthropology* 32.

Brown, Judith K.
1970. Economic organization and the position of women among the Iroquois. *Ethnohistory* 17:151–67.

Buettner-Janusch, John.
1967. *Origins of man: physical anthropology.* New York: John Wiley and Sons.

Buss, A. H.
1963. Physical aggression in relation to different frustrations. *Journal of Abnormal and Social Psychology* 67:1–7.

Buss, A. H., and T. C. Brock.
1963. Repression and guilt in relation to aggression. *Journal of Abnormal and Social Psychology* 66:345–50.

Carpenter, C. R.
1964. A field study in Siam of the behavior and social relations of the gibbon. In *Naturalistic behavior of nonhuman primates,* ed. C. R. Carpenter, pp. 145–271. University Park, Pennsylvania: The Pennsylvania State University Press.
1965. The howlers of Barrow Colorado Island. In *Primate behavior: field studies of monkeys and apes,* ed. Irven DeVore, pp. 250–91. New York: Holt, Rinehart and Winston.

Carr, Donald E.
1970. *The sexes.* New York: Doubleday.

Carstairs, G. M.
1958. *The twice-born.* Bloomington: Indiana University Press.

Chance, M. R. A.
1961. The nature and special features of the instinctive social bonds of primates. In *Social life of early man,* ed. Sherwood Washburn, pp. 17–33. Chicago: Aldine.

Child, I. L., T. Storm, and J. Veroff.
1958. Achievement themes in folktales related to socialization practice. In *Motives in fantasy, action, and society,* ed. J. W. Atkinson, pp. 479–92. Princeton: Van Nostrand.

Childe, V. Gordon.
1942. *What happened in history.* Harmondsworth, England: Penguin.
1951. *Man makes himself.* New York: New American Library.

Cipolla, Carlo M.
1970. *The economic history of world population.* Baltimore: Penguin Books.

Clignet, Remi.
1970. *Many wives, many powers: authority and power in polygynous families.* Evanston, Illinois: Northwestern University Press.

Cohen, Ronald.
1967. *The Kanuri of Bornu.* New York: Holt, Rinehart and Winston.

Conklin, Harold C.
1955. Hanunóo color categories. *American Anthropologist* 11:339–44.

Cowgill, Ursula M.
1970. The people of York: 1538–1812. *Scientific American* 222(1):104–12.

D'Andrade, Roy.
1966. Sex differences and cultural institutions. In *The development of sex differences,* ed. Eleanor Maccoby, pp. 174–204. Stanford: Stanford University Press.

Darwin, Charles.
1874 (orig. 1871). *The descent of man and selection in relation to sex.* New York: Thomas Y. Crowell.
1958 (orig. 1859). *Origin of species.* New York: New American Library.

Debetz, G. F.
1961. The social life of early Paleolithic man as seen through the work of the Soviet anthropologists. In *Social life of early man,* ed. Sherwood Washburn, pp. 137–49. Chicago: Aldine.

Delgado, José M. R.
1967. Social rank and radio-stimulated aggressiveness in monkeys. *The Journal of Nervous and Mental Disease* 144(5):383–90.

Dennis, Wayne.
1955. Are Hopi children noncompetitive? *The Journal of Abnormal and Social Psychology* 50:99–100.

Devereux, George.
1937. Homosexuality among the Mohave Indians. *Human Biology* 9:498–597.
1961. Mohave ethnopsychiatry and suicide: the psychiatric knowledge and the psychic disturbances of an Indian tribe. *Bureau of American Ethnology, Bulletin 175.*

De Vore, Irven.
1963. A comparison of the ecology and behavior of monkeys and apes. In *Classification and human evolution,* ed. Sherwood L. Washburn. *Viking Fund Publication in Anthropology* 37:301–19.

De Vore, Irven, and K. R. L. Hall.
1965. Baboon ecology. In *Primate behavior: field studies of monkeys and apes,* ed. Irven De Vore, pp. 20–52. New York: Holt, Rinehart and Winston.

D'Hertefelt, Marcel.
1965. The Rwanda of Rwanda. In *Peoples of Africa*, ed. James Gibbs, pp. 403–40. New York: Holt, Rinehart and Winston.

Distant, W. L.
1874. On the mental differences between the sexes. *Royal Anthropological Institute of Great Britain and Ireland, Journal*, pp. 78–87.

Dobzhansky, Theodosius.
1962. *Mankind evolving: the evolution of the human species.* New Haven: Yale University Press.

Dodge, Norton.
1966. *Women in the Soviet economy: their role in economic, scientific, and technical development.* Baltimore: Johns Hopkins University Press.

Dupire, Marguerite.
1963. The position of women in a pastoral society. In *Women of tropical Africa*, ed. Denise Paulme, pp. 47–92. Berkeley and Los Angeles: University of California Press.

Earthy, E.
1933. *Valenge women: the social and economic life of the Valenge women of Portuguese East Africa.* Oxford: Oxford University Press for International African Institute.

Edgerton, Robert B.
1964. Pokot intersexuality: an East African example of the resolution of sexual incongruity. *American Anthropologist* 66:1288–99.

Engels, Frederick.
1972 (orig. 1884). *The origin of the family, private property and the state,* ed. Eleanor Burke Leacock. New York: International Publishers.

Fernea, Elizabeth Warnock.
1965. *Guests of the sheik.* New York: Doubleday.

Fernea, Robert.
1970. *Shaykh and effendi.* Cambridge, Massachusetts: Harvard University Press.

Field, Mark G., and Karin I. Flynn.
1970. Worker, mother, housewife: Soviet woman today. In *Sex roles in changing society*, eds. Georgene Seward and Robert Williamson, pp. 257–84. New York: Random House.

Flecher, Alice C., and Francis La Flesche.
1905–6. The Omaha tribe. *Bureau of American Ethnology, Annual Report* 27.

Ford, Clellan S., and Frank A. Beach.
1951. *Patterns of sexual behavior.* New York: Harper and Brothers.

Forde, Daryll.
1949. *Habitat, economy and society.* New York: E. P. Dutton.

Fox, Robin.
1967. In the beginning: aspects of hominid behavioral evolution. *Man* 2:415–33.

Freud, Sigmund.
1938 (orig. 1913). *Totem and taboo.* London: Penguin Books.

Garcia, John.
1972. I.Q.: the conspiracy. *Psychology Today* 6(4):40–94.

Gessain, Monique.
1963. Coniagui women. In *Women of tropical Africa,* ed. Denise Paulme, pp. 17–46. Berkeley and Los Angeles: University of California Press.

Gleason, Harold.
1955. *An introduction to descriptive linguistics.* New York: Holt, Rinehart and Winston.

Goffman, Erving.
1966. *Behavior in public places: notes on the social organization of gatherings.* New York: The Free Press.

Goldin, George J., Sally L. Perry, Reuben Margolin, and Bernard Stotsky.
1972. *Dependency and its implications for rehabilitation.* Lexington, Massachusetts: D. C. Heath.

Goodale, Jane.
1971. *Tiwi wives.* Seattle and London: University of Washington Press.

Goodall, Jane. (*see also,* Van Lawick-Goodall, Jane)
1965. Chimpanzees of the Gombe Stream Reserve. In *Primate behavior: field studies of monkeys and apes,* ed. Irven DeVore, pp. 425–73. New York: Holt, Rinehart and Winston.

Goodman, Louis Wolf, and Janet Lever.
1972. Children's toys and socialization to sex roles. Department of sociology, Yale University. Mimeographed.

Gough, Kathleen.
1961. The modern disintegration of matrilineal descent groups. In *Matrilineal kinship,* eds. David M. Schneider and Kathleen Gough, pp. 631–52. Berkeley: University of California Press.

Hampson, J. L., and Joan Hampson.
1961. The ontogenesis of sexual behavior in man. In *Sex and internal secretions, vol. 2,* ed. William C. Young, pp. 1401–32. Baltimore: Williams and Wilkins.

Harlow, H. F., M. K. Harlow, and S. J. Suomi.
1971. From thought to therapy: lessons from a primate laboratory. *American Scientist* 59:538–49.

Harris, Marvin.
1968. *The rise of anthropological theory.* New York: Thomas Y. Crowell.

Harrison, Richard J.
1971. *Reproduction and man.* New York: W. W. Norton and Company.

Hart, C. W. M., and Arnold Pilling.
1960. *The Tiwi of North Australia.* New York: Holt, Rinehart and Winston.

Heckhausen, Heinz.
1967. *The anatomy of achievement motivation.* New York and London: Academic Press.

Heim, Alice.
1971. Intelligence and personality: their relationship and appraisal. *Impact of Science on Society* 21:347–55.

Herskovits, Melville.
1926. The cattle complex in East Africa. *American Anthropologist* 28:230–72, 361–80, 494–528, 663–64.

Hill, W. W.
1935. The status of the hermaphrodite and transvestite in Navaho culture. *American Anthropologist* 37:273–79.
1938. Note on the Pima berdache. *American Anthropologist* 40:338–40.

Holder, A. B.
1889. The *bate. New York Medical Journal* 50:623–25.

Honigmann, John.
1959. The world of man. New York: Harper.

Hudson, Charles.
1966. Folk history and ethnohistory. *Ethnohistory* 13:52–70.

Ibn Khaldun.
1958. *The Mugaddimah: an introduction to history, vol. 1.* The Bolligen Foundation, New York.

Itani, J.
1967. From the societies of non-human primates to human society. *Kagaku Asahi* 27:170–74.

Itani, J., and Suzuki, A.
1967. The social unit of chimpanzees. *Primates* 8:355–82.

Jay, Phyllis.
1963. The female primate. In *Man and civilization: the potential of women; a symposium*, eds. Seymour M. Farber and Roger H. L. Wilson, pp. 3–12. New York: McGraw-Hill.
1965. The common langur of North India. In *Primate behavior: field studies of monkeys and apes*, ed. Irven DeVore, pp. 197–249. New York: Holt, Rinehart and Winston.

Jensen, Gordon D., Ruth A. Bobbitt, and Betty N. Gordon.
1968. Sex differences in the development of independence of infant monkeys. *Behaviour* 30:1–14.

Jolly, Alison.
1967. Breeding synchrony in wild *Lemur catta*. In *Social communication among primates*, ed. Stuart A. Altmann, pp. 3–14. Chicago: University of Chicago Press.
1972. *The evolution of primate behavior*. New York: Macmillan.

Jolly, C.
1970. The seed-eaters: a new model of hominid differentiation based on a baboon analogy. *Man* 5:5–26.

Kagan, Jerome, and Howard A. Moss.
1962. *Birth to maturity*. New York: John Wiley.

Kardiner, Abram.
1939. *The individual and his society*. New York: Columbia University Press.
1945. *The psychological frontiers of society*. New York: Columbia University Press.

Katchadourian, Herant A., and Donald T. Lunde.
1972. *Fundamentals of human sexuality*. New York: Holt, Rinehart and Winston.

Kaufmann, Harry.
1970. *Aggression and altruism: a psychological analysis*. New York: Holt, Rinehart and Winston.

Klah, Hasteen.
1942. *Navajo creation myth*. Santa Fe, New Mexico: Museum of Navajo Ceremonial Art.

Klopfer, Peter H.
1971. Mother love: what turns it on? *American Scientist* 59:404–7.

Kormondy, Edward J.
  1969. *Concepts of ecology.* Englewood Cliffs, New Jersey: Prentice-Hall.

Kroeber, A. L.
  1919. On the principle of order in civilization as exemplified by changes in fashion. *American Anthropologist* 21:253–63.
  1940. Psychosis of social sanction. *Character and Personality* 8:204–15.

Lancaster, Jane B., and Richard B. Lee.
  1965. The annual reproductive cycle in monkeys and apes. In *Primate behavior: field studies of monkeys and apes,* ed. Irven De Vore, pp. 486–513. New York: Holt, Rinehart and Winston.

Laufer, Berthold.
  1920. Sex transformation and hermaphrodites in China. *American Journal of Physical Anthropology* 3:259–62.

Laughlin, William S.
  1968. Hunting: an integrating biobehavior system and its evolutionary importance. In *Man the hunter,* eds. Richard B. Lee and Irven De Vore, pp. 304–20. Chicago: Aldine.

Laurentin, Anne.
  1963. Nzakara women. In *Women of tropical Africa,* ed. Denise Paulme, pp. 121–78. Berkeley and Los Angeles: University of California Press.

Lee, Richard.
  1968. What hunters do for a living, or, how to make out on scarce resources. In *Man the hunter,* eds. Richard B. Lee and Irven De Vore, pp. 30–48. Chicago: Aldine.

Leith-Ross, Sylvia.
  1939. *African women: a study of the Ibo of Nigeria.* London: Faber and Faber.

Lerner, I. Michael.
  1968. *Heredity, evolution and society.* San Francisco: W. H. Freeman.

Levine, S. N.
  1966. Sex differences in the brain. *Scientific American* 214(4):84–90.

Lewis, Oscar.
  1941. Manly-hearted women among the North Piegan. *American Anthropologist* 43:173–87.

Linton, Sally.
  1970. Woman the gatherer. Paper presented at the 69th Meeting of the American Anthropological Association, San Diego.

Lorenz, Konrad.
1966. *On aggression.* New York: Harcourt, Brace and World.

Lowie, Robert.
1920. *Primitive society.* New York: Boni and Liveright.
1935. *The Crow Indians.* New York: Farrar and Rinehart.

Lubbock, John.
1873 (orig. 1870). *The origin of civilization and the primitive condition of man; mental and social condition of savages.* New York: D. Appleton.

Lurie, Nancy.
1953. Winnebago berdache. *American Anthropologist* 55:708–12.

Maccoby, Eleanor E.
1966. Sex differences in intellectual functioning. In *The development of sex differences,* ed. Eleanor E. Maccoby, pp. 25–55. Stanford: Stanford University Press.

Mace, David, and Vera Mace.
1963. *The Soviet family.* New York: Doubleday.

Maine, Henry.
1861. *Ancient law.* London: J. Murray.

Marshall, Carol Helman.
1970. The Soviet family and Soviet family law: a functional analysis of change. *New Scholar* 2:49–70.

Martin, M. Kay.
1974. *The foraging adaptation: uniformity or diversity?* Addison-Wesley Modular Publication No. 56. Reading, Massachusetts: Addison-Wesley.

Marx, Karl.
1965 (orig. 1857–58). *Pre-capitalistic economic formations,* ed. Eric J. Hobsbaum, trans. Jack Cohen. New York: International Publishers.
1888 (orig. 1848). *The communist manifesto.* London: W. Reeves.

McClelland, D. C.
1961. *The achieving society.* Princeton: Van Nostrand.

McLennan, John.
1865. *Primitive marriage.* Edinburgh: Adam and Charles Black.

McWhirter, Norris, and Ross McWhirter.
1971. *Guiness book of world records.* New York: Sterling Publishing Co.

Mead, Margaret.
1961. Cultural determinants of sexual behavior. In *Sex and internal secretions, vol. 2*, ed. William C. Young, pp. 1433–49. Baltimore: Williams and Wilkins.
1963. *Sex and temperament in three primitive societies*. New York: William Morrow.

Meek, C. K.
1931. *Tribal studies in northern Nigeria*. London: K. Paul, Trench, Trubner.

Mischel, W.
1961. Delay of gratification, need for achievement, and acquiescence in another culture. *Journal of Abnormal and Social Psychology* 62:543–52.

Mohsen, Safia.
1970. Aspects of the legal status of women among Awlad 'Ali. In *Peoples and cultures of the Middle East, vol. 1*, ed. Louise E. Sweet, pp. 220–33. Garden City, New York: The Natural History Press.

Money, John.
1965. Psychosexual differentiation. In *Sex research; new developments*, ed. John Money, pp. 3–23. New York: Holt, Rinehart and Winston.
1971. Pre-natal hormones and intelligence; a possible relationship. *Impact of Science on Society* 21:285–90.

Money, John and Anke A. Ehrhardt.
1972. *Man & women; boy & girl*. Baltimore and London: The Johns Hopkins University Press.

Morgan, Elaine.
1972. *Descent of woman*. New York: Stein and Day.

Morgan, Lewis Henry.
1851. *League of the Ho-de-no-sau-nee, or Iroquois*. Rochester: Sage.
1870. *Systems of consanguinity and affinity of the human family*. Washington, D.C.: Smithsonian Institution.
1877. *Ancient society*. New York: World Publishing.
1881. *Houses and house-life of the American aborigines*. Washington, D.C.: Government Printing Office.

Morris, Desmond.
1967. *The naked ape*. London: Jonathan Cape; New York: McGraw-Hill (1968).

Murdock, G. P.
1937. Comparative data on the division of labor by sex. *Social Forces* 16:551–53.

1949. *Social structure.* New York: Macmillan.
1959. *Africa: its peoples and their culture history.* New York: Mc-Graw-Hill.
1967. *Ethnographic atlas.* Pittsburgh: University of Pittsburgh Press.

Murphy, Robert.
1970. Social distance and the veil. In *Peoples and cultures of the Middle East, vol. 1,* ed. Louise Sweet, pp. 290–314. Garden City, New York: The Natural History Press.

Nadel, S. F.
1942. *A black byzantium.* London: Oxford University Press.
1952. Witchcraft in four African societies: a comparison. *American Anthropologist* 54:18–29.

Napier, J. R., and P. H. Napier.
1967. *A handbook of living primates.* London and New York: Academic Press.

Oberg, Kalervo.
1955. Types of social structure among lowland tribes of South and Central America. *American Anthropologist* 57:472–88.

Oetzel, Roberta M.
1962. Sex typing and sex role adoption in relation to differential abilities. In *Differential cognitive abilities,* ed. Eleanor E. Maccoby and Lucy Rau, pp. 126–45. Stanford: Stanford University Press.

Opler, Morris E.
1960. The *hijarā* (hermaphrodites) of India and Indian national character: a rejoinder. *American Anthropologist* 62:505–11.

Ottenberg, Phoebe.
1959. The changing economic position of women among the Afikpo Ibo. In *Continuity and change in African cultures,* ed. W. R. Bascom and M. J. Herskovits, pp. 205–23. Chicago: University of Chicago Press.

Otterbein, Keith, and Charlotte Swanson Otterbein.
1965. An eye for an eye, a tooth for a tooth: a cross-cultural study of feuding. *American Anthropologist* 67:1470–82.

Parens, Henri, and Leon J. Saul.
1971. *Dependence in man: a psychoanalytic study.* New York: International Universities Press.

Pilbeam, David.
1972. *The ascent of man: an introduction to human evolution.* New York: Macmillan.

Pilling, Arnold.

1957. Law and feud in an aboriginal society of North Australia.
    Ph.D. dissertation, Department of Anthropology, University of
    California, Berkeley.

Plato.

1970. *The symposium of Plato.* Trans. Suzy Q. Groden, ed. John A.
    Brentlinger. Amherst: The University of Massachusetts Press.

Richards, Cara.

1957. Matriarchy or mistake: the role of Iroquois women through
    time. *Proceedings of the 1957 Annual Spring Meeting of the
    American Ethnological Society,* pp. 36–45. Seattle: American
    Ethnological Society.

Rosenberg, B. G., and Brian Sutton-Smith.

1972. *Sex and identity.* New York: Holt, Rinehart and Winston.

Rowell, Thelma.

1966. Forest living baboons in Uganda. *Journal of Zoology*
    149:344–64.

Russell, Claire, and W. M. S. Russell.

1968. *Violence, monkeys and man.* London, Melbourne: Macmillan.
1971. Primate male behaviour and its human analogues. *Impact of
    Science on Society* 21:63–74.

Sahlins, Marshall.

1960. The origin of society. *Scientific American* 203(1):76–87.
1961. The segmentary lineage: an organization of predatory expan-
    sion. *American Anthropologist* 63:322–43.

Schaller, George.

1963. *The mountain gorilla: ecology and behavior.* Chicago: Univer-
    sity of Chicago Press.

Schneider, David, and Kathleen Gough, eds.

1961. *Matrilineal kinship.* Berkeley and Los-Angeles: University of
    California Press.

Schonfeld, W. A.

1943. Primary and secondary sexual characteristics: study of their
    development in males from birth through maturity, with bio-
    metric study of penis and testis. *American Journal of Diseases
    of Children* 65:535–49.

Schultz, A. H.

1956. Postembryonic age changes. *Primatologia* 1:887–964.

Seligman, Charles G., and Brenda Z. Seligman.

1932. *Pagan tribes of the Nilotic Sudan.* London: George Routledge
    and Sons.

Service, Elman.
  1962. *Primitive social organization.* New York: Random House.

Simms, S. C.
  1903. Crow Indian hermaphrodites. *American Anthropologist* n.s.
  5:580–81.

Simpson, G. G., C. S. Pittendrigh and L. H. Tiffany.
  1957. *Life: an introduction to biology.* New York: Harcourt, Brace.

Smith, Mary Felice.
  1954. *Baba of Karo: a woman of the Muslim Hausa.* London: Faber.

Smith, Philip.
  1972. *The consequences of food production.* Addison-Wesley Modular Publication No. 31. Reading, Mass.

Smuts, Robert.
  1959. *Women and work in America.* New York: Columbia University Press.

Stannard, Una.
  1971. The mask of beauty. In *Woman in sexist society: studies on
  the power and powerlessness,* ed. Vivian Gornick and Barbara
  K. Moran, pp. 187–203. New York: New American Library.

Steward, Julian.
  1955. *Theory of culture change.* Urbana: University of Illinois Press.

Strathern, Marilyn.
  1972. *Women in between.* London and New York: Seminar Press.

Sturtevant, William C.
  1964. Studies in ethnoscience. *American Anthropologist* 66:99–131.

Thompson, Richard W. and Michael C. Robbins.
  1973. Seasonal variation in conception in rural Uganda and Mexico.
  American Anthropologist 75:676–86.

Tiger, Lionel.
  1970a. *Men in groups.* New York: Vintage Books.
  1970b. The possible biological origins of sexual discrimination. *Impact of Science on Society* 20:29–44.

Tiger, Lionel, and Robin Fox.
  1971. *The imperial animal.* New York: Holt, Rinehart and Winston.

Trager, George L.
  1962. A scheme for the cultural analysis of sex. *Southwestern Journal of Anthropology* 18:114–18.

Travis, Carol.
  1971. Woman and man: a *Psychology Today* questionnaire. *Psychology Today* 4(9):82–85.

1972. Woman and man. *Psychology Today* 5(10):57–85.

Turgot, A. R. J.
1844 (orig. 1750). *Plan de deux discours sur l'histoire universelle. Oeuvres de Turgot.* Paris: Guillaumin.

United States Bureau of the Census.
1973. *Current Population Reports,* Series P-60, No. 90. Washington, D.C.: United States Government Printing Office.

Urdy, J. Richard, and Naomi M. Morris.
1968. Distribution of coitus in the menstrual cycle. *Nature* 220:593–96.

Van Lawick-Goodall, Jane.
1968. The behavior of free-living chimpanzees in the Gombe Stream Reserve. *Animal Behavior Monographs* 1:165–311.
1971. *In the shadow of man.* Boston: Houghton Mifflin Company.

Washburn, S. L., and Irven De Vore.
1961. Social behavior of baboons and early man. In *Social life of early man,* ed. S. L. Washburn. *Viking Fund Publications in Anthropology* 31:91–105.

Washburn, S. L., and C. S. Lancaster.
1968. The evolution of hunting. In *Man the hunter,* eds. Richard B. Lee and Irven De Vore, pp. 293–303. Chicago: Aldine.

Weisstein, Naomi.
1971. Psychology constructs the female. In *Woman in sexist society,* eds. Vivian Gornick and Barbara Moran, pp. 207–224. New York: Basic Books.

Weitzman, Lenore J., Deborah Eifler, Elizabeth Hokada, and Catherine Ross.
1972. Sex-role socialization in picture books for preschool children. *American Journal of Sociology* 77:1125–50.

Winton, F. R. and L. E. Bayliss.
1962. *Human physiology.* Boston: Little, Brown.

Young, William C.
1961. The mammalian ovary. In *Sex and internal secretions, vol. 1,* ed. William C. Young, pp. 449–96. Baltimore: Williams and Wilkins.

Young, William C., Robert W. Goy, Charles H. Phoenix.
1964. Hormones and sexual behavior. *Science* 143:212–18.

Index